Introduction to Educational Psychology

AN OPERANT CONDITIONING APPROACH

Introduction to
Educational Psychology

CARL E. PITTS

Thomas Y. Crowell Company

AN OPERANT CONDITIONING APPROACH

United States International University
CALIFORNIA WESTERN CAMPUS

NEW YORK   Established 1834

L C Card 77–146070
ISBN 0–690–44798–1

Manufactured in the United States of America
Designed by Judith Woracek Barry

Dedication

Writing a book is an inordinately dependent undertaking. One must rely upon the help of many others if the final product is ever to emerge. Deep and grateful appreciation is due:

To Webster College, a small but courageous institution

To "J" and Joe, for allowing time away from the vicissitudes of institutional life

To Jim, for the encouragement and personal support in translating what began as a casual idea into a book

To my overworked colleagues in the social and behavioral science department, who graciously adjusted to my absence for an academic year

To Virginia, for unfailing perseverance in bringing order out of an almost illegible manuscript

To a host of students and their ever-present demands for clarity

To Janna, Andy, and Murray, for much needed and delightful respites from the deprivation chamber known as a study

And especially to Joann, without whom any undertaking would be hollow.

Why Another Text in Educational Psychology?

Some years ago in the dark past of my educational history I was a student in a course called Educational Psychology. There are still some vivid memories of that experience; it met at the ungodly hour of 8 a.m. three times a week, the textbook was red, the professor was an ex-superintendent of schools, and a very attractive blonde and I worked out an ingenious method of sharing notes in preparation for the many true-false, multiple-choice tests we were required to take. There may be other memories latent in the recessed cortical folds of my brain, but at the moment they escape me.

I am not sure how far the field of educational psychology has come since those days. Certainly much more research has accumulated. I suspect that there are fewer ex-superintendents teaching the course. I know that the instructor today has a much wider choice in the color and variety of the text and, according to observation from reliable sources, students are more ingenious than ever. But even with these sweeping changes, I have a hunch that things are pretty much as they were when I was a student. Educational institutions have an amazing ability for holding on to the way things have been done in the past.

Why, then, add to the already large agglomeration of educational psychology texts? Since this book is a calculated departure from traditional books in educational psychology, you are due some explanation of its rationale.

Today there is a greater knowledge of human behavior than ever before. Books and journals line the shelves of libraries in universities, colleges, cities, communities, and even in many homes. Popular magazines of all varieties rarely fail to devote space to that most fascinating of all subjects, the human organism and why it behaves like it does. Confidence that true answers have been found has reached a new peak. The dust jacket of a recent publication simply entitled *Human Behavior* describes the contents as:

the first comprehensive attempt to summarize what social scientists believe they have substantiated about the ways humans behave. . . . stated in plain, non-technical language, these significant and revealing propositions cover almost every aspect of human activity. . . . They answer such questions as: How widespread in human societies are premarital and extramarital relations? How do the IQ's of men compare with those of women, of Negroes with whites? How effective is psychotherapy? Does hypnosis really work? Do television viewers read less than non-viewers?
The book is a landmark in the social sciences. *It should be of value to leaders of all institutions whose success depends on understanding people.*[1]

The implication is that the knowledge presented in the book can be *used* by practitioners—psychotherapists, industrial psychologists, teachers, religious leaders, college deans, personnel directors, chairmen of the board, YMCA directors, and so on—who, in working with others, desire to bring about certain predictable changes in human behavior.

A similar optimism about our accumulated insight into human behavior and its usability is reflected in a recent fourth edition of a text for college students preparing for the teaching profession:

If we have made no signal discoveries [in the behavioral sciences] we certainly have achieved a .more comprehensive understanding of the structural and behavioral development of man. . . .
A text, such as this, in applied psychology, is concerned with understanding human capabilities and *the means* to bring about their most favorable growth and development.[2]

Here, the author is quite explicit about what the book has to offer the teacher —"the means" for changing human behavior. This is, in fact, at least the implicit promise of all educational psychology texts. It is also, however, the too-often-frustrated hope of the readers of such texts. Students and teachers characteristically rate their educational psychology courses near the bottom of those studies designed to prepare them for the classroom. Their comments are seldom enthusiastic and tend to range from the tepid "Well, it was all right, I guess" to the less solicitous "Complete waste of time." There could be a variety of explanations for their attitudes.

---

[1] B. Berelson and G. Steiner, *Human Behavior: An Inventory of Scientific Findings* (New York: Harcourt, Brace and World, Inc., 1964). Italics added.
[2] Herbert Sorenson, *Psychology in Education* (New York: McGraw-Hill Book Co., 1964), p. v. Italics added.

All educational psychology courses are poorly taught.
Those who take educational psychology are inferior students.
Educational psychology texts are not designed to help the teacher.
The fund of knowledge in the psychology of education is not presented in a manner
that is helpful to teachers in the classroom.

After careful consideration it was decided that:

All courses in educational psychology are not poorly taught.
Students who take educational psychology are as capable as students who take other
courses.
Educational psychology texts are written with the hope that the information contained will be helpful to teachers in the classroom, but
The accumulation of knowledge about teaching and learning *has not been presented
in a way that can be of appreciable help to the teacher in the classroom.*

The last statement, the crux of the problem, needs further explanation
inasmuch as this book is designed to bridge the chasm between educational
psychology texts and the classroom.

First of all, this text takes the position that the science of psychology is
essentially a problem-solving *process*. What John Maynard Keynes, the eminent economist, said about economics is applicable to this book: "It is designed to present a method rather than a doctrine, an apparatus of the mind,
a technique of thinking which helps its possessor to draw correct conclusions." Contrary to a widespread popular view, science is not so much a
compilation of facts as it is a willingness to work at problems following the
rules of the scientific game. Facts have an annoying way of changing, and
what is fact today may become fallacy tomorrow. It is a fundamental error to
regard our knowledge of human behavior at any given point in time as
immutable.

Second, inasmuch as the teacher's role is often that of problem solver,
it follows that effective problem-solving tools are needed. This is not to say
that accumulated information is unnecessary or irrelevant; it *is* to say that
because the teacher's concerns about students' behavior are more specific
than general, the teacher must have the equipment to deal with situations as
they arise. In the final analysis, most teachers are more interested in *their*
class, *their* individual students, rather than in generalized, normative statements about motivation, learning, child development, and the many other
topics making up the chapters of the traditional educational psychology texts.

Unfortunately, those of us who teach educational psychology do not
always view our discipline as a process of problem solving. We have become
enamored of the "fact," the product of research. Perhaps the fallacy of the
factual-teaching approach is best demonstrated by pushing it to its logical
conclusion: If those of us who teach educational psychology know so much
about classroom environment, learning, teaching, and students, it follows that
our classes are the most exciting and intellectually stimulating courses on
campus. Present evidence does not support that hypothesis.

But how do you replace product with process?

This text is a first approximation in translating the concepts and tools of the social-behavioral sciences into vocabulary and skills for the classroom. It is designed to help the teacher behave as a researcher, with the classroom and the school as the principal source of data. To become trained as a researcher means to learn to use such tools of the social-behavioral sciences as methods of observation, ways of investigating group structure, and the gathering and interpretation of statistics. These methods produce what one might call "snapshots" and are standard research techniques for describing behavior at a point in time.

But the teacher's job is more than one of description. Given the above "snapshots," his primary concern is to change behavior. Having decided on objectives, his role must be that of an agent of change, providing an environment of individual and group experiences that increases the probability that students will progress from where they are to where the teacher wants them to be. Student A does not read well for his age. How can his reading ability be increased? Student B continues to have difficulty with algebra. What method can be employed to improve his ability to solve algebraic problems correctly? The class gets out of hand. What can be done to change the group's behavior? These and many other similar problems besiege the sensitive teacher. Therefore, in addition to training the neophyte teacher to become a good describer (researcher), the second and equally important goal of this text is to give him a methodology for creating the conditions that facilitate reaching objectives with maximum satisfaction for both teacher and student.

This text does not present an eclectic approach to teaching and learning. Its orientation, or methodology, is that of *reinforcement theory* or, more specifically, *operant conditioning* as developed primarily by the psychologist B. F. Skinner and extended by an ever-increasing number of his disciples. Operant conditioning is an applied psychology designed to help the practitioner achieve certain predetermined, concrete ends. It is a deliberate psychology, a psychology designed to *do* something. Therein lies the suitability of the operant conditioning technique to teaching. The teacher, too, wants to do something with students—help them become more adept at solving problems, thinking logically, critically, analytically, and creatively.

No new skill that involves the interaction of human beings can be mastered merely by reading about it. The student must not assume that, because he has read and understood the contents of this book, he will be able immediately to use the techniques of behavior modification with ease or success. In addition to understanding the principles of how to change performance, one must have the opportunity to practice and experiment with the principles. Ideally, the two should be concurrent. Unfortunately, the matter of practice and experimentation is made difficult by the fact that many schools are simply not geared to handle the techniques or procedures called for by this or any other systematic teaching-learning approach. Our schools have become the victims of a tradition of educational style that tenaciously resists change. Though the broader problem of educational change is an area beyond the scope of this book, there is little doubt that facilitation of the position suggested here—that of the teacher as describer (researcher) and behavioral modifier—is intricately bound to a supportive institutional environment.

It is not my intent to point the finger of blame at the amorphous "they" responsible for the many shortcomings of our educational institutions, but there are many factors determining what goes on in the classroom over which the teacher has little control. Texts in educational psychology have been remiss in not pointing out that the particular psychological school they represent must have institutional sanction if it is to be successful in the classroom.

As broad and as deep as the faults and fissures in our educational system are, though, we still have grounds for optimism. Demands for change are coming from all quarters, and there is developing a new breed of educator—the dissatisfied student of yesterday—as well as a new technology of teaching. This book has been written to help meet the emerging needs of both pre-service and inservice teacher-training programs dedicated to an applied educational psychology.

The pattern and purpose of this text began with my own disquiet over educational psychology textbooks, but the impetus to get it down in writing came largely from the response of students and teachers. Their perceptive comments over several years of my and their struggling with what should go into the course have been invaluable and have had a great deal to do with the final product. Undergraduate students can become good researchers, and that fact has led me to a deeper conviction that students really are more ingenious than ever.

C. E. P.

CONTENTS

I / THE WAY THINGS ARE

Describing the Way Things Are

Part I is designed to introduce you to a variety of the tools of the social behavioral sciences. A consideration of some of the rules of the scientific game
in Chapters 1–3 is followed by a method for observing the behavior of others
in Chapter 4. Quite legitimately you might wonder why you need to be
trained to observe, since it could hardly be said that you have been oblivious
to the behavior of others. But, as you will see, several knotty problems arise
when you set out to observe as a scientist. Chapter 5 discusses the most
obvious method of getting information about others' behavior, simply asking
them. Although social scientists have relied upon this method quite exten-
sively, again there are important precautions necessary to insure that information got by asking questions is accurate. The same chapter considers other
methods, whereby the investigator is not so apparent to those being studied.
Chapter 6 is devoted to a technique for studying the social structure of the
classroom, with some suggestions of how the established system has been
changed. Chapter 7 raises the ethical problems one invariably runs into when
studying the behavior of others.

Part I deals primarily with descriptive tools and techniques for gaining
insight to the way things are. It is a noun-like section in comparison with
Part II, which emphasizes the more verb-like concepts of changing behavior
once it has been described.

1 / What Is This Thing Called Science?

A logical first step in training you to be a teacher-researcher is to provide a backdrop about scientific methodology, particularly as that methodology applies to the study of human behavior. Such is the intent of this and the next two chapters. The essential problem has to do with the nature of data and the researcher's struggle for assurance that the data meet certain criteria.

The Game of Science

To try to capture in a few chapters the essence of such a diverse undertaking as science is almost folly. The many strands of methodology, measurement devices, objects of study, and personalities make science somewhat akin to the fabled elephant inspected by the five blind men, each of whom, investigating a different portion of the unknown beast, reported on the limited data available to him. But their elephant was more than just a trunk, a leg, a tail, a tusk, or an ear; it was more even than the combination of all those parts. "Scienceness" like "elephantness" is difficult to capture without extensive description.

Nevertheless, the invitation has been extended in this text to play the game of science, and some general guidelines must be set forth if that game is to have meaning. Fortunately, there is more to go on than that available to the blind men, but as yet the photographs taken of illusive science, while allowing a general image, are nonetheless blurred. Among other reasons science has never been known to stand still long enough to be other than blurred.

3

Measurement and Criteria

The internal core around which science revolves can be described as measurement. There is no special or esoteric meaning attached to the notion of measurement. It is used here in much the same fashion as one would use it in everyday conversation. What is important is its centrality to science. "I often say that when you can measure what you are speaking about and express it in numbers, you know something about it, but when you cannot measure it, when you cannot express it in numbers, your knowledge is of a meager and unsatisfactory kind." So spoke an eminent metrologist, Lord Kelvin.[1]

Implicit in measurement is a specified standard or criterion to which that to be measured can be compared. For example, the unit of measurement when one measures length may be a meter, inch, foot, mile, or centimeter. The criterion for the standard meter of the world is the distance between two marks on a platinum-alloy bar kept at the International Bureau of Weights and Measures in France.

This standard to which other lengths could be compared was agreed upon in 1889. Before that, there were a variety of ways of measuring distance between points. Some were complicated and unwieldy. In 1824 the standard yard was the length of the pendulum that produced a beat every second at sea level in the latitude of London. Others—for example, the measurement of a horse's height by the number of hands high it stood—were grossly imprecise. In time, one standard was selected, and with minor changes that standard has remained until today. Even the lowly wooden yardstick available at most lumberyards can be traced back to its progenitor established in 1889. An explicit standard to which something can be compared (measured) is also used for other variables such as mass, time, frequency, volume, velocity, acceleration, pressure, and temperature.

For purposes of contrast, consider another form of comparing something to a criterion. The critic Irving Kolodin comments on a recent recording of Tchaikovsky's *Serenade for Strings* and *Nutcracker Suite:*

The strings of the Berlin Philharmonic have rarely shown greater claim to be considered among the great ensembles of the world than in this finespun performance. In Karajan's fashion the fast tempi tend to be faster, the slow to slower, but he draws so strong a line from phrase to phrase that the touches of excess are smoothed out. It is, in short, an instance in which virtuosity is expended virtuously, and to the advantage of the end result. The Nutcracker is rather a different matter, for here the relationship to anything meant to be danced is remote (more than second cousin twice removed). Thus, the pace at which the "Trepak" is taken is headlong rather than footsure, while

---

[1] William Thomson Kelvin, *Popular Lectures and Addresses,* 3 vols. (New York: The Macmillan Company, 1891), 1:80.

the "Danse de Mirlitons" is slowed down to a stately tread. Everything comes out immaculately, but not in conformity with the character of the music.[2]

Here, although the criteria are implicit rather than explicit, it is not difficult to see that there are several sources of standards for the critic to make a judgment (measurement) of the new recording: the composer's notations of how the music should be played, historical precedence, and what might be called common sense. The phrases in which comparisons are made between performance and criteria and the possible sources of the criteria (which Kolodin does not specify) are:

. . . the fast tempi tend to be faster, the slow to slower . . . [Compared to composer's markings of tempi?]
. . . he draws so strong a line from phrase to phrase . . . [Compared to other, more segmental performances?]
. . . the relationship to anything meant to be danced is remote . . . ["Trepak," a Russian form of dance, could hardly be danced at this speed.]
. . . everything comes out immaculately, but not in conformity with the character of the music. [As other recordings and performances have displayed it?]

Specifically, when the scientist is set alongside the critic, particularly in the examples used here, one notes that the criteria for measurement in science approach absoluteness whereas the criteria for evaluation in music are much less absolute. Hence two critics hearing the same performance may write diametrically opposed reviews, but such disagreement would hardly seem possible between two scientists measuring the weight of a fluid.

The difference between science and nonscience is not always that clear, however. Criteria for weight, mass, and velocity do have an absoluteness about them, but many other phenomena in which scientists, notably social-behavioral scientists, are interested have criteria less clear than one would wish. An example is the quasi-scientific term *emotion,* a favorite of the social scientist, which frequently appears in psychological literature.

What is emotion? What does one do that allows an observer to classify what he observes as an emotional state or emotional quiescence? There are several standard ways that emotion has been measured. One of the more popular laboratory techniques is to measure it with a galvanic skin response (GSR). With this instrument, electrodes are attached to the skin, usually on the palms of the hand, and under conditions of emotionality the conductivity between the two electrodes changes. The changes are associated with the increase or decrease of minute amounts of perspiration, which, in turn, increase or decrease the conductance between the electrodes. Other physiological measures used to quantify emotional states are blood pressure, heart rate, respiration, dilation and constriction of the pupils of the eye, salivary

[2] Irving Kolodin, "Miscellaneous LP Recordings Report II," *The Saturday Review,* April 27, 1968, p. 76, reprinted by permission of Irving Kolodin and *The Saturday Review.*

secretion, muscle tension, and blood composition. These measures have a nice scientific ring to them, but it is not that simple because they are not related even though they are often treated *as if* they measured the same condition.

Furthermore, what if these instruments are not practical, as in the case of studying a student's behavior during a midterm exam? The problem of having commonly agreed upon criteria becomes more and more immense because, as you know, emotionality is expressed in different ways by different people. Behaviorally, what may appear to be anxiety to one observer may appear to be confidence to another.

There are a variety of ways such phenomena can be studied and these will be considered later. For now, the important point to remember is that one way science is distinguished from nonscience is by its concern for the establishment of commonly agreed upon criteria or, for lack of consensus, a clear statement of the criteria used in any particular investigation. Without an agreed upon or a careful definition of criteria, science would be unable to exist as science because it would be robbed of its most essential element, measurement.

Measurement and Validity

The term validity refers to the degree to which a measure actually gets at that which it purports to be measuring. Does I.Q. measure intelligence? Do achievement tests measure the student's knowledge in a particular area? Does a GSR measure emotionality?

One way validity can be determined is by applying some other criterion designed to measure the same thing. Let us say that one wants to measure the pattern of likes and dislikes among a group of high school students. One technique is *sociometry,* in which persons are simply asked to rank the others in the group in an order of preference. With proper treatment of the data, the investigator may come up with a rank ordering of social power; not only will the highly chosen stars be identified but, equally important, so will the social isolates. Further analysis will give the social network, the cliques and the mediators between subgroups.

How is the investigator sure that in taking a sociometric measure he has gotten at the real picture? Asking students for likes and dislikes is open to serious question as a source of valid data. Perhaps the students did not understand the task correctly or they may not like the teacher prying into their affairs. Under these conditions the data could be *une grande attrape* leading the investigator to heaven knows how many inaccurate conclusions.

A way to check a social system beyond sociometry is to observe carefully the behavior of the students in a variety of situations both in and out of the class. The stars, as determined by the sociometric or paper-pencil method, ought to be treated as stars by other members of the class. That is, on the assumption that one who likes another would prefer to be around the other, you would expect that the socially powerful would be invited, talked with, visited more frequently than the less powerful. Similarly, those who have no power would be less visible to the others in the class. Their opinion would seldom be asked, and they would frequently be left out of social occasions.

Still another means of ascertaining validity would be to study the research in sociometry to see if the paper-pencil method is supported by investigators of other groups.

If these three sources of information (paper-pencil sociogram, behavioristic observation, and previous research) are mutually supportive, it can be safely assumed that the sociometric measure originally taken is valid. If not related, one would not know which measure was more accurate, and, as the engineer said when his beautifully designed boat sank, "Back to the drawing board!"

There are several kinds of validation. The simplest is "face validity"; the relevance of the measuring instrument to what one is trying to measure is apparent "on the face of it." Were one interested in evaluating the adequacy of a student's knowledge of a particular unit in math, the measurement would consist of a series of problems from the unit. The student would not be measured with a foreign language test, to use an absurd example. Compared to other forms of validity, face validity is clearly the least complicated, but this does not make it any less significant. Included in face validity are all those measures based directly on behavior of the kind in which the investigator is interested. For example, if one wants to evaluate the ability of an aircraft pilot, a first step might be to rate him by obvious criteria necessary for flying. Does he observe safety regulations? Is he able to perform with efficiency under pressure? Does he have a sound heart, 20-20 vision, and so on? It would seem that in order to evaluate him "on the face of it," these and other kinds of information should be known about the pilot. It may happen, however, that what appears to be measuring one quality is actually measuring another. In some situations the obvious or logical measure is in fact inappropriate. A teacher might want to identify the leaders in her class by their behavior, but it is often demonstrated that teachers are not always the best at identifying leaders because their criteria of what constitutes a leader is not similar to the way students define a leader. Again, that a measure is behavioral or appears to be appropriate does not necessarily make it valid, and the researcher must always be sensitive to such possibilities.

Construct validity, another form of assurance that the measure is measuring what it purports to measure, means that two independent measures seem to "fit" logically together and that both are measuring the same general abstract quality or construct. Let us say that a teacher gets two separate measures on a child, an I.Q. test and an achievement test, and finds that he ranks first in his class on both. The relationship of two measures, ostensibly getting at a common factor, obviously leads to more assurance about the child's ability than is possible with just one measure. Or, in a less rigorous way, if a high-school student achieves success on the football field, the basketball court, and the baseball diamond, the construct of athletic ability might be inferred with a fairly high level of conviction.[3]

Another test of validity in measurement is called pragmatic or predictive validity. Does the instrument predict? Can one make better decisions with its help than without it? What is essential in this kind of validity is that there is a reasonable criterion to which the data from the measuring device can be compared. The electroencephalograph (EEG) measures brain wave patterns. It was found that with patients who report particular symptoms the EEG pattern could be used to diagnose the presence and position of a tumor on the brain. The pragmatic validity of the instrument is clearly demonstrated when the surgeon operates and finds the tumor in that portion of the brain predicted by the electronic reading.

In the study of human behavior few measurement devices have the predictive validity of such physiological equipment as the EEG. As often as the I.Q. test is administered, it is not an especially good predictor of a student's academic behavior. Similarly, achievement, personality, and interest tests, when used as the only source of data, leave much to be desired in predicting future behavior. The marvelous ability of the human organism to adapt in unpredictable ways to new situations is too often minimized by decision makers who rely upon a few tests to predict the future. The theme of tentativeness, especially in predicting behavior, will be encountered again and again throughout this text.

Measurement and Reliability

Another quality in measurement for which the researcher strives is reliability: the stability or consistency of the measure. Say that you measured the length of your desk every morning for a week and attained the following results:

Monday	65 inches
Tuesday	67 inches
Wednesday	64 inches
Thursday	69 inches
Friday	72 inches
Saturday	51 inches
Sunday	51 inches

[3] Be careful when there is too little data—the student could have been the team manager.

One of three conclusions could be made: someone is switching desks on you, you are using a rubber ruler, or you badly need glasses. At any rate, your measurement reflects an unusual amount of variability, and with the data on hand you would be hard pressed to give an accurate description of the length of your desk.

Another example more closely related to this text: a teacher administers different but equivalent forms of an I.Q. test to her class on Monday, Wednesday, and Friday. It is found that the average score on Monday is 98, Wednesday 116, and Friday 90. What conclusion about the average I.Q. of the class could be made? Obviously little or no confidence could be put in these scores.

The more perceptive reader will have already discovered that reliability is actually a special way to test validity, a way to give greater assurance that what is being measured is what the investigator believes it to be. Consequently, any valid measure is reliable, but a reliable measure is not necessarily valid. A reliable instrument is consistent in measurement when conditions remain the same, but a systematic bias may render it invalid. The weightwatcher may have a reliable bathroom scale, but how disconcerting it would be to discover that it is consistently seven pounds light!

Measurement and Objectivity

A feeling most persons assume to be an integral part of science but which is sometimes difficult to impart to the budding scientist is objectivity. In a way, objectivity is like validity, for it is a frame of mind, a way of operating designed to give assurance that one's information is accurate. It requires that one comes to the task with tentativeness, with reservations, with caution, with a minimum of subjective involvement. To do otherwise would open up the possibility of finding whatever one wants to find, for subjectivity often leads to selective perception, to seeing only what one wants to see.

To have greater assurance of objectivity, the scientist often tries to remove himself as the only observer. He may rely not only on instrumentation to assure objectivity but also on colleagues who are not as involved as he; the design of a study can often rule out whatever biases he may have, as can the possibility of criticism from fellow scientists who read his published reports. Ray Hyman catches the essence of this in describing the science of psychology:

The psychologist as a scientist, then, rejects many sources of observations—of his own as well as of others. He knows that man is a highly fallible observer. Despite the best intentions the human onlooker is limited by the sensitivity of his perceptual apparatus, by the frameworks and categories he has for ordering his perceptual experience, by the limited span of things he can attend to at any one time, and by motivational and physiological aspects that lead to self-deception. The growth of psychology as a science goes hand in hand with the gradual discovery and elimination of these human defects in the gathering of data.[4]

This quality of objectivity will be considered in much greater detail in ensuing chapters because of its centrality to the purposes of this text, namely to help you become a better, more scientific observer of the classroom scene. The key notions about science that have been considered thus far are:

1. The necessity for a clearly established statement of criteria to facilitate measurement.
2. Validity in measurement, including the varieties of face, construct, pragmatic-predictive.
3. Reliability, the constancy of a measure under similar conditions.
4. Objectivity.

All of them are related in one way or another to measurement. They are aspects of a quality that leads the scientist to higher levels of assurance about his data. Now consideration will be given to kinds of scientific measurement.

Kinds of Measurement

Remember that once a criterion has been chosen, measurement is a matter of determining the relationship of the phenomena under investigation to the criterion. Traditionally, the categories used to describe this relationship have been of four varieties: nominal, ordinal, interval, and ratio. For the purposes of this text, interval and ratio measures will be combined, making three kinds of relationships: nominal, ordinal, interval-ratio.

To illustrate the distinctions among these three, select a book other than this, put it and this book side by side on the desk in front of you, and on a sheet of paper list all the ways the two books are different.

Yes, go ahead and do it. it will be more effective if you get involved.

Look carefully at what you have written. Do you discover qualitative differences in your statements? You probably have listed things like:

One is an educational psychology text; the other is a history text.

One is a hardback; the other is a paperback.

Statements of this kind are nominal differences, differences in name. The nominal category consists of distinctions based on name or class, whatever the compared objects are, for example, sexes (male or female), trees

---

[4] Ray Hyman, *The Nature of Psychological Inquiry* (Englewood Cliffs, N.J.: Prentice-Hall, Inc., 1964), p. 40, copyright © 1964 by Prentice-Hall, Inc., reprinted by permission of the publisher.

(maple or oak), cars (Oldsmobile or Ford), books (encyclopedia or dictionary), or colors (green or sienna).

Other differences you noted might be:

One is bigger than the other.
One has fewer pages than the other.

Here the relationship, called ordinal, is that of size, with a specification of bigger than, equal to, or smaller than. Other examples are faster, shorter, less intelligent, sexier, and fuller. Note that the relationship is one to which numerical rank can be attached, as one might rank in first, second, and third order the best restaurants in San Francisco without specifying how much one is better than the other.

The how-much quality in describing relationships, to return to your listing of differences between this and another book, is an interval-ratio measure. You might have said:

One weighs twice as much as the other.
One has 242 pages; the other has 320 pages.

The interval-ratio measurement consists of numbers, quantitative data that can be added, subtracted, divided, and multiplied. In ordinal measurement one does not know how much, but with an interval-ratio relationship there is a specified quantitative distinction describing how much difference exists.

The three kinds of measures—nominal, ordinal, and interval-ratio—yield differences between phenomena or events. Nominal measures contrast names such as black-white or good-bad; ordinal measures show rank order such as first, second, and third; and interval-ratio measures tell how much difference exists between ranks. For the results of a swimming race, a nominal reporting would yield winner and loser data; an ordinal would list who was first, second, third, etc.; and an interval-ratio would give the time in seconds for each swimmer. Notice that both the nominal and ordinal measures can be derived from an interval-ratio measure, but, the process is not reversible; that is, the interval-ratio measure could not be determined from either a nominal or an ordinal report of the race.

Science and Morality

Because of the importance in science of a firmly established standard, unit, or criterion to which other phenomena are compared, it can now be seen why science as science cannot become involved in questions of value, morality, or ethics, conditions in which the criterion is often not commonly shared. If there is no clear standard agreed upon by participants, it is impossible to measure departures from the standard. What constitutes moral or immoral behavior may be agreed upon within one subculture but may be seen from an entirely different perspective by another. Indeed, the scientist may have important scientific information to facilitate value decisions, but as a scientist he has no more insight into what decision ought to be made than any one else. Such was the case in the Manhattan Project, which developed the atomic bomb. Scientists were needed to build the bomb, but the decision of whether to use it in warfare is not a scientific one. Certainly, the Japanese scientist in Hiroshima did not share the position of the American scientist who felt the bomb should be dropped. The scientific community can function best when criteria for measurement are established and agreed upon by other scientists. A decision based upon conflicting or fuzzy criteria, which unfortunately are involved in a good deal of decision making, is not compatible to science.

Science and the Study of Man

The dispassionate, tentative, objective view is not easy to maintain when the scientist turns to the study of his fellow man. In a sense, it requires that man be viewed as an object not unlike a chemical or a piece of metal. Otherwise, the scientist opens himself up to subjective observation where his feelings may well obscure the facts. An eminent psychologist, David C. McClelland comments on the scientific study of man:

Acquiring a scientific attitude toward human personality is not easy. There are all sorts of emotional and theoretical problems involved, all sorts of implicit assumptions that tend to color thinking and distort judgement unless they are made explicit to begin with. After all, to take a detached scientific attitude toward a human being is to do a somewhat peculiar, "unnatural" thing. It involves treating another human being as if he were a thing—a tree or a stone—to be analyzed and conceptualized, rather than loved, hated, judged sinful or successful, appreciated or derogated. It involves the assumption that human nature *can* be understood in the same way a tree or stone can be understood. This daring assumption is by no means shared by everyone.[5]

How does the scientific student of human behavior resolve the dilemma? Can man maintain his transcendent nobility and still be the object of inquiry by the social-behavioral scientist? McClelland continues:

After all, the scientific mode of apprehending reality is only one possible mode. A person may put it on or take it off according to the demands of the occasion. A chemist can enjoy a steak; he can also analyze it into its organic compounds if he wants to. He need not do both at once. A physiologist can enjoy a cocktail without mentally tracing the deleterious influence of alcohol on the various functions of the body. A physicist can enjoy a sunset without giving a thought to the principles of optics and

⁵ David C. McClelland, *Personality* (New York: Holt, Rinehart and Winston, Inc., 1951), p. 3, reprinted by permission of the publisher.

refraction. A psychologist can love his wife without perceiving that she is "really" a mother figure for him.[6]

To use a trite image, social scientists are destined to wear two hats, one while in the laboratory or the field as they study behavior, the other as less scientific members of the human race. The two roles are not mutually exclusive, however. The scientist may and often does become involved in humanitarian research, but he also knows his findings should not become contaminated by personal biases and predispositions more readily acceptable in the less scientific world. This is the basis for the regulation in the medical profession that prohibits a physician from operating on members of his immediate family or a clinical psychologist from being a therapist to his wife. Neither could be objective in performing his professional duties. The social scientist must be able to discriminate between appropriate and inappropriate headgear for different occasions, for problems are inevitable when the hats get mixed.

Summary

Although there are specific guidelines such as the need for measurement, clearly defined criteria, and conditions of validity and reliability, science in the final analysis is a frame of mind seeking to establish accurate and powerful kinds of knowledge about a subject. When scientific methodology turns from the inanimate or nonpersonal to the personal, when man studies man, the task becomes more difficult because of the danger of allowing subjectivity to creep in. The careful social-behavioral scientist is always sensitive to the possibility that his own biases may distort his judgment.

This chapter has focused on the broad concept of science as a method, a "feeling-tone" for generating knowledge. There is a need to direct attention now to that youngster of the sciences, psychology. The guidelines established in this chapter will still be appropriate, but more needs to be said about the application of these guidelines to the scientific study of human behavior. Such is the task of Chapter 2.

[6] Ibid., p. 15.

2 / Psychology and the Scientific Process

The first chapter dealt with the broad concept of science as it transcends specific disciplines such as physics, chemistry, and biology. There is a need for special attention here to the science of psychology, in particular the changes that have occurred over the last thirty years. You will discover that psychology, particularly that branch called personality theory, is not rooted in science as that term has been discussed in Chapter 1. The purpose of this chapter is to help you understand where and what psychology is today, so you may avoid using an antiquated system.

The Naming-Is-Explaining Fallacy

A good starting point to consider changes in psychology is about thirty years ago, the period of the death of a man who has probably made more impact on the interpretation of behavior than any other contemporary figure: Sigmund Freud, who, though called by one wag "the brilliant little genius with the dirty mind," established a frame of reference that is now almost second nature to interpretations of behavior. That frame of reference is clear in the following two quotations from Freud. In particular, note his statements about the causes of the described behavior.

A woman who was living apart from her husband was subject to a compulsion to leave the best of whatever she ate; for example, she would only take the outside of a piece of roast meat. This renunciation was explained by the date of its origin. It appeared the day after she had refused marital relations with her husband, that is to say, had given up the best. . . .

The same patient could only sit on one particular chair, and could leave it again only with difficulty. In connection with certain details of her married life the chair symbolized to her her husband, to whom she remained faithful. She found the explanation of her compulsion in the sentence, "It is so hard to part from anything (chair or husband) in which one has once settled oneself."[1]

Freud's method for understanding man's behavior begins with observation, moves to a curiosity about what might have caused it, and results in a logical imputation about antecedent conditions.

A more recent example of this model can be found in the best seller of several years ago *African Genesis*, by Robert Ardrey. Ardrey quotes C. R. Carpenter, an American zoologist, to support Ardrey's thesis that a good deal of human and subhuman behavior can be understood by the innate or unearned need to defend one's territory. Carpenter says:

It would seem that possession and defense of territory which is found so widely among vertebrates, including human and sub-human primates,[2]

This is the observation stage leading to the imputation of causality; Carpenter continues that this behavior

may be a fundamental biological need.[3]

Note the conditional quality in the term "may be." But that quality is dismissed in the next sentence:

Certain it is that this possession of territory motivates much primate behavior.[4]

The model just expressed is the same as Freud's:

Observation → imputation of causes → acceptance of the imputation as fact.

What has happened is a subtle transmutation of inference to truth. B. F. Skinner describes the process:

Trait-names usually begin as adjectives—"intelligent," "aggressive," "disorganized," "angry," "introverted," "ravenous," and so on—but the almost inevitable linguistic result is that adjectives give birth to nouns. The things to which these nouns refer are then taken to be the active causes of the aspects. We begin with "intelligent behavior," pass first to "behavior which *shows* intelligence," and then to "behavior which is the *effect* of intelligence." Similarly, we begin by observing a preoccupation with a mirror which recalls the legend of Narcissus; we invent the adjective "narcissistic," and then the noun "narcissism," and finally we assert that the thing presumably referred to by the noun is the cause of the behavior with which we began. But at no

[1] Sigmund Freud, "Obsessive Acts and Religious Practices," *Collected Papers*, ed. Ernest Jones, 5 vols. (New York: Basic Books, Inc., Publishers, 1959), 2:28.
[2] Robert Ardrey, *African Genesis* (New York: Atheneum Publishers, 1961), p. 83.
[3] Ibid.
[4] Ibid.

point in such a series do we make contact with any event outside the behavior itself which justifies the claim of a causal connection.[5]

For example, in a study by Eric Haughton and Teodoro Ayllon a particularly lethargic woman patient who had been hospitalized for twenty-three years was trained to stand by her bed and hold a broom. Two psychiatrists were asked to observe and evaluate the patient from behind a one-way mirror. They did not, however, know of her training. Their evaluations, based upon a Freudian interpretation, are good illustrations of how the naming-is-explaining phenomenon sometimes operates. Psychiatrist A interpreted the broom-holding as a symbolic act and equated the broom with the way a child treasures a toy. Psychiatrist B went a little further and said:

Her constant and compulsive pacing holding a broom in the manner she does could be seen as a ritualistic procedure, a magical action. When regression conquers the associative process, primitive and archaic forms of thinking control the behavior. Symbolism is a predominant mode of expression of deep-seated unfilled desires and instinctual impulses. By magic, she controls others, cosmic powers are at her disposal and inanimate objects become living creatures.
    Her broom could be then:

1. A child that gives her love and she gives him in turn her devotion.
2. A phallic symbol.
3. The sceptre of an omnipotent person.[6]

But of course the broom holding was the result of a simple training procedure by the experimenters.

One major change in psychology since Freud, to say it as succinctly as possible, is that psychologists have more and more imposed upon themselves the rigors of scientific methodology as described in Chapter 1. They now recognize the necessity to build their studies upon measurement that approximates the qualities of validity and reliability rather than upon imputations or intuition. It is not to say that hunches and guesses are ruled out of the psychologist's method. Social scientists could hardly function without them. It is to say that intuitions are seen for what they are and today are much less likely to achieve the status they had in Freud's day. Perhaps this is another way of reiterating a theme of Chapter 1; the scientific process necessitates measurement, and unless measurement is taken, one begins to move outside the scope of science. Those who view Freud's statements as scientific have done so without a careful reading of his works. "I am not really a man of science," Freud himself states. "I am not really an observer, not an experimenter and not a thinker. I am nothing but by temperament a conquista-

---

[5] B. F. Skinner, *Science and Human Behavior* (New York: The Macmillan Company, 1953), p. 202.
    [6] E. Haughton and T. Ayllon, "Production and Elimination of Symptomatic Behavior," in *Case Studies in Behavior Modification,* ed. Leonard P. Ullmann and Leonard Krasner (New York: Holt, Rinehart & Winston, Inc., 1965), pp. 94–98.

dor—an adventurer—with the curiosity, the boldness, and the tenacity that belong to that type of being."[7]

Removing Oneself as a Source of Bias

Another trend in psychology has been to decrease the possibility of the investigator's bias. Observers are prone to see what they want to see, that which fits their predispositions, and the psychologist is not exempt from that danger. Consequently, psychologists have deliberately moved away from primary reliance upon subjective observational data. The March, 1969, issue of the *American Psychologist* hints strongly how this may be done. This issue devotes itself exclusively to instrumentation, to electro-mechanical-chemical devices designed to help the researcher become more objective in gathering data. In the lead article, the authors state:

These 29 contributions [in this issue] . . . cover many facts of psychological instrumentation. They represent, however, a small sampling of the many techniques used in the behavioral sciences. But they do suggest that the search for a surer understanding of behavior is being influenced at an accelerating rate by technological developments in electronics and computer sciences.[8]

Several years ago pupillometry (measurement of changes in the size of the pupil of the eye) interested many psychologists. Among other things, it was felt that pupillary response might be an excellent way to study motivational states since dilatation was assumed to be related to conditions of interest or curiosity. Typically, motivation had been studied by rather ephemeral measures like asking the subject if he was aroused, asking him to fill out questionnaires, respond to projective tests, or mark on some sort of scale. These measures left much to be desired because the subject always had the option of deception, that is, of responding in the ways he thought the experimenter wanted him to respond. Subjects for psychological experiments, curiously enough, often strive to please the experimenter. Two investigators[9] had an electronic pupillometer built to measure accurately when and how much the pupil changed under given stimulus conditions. The advantage of such an instrument is that pupillary constriction and dilatation are part of the autonomic nervous system and as such are reasonably free from the subject's

---

[7] Sigmund Freud, quoted in Ernest Jones, *The Life and Work of Sigmund Freud,* ed. Lionel Trilling and Steven Marcus (Garden City, N.Y.: Anchor Books, Doubleday & Co., Inc., 1961), p. xi.

[8] J. B. Sidowski and S. Ross, "Instrumentation in Psychology," *American Psychologist,* March 1969, 24:191.

[9] C. E. Pitts and E. N. Ernhart, "Progress Report—Pupillometrics," August 1, 1967, Central Midwestern Regional Laboratory Grant #28 performed pursuant to contract No. OEC 3-7-063875-3056. Copies may be secured from the U.S. Department of Health, Education and Welfare.

deliberate control or the investigator's subjective interpretations. Therefore these researchers were able to study motive states without having to ask the subject for any verbal information.

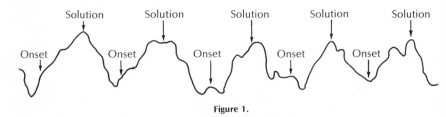

Figure 1.

Figure 1 illustrates how problem solving was studied using an electronic-physiological measure rather than a verbal-introspective measure. Even the casual reader can see the advantage of this method when a subject like "thinking" is studied. No one would doubt that persons think; the difficulty arises when you set out to measure it. The data indicates quite clearly by the dilatation of the eye when the subject was attending to the mathematical problem. Moreover, it is equally clear when the subject solved the problem. Without the pupillometer the quality of the data would have been considerably weakened by human inaccuracy and the subject's or experimenter's predisposition.

Advances in the Design of Psychological Research

It is not intended to give the impression that all of psychology is moving into the brass instruments business. A great deal of research requires relatively little hardware but relies on research design for objectivity. For example, a young child in a preschool exhibited marked isolation behavior. The Freudian could have a field day explaining why the child was asocial, but the principal investigators[10] in this study chose a learning rather than a psychoanalytical model to analyze and change the behavior. Their purpose was to get the child to achieve and maintain more play relations with other children. Their method was to pay attention to her—by talking to her, smiling, touching her, and assisting her—whenever she played with others. When she engaged in isolate behavior no attention was paid to her.

The first step in this study was to get what is known as a baseline, a picture of the child's behavior under nonexperimental conditions. In figure 2 this included days one through five. Here you will note that over the nonexperimental, observational period the highest level of social interaction

[10] K. E. Allen, B. M. Hart, J. S. Guell, F. R. Harris, and M. M. Wolf, "Effects of Social Reinforcement on Isolate Behavior of a Nursery School Child," *Child Development* 35 (1964): 511–18.

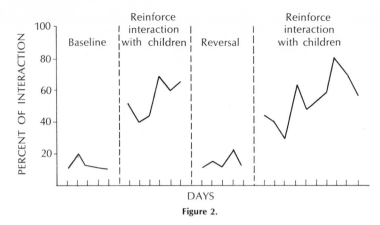

Figure 2.

was about 22%, with an average of 19% for a morning session. Under the experimental conditions of attending to her when and only when she interacted with other children, interaction behavior jumped to an average of about 63% for the next six sessions.

You might quite legitimately say that there had been factors other than attention to account for the change. The only way to test whether or not attention was the variable would be to withhold attention and see if the behavior returned to baseline. As you can see, interaction did drop just about to the level prior to introduction of the change agent.

What you have just seen is what is called an ABA design, a research strategy to determine causal conditions by determining the baseline (condition A), inserting the experimental variable (condition B), and then withdrawing it (condition A). If B is a causal agent, the data one gets during that period ought to be different from those periods when the variable is absent. Moreover, both A conditions would yield similar data.

The example just presented was drawn from the field that has come to be known as behavior modification, a kind of psychology where the purpose is to discover ways behavior may be changed. Another emphasis in psychology has the purpose of description. Here the intent is simply to document in objective terms how a person behaves with no particular interest in modification. A good example of the use of this type of research design can be found in a study by Ogden Lindsley[11] of television viewing with particular concern for what happens when a commercial comes on.

Lindsley developed a simple measurement device based on the principle that the amount of effort one exerts to maintain a condition is a sensitive measure of one's interest. He rigged up a telegraph key which, if depressed sixty times per minute on a near one-per-second schedule, a clear picture was maintained on the tube. If the rate dropped, the picture would fade and

[11] Ogden Lindsley, "A Behavioral Measure of Television Viewing," *Journal of Advertising Research* 2 (1962): 2–12.

blur although there was no effect on the audio. Essentially he wanted to see how much work one would put out to maintain clear viewing. He used actual television productions, and his data was automatically and objectively recorded on a cumulative recorder. The cumulative recorder is an instrument where recorder paper flows beneath a pen at a constant rate. Whenever a response is made, in this case, in pressing the key, the recording pen jumps up a notch. When no response is made, the pen stays in the same position, producing a line horizontal to the side edges of the paper. Steady responses give a rather flat line; no responses give a perfectly flat line.

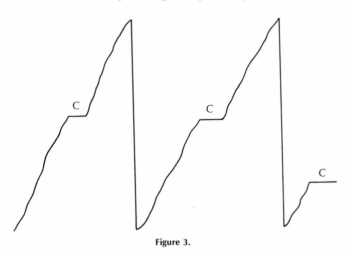

Figure 3.

Figure 3 presents the data from one of Lindsley's subjects viewing the late show. Notice that there is a steady output of key pressing to maintain picture clarity during the movie. When the commercial begins (plateau marked C), there is no output, but when the movie starts again, key pressing returns to its original rate. One does not have to stretch his imagination to interpret how this subject views the merits of the movies in relation to the commercials. In effect, what Lindsley has developed is an attitude measure without having to go through the less objective technique of asking a person how he feels about something.[12]

So What, for Teachers?

This chapter has traced some of the recent trends and shifts of interest in psychology. Since this text is not for the professional psychologist but for

[12] For purposes of clarity, this study has been described here in brief. For more details, the reader is referred to Lindsley's article.

ısers of psychological knowledge, it is appropriate to ask, "So what?" Why nclude what appears at first glance to be a somewhat esoteric, historical liscourse on how psychology has changed?

The primary purpose of this chapter has been to help you develop a ensitivity for and a discriminative framework about data. In its early beginings, psychology—referring now to personality theory—was a social phiosophy rather than a science. It often accepted inference as objective fact,)artly because it had neither the conceptual tools nor the instrumentation to ıchieve those two important conditions of scientific measurement: reliaּility and validity. Much of its terminology was vague even though it oc-:asionally had a deceptive sound of science. Psychology has grown beyond ׀hat early stage, but unfortunately many of the users of psychology, such as eachers, have not. They persist in relying on an outdated and frequently ınusable system. For some reason there is a strong resistance to giving it up. ׀s weakness is pointed up in a study by R. E. Ulrich, T. J. Stachnik, and N. R. ;tainton.[13] One hundred thirty-six students in an educational psychology :lass were given two personality tests. Their instructor returned to each stu-ּent an interpretation of his answers with the request that he evaluate the ınterpretations. By and large, the students praised their instructor's comments ᴠith phrases like "surprisingly accurate," "unbelievably close to the truth," 'on the nose," "very good." What the students did not know was that the ınterpretive comments were the same for each member of the class! Another ᗞroblem of the old personality theory is that it is of questionable value to the ᗞractitioner. What does one *do* if a student has been diagnosed as having ᴠeak ego strength, father fixation, oedipal complex, is insecure, anxious, ense, or dumb? None of these categories—purportedly "causes" of behavior —carries with it any notion of ways to change the behavior related to the 'cause." Much of contemporary psychology is impatient with the naming-is-ׇxplaining fallacy.

In its place, psychologists today prefer to deal with more tangible, ᴨeasurable variables, and they turn to ways of designing environmental :onsequences that will effectively change inappropriate behaviors. The ᴦend is toward clearer specification and quantification of change agents as ᴠas found in the study by Allen with the withdrawn preschoolers. There the ᴠariable directly related to changing the child's asocial behavior was atten-ion. There was no mystery about what that meant for the teacher and, ac-:ordingly, was a readily usable tool for therapy.

The teacher is the recipient of a considerable amount of information ıbout a class and the individuals within that class. What will you accept and ᴡhat will you reject as datum? How will you respond if someone tells you ׀he cause of a child's poor academic record is laziness? Or that a student

[13] R. E. Ulrich, T. J. Stachnik, and N. R. Stainton, "Student Acceptance of Generalized ᗮersonality Interpretations" in *Control of Human Behavior*, ed. R. E. Ulrich, T. J. Stachnik, and . Mabry (Glenview, Ill.: Scott, Foresman and Company, 1966).

cannot succeed because he is dumb? How will your attitude toward a studen whom you do not like affect his performance scores on an essay test?

There is an interesting self-fulfilling prophecy about information and predispositions of this variety. In a study conducted in a number of classe on the West Coast[14] teachers were informed that they had several "spurters" in each class, children who could be expected to show significant increase during the year. These students were identified to the teacher, and as pre dicted they did show the expected increases. The "spurters" gained sig nificantly more than the other children in their classes on the post-test. It wa only until after the experiment that the schools were informed that the "spurt ers" were chosen at random. As the authors put it, "the difference between the special children and the ordinary children was only in the mind of the teacher."

Summary

This chapter, designed to inform you of some recent trends in the field c psychology, considered the following major points:

1. Much of historical psychology—in particular, personality theory—has been guilty of the scientifically questionable assumption that naming a behavio explains the cause of that behavior.
2. Psychology has increasingly imposed upon itself a more rigorous scientifi methodology.
3. Psychologists, as part of their self-imposed rigor, have become more con scious of the possibility of subjective interpretation of their observations an have devised ways to insure greater objectivity.
4. One way objectivity can be increased is by the appropriate use of electro mechanical devices and more careful research design.
5. Scientific knowledge developed from more objective measurement and controlled research procedures has greater possibility for application b practitioners than ever before because of the knowledge now available abou change agents and processes.

The next chapter is a further extension of the scientific process in understanding behavior. An actual study is presented and criticized from the point of view discussed in Chapters 1 and 2.

---

[14] R. Rosenthal and L. Jacobsen, *Pygmalion in the Classroom* (New York: Holt, Rineha and Winston, Inc., 1968).

3 / A Case Study

The first chapter was designed to highlight the principal guidelines in scientific investigation. This chapter is designed to show how some of these were put into operation in an actual study of children in a kindergarten.

The study to be presented in full is a descriptive study. That is, its purpose is not to change the children's behavior but rather to describe how ten five-year-old boys behave toward each other in a reasonably natural environment. Notice that the study was done in 1935, which in the history of the social-behavioral sciences makes it an old study. Nonetheless, it is one which has often been reprinted largely because of the author's adherence to a careful methodology and measurement technique.

As you read the study, keep in mind the concepts of science discussed in Chapter 1.

Social Structure of a Group of Kindergarten Children
EUGENIA HANFMANN[1]

In order to investigate the interrelationship of dominance within a kindergarten group consisting of ten five-year-old boys, the method of comparison in pairs was introduced. Two children at a time were taken to a separate room and allowed to play freely with colored blocks for fifteen to thirty minutes, while two observers recorded everything both children did and said. Every child was to be paired with every other child of the group and was thus to be observed playing with nine different partners.

[1] Eugenia Hanfmann, "Social Structure of a Group of Kindergarten Children," *American Journal of Orthopsychiatry* 5 (October 1935): 407–10, copyright © 1935 by the American Orthopsychiatric Association, Inc., reprinted by permission of Eugenia Hanfmann and the American Orthopsychiatric Association, Inc.

For control purposes some of the combinations were repeated with changed play material.

After each session an estimate was made by two observers as to which child of the pair was the dominant one. The child who was considered dominant was the one who in his play carried through what he himself wanted and also had the other child do what he—i.e., the first child—wanted. In other words, he controlled both his own play and that of his companion. In doubtful cases the decision was reached by determining how frequently during a session each child controlled the other and was himself controlled. Usually the impression of the observers was confirmed by this analysis.

On the basis of these estimates we arrived at a rank order of dominance measured by the number of partners whom the child dominated. This rank order is shown on the chart [figure 4]. One child is omitted from the chart because he was not paired with all nine children. If the dominance were based upon one factor, varying in degree from child to child but constant for each child, we would expect to find that if child X dominated child Y, and the latter in his turn dominated child Z, then X would also dominate Z, and we would have a linear rank order. Such relationship is actually found in the lower half of our rank order. However, the interrelationship of the four children ranking highest is more complicated; while A dominates B and B dominates C and D each of these, C and D in his turn dominates A. This circular connection suggests that the dominance does not mean the same thing in all cases, and actually we find that these four or five children represent different patterns and different methods of dominance.

We start with child E who occupies the middle position: He is dominated by four children and he himself dominates four. His dominance, however, conforms only to the first part of our criterion: he plays as he wants, but he does not control the play of his partner except by resisting the latter's wishes. He anxiously protects the blocks that have become his and consistently opposes the attempts of any other child to bring about joint play. In seven of the nine combinations in which E takes part, the play is parallel play throughout, each child building by himself. Thus the dominance is reached by this apprehensive child by way of isolation: it is a negative rather than a positive dominance.

The opposite tactics are employed by the four highest ranking children who actively control the others: every one of them tends to break rather than to strengthen the barrier between himself and his associate, but each does it in a different way and to a different extent.

Child C is himself dominated and dominates the other children by his strong interest in the constructive play, of which he is a great master. He has very definite plans for his play; usually he succeeds in imparting them to the other child and then he will lead and direct the joint activity, mostly giving suggestions but also frequently taking them. He gets what he needs from his companion—his play material, his assistance—by clearly explaining to the latter his purpose and needs, by earnestly stressing the requirements of the play and insisting on them but never by violence. If a conflict arises, he tries to solve it by a compromise, e.g., by giving a block in exchange for the one he needs, by making a pact about taking turns, or by combining ingeniously two proposed activities into one. If the conflict cannot be solved by any one of these methods, he will occasionally deliberately dissolve the joint play declaring, for instance: "I'll make a chimney, and you make what you like!" Thus, on the whole, his play with another child results as frequently in parallel as in joint play, the social aspect being subordinated to the requirements of the play activity as such. We could speak of this child as an *objective leader*.

For child D, on the other hand, not play in itself but play with another child is the ultimate goal. He tries to induce and to maintain the joint play whenever he can

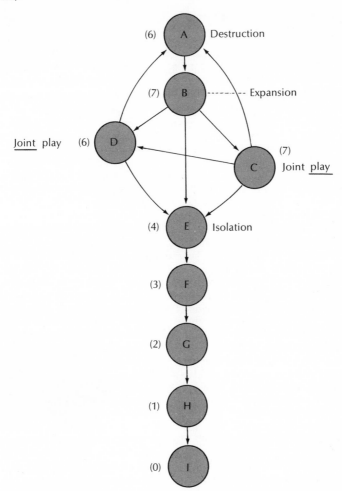

(6) A Destruction

(7) B ------- Expansion

Joint play (6) D

(7)
Joint play

C

(4) E Isolation

(3) F

(2) G

(1) H

(0) I

Figure 4. Figures in parentheses refer to the number of partners dominated by the child.

and actually succeeds with six children out of nine. His methods of controlling the other child are similar to those of C, for he bases his demands upon the requirements of the play, never coercing his playmate and never flatly refusing his requests. But he goes further than that: he actually takes into account the attitude of his companion and displays an astonishing skill and flexibility in trying to remove rather than break his resistance. He introduces mutual play not by taking the other child's blocks but by offering his own; he takes care to announce and to explain his actions in advance, especially when taking the blocks away; while the blocks are in his possession, he keeps telling the other one reassuringly that he will return them soon and actually does so; if he meets with resistance, he never presses the point and lets some time pass before repeating his request, usually in a modified form; occasionally he simply ignores a refusal or by treating it as a joke makes the other child treat it in the same way. Usually these varied diplomatic methods are successful but in the case of a serious conflict he will give way, at least temporarily, to his comrade's plans rather than give up the joint play. We may speak of this child as a *social leader*.

For child B social play has a totally different function—it is a means of expanding and displaying his own power. Though extremely active, he is less interested in the play itself than in getting all blocks for himself, in being the initiator of all activities, and in having an unrestricted command over the other child. This latter is not allowed any possession or any activity except in a subordinate role; he is practically thrust out of the play. Yet C does not leave him alone; he keeps requiring the other's services and attention and refers to his own activities as if they were a joint enterprise: "We are making a big train," etc. Thus with this boy social play degenerates into pseudo-social play, with one child having no real part in it. The methods he uses to bring about this situation are as primitive as they are effective: grabbing blocks violently; disregarding protestations; denying the other's requests by saying merely "No, you can't. They are mine. I will do it myself"; suppressing the other's attempts at activity by force, for instance, by holding his hands; boasting of his own possessions and actions and belittling his partner. In short, the methods used are those of a little *gangster*. They are characterized by great forcefulness and by complete disregard for the rights and wishes of the other child.

It seems that the child using such methods should be invincible. Yet as the medium for his expansion and dominance is still play activity, he is powerless against the child (A) who deliberately disrupts the situation of orderly play. The method of child A is destruction. He himself does not build, and when the other child starts building, he purposely destroys his work, throwing the blocks to the floor and meeting protests merely with outbursts of laughter. This procedure is repeated until the other child gives up all attempts at continuing his play. (At this point A usually introduces a new activity, e.g., counting objects in the room—an activity in which he takes the lead or in which both children continue relatively independent of each other.) As *destroyer* this child is invincible. Yet with children C and D he made only half-hearted attempts at destruction and mostly observed with interest their intensive play. Another time he watched for a while spell-bound, observed the constructive play of the other child for a moment, tried to imitate him, and then suddenly burst into wild destruction. These variations of his usual behavior suggested that, with play material sufficiently interesting and yet not too difficult for him, the destructive behavior of this child could be checked. This expectation was fulfilled. With the new play material, the behavior of A changed to a quiet absorption in his play, and he assumed methods of controlling the other child similar in all details to those of C and D. This shows that even though a pattern of dominance can be typical for one child, it is not rigid and unchangeable and depends both upon his partner and upon the activity. That is why we prefer to speak of the patterns of dominance rather than of the types of dominators.

We cannot discuss here what conflicts arise when the different dominance patterns meet, but we must consider briefly how these different patterns affect the dominated children. Patterns represented by C and D make for a happy and harmonious play, those represented by A and B lead to continuous conflict and dissatisfaction. When the children were asked by their teacher, after the completion of the experiment, with whom they liked best to play, eight of the ten named either C or D, thus proving that they preferred the leadership of this type both to the other patterns of dominance and to the absence of any strong leadership.

Summarizing, we find that the pattern of dominance by destruction is the most effective but also the least stable one, because it disappears as soon as interest in the play is aroused. That is why the "destroyer" may dominate the "gangster," yet be himself dominated by children whose primary interest is play and whose methods are far from violent. The pattern of dominance based upon expansion of personal power is a much stabler one, even though it can also be modified by a strong interest in play as such.

Both of these patterns, however, are unacceptable to the dominated child. Only the child who is mostly interested in play as such or in social play becomes a real leader, gladly followed by other children. In every instance the social behavior of a child is part of a total structure including the interrelationship of both children involved and the medium in which it takes place and can be influenced and changed through changes of this structure.

Dissecting a Study

Now that you have read the study, it would be advantageous to go back over it in some detail.

Miss Hanfmann states that her intent is to study ten children. Nowhere does she say that she is trying to describe *all* children or even *all kindergarten* children. Rather, she confines her explanation to the data at hand and is careful not to generalize to other groups. The beginning point, then, is with her group of ten children.

The next step in the study is to arrange an experimental setting in which each child plays with each other child for a period of fifteen to thirty minutes. Two observers watched the children as they played, but here she is not too specific about the conditions of observation. Were the observers behind a one-way mirror or were they seated away from the children but within the children's view? If the latter, could there not have been some confounding influence by the observers' presence? Would the children have played the same way if the observers were out of view? It is difficult to say, but for the moment charity will be extended and it will be assumed that the presence of the observers was not disruptive to the children's play.

The criteria used by each observer was clearly defined; they were to select the dominant child from each pair, based upon two kinds of behavior, the child "who in his play carried through what he himself wanted and also had the other child do what he—i.e., the first child—wanted. In other words, he controlled both his own play and that of his companion." The study does not state how the observers quantified "dominating" behavior, but presumably a running tally of instances of domination was kept and the child with the largest number was classified as dominant. Nor does the study report differences in amount of domination. For example, if child A dominates child E twenty times and child B dominates child C two times is it legitimate to classify both A and B as dominant even though there was a difference of eighteen acts of domination between A and E and B and C? This kind of data could and perhaps should have been included in the study.

Why two observers? This seems to be a case where two heads are better than one to assure a more reliable measure. Typically, when measures are of the observational variety, observers are well trained before embarking on the study, and as a rule of thumb observers have to reach an agreement of 85% or better in whatever they are observing before the measurement is considered adequate. In the case of this study, it appears that what was being observed was sufficiently obvious that there was little disagreement between observers.

One particularly interesting finding was that when the play situation was changed for child A, he engaged in social rather than destructive behavior. "This shows that even though a pattern of dominance can be typical for one child, it is not rigid and unchangeable and depends both upon his partner and upon the activity." Dominance seems to be a function of the environment of the child as well as habitual patterns. A finding such as this is provocative of many other testable hypotheses for the teacher who has great control over the kind of activities in which the children engage.

Finally, the question of validity of the measure needs to be asked. The behavioral definition of dominance was clearly stated by the investigator, leading to reasonable assurance that what was quantified by the observers was what Miss Hanfmann chose to call "dominance." Another investigator might have preferred "social power" or "aggression"; the term becomes understandable only by the criteria used in measurement. Since the study became public by having appeared in the *American Journal of Orthopsychiatry,* one can assume that it was read by the editor and in all probability by other experts in the field before it was recommended for publication. Studies submitted for professional journals go through quite a critical gauntlet before they appear in print, and they are sometimes rewritten several times in the process. Here it is obvious that the editorial readers accepted the author's measure of dominance without question, a second-order validation through consensus by a panel of experts. Even so, a reader may still want to disagree and if a reasonable case is made and submitted to the journal, the reply to the study will in most cases be printed. The history of research includes many running battles of presentation, disagreement, rebuttal, and so on.

The major portion of Miss Hanfmann's article is devoted to an analysis of the kinds of dominance in the children's behavior. She seldom goes beyond the immediate data, but one does occasionally get the impression that her own values have entered: child B's behavior is that "of a little *gangster . . .* characterized . . . by complete disregard for the rights and wishes of the other child." Obviously one must exert extreme caution not to let his own biases enter into interpretation. Terms that connote good-bad qualities to persons being studied, such as "dominance," "destroyer," "gangster," and "real leader," are usually to be avoided in research, or if they are difficult to avoid, it is incumbent upon the investigator to admit openly his feelings.

Summary

A case-study approach using an actual study has been presented and discussed on the basis of scientific guidelines. In particular, reliability, validity, and the necessity for science to be public have been emphasized. Suggestions were made for the inclusion of some additional details.

The next chapter is typical of the two to follow it. Specific tools of the social-behavioral sciences are presented in the hope that these tools will become a part of your repertoire of skills.

4 / Observation

Our visitor bore every mark of being an average common-place British tradesman, obese, pompous, and slow. He wore rather baggy gray shepherd's check trousers, a not over-clean black frock coat, unbuttoned in the front, and a drab waistcoat with a heavy brassy Albert chain, and a square pierced bit of metal dangling down as an ornament. A frayed top hat and a faded brown overcoat with a wrinkled velvet collar lay upon a chair beside him. Altogether, look as I would, there was nothing remarkable about the man save his blazing red head and the expression of extreme chagrin and discontent upon his features.

Sherlock Holmes's quick eye took in my occupation, and he shook his head with a smile as he noticed my questioning glances. "Beyond the obvious facts that he has at some time done manual labor, that he takes snuff, that he is a Freemason, that he has been in China, and that he has done a considerable amount of writing lately, I can deduce nothing else."

Mr. Jabex Wilson started up in his chair, with his forefinger upon the paper, but his eyes upon my companion.

"How, in the name of good fortune, did you know all that, Mr. Holmes?" he asked.[1]

It seems appropriate in this chapter to begin with the greatest observer of them all. Arthur Conan Doyle created in Sherlock Holmes an unforgettable character with an uncanny ability to discover subtle cues, to synthesize them into a patterned whole, and to add meaningful order in a style that escapes most of the rest of us. Let it be quickly stated, however, that reading this chapter will not make you a Sherlock Holmes or even a less perceptive Dr. Watson. Perhaps such astute observational powers can only be found in fiction. Nonetheless, this chapter is designed to sharpen your already well-

---

[1] Arthur Conan Doyle, "The Red-Headed League."

developed skills by providing precautions, guidelines, and a methodology for observing and recording the behavior of others.

The Problem of Selective Perception

What a person sees as he views another's behavior is always the result of a process of selection and interpretation. One cannot pay attention to everything nor does one usually accept behavior for its face value without adding some kind of interpretative "causes." There is an old trick often performed in introductory psychology courses of having one of the class members behave in a shocking manner during class. The class does not know that the professor and the student have rehearsed the bit beforehand. When the class is questioned about the details of the event—what kind of sweater did the student wear, how much did he weigh, what was the cause of the event, was he wearing a ring, what did he say, was he angry, and so on—it is surprising how little agreement there is in description and interpretation.

Perception may also be swayed by one's own needs and predispositions. David C. McClelland cites an example of how manipulation of instructions may affect one's perception. When asked to interpret a picture of a boy sitting at a desk with an opened book before him, one typical male college student's response is:

A boy in a classroom who is daydreaming about something. He is recalling a previously experienced incident that struck his mind to be more appealing than being in the classroom. He is thinking about the experience and is now imagining himself in the situation. He hopes to be there. He will probably get called on by the instructor to recite and will be embarrassed.[2]

If the request for interpretation is modified by the statement that their response is a measure of their level of intelligence, administrative capacity, and leadership potential, the subjects usually respond quite differently:

The boy is taking an hour written. He and the others are high-school students. The test is about two-thirds over and he is doing his best to think it through. He was supposed to study for the test and did so. But because it is factual, there were items he saw but did not learn. He knows he has studied the answers he can't remember and is trying to summon up the images and related ideas to remind him of them. He may remember one or two, but he will miss most of the items he can't remember. He will try hard until five minutes is left, then give up, go back over his paper, and be disgusted for reading but not learning the answers.[3]

The more one gets committed to a point of view the more he is susceptible to seeing what he wants to see. Ray Hyman recounts an example of

[2] David C. McClelland, *The Achieving Society* (New York: The Free Press, 1961), p. 41, copyright © 1961 by D. Van Nostrand Co., Inc., reprinted by permission of The Macmillan Company.

[3] Ibid., p. 41.

subjective viewing in the physical sciences:

The n-ray was discovered in 1902 by the eminent French physicist M. Blondlot. The discovery was confirmed and extended by other French scientists. In the year 1904 alone, there appeared 77 different scientific publications devoted to the n-ray. Controversy over the n-ray quickly arose when it was realized that German, Italian, and American physicists could not duplicate Blondlot's findings. The n-ray, it seemed, could be observed only on French soil. Eventually, the American physicist R. W. Wood, who had unsuccessfully attempted to duplicate n-rays in his own laboratory at Johns Hopkins, visited Blondlot in Nancy. Woods own encounter with Blondlot is best described in his own words.

> He first showed me a card on which some circles had been painted in luminous paint. He turned down the gas light and called my attention to their increased luminosity when the n-ray was turned on. I said I saw no change. He said that was because my eyes were not sensitive enough so that proved nothing. I asked him if I could move an opaque lead screen in and out of the path of the rays while he called out the fluctuations on the screen. He was almost 100% wrong and called out fluctuations when I made no movement at all, and that proved a lot, but I held my tongue.

Wood conducted other tests which clearly demonstrated that the n-rays existed only in Blondlot's imagination. By 1909 there were no more publications involving the n-ray. Blondlot himself never recovered from this incident and died in disgrace.[4]

Other examples could be given for further support to the fact that one's predispositions—values, moods, needs, and expectations—are important factors in what is seen and how it is interpreted. In one way the human organism, because of its unusual level of sensitivity and ability to respond to many cues, is an exceptionally good observer; in another way, its penchant for selective perception and subjective interpretation leaves much to be desired if the purpose of observation is to secure scientifically respectable data.

Fortunately, persons can be trained to increase their objectivity in observation. A psychiatrist or clinical psychologist who engages in interpretive verbal therapy has to have a deep insight into his own problems and inabilities. It is not unusual for such a person to go through extensive psychotherapy or even psychoanalysis in order to achieve some objectivity about himself. Unless one is extremely well trained and sensitive to his own biases, the act of watching and interpreting the behavior of others could become an expression of the observer's needs and values with little to do with the behavior of the one observed. And science, as considered in Chapter 1, goes out the window when it becomes so individualistic.

What alternative is there for the person who wants to be an objective observer without becoming a psychiatrist or earning a Ph.D. in clinical psychology? The answer is deceptively simple. Stick as close as possible to the actual data of behavior, and be careful of interpretive remarks that are based

---

[4] Ray Hyman, *The Nature of Psychological Inquiry* (Englewood Cliffs, N.J.: Prentice-Hall, Inc., 1964), p. 38, copyright © 1964 by Prentice-Hall, Inc., reprinted by permission of the publisher.

upon inferences. The answer is *deceptively* simple because it takes discipline not to go beyond the data at hand. As one first begins objective observation, it feels unnatural because of the novelty of its style. Obviously, a certain richness will be lost when one sticks just to the behavior that occurs. A novelist could hardly hope to write a work of art by following the rules of objective observation, but a novelist (thank goodness) is primarily interested in creative portrayal and not in scientific reporting.

Herbert Wright expresses in more detail the guidelines for behavioral observation:

The observer is not asked to theorize; he is asked not to theorize. He is asked to suspend biases from formal psychological training, and to fall back on the elementary, garden variety, spur-of-the-moment notions and hunches about behavior that are common to man as a socialized being, that could never be abolished or appreciably suppressed if this should seem desirable, and that cannot help but astonish anyone who stops to reflect upon them with their high ratio of accuracy to error.

A rough three-level classification of psychological descriptions may now be useful.

There are, first, running accounts of what a person is doing and of his situation on the level of direct perception or immediate inference. Here are some samples from one of our records. What we take to be immediate inferences are italicized.

> Suddenly Raymond ran *eagerly* to another tree. He started climbing the tree with great energy. He remarked *in an offhand way,* but with slight emphasis on the second word, "I hope I can climb this tree." *He seemed to say this to himself as a form of encouragement.* In a high-pitched, soft sing-song he said, "I hope, I hope, I hope." Raymond continued climbing the tree *cautiously,* grasping one branch and then another and fixing his feet firmly. He called out to Stewart in a *playfully boastful manner,* "Stewart, this tree is harder to climb than the other one." Stewart called back very firmly and definitely, "No, it isn't." . . .

Second, there are minor interpretations in the form of statements *about* rather than descriptions *of* behavior or situation. Usually these are based upon observations covering a more or less extended sequence of behavior. Always they are couched in the idiom of everyday social experience, as below.

> *I had the feeling that, although the story wasn't especially interesting, he liked this restful part of the day when he could just sit. In handing his father the sugar bowl and salt shaker, Raymond was helping. Of course, he would have helped more if he had gotten up and put them in (the cupboard) himself, . . . I think Raymond wanted to be in on what was going on that he wanted his father's continued attention more than to help. But the efforts were accepted as help. . . .*

Minor interpretations like these often may be included advantageously in a record when the behavior and circumstances of the subject would otherwise remain obscure. They appear rather infrequently in our reports, however, and the observers are not pressed to offer them. When any such interpretation does occur in a record, it is set apart in an indented paragraph, where it can be studied for what it may be worth.

Finally, there are the technical or professional interpretations. We mean by these: generalizations based upon quite explicit theories about behavior.

The evidence suggests that in "accidentally" breaking the new briar pipe, after listening in on the argument between his parents, Tom was manifesting repressed aggression against his father. . . .

These statements exemplify the theorizing that the observers are asked not to do. The psychology of observing for a specimen record is not a depth psychology or a textbook psychology, but whatever psychology there is in common understanding of behavior.[5]

An Observational Technique Applicable to the Classroom

Every teacher sooner or later would like to have objective observational data on one or several students in the class to help give insight into a problem situation. What is to follow is an explanation of a helpful technique for gathering observational information.

During World War I a citizen of Polish Austria, Bronislaw Kasper Malinowski, was made to disembark from the ship on which he was traveling and was "interned" for the major portion of the war on the Trobriand Islands. The fact that Poland had become involved in the war while Malinowski was on the trip accounted for his abrupt disembarkation. The islands where he was to spend several years constitute part of the Melanesian community and lie directly north of the eastern tip of New Guinea. With no place else to go and time on his hands, Malinowski became preoccupied with observing and recording the behavior of the Trobrianders and in the process began to develop a system that later became a major school of anthropology. It is known as functionalism, and it maintains that culture is an integrated whole, analogous to a single organism, and that no part of a culture may be understood except in relation to the whole. Contrary to other anthropological methods, functionalism is less concerned about the history or evolution of a culture than it is in the totality of what is currently going on.

The functionalist point of view is not confined to anthropology, however, for the technique has been used in sociology, social psychology, and psychology. Essentially, it involves an observer in a naturally occurring environment rather than an experimentally induced environment. The observer seeks through first-hand observation to construct the network of interrelationships between people and their environments. The technique goes beyond mere description to analysis and comparison. Two of the better-known exponents of the functionalist position in psychology (they call their methodology *behavioral ecology*) are Roger G. Barker and Herbert F. Wright. The two of them have amassed an impressive body of observational data on the behavior of children. Probably their best-known work is an extensive obser-

---

[5] Herbert F. Wright, *Recording and Analyzing Child Behavior* (New York: Harper & Row, Publishers, 1967), pp. 38–40, copyright © 1967 by Herbert F. Wright, reprinted by permission of the publisher.

vational tour de force which documents and analyzes the behavior of a boy
from early rising to bedtime, *One Boy's Day*.[6]

Analysis of Observational Data

Following in the Barker-Wright tradition the purpose of this section is to
define ways by which the "stream of behavior"[7] can be arranged for purposes of analysis.

It will be remembered that at the beginning of this chapter it was
stated that the purpose was to increase your already well-developed skills
of observation. That phrase was used not to boost your ego but was meant
literally because persons without training do perceive the behavior of others
in terms of units. Harold R. Dickman designed a study to answer the question,
"to what extent is there communality of agreement among independent
observers relative to the units of behavior contained in a given sequence."[8]

He selected an eight-minute section from the sound movie *A Gift from
Dad* dealing with a little girl who had accidentally killed a squirrel and who
subsequently received a baby calf from her father to alleviate her guilt. Each
subject was asked to view the segment as they would in the theater. After
presentation of the segment, the subjects were given a series of 140 three-by-
five cards each of which had a small part of the movie described on it. The
cards were arranged in a sequential order to correspond to the events in the
movie and subjects were asked to

divide the cards into groups so that each group represents a happening in the movie.
There is no "right" answer to this test. You may have as many or as few groups as
you would like as long as each group represents a happening in the movie. . .[9]

The subjects, thirty-eight students in a beginning psychology course,
had little difficulty completing the task. Their responses are shown in figure 5.
Each vertical line represents one subject's division of the film sequence. Interruption of the line indicates that subject's choice of a breaking point in
the sequence. Dickman concludes his analysis of the data gathered from
untrained observers:

we may summarize our conclusions by saying that the "stream of behavior" attains
orderliness in the eyes of other humans to the extent that goals and motives are im-

---

[6] Roger G. Barker and Herbert F. Wright, *One Boy's Day* (New York: Harper & Row,
Publishers, 1951).
[7] A term used by Barker to describe behavioral flow which became the title of a book of
readings using the Barker-Wright technique: Roger G. Barker, ed., *The Stream of Behavior* (New
York: Appleton-Century-Crofts, 1963).
[8] Harold R. Dickman, "The Perception of Behavioral Units," in *The Stream of Behavior*,
ed. Barker, pp. 25–26, reprinted by permission of the publisher.
[9] Ibid., p. 26.

puted to the behavior. Independent observers of such a behavior continuum demonstrated significant agreement on general patterning and specifically on the points at which units began or ended.[10]

Beverly Is a Problem

Beverly is a five-year-old child enrolled in a preschool, Head Start center in a rural, midwestern area. Her teacher was concerned about her behavior because, as she put it, "Beverly seems very immature for her age. She's shy. Very seldom does she talk with the other children or take part in our general activities, except to stand by and watch. How can we get her involved?"

A trained observer recorded Beverly's behavior for one hour. Part of these observations are reproduced as a sample of a technique of recording behavior from which analysis can later be made.

Upon entering the room, the observer made a rough sketch of the room space, using roman numerals to designate portions of the room. In the report the teacher is identified by "L"; the teacher's aide by "GA"; Beverly by "B." There were fourteen children.

10:45:30 / (Forty-five minutes and thirty seconds after ten o'clock) I walked in during a free time period where children were engaged in a variety of self-selected activities. Beverly (B) was standing by herself next to table in area II cutting paper. She looked toward me, looked back at paper, turned again to me and back to paper. Cutting small pieces.

10:47:50 / Teacher aide (GA) walks over, puts hands on B's shoulder and talks to her. I could not hear. GA walks to easel, turns, looks to B. B continues to cut. GA walks to B, again places hands on shoulders, talks to her. B puts down scissors, GA walks to easel. B follows: GA puts up paper on easel. B stands before easel and watches with hands behind her back—glances over to me—turns back—stands quietly, mouth open, watching GA. GA gets apron and ties it on B, gets paint brush, puts brush in B's left hand and lifts her hand into position.

10:50:07 / B stands before easel, holding brush, looking at paper. Another child, painting on easel next to her, talks to B. B turns, looks at her. No response from B. Turns back to easel.

10:54:22 / Slowly dips brush in paint and begins to make ovals on paper. GA, who had gone to area V, returns: "Want another color?" B nods affirmative. "Green?" B shakes her head. "Red?" B shakes her head. "What color do you want?" B drops her head, turns to face easel, puts her finger up to mouth as GA watches. GA turns and walks away. B begins painting again.

10:57:15 / GA returns: "Here I'll put your name on your picture." B watches while GA writes her name in upper right corner.

10:57:30 / B turns to watch girl next to her. She (neighbor) rattles off several ques-

[10] Ibid., p. 41.

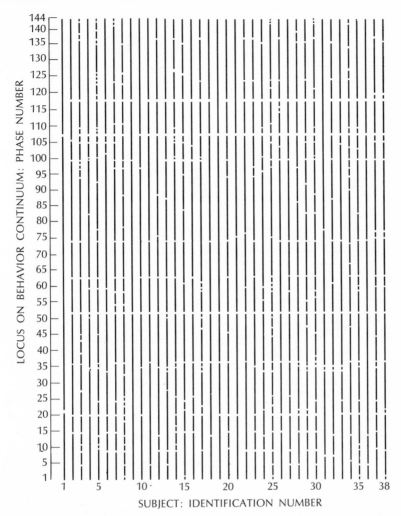

LOCUS ON BEHAVIOR CONTINUUM: PHASE NUMBER

SUBJECT: IDENTIFICATION NUMBER

Figure 5. Units of behavior identified by each subject on first behavior grouping test. Phases of the behavior continuum are numbered in consecutive order.

tions. B just looks at her. No change in expression (actually no change in expression up to now).

11:00:15 / "Time to get ready for lunch," general announcement by teacher (L). B puts down brush, turns, starts to take off apron. GA helps her take it off.

11:03:05 / GA untacks her picture. "Good, B. Now go to the bathroom and wash your hands."

11:03:35 / B turns and walks out door at II.

11:08:55 / B walks into room. Most of the children are already back. Goes to table

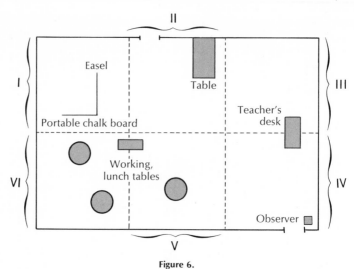

Figure 6.

at II where two other children are standing. Picks up scissors and begins cutting. Appears to be same activity when I first entered.

11:09:45 / Looks at me. Watches girl next to her. Looks back at me. Puts down scissors, walks to VI. Sits down at far table. GA talks to her. No verbal response from B. Rolls small plastic horse back and forth across table.

11:12:15 / Gets up, goes to II. Generally, most of the children moving toward or around tables in area VI. Teachers bringing in trays of food.

11:14:30 / Returns to II and begins sweeping floor. B goes to IV, gets broom, picks up scraps of paper on floor, and deposits in cardboard box.

11:16:17 / "Come on B. Sit down at the table." L spoke softly but firmly. B goes slowly to area VI and sits in chair. Girl next to her hands her a cut-out Santa. B accepts. Looks at it. Places it on table.

11:16:20 / L gives tray to B. She sits quietly looking at her food.

11:18:05 / Grace said by one of the children. Most begin eating. B continues looking at her food. GA says, "Beverly, why don't you eat?" B ducks her head, GA comes over, talks with her silently. B does not look at GA, just sits with head down. GA pulls a chair over, sits down next to B, picks up her plastic spoon, and begins feeding her. B accepts the food but after each bite lowers her head.

Analyzing the Behavioral Stream

Analysis of behavioral sequences must be tailored to fit the kind of problem one is investigating. In the case of Beverly, whom the teacher wanted to get more involved, several aspects of her behavior are evident.

1. Beverly often gets what she wants by noninvolvement.
2. Withdrawal consistently gets attention from the teacher or teacher aide.
3. Direct attempts to bring her into the group activities usually fail.
4. Most of her play during the observational period was solitary play. She watched other children but seldom responded to them.

Given longer observational periods, the record could be reviewed in a variety of ways. Some of the questions one might ask of the data are:

1. When the teacher or teacher aide gives general directives to the group such as "Let's put away our paints now," what does Beverly typically do? The intent here is to discover what Beverly does when indirect methods are used.
2. Does Beverly usually resist direct invitations to participate with the group? Such was the case during the period recorded here, but it may not be true over longer observational time.
3. Under what conditions is she noncontingent upon external influences; that is, when does she fail to respond to opportunities for involvement from teachers or other students?
4. Under what conditions is she more contingent upon teachers or other students? If these can be documented from observational data, they might be good beginning points for more general contingency training.
5. Are there children in the group to whom Beverly is responsive either in a positive or negative fashion? Children with whom she spends most of her time could become important agents in changing Beverly's behavior.
6. In what activities does Beverly spend most of her time? Such activities could become important rewards for other "involvement" behavior which in turn might increase the probability of her becoming more involved.

These particular questions seem appropriate in the case of Beverly's noninvolvement because they are designed to discover the conditions to which she was positively responsive so that they in turn could be used to bring about a change in her behavior. Since this is an actual case, partial answers based upon more lengthy observation can be given.

Generally, Beverly was quite responsive to requests made by the teacher to the whole group, but Beverly rejected the greater percentage of direct appeals, requests, or invitations. Knowing this, the teachers changed their approach to Beverly, and whenever possible their directions to Beverly were given to several children. Beverly seemed perfectly willing to become involved when others were included but continued to resist being singled out.

Because Beverly would get the teachers' attention (which she obviously wanted) by failing to respond to requests, it appeared as though the teachers by their attention were building in the very behavior they did not want. Consequently, they stopped attending to her withdrawal. Beverly did miss one meal because she refused to feed herself, but that was the last meal she missed.

Having established from the observational data that adult attention was important, both teachers became much more attentive to her when she became involved. In time the fun of the activities was sufficient to replace their attention.

Beverly still has a long way to go to catch up with the other children, but appreciable progress has been made. The observational study turned out to be an important source of information to help the teachers change their behavior so that Beverly could become more comfortable with them and with the class. Remember that what was done with Beverly is not offered as a master plan for all shy children. Beverly's "therapy" grew out of a specific situation that was thoroughly understood because of systematic observation from which a definite plan could be derived.

Summary

To be able to observe someone else's behavior takes both training and self-discipline, for without either there is a strong and very natural tendency to emphasize and interpret those aspects of behavior which fit our own predispositions.

This chapter presented a method of behavioral observation that minimizes subjective interpretation while emphasizing objective recording of the stream of behavior. Once observational data has been gathered, it may be analyzed in whatever ways seem appropriate to the original reason for observation. An example of data covering about thirty minutes was presented from an actual situation involving a five-year-old child in a preschool program. An analysis was made with respect to the teacher's concern that the child was not sufficiently involved in the activities, with samples of relevant questions.

5 / Obvious and Not-So-Obvious Measures

The eminent psychologist G. W. Allport once said, "If you want to know how people feel: What they experience and what they remember, what their emotions and motives are like, and the reason for acting as they do —why not ask them?"[1] Certainly Allport's view seems reasonable. Indeed, social scientists appear to have taken him seriously if their type of research reflects their view of sources of information. Social scientists are continually asking people how they feel about something. Questionnaires, interviews, self reports, case studies, rating scales, and opinion polls abound in the professional journals as measuring devices.

Not all researchers engaged in the study of human behavior agree that verbal reports should be granted the degree of respectability the literature affords them. There are a variety of reasons for the dissenters' arguments against verbal reports. A person may not want to express his opinion because it is unpopular. Consequently, his response would be couched in socially acceptable terms rather than in accordance with how he actually felt. The respondent may want to ingratiate himself to the interviewer to gain respect or status. He may want to amuse. He may resist someone prying into his affairs. He may find it impossible to respond within the questioner's broad categories such as "like" or "dislike" because of ambivalent feelings. Parry and Crossley have found that even with straightforward factual ma-

---

[1] G. W. Allport, quoted in Eugene J. Webb, Donald T. Campbell, Richard D. Schwartz, and Lee Sechrest, *Unobtrusive Measures: Nonreactive Research in the Social Sciences* (Chicago: Rand McNally & Co., 1966), p. 23.

terial adults exaggerate: on registration and voting behavior, contributions, possession of telephone, home and car ownership, and even library cards.[2]

Those who rely on verbal reports as legitimate data reply to their critics that even though some reports may be inaccurate, asking is the best method to get at deeper feelings, perceptions, beliefs, expectations, and motivations. Without such information, one is left, continues the advocate of asking, with a limited and sterile data that can never do justice to the complexity of the human organism. Besides, not all verbal reports are inaccurate, they contend. Normally, with some care most respondents are perfectly willing to state opinions, beliefs, and past behavior with a high degree of honesty and self-perceptiveness.

For purposes of contrast, the issue of validity or invalidity of verbal reports has been unrealistically cast here in an either/or framework. There are those who would be satisfied with abolishing the interview, but most researchers are willing to accept interviews and questionnaires as sources of data as long as certain conditions are satisfied. One of the purposes of this chapter is to explicate these conditions.

The Kinsey Report

Perhaps you have noticed in baseball that the on-deck batter often swings several bats as a warm up before he steps up to the plate. The extra weight of two bats makes it easier to use one. In much the same spirit, a very difficult kind of interview process will be considered to present in bold form the problems of interviewing and the ways of including checks and balances to assure greater validity of verbal responses.

In 1939 Alfred Charles Kinsey, then professor of zoology at Indiana University, began a massive investigation of human sexual behavior. Since then there have appeared many reports and two major books, *Sexual Behavior in the Human Male* and *Sexual Behavior in the Human Female*,[3] probably the most extensive study of sexual behavior in the scientific literature.

Kinsey and his associates relied principally on the interview as the source of their data. Because of the personal nature of the subject, there are few if any areas more difficult to study, but Kinsey was well aware of the difficulty of his task and the necessity that scientific data meet certain criteria:

The quality of a case history study begins with the quality of the interview by which the data has been obtained. If, in lieu of direct observation and experiment, it is neces-

---

[2] Reported in Daniel Katz, "Social Psychology and Group Process," in *Annual Review of Psychology*, ed. C. P. Stowe (Stanford, Calif.: Annual Review, Inc., 1951).

[3] Alfred C. Kinsey, W. B. Pomeroy, and C. E. Martin, *Sexual Behavior in the Human Male* (Philadelphia: W. B. Saunders Company, 1948); Alfred C. Kinsey, W. B. Pomeroy, and C. E. Martin, *Sexual Behavior in the Human Female* (Philadelphia: W. B. Saunders Company, 1953).

sary to depend upon verbally transmitted records obtained from participants in the activities that are being studied then it is imperative that one become a master of every scientific device and of all the arts by which any man has ever persuaded any other man into exposing his activities and his inner-most thoughts. Failing to win that much from the subject, no statistical accumulation, however large, can adequately portray what the human animal is doing. . . .

Learning how to meet people of all ranks and levels, establishing rapport, sympathetically comprehending the significance of things as others view them, learning to accept their attitudes and activities without moral, social or esthetic evaluation, being interested in people as they are and not as someone else would have them, learning to see the reasonable bases of what at first glance may appear to be most unreasonable behavior, developing a capacity to like all kinds of people and thus to win their esteem and cooperation—these are the elements to be mastered by one who would gather human statistics.[4]

It is worth going through Kinsey's project in some detail to see how he gathered his data and sought validation, for it demonstrates clearly the kinds of cautions necessary to any good interview.

The Contact

Kinsey and the interviewing team gained entrée into communities through college, professional, church, YMCA, and other institutions. Hundreds of lectures emphasized the opportunity to contribute to basic research and to help others by sharing one's experience. Kinsey found an amazing amount of response to the altruistic appeal. He describes one gray-haired woman's reply to the interviewer's request as typical: "Of all things—! In all my years I have never had such a question put to me! But—if my experience will help, I'll give it to you." Data was gathered from a wide variety of sources including professional groups such as college professors, editors, clergymen, marriage counselors, psychiatrists, and YMCA secretaries, as well as less professional groups such as pimps, male and female prostitutes, prison inmates, gamblers, and bootleggers.

The key to cooperation from a community was by identification of those who through an interest in the research had submitted to an interview and who could convince others to be interviewed, from a local clergyman, housewife, successful businessman, underworld kingpin (with the longest FBI record and the fewest convictions), student leader, to a Salvation Army worker—anyone who was trusted and who had contacts with others.

After these significant persons were interviewed, the interviewer took time to become further acquainted with them and their community. The process included going with them to dinner, concerts, nightclubs, poolrooms, taverns, and garden clubs. In short, the investigators became identified

[4] Kinsey et al., *Sexual Behavior in the Human Male*, p. 35, reprinted by permission of Paul H. Gebhard, Director of the Institute for Sex Research.

with the community in a wide variety of ways. In time they developed a broad range of contacts who were willing to be interviewed on their sexual behavior.

The Interview Process

For carrying out the actual interview, Kinsey describes certain conditions that must be met to yield the best (most valid) data. Obviously there must be a feeling of trust or rapport between interviewer and interviewee if the data is to reflect the subject's behavior. The interviewer must be careful not to register surprise, disapproval, condemnation, or disinterest. Sexual behavior or any behavior must be treated as factually as possible during the interview. Whether positive or negative, all judgment must be forgone or the interviewee might withhold information or fabricate data if encouraged in a certain direction.

Assurance of confidentiality was essential. In part, this was secured when the subjects were contacted by their friends whom they trusted and whom they knew had already been interviewed. Further, the interviewer went to great lengths to explain the confidential nature of the interview material and that none of the information, which was recorded in a code, was to be translated into words. Actually, when *Sexual Behavior in the Human Male* was written, there were only four persons acquainted with the whole code, each of whom had memorized it since Kinsey refused to have it written down.

Kinsey adds further technical information in statements that might serve as a convenient checklist for evaluating or constructing an interview:

1. Putting the subject at ease. Many of the persons who contribute to a sex study manifest some uneasiness at the beginning of an interview and from the start particular attention needs to be given to putting the subject at ease. . . .
2. Assuring privacy. Places where the interviews are held should be reasonably soundproof and there should be no unexpected interruptions from other persons entering the room. . . .
3. Sequence of topics. . . . it is advisable to begin a conference with items that are non-sexual and least likely to disturb the subject. . . .
4. Recording at time of interview. . . . we began to record in code all of the data directly in the presence of the subject, and there has been no indication that this has been responsible for any loss of rapport or interference with the subjects' free exposure of confidences. . . .
5. Supplementary exploration. While there may be a basic minimum of material that is covered on each history, the interviewer should not hesitate to secure additional data on special situations that are outside the routine.
6. Avoiding bias. . . . In his tone of voice and in his choice of words, the interviewer must avoid giving the subject any clues as to the answers he expects. For example, when the subject is at a loss as to how to estimate the frequencies with which he has engaged in a particular sort of activity, the interviewer can

explain what sorts of frequencies are possible, provided he is careful not to give any idea what frequencies are common in the population or what frequencies he, the subject, might be expected to have. . . .

7. Direct questions. . . . Ask direct questions, without hesitancy and without apology. If the interviewer shows any uncertainty or embarrassment, it is not to be expected that the subject will do better in his answers. . . .

8. Avoid multiple questions. . . Multiple questions usually bring replies that are ambiguous. . . .

9. Cross-checks on accuracy. . . . The best protection against cover-up lies is a considerable list of inter-locking questions which provide cross-checks throughout the history, and particularly in regard to socially taboo items.[5]

Validity Checks

Kinsey was not naive to the possibility of inaccuracy in his data. In an effort to measure the size of error that might have occurred in initial interviews, retakes of histories were made on some of the subjects. The minimum elapsed time for retakes was eighteen months; in some cases as many as seven years separated the first and second interviews. The mean lapse was a little over three years. After the second interview, correlations were run between the two histories for a diverse list of items to see the strength of the relationship of the first and second measures.

Another check on the data was achieved through separate interviews of a husband and wife on those items for which there would be common knowledge. When there were other sexual partners than a wife, each person was interviewed independent of the other.[6] Other validity information consisted of the internal constancy of an interview. Within each history there were a number of similar questions phrased differently to provide an internal check, as Kinsey notes in his ninth item. When possible, Kinsey sought construct validity by comparing his findings with other studies. Finally, the data gathered by the three principal investigators, Kinsey, Pomeroy, and Martin, were compared one with the other to see if the interviewer himself might have been a source of bias.

The Kinsey Data—Valid or Invalid?

As one might suspect, there was a flurry of comment from social-behavioral scientists following publication of Kinsey's report. As nearly as can be determined, the critics of the report were almost equal to the enthusiasts. Even though Kinsey had gone to great length to establish that his interview data were valid, many scientists disagreed with the research on methodological grounds. Others contended that the findings approached the best possible

[5] Ibid., pp. 47–58.

[6] This variety of cross-checking was particularly helpful in penal institutions where normal sexual outlets were impossible.

with the most frequently used method in the social sciences, interviewing. "If this study with its checks on validity is not acceptable," the Kinseyite argued, "what about all the thousands of other published studies relying on verbal reports that have hardly had the care this data has received?"

Again, we see an issue about the credibility of data to which no definite yes or no answer can be given. Had there been other studies after the Kinsey report of the same scope and interest, they could have served as an independent check of validity, but no such studies exist. Has the study been useful in a predictive sense? Has it proved useful to practitioners such as marriage counselors, clergymen, the courts? The answer is both yes and no. Some have found it helpful; others have not.

The direct approach of asking the subject has obvious disadvantages and advantages. The main advantage is that asking is the most direct and generally speaking the least complex way to get data. The main disadvantage is that one is not always sure of the validity of verbal reports when it is the principal or sole source of data.

In addition to the guidelines from Kinsey, which are applicable to any interview, on sex or whatever, the chief research dictum, to which reference has already been made, is *do not rely on a single source of data when there is a possibility of several.* Verbal reports, then, can become an important data dimension, but it is strongest when used in conjunction with other kinds of supportive data.

The Not-So-Obvious Measures

To the sensitive observer there is a plethora of data on human behavior just waiting to be analyzed, but perhaps because it is so obvious, much of it is often missed by the less skilled. For example, there are a variety of persons who have access to a great deal of information about man's behavior: the maid in a hotel, a janitor, the trashman, the postman, or as they were once described, the invisible observers—each is privy to many facts about our comings and goings, our likes and dislikes, our pretenses, attitudes, and beliefs. Similarly, many other second-order unobtrusive measurement possibilities, readily accessible but often untapped and unexploited, can be adapted by the creative researcher for the school setting. Note that the emphasis is upon adaptation rather than replication since most of the following models involve sources other than the school.

In an attempt to sensitize researchers to the not-so-obvious measures, four social scientists, Eugene J. Webb, Donald T. Campbell, Richard D. Schwartz, and Lee Sechrest, have written an engaging paperback entitled *Unobtrusive Measures: Nonreactive Research in the Social Sciences.*[7] The

[7] This section on off-beat measures is largely drawn from Webb et al., *Unobtrusive Measures.*

hesis of their work is captured in the first three paragraphs of Chapter 1:

This survey directs attention to social science research data *not* obtained by interview or questionnaire. Some may think this exclusion does not leave much. It does. Many innovations in research method are to be found scattered throughout the social science literature. Their use, however, is unsystematic, their importance understated. Our review of this material is intended to broaden the social scientist's currently narrow range of utilized methodologies and to encourage creative and opportunistic exploitation of unique measurement possibilities.

Today, the dominant mass of social science research is based upon interviews and questionnaires. We lament this overdependence upon a single, fallible method. Interviews and questionnaires intrude as a foreign element into the social setting they would describe, they create as well as measure attitudes, they elicit atypical roles and responses, they are limited to those who are accessible and will cooperate, and the responses obtained are produced in part by dimensions of individual differences irrelevant to the topic at hand.

But the principal objection is that they are used alone. No research method is without bias. Interviews and questionnaires must be supplemented by methods testing the same social science variables but having *different* methodological weaknesses.[8]

The authors use as their major outline three classes of unobtrusive measures: the physical traces of erosion and accretion, archival records, and contrived observation.

Erosion

Comparative wear of selected physical elements is the object of investigation in erosion measures. That is, objects that are continually used show more evidence of wear than do objects infrequently used. For example, if one wanted to know the comparative attractiveness of long-term exhibits in a museum, as once was the case at Chicago's Museum of Science and Industry, one measure to be used in conjunction with observational data might be the replacement rate of vinyl tile around each exhibit.[9] The assumption, of course, is that the popular displays attract more people, who in turn wear out a greater amount of tile.

One way to check the readership of books is to note the amount of deterioration over time. Frederick Mosteller studied the use of different sections of a library encyclopedia by the criteria of dirty edges of pages, amount of torn pages, smudges, finger markings, and underlining.[10] As any librarian well knows, the obvious information of how often a book is checked out is

[8] Ibid., p. 1.
[9] C. P. Duncan, personal communication, 1963, to Webb et al., reported in *Unobtrusive Measures,* p. 36.
[10] Frederick Mosteller, "Use as Evidence by an Examination of Wear and Tear on Selected Sets of ESS," in "A Study of the Need for a New Encyclopedia Treatment of the Social Sciences," ed. K. Davis et al. (unpublished manuscript, 1955), pp. 167–74.

not always a measure of its use, but when the rates of check-out *and* wear are highly related, one can be more confident of the use of the book. The activity level of children might be measured by the rate at which they wear out the soles of their shoes. Any physical object that deteriorates or is used up over time may become a source of insight for a comparison of differences in behavior. Possible erosion measures are such things as pencils, laboratory supplies, books, paper, chalk, chairs, and desks, and playground equipment. The particular meaning of the rate of erosion must always arise out of the nature of the problem in which the investigator is interested.

Accretion

Measures of accretion include accumulation or deposits that occur over time. The fact that one library book has more dust on it than another may say something about its interest value, assuming that a fastidious librarian has not disturbed the accumulation. One researcher set a difficult task for himself when he became curious about measuring liquor consumption in a city without package stores.[11] With the obvious source of data gone, he counted the number of empty liquor bottles in trash cans. Not only could he determine the rate of consumption but he could also find out how intake varied as a function of weather, holidays, and seasons, what brands, cost, blends, and alcoholic content were popular, and what neighborhood consumes what kind of alcohol, and so on. Cafeterias and automated food and beverage dispensers are fertile sources of data on eating behavior, as are trash cans with their accumulations of candy wrappers, milk cartons, uneaten food, and so on. Brown (1960) used the simple measure of the weight of incoming food compared to outgoing garbage in a study of food intake of institutionalized patients.[12]

To decide which radio station would be best for him to advertise on, an automobile dealer asked his mechanics to gather a frequency count on the radio dial settings of all the cars that came into the shop. With the obvious precaution of avoiding duplication—each car was counted only once—and with the large sample of 50,000 dials a year, the dealer found that his data were highly correlated with independent rating reports on the radio stations.[13]

Popularity among glass-enclosed exhibits for children could be studied by counting the number of noseprints deposited on the glass each day. Not

[11] H. G. Sawyer, "The Meaning of Numbers" (speech before the American Association of Advertising Agencies, 1961).

[12] J. W. Brown, "A New Approach to the Assessment of Psychiatric Therapies" (unpublished manuscript, 1960).

[13] "Z. Frank Stresses Radio to Build Big Chevy Dealership," *Advertising Age* 33 (1962): 83.

veryone will leave a noseprint, obviously, but one might assume that con-
itions would be the same for each exhibit and that the noseprints, though not
eflective of all who viewed the exhibit, would provide a relative index for
imilar glass-enclosed exhibits.

Archival Records

Archives, public records, hold an immense quantity of rich, descriptive data
anging from inscriptions on an old tombstone to the current data on students
n a principal's office. Though normally thought of as data for the historian,
rchival records are equally usable by the social scientist. The problem with
uch records is that they have often been developed and kept by nonscientists,
nd as a consequence they may have substantial errors. But, to repeat the
itany, if records of the past are used in conjunction with other measures, they
an become a valuable source of information. Archeologists, for example,
vould seldom rely on one kind of data when there is the possibility of adding
imilar but independent data from another source.

Schools usually have extensive records gathering dust in some out
of the way repository. These records include grades, school activities, standardized test scores, family backgrounds of students, scholastic achievements, athletic scores, budgets, teachers' salaries, enrollment figures, teacher-
pupil ratio, library withdrawals, heights and weights of students, ticket sales
to school events—the listing could be extensive and will, of course, vary
from school to school. These records continue to gather dust unless some
creative researcher comes along and puts them to use.

Contrived Unobtrusive Observation

Chapter 4 was devoted to an observational technique adapted from the work
of Barker and Wright, where the methodology consisted of analysis of behavioral recording of the stream of events, generally with no hypothesis in
mind. There is another type of more deliberate observation in which the
observer becomes an experimenter by setting certain preconditions and
watching how persons respond without knowing that their behavior is being
studied. Sechrest selected a frequently used door and affixed to it a sign reading USE OTHER DOOR.[14] He recorded how many heeded the directive. Later
he put up a sign PLEASE DO NOT USE THIS DOOR, gathering similar data on how
many paid attention.[15]

[14] Lee Sechrest, "Handwriting on the Wall: A View of Two Cultures" (unpublished
manuscript, Northwestern University, 1965).
[15] The polite appeal won, eliciting fewer violations.

Lefkowitz, Blake, and Mouton studied the effect on conformity of high or low status clothing.[16] Their experimental setting was a stoplight in the city of Austin, Texas. A confederate would violate the light by walking across when the caution *wait* was lighted. The investigators were interested in seeing how many bystanders would follow as they varied the clothing of the confederate from banker to bum.[17]

In an ingenious study to discover the effects of a unit of instruction on communicable diseases, four high school biology classes were observed before and after the unit was taught.[18] Two classes studied the unit; two, an unrelated unit. Evaluation of the courses' effectiveness was based upon differences observed during selected periods between the experimental and control groups on the following categories:

1. Putting foreign articles in mouth.
2. Biting fingernails.
3. Picking nose with finger.
4. Rubbing eyes with fingers.
5. Coughing or sneezing without handkerchief.[19]

A driving study by Lee Sechrest set out to determine the conditions under which fellow motorists could be challenged to "drag" at stop signals.[20] The investigators would pull up alongside a car, gun their motor, and look once at their potential opponent to entice them into combat. The variables of interest were the make of the stimulus car, the age of the driver, and the effect of the passengers in the stimulus car.[21]

There have been a host of studies of persuasive techniques to see the effect of various kinds of appeals on specified behavior. Stanley Schachter and Robert Hall studied the effect of differing restraints upon college students volunteering for an experiment.[22] There were four conditions, one for each group. After a verbal presentation of the "study" for which they were to volunteer, group 1 was asked to fill out a questionnaire indicating whether or not they wished to take part in the experiment. Group 2 had forms passed around with instructions to take one if the student wished to participate. Group 3 was asked to raise hands if interested. And group 4 was asked to

[16] Lefkowitz, Blake, and Mouton, "Status Factors in Pedestrian Violation of Traffic Signals," *Journal of Abnormal and Social Psychology* 51 (1955): 704–6.
[17] As might be expected, high status clothing elicited more violations than did low status clothing.
[18] J. Urban, "Behavior Changes Resulting from a Study of Communicable Diseases," *New York Bureau of Publications* (Teachers College, Columbia University) 1943.
[19] The unit was effective! Significant differences in total score favored the experimental group even up to twelve weeks later.
[20] Lee Sechrest, "Situational Sampling and Contrived Situations in the Assessment of Behavior," mimeographed (Northwestern University, 1965).
[21] They found that as age and number of passengers increased, fewer challenges were accepted. When the stimulus car was a Volkswagen, not many responded to the invitation.
[22] Stanley Schachter and Robert Hall, "Group Derived Restraints and Audience Persuasion," *Human Relations* 5 (1952): 397–406.

raise hands, but half the group was comprised of confederates of the experimenter, all of whom volunteered. The measure of effectiveness of high or low restraint conditions for volunteering was whether or not the volunteer showed up for the experiment.[23]

A good many of the unobtrusive observational studies gather data by experimental hardware such as hidden tape recorders, cameras, video-tape recorders, and a variety of other electro-mechanical devices. Miniaturization of electronic equipment, in particular, has afforded a great advantage when the researcher wants to study phenomena where his physical presence would affect the responses of those being studied.

A serious question must be raised, however. With increased technology—long range hearing devices, electronic "eyes," miniature transmitters, and the countless other unobtrusive information-gathering devices—what about the ethics of invasion of privacy? Or, more broadly, might not the whole research process, the studying of the behavior of others, be a violation of the constitutional concepts of human dignity and freedom? These questions are not to be answered lightly, and it is incumbent upon anyone who studies human behavior to give serious attention to them. Following the next chapter, on techniques of discovering the social structure of a group, the question of ethics in research will be considered in some detail.

Summary

This chapter considers both the obvious and the not-so-obvious sources of data for the researcher. The obvious method is the interview: if you want to find out something, the most immediate method and the one most frequently used by researchers is the verbal report. The eternal problem of validity is probably more apparent in the interview than in any other methodology. A consideration of one of the more difficult studies using the interview, the Kinsey Report, reveals a series of ways to assure greater validity.

The not-so-obvious sources of data for researchers are unobtrusive in nature; that is, they do not intrude upon the persons being studied. They include erosion, accretion, archival, and contrived observational sources of data.

---

[23] If it was easy to refuse (low restraint) there was a high refusal rate but high attendance of those who volunteered. If it was difficult to refuse (high restraint) there were more volunteers but fewer came to the experiment.

6 / Sociometry

Up to this point, emphasis has been upon the method of science by considering briefly its historical roots, the guidelines of science, and its key concepts and limitations. This introduction to scientific method has been followed with samples of specific tools of the social-behavioral sciences. This chapter introduces a technique for insight into the social structure of the classroom group. It is based upon the obvious assumption that the structure of the group is an important factor in human learning. The technique to be considered, sociometry, is one of several means to measure the socio-emotional and task-oriented climate of the classroom.

Development of Sociometry

As early as 1923 Jacob L. Moreno, a psychiatrist by training, became interested in the study of small groups, but it had been during World War I that he discovered the power of knowledge about social systems when he was administrative director for a camp of displaced persons in Switzerland. There was a serious problem of morale, as one would expect. Moreno observed that the adjustment of people seemed to be better if they were allowed to form their own groups within the camp than if groups were arbitrarily formed. This observation was followed by systematic research in schools and reformatories when Moreno became a citizen of the United States.

Here he developed a measurement device for research that consisted of a simple questionnaire requesting persons to designate others in their group whom they liked or disliked. The result was called a sociogram, a schematic picture of group members' preferences, dislikes, and indifferences. Since these early beginnings there have been adaptations and variations of Moreno's technique, and an impressive number of studies have resulted by Moreno and others. In 1937 the advent of a professional journal, *Sociometry: A Journal of Interpersonal Relations,* provided a vehicle for the development of a fairly cohesive body of knowledge.

Number of Choices

The process for gathering sociometric data begins with deciding, first, the number of choices each group member will be requested to make, and, second, the type of question to be the basis for choice. Essentially there have been three methods followed. In the first the participant is not told how many or how few group members he is to list. He is free to rank every member or none at all. The second method is to limit the number of preferences or rejections. Conventionally, the limit is three "likes" and three "dislikes." The third method requests from each member a complete listing by rank of all the other members in the group. Each of the three methods has advantages and disadvantages in the analysis of the data.

The first, unspecified method as originally described by Moreno allows examination and comparison of each respondent according to the number preferred or rejected and the relationship of the preferred to the rejected. For example, student A may identify seven friends and reject no one, whereas student B may reject seven and like two. Such data may be important in view of other information the teacher has. Furthermore, if one is interested in ascertaining the true isolate—the person who neither chooses nor is chosen— the unspecified method is the only one of the three capable of giving that kind of datum because it affords the possibility of a group member's choosing no one. The unspecified method is inappropriate if one wishes to make statistical comparisons because for lack of data the isolate will have to be dropped from the analysis.

The specified method consisting of three likes and three dislikes is convenient because it usually takes less time to administer, it allows statistical treatment, and it has been found to yield much the same kind of general pattern as the unspecified method.[1] The disadvantage is that the isolate cannot be identified because each member must make six choices and the isolate by definition neither chooses nor is chosen.

Ranking each group member has the obvious advantage of yielding data on each person, which in turn affords more powerful statistical analysis.

[1] Norman E. Gronlund, *Sociometry in the Classroom* (New York: Harper & Row, Publishers, 1959), pp. 93–113.

The method cannot be used effectively, however, unless every person knows every other person in the group. Otherwise, asking the participant to rank an unknown person in terms of like-dislike is to force him to an impossible task. This method is most often applicable to small, fairly well established groups.

The Criterion Question

In addition to deciding the number of choices, the sociometric investigator decides what kind of question, called the criterion question, to which the group will respond. It may be social (for example, Whom would you like to spend a Saturday afternoon playing with?), task oriented (for example, Whom would you prefer to work with?), or designed to identify leaders (for example, Who could best represent the group on the school council?)

In a review of a good many studies using the sociometric technique, N. E. Gronlund found that up to about the age of twelve it makes little difference what question is asked. In analyzing data from forty sixth-grade classes he found that

... there was a tendency for pupils to remain in the same sociometric position on all three sociometric questions [as to seating companion, work companion, and play companion]. Those with high sociometric status as seating companions tended also to have high status as work companions and play companions. Conversely, pupils least accepted as seating companions tended to remain in this position as work companions and play companions. . . .[2]

Beyond the age of twelve the criterion question seems to become more important. The rule of thumb is to use the question most appropriate to what you want to find out, recognizing that there will probably be little difference regardless of the criterion question for younger children. Relevant to the matter of the criteria question, Lois H. Criswell[3] makes a distinction between one-way questions and two-way questions. She points out that certain sociometric criteria (for example, those of seating or rooming arrangement) refer to relationships that are potentially reciprocal. Other criteria (for example, those of leading a squad or representing a school at a conference) deal with relationships where mutual choice is relatively unimportant. In the former situation the researcher would be more interested in reciprocal or mutual choices among persons within the group; in the latter, in the frequency with which a person is chosen, not in whether he is chosen by those whom he chooses.

    [2] Ibid., p. 98, reprinted by permission of the publisher.
    [3] Lois H. Criswell, "Sociometric Concepts in Personnel Administration," *Sociometry* 12 (1949): 287–300.

Graphing Sociometric Data

It is often helpful in analysis to translate sociometric data into visual form. In drawing the sociogram, symbols (usually a symbol with a name inside) represent each individual. Circles have been used to designate girls; triangles, boys, as in figure 7.

Figure 7.

These symbols should be placed around the edge of a large work sheet to facilitate the next step, which is to connect the symbols by lines representing the choices from the sociometric test. Traditionally, lines emanating from the edge of a circle signify that person's choice; lines going into a circle signify a choice of that person by someone else, as in figure 8.

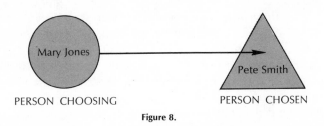

PERSON CHOOSING   PERSON CHOSEN

Figure 8.

If the method of specifying the number of choices is used, colors or different kinds of lines may be utilized to signify first, second, and third choices, as in figure 9.

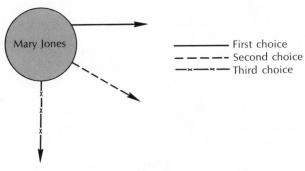

——————— First choice
— — — —– Second choice
—×——×—— Third choice

Figure 9.

Distinctive lines should be used to stand for conditions of rejection. One method is to use wavy lines for such a designation, as in figure 10.

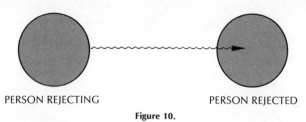

PERSON REJECTING   PERSON REJECTED

Figure 10.

Sociometric Roles

Three kinds of characters in the sociometric drama are easily recognized when the data is in graphic form. Highly chosen members have been dubbed "stars" or "overchosen." Often the star may be viewed as having social power. In a frequently cited study, Helen H. Jennings[4] investigated the social structure in a school for delinquent girls. Using as a criterion the choice of an eating companion, she took periodic measures and among other things discovered that eighteen of the twenty identified as overchosen were elected to the house council, an unusually good example of predictive validity. Furthermore, the two overchosen girls not elected closely missed the required number of votes for election. Other studies have supported Miss Jennings's findings, but a word of caution is in order. Social power is a complicated phenomenon, and it is not always tapped through sociometry. Obviously, persons can achieve positions of social power in a variety of ways other than by group acceptance.

The isolate, that person who receives no choices and makes none, is for all practical purposes an invisible member of the group. Others are indifferent or unresponsive to him. Although the label "isolate" connotes poor adjustment to the group, such is not always the case unless it is known that the isolate is dissatisfied or uncomfortable. Some isolation is by voluntary choice; the person simply does not wish to become visible. Mary L. Northway has suggested reasonably that sociometric data provide evidence of a person's acceptance but not necessarily of his acceptability.[5] *Acceptability* is a much broader concept than *acceptance,* and the imputation of poor mental health from sociometric data must be extremely tentative awaiting other kinds of supportive evidence.

[4] Helen H. Jennings, *Leadership and Isolation,* 2nd ed. (London: Longmans, Green & Co., Ltd., 1950).

[5] Mary L. Northway, "Outsiders: A Study of the Personality Patterns of Children Least Acceptable to their Age Mates," *Sociometry* 7 (1944): 10–25.

The rejected person is the recipient of negative votes. Because sub-groups are occasionally rejected, some investigators use sociometry for identifying ethnic cleavages. Charles P. Loomis found in two southwest high schools a racial split between Spanish-American and American students.[6] As one might expect, the minority group tended toward preference of racially similar and rejection of racially dissimilar students. Other studies too numerous to mention here have reported the same kinds of findings to support the general notion that sociometry provides a sensitive measure of group disruption and division caused by racial prejudice. Jacob L. Moreno has an interesting addendum: minority group cleavages were observed only beyond the fourth grade; younger children do not seem to make friendship choices on the basis of racial identity.[7]

Using Sociometry

A Study of Group Structure in a Fourth-Grade Class
TRUDY VILLARS[8]

An objective measure of group interaction such as the sociogram can be a valuable asset to anyone who must understand a group and work with it effectively. The sociogram is a graphic representation of the likes and dislikes of the individuals of a group from which data is obtained by asking each individual to list his preferences for other members in the group.

This paper is a study of a fourth-grade class using sociometric techniques.[9] The students were unknown to the investigator. Analysis of the group structure was based primarily on data obtained from the students' written responses to three questions. The class was composed of thirteen children, eight boys and five girls who were above average in intelligence.

METHOD
The study was conducted in a large room in which the students arranged tables and benches according to their own choosing. See figure 11.

They were given a sheet of paper and a pencil and were asked to list the students in the group. Then they were given the following instructions:

I am going to ask you a few questions that should not take too long to answer. Try to answer them as honestly as you can. This is not an examination that can be graded. It is simply asking for your opinion and is information for a study I am doing.

The questions in this study dealt with a limited, three-choice social companion question, a rejection question, and a ranking question to select representatives for

[6] Charles P. Loomis, "Ethnic Cleavages in the Southwest as Reflected in Two High Schools," *Sociometry* 6 (1943): 6–26.
[7] Jacob L. Moreno, *Who Shall Survive?*, Nervous & Mental Disease Monograph 58 (Washington, D.C., 1934).
[8] This paper was written especially for this book.
[9] The class was from an experimental laboratory school.

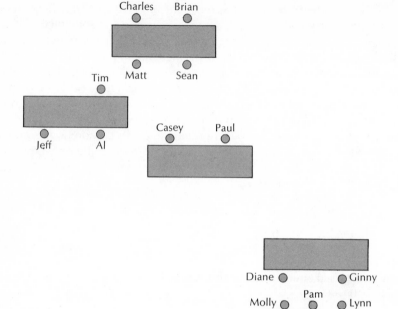

Figure 11. Seating arrangement selected by students as they prepared for the socio-metric measure.

the group. The questions were asked one at a time and the students were given as much time as they needed to answer them. If they were unsure of the meaning of a question it was further explained. The following questions were asked:

1. If you could take three people, in addition to yourself, to the movies, whom would you take?
2. Is there anyone in this group you would not want to come with you?
3. If you were having a class party and were electing a chairman from this group, whom would you choose, first, second, etc.? Put a number next to each name indicating where you would rank that person.

RESULTS AND DISCUSSION

In developing the sociogram, all three questions were used. Question 1 was viewed as a measure of positive affect for social companion; question 2, as a measure of negative affect; and question 3, as a kind of electoral choice or leadership measure.

Figure 12 is the sociometric diagram of the group. The vertical dimension is based upon the group's response to question 3 with those receiving the most votes at the top, the least or nonselected at the bottom.

Several findings are obvious: the two groups are split by sex (not unusual for fourth-graders); both groups are fairly cohesive (only two boys and one girl has an inner, reciprocal choice core. If one were concerned with the children on the fringe, Al, Casey, and Diane would bear watching.

Sociometric data can be valuable both to provide a descriptive understanding

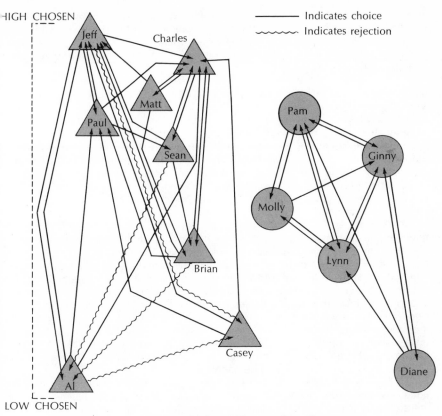

HIGH CHOSEN ——————————— Indicates choice

~~~~~~~ Indicates rejection

LOW CHOSEN

Figure 12. Sociogram of fourth-grade class of thirteen students. The two groups are split by sex, and choices as well as rejections were within the same sex group.

of the group's structure and to develop methods of altering the group's structure to reach desired goals. The data, of course, must be used with other data available to teachers such as choice of seating companions as in figure 11. In applying the data to alter the group structure in order to reach desired goals, however, there should be a relationship between the type of situation to which the data will be applied and the situation to which the questions explicitly applied. The questions used in this study dealt with a social situation, but because of the age group the results could probably be generalized to other types of situations. Research by Norman E. Gronlund has indicated that for subjects beyond the age of twelve a generalization should be made with caution.[10]

The obtained data can be applied to the restructuring of either an individual in a group or of subgroups within a total group. There are a number of approaches which can be used, separately or together, to bring a low-ranking member closer into a group. The most important information supplied by the sociogram is the other group members with whom a particular low-ranking individual could best associate. The sociogram could yield data about an individual or individuals who would be most open to the low-ranking person and who at the same time would be most likely and able to integrate this person into the group.

[10] Gronlund, *Sociometry in the Classroom*, p. 98.

The exact method of integrating would depend very much on the particular situation. The individual obviously should be paired with those with whom there is the greatest chance of entrance into the group. There are innumerable opportunities in a classroom to pair or group students for work on projects and even more opportunities outside of the classroom.

The talents of the low-ranking person can and should have an effect upon the activity used to raise his rank. Obviously if the student is shy, putting him in a speaking activity might only result in his becoming more isolated from the group. That same person, if he were artistically adept, might become quite involved if he were to work on the decorations for a Christmas party.

Another aspect of the activity that can greatly affect the acceptance of an individual is how much the results of a project affect the group as a whole. The low-ranking person with artistic ability, were he to encourage and aid the other students in preparing posters for a contest between classes, would be aiding the others in reaching a desired goal, and the chance of his becoming more involved in the group would be heightened.

A personal observation of the author might serve as a further example of this point. In a small group of high-school students working on the development of speaking skills, there was one member whose silence kept him from participating in the group discussions or projects. Although he did not seem disliked, neither did he show much involvement in the group. Near the end of the semester a debate between two sections of the class was to be presented to an audience of students from other classes. The topic decided upon for the debate turned out to be of special interest to the shy student, and as a consequence he spent much time explaining the background to the other students in the group. When the day of the presentation came, he spoke quite assuredly on the topic, visibly impressing the audience and the class. His efforts, instrumental in the successful presentation of the debate, apparently brought him closer to the students with whom he had worked.

Returning to the sociogram obtained from the fourth-grade class, there are three low-ranking members, Al, Casey, and Diane. With Al advantage should obviously be taken of the mutual choice between him and Jeff. Not only do they show mutual acceptance but Jeff is also a star of the class and might be expected to be able to bring Al closer given the opportunity. Charles or Matt might also be a good choice to group with Al.

Using group members to facilitate Casey's integration would be more difficult since no students chose him on the limited choice question.

Diane does not present as great a problem as do Al and Casey, even though she ranks lower than either of them in the total group. Her sex group is very close, and she is completely a part of that group, as is indicated by the lack of rejection lines between boys and girls. One way to bring up her rank in the total group would be to raise the rank of the girls as a whole.

The relationship between the two major subgroups is another problem that might be handled. It would be expected that with this age total integration of the two groups would be difficult. It might be hoped, however, that the social distance between the two could be lessened. One method of accomplishing this would be to get the groups involved in a project that supersedes the two groups' interests, a superordinate goal transcending the sexes. An attempt to use small mixed groups might bring about greater unification, but it probably would fail because of the isolation of the sexes.

A further application of the sociogram would be to integrate a problem group into the total group in order to dissolve its undesirable effectiveness. For example, data from a sociogram might be used to diffuse disruptive behavior of a "gang" by designing a seating arrangement such that each member of the gang would be near someone outside the gang with whom he had indicated positive affect. This method of careful attention to seating arrangement is well known to many successful teachers.

SUMMARY

This paper presents some uses of the sociogram in working with groups, especially groups of children. It examines various methods of data gathering and the analysis of this data. Discussion focuses on integration of low-ranking group members, the shortening of social distance between conflicting groups, and the dissolution of problem groups.

Validity of Sociometry

The sociometric technique is one of those instruments referred to previously where face validity is assumed. It is based on the notion that if you want to get information about individual and group choices, ask the group. How does one know or how does one have assurance that the individual-group response is an honest one, that is, that the respondents are giving what you think they are giving? As with all measures where persons are asked their attitude toward something else, there is always the possibility of conscious or unconscious falsification. Little can be done about unconscious responses overriding the conscious; the condition, when it does exist, is assumed by most investigators to be atypical and therefore not a major source of invalidity. Deliberate falsification, however, is an ever-present source of difficulty in research. The best precaution is that the investigator create in the respondent the assurance that an honest response will not be harmful to him, that he will not be judged in his response, and, more positively, that his response will help the investigator and the respondent achieve a better state of affairs. In short, rapport between investigator and respondent is critical. Moreno seeks to assure rapport by including in his general directions for the use of sociometry the dicta that sociometric data should be used to restructure the group and that the group members should be informed of this fact.[11] Not all investigators have followed his advice, primarily because they are not in a position to change the group as is the teacher, but the value of restructuring where problems exist is obvious.

In addition to face validity, two other kinds of validity are possible: construct validity (that is, a correspondence between the sociometric test with other behavioral data) and pragmatic validity (that is, an ability to alleviate undesirable group situations). An interesting example of construct validity is provided in a study by Manuel Ramirez and Alfred Castaneda.[12] A com-

---

[11] Moreno, *Who Shall Survive?*

[12] Manuel Ramirez and Alfred Castaneda, "Paired Associate Learning of Sociometrically Ranked Children's Names," *Child Development* 37 (1966): 171–79.

parison was made between the standard sociometric measure and the learning of nonsense syllables associated with group members' names. The results clearly support the sociometric measure in that the nonsense syllables paired with overchosen students were learned more easily than the syllables associated with lower-ranked children. Generally, other investigators have found sociometry to be a valid measure given the conditions of rapport outlined above.[13]

There is another problem to which one must always be sensitive when groups are studied longitudinally (that is, over a period of time): is the data a function of memory or of actual shifts in choice-rejection patterns? For example, there might be a tendency for a person to respond the second time as he did the first time even though changes may have occurred in his choices. He may resist changing his previously written-down response because of the value our society places upon consistency. Lois H. Criswell has suggested a way out of the test-retest problem.[14] If the investigator has established at the time of the first test a relationship between the sociometric device and an independent criterion, that same relationship should exist if the sociometric measure shows little change on the retest. Stars and isolates who remain stars and isolates on the retest should behave and be treated as stars and isolates at the time of the second test. Measurement error can usually be reduced when the investigator relies upon more than one measure.

The Sociometrically Rich and Poor

Gronlund's research conducted in a variety of classrooms leads him to distinguish two general characteristics of instructional groups, both of which are similar to findings in settings outside the school. The first characteristic is that the highly chosen persons, the stars, make up a small percentage of the group.

At all grade levels, there are almost twice as many pupils in the below average category as there are in the above average group. The combined percentages in the neglected and isolate categories also exceed those in the star category, at all grade levels except the fourth. Thus there is a tendency for groups to contain more pupils with extremely low socio-metric status than with high status. An analysis of the percentage of choices received by these extreme groups revealed that the 7 to 17 percent of the pupils in the star category captured between 17 and 41 percent of all the choices given. In contrast the pupils in the neglectee and isolate categories received less than 3 percent of the choices although there were between 11 and 22 percent of the pupils in these groups.[15]

[13] See Gronlund, *Sociometry in the Classroom*, p. 97.
[14] Lois H. Criswell, "Foundations of Sociometric Measurement," *Sociometry* 9 (1946): 7–13.
[15] Gronlund, *Sociometry in the Classroom*, p. 106.

Choices Between Boys and Girls

The second characteristic noted by Gronlund is that boys and girls strongly tend to limit their choices to members of their own sex. When viewed over the range of third grade to college, sex cleavages become less apparent, though there is not the striking interest in the other sex often assumed to occur during the junior and senior high school level. Even at the collegiate level, boys tend to choose boys and girls to choose girls, though the differences are not nearly as marked as they are at the third to eighth grade levels.

In the study of forty-six sixth-grade classes referred to previously, the criteria for choosing—seating, working and play—were compared, and it was found that cleavage is most obvious for play, less obvious for work, and least obvious for seating. Gronlund notes that there is a wide range of differences among schools on the amount of sex cleavage:

. . . the nature of the school influences the extent to which pupils express a desire to associate with members of the opposite sex for certain activities. Schools with a relatively small percentage of cross-sex choices . . . in all probability have separate play-grounds for boys, encourage boy-girl competition in the classroom, and in other ways widen the cleavage between the sexes. In contrast, those schools with a relatively large percentage of cross-sex choices probably encourage and arrange for boy-girl interaction. Although we can only speculate concerning the probable causes of the differences between these schools, the fact that boy-girl relations can be modified is noteworthy.[16]

Using Sociometry to Facilitate Group Change

Sociometry can be an important tool to describe the way the group is structured, the first step in defining what changes should occur. The uses made of sociometry have been largely to determine ways of restructuring the group so that children showing signs of adjustment difficulties could be given positions of positive interaction with others[17] and so that more effective subgroups could be created.[18] Sociometry has also been used to indicate whether or not attempts toward social integration were successful.[19]

Polansky, in a provocative study of group climate, found that teachers in "good climate" classrooms supported the group's status system whereas

[16] Ibid., pp. 103–4.
[17] F. M. McLelland, and J. A. Ratliff, "The Use of Sociometry as an Aid in Promoting Social Adjustment in a Ninth-Grade Home-Room," Sociometry 10 (1947): 147–53.
[18] D. Faunce and J. A. Beegle, "Cleavages in a Relatively Homogeneous Group of Rural Youth," Sociometry 11 (1948): 207–16.
[19] Muzafer Sherif, "Experiments in Group Conflict," Scientific American, Nov. 1956.

teachers in "poor-climate" classrooms did not.[20] Although extrapolation must be cautious, Polansky's finding suggests that one ought not set out to disrupt the structure of a group without expecting resistance. A more prudent approach when change in structure is considered important is to leave the ranking as it is (see figure 4, p. 25) and work at reducing social distance between stars and isolates. That is, tighten up the structure without rearranging it.

In an unpublished study sociometry was used in a variety of ways to help solve group problems of a particularly troublesome fourth-grade class.[21] This group of twenty-five children was notorious for its inability to function as a group. Every teacher who had come in contact with them complained about the difficulty of getting them to work together. Preliminary sociometric data indicated four loosely organized clusters and an unusually high percentage of isolates. For a week-long school camping excursion the class was separated into five-man task groups, each of which contained a natural leader and a college student counselor. The isolates and rejectees were distributed among groups where there seemed to be the highest probability of successful integration into the group. For example, a rejectee was placed with four other children, none of whom indicated dislike for him, and two competing stars were never put together.

During the camp, each group was observed by a trained observer who kept a running record of group interaction. Most daily activities involved small groups for nature hikes, craftwork, games, horseback riding, and so on, but the campers met for such general activities as meals, evening activities, and large group games. As the week progressed the children during the general activities did not revert to the previous stratification; rather, there was a tendency for more widespread interaction.

One of the stars, the smallest boy in the class, figured out early in the game that he had better team up with someone who could cope with the more physically demanding camp environment. He chose the largest boy in the group, a member of his five-man group, who happened to be an isolate. The two of them became almost inseparable with this highly successful brain-and-brawn combination. It was the same large boy who on the last night of camp defended the campers' honor in a game of "hot pepper."

In this game the players form a large circle, each about two feet apart. As a basketball is thrown around and across the circle, whoever misses the ball drops out, and the circle becomes smaller and smaller. This time when the others had been eliminated, the two remaining were the boy and a counselor. It immediately became a contest of campers versus counselors, and as fortune would have it, the campers won. In spontaneous acclaim, the boy

[20] Lois Polansky, "Group Social Climate and the Teacher's Supportiveness of Group Status Systems," *Journal of Educational Sociology* 28 (1954): 115–23.

[21] Carl E. Pitts, "Changing Group Structure by Lessening Social Distance" (unpublished manuscript prepared for staff of Webster College School, 1964).

was hoisted to the shoulders of the other campers, who marched around the room cheering the victor. As one might expect, post-test sociometric data supported the obvious. But there were other less dramatic but nonetheless important changes: the number of isolates went from three to one; no child was rejected on the post-test measure; choices were more evenly distributed throughout the group; and the number of mutual choices increased. Follow-up measures of the class indicated that out of the camping experience grew a new social system, which had stabilized with minor changes when the last sociometric measure was taken six months after camp.

Cautions in Using Sociometry

The relative simplicity of the sociometric measure plus the orientation of the teacher toward *doing* something has led to widespread use of socio-metry in the classroom, but there are important considerations to be kept in mind when this instrument is used. In a sense, the cautions with sociometry are those that could be brought to bear upon all of the measurement pro-cesses. The chief pitfalls are the attribution of validity where it may not exist and the stretching of findings beyond the warranted limits.

Validity has been discussed, but it is worth reemphasizing. How do you know that the sociometric data is an accurate picture of the group structure? That a measure has been taken does not ipso facto assure validity. Rapport with the students and the agreement of sociometric data with data from inde-pendent measures and observations are important sources of validation, as is the degree to which the structural changes based upon the measure achieve the desired results.

Interpretation of sociometric data invites speculation, but it must be done with care. For example, sociometry is a measure of group choices; it is not necessarily a measure of leadership, mental health, anxiety, or group morale. Inferences to constructs other than those the instrument measures can, of course, be made, but they must be recognized as inferences and not fact. Other corroborating evidence may strengthen the hunch and should be sought out. If a child is rejected by the group sociometrically, demonstrates aggressive behavior, is described by his mother as a problem at home, and has social difficulty in other classes, then inferences about the child's mental health are more accurate than if there were only one source of data.

Summary

This chapter extended the samples of social-behavioral science tools intro-duced earlier. Several sociometric techniques were described, and the procedure for constructing a sociogram was considered in detail. Three kinds of roles people play in groups were designated: the star, the isolate, and the rejectee. An actual example of the use of sociometry in a fourth-grade laboratory school class was given, and some of the general findings from sociometry were discussed.

Sociometry is a widely used classroom tool and is supported by an impressive number of studies, but the ease of gathering sociometric data may lead to excessive reliance on it as a measure. Various precautions were presented to guard against unwarranted interpretation of sociometric data.

7 / Research and Ethics

Recall that in Chapter 1, "What Is This Thing Called Science?" it was pointed out that science *as science* has difficulty in questions of ethics or morality. The reason given was that one of the important conditions for science to operate effectively is the establishment of criteria acceptable to the scientific community to be used as standards for evaluation and measurement. If there are no shared standards, there can be no science.

It is not to say that scientists as members of the human race are unconcerned with or oblivious to the moral and ethical issues arising out of the scientific process. Because of the tremendous increase in technological know-how within the last twenty years, it is safe to say that the scientist is more concerned with the use of that power than ever before. This is as true in the scientific study of human behavior as it is in the natural and physical sciences. In the case of the social-behavioral sciences, two concerns are paramount, both of which are questions of ethics. The first deals with the process of gathering data and the invasion of privacy. The second has to do with the use of the gathered data in making decisions. Both are legitimate concerns of the teacher-researcher.

Two recent articles raise these issues: the first, which is reproduced in part, comes from a panel of distinguished scientists; the second comes from the comedy team of Bob Elliott and Ray Goulding, more familiarly known as Bob and Ray.

Privacy and Behavioral Research: Preliminary Summary of the Report of the Panel on Privacy and Behavioral Research[1]

In recent years there have been growing threats to the privacy of individuals. Wiretapping, electronic eavesdropping, the use of personality tests in employment, the use of the lie detector in security or criminal investigations, and the detailed scrutiny of the private lives of people receiving public welfare funds all involve invasions of privacy. Although the social purpose is usually clear, the impact on the persons involved may be damaging. Our society has become more and more sensitive to the need to avoid such damage.

This concern has led to extensive discussion about the propriety of certain procedures in behavioral research, by the Congress, by officials in the various agencies of the Government, by university officials, by the scientific community generally, and by leaders in professional societies in the behavioral sciences. The Office of Science and Technology appointed a panel, in January 1966, to examine these issues and to propose guidelines for those who are engaged in behavioral research or associated with its support and management. . . .

THREATS TO PRIVACY

The right to privacy is the right of the individual to decide for himself how much he will share with others his thoughts, his feelings, and the facts of his personal life. It is a right that is essential to insure dignity and freedom of self-determination. In recent years there has been a severe erosion of this right by the widespread and often callous use of various devices for eavesdropping, lie detection, and secret observation in politics, in business, and in law enforcement. Indeed, modern electronic instruments for wiretapping and bugging have opened any human activity to the threat of illicit invasion of privacy. This unwholesome state of affairs has led to widespread public concern over the methods of inquiry used by agencies of public employment, social welfare, and law enforcement.

Behavioral research, devoted as it is to the discovery of facts and principles underlying human activity of all types, comes naturally under scrutiny in any examination of possible threats to privacy. All of the social sciences, including economics, political science, anthropology, sociology, and psychology, take as a major object of study the behavior of individuals, communities, or other groups. In one context or another, investigators in all these disciplines frequently need to seek information that

[1] Reprinted from *Science* 155 (1967): 535–38. Copyright © 1967 by The American Association for the Advancement of Science. The Panel on Privacy and Behavioral Research was appointed by the President's Office of Science and Technology. The members of the panel are Chairman Kenneth E. Clark, Dean of the College of Arts and Sciences, University of Rochester, Rochester, New York; Bernard Berelson, Vice-President of the Population Council, Inc., New York, New York; Edward J. Bloustein, President of Bennington College, Bennington, Vermont; George E. Pake, Provost of Washington University, St. Louis, Missouri; Colin S. Pittendrigh, Dean of the Graduate School, Princeton University, Princeton, New Jersey; Oscar M. Ruebhausen, Debevoise, Plimpton, Lyons & Gates, New York, New York; Walter S. Salant, Economics Studies Division, Brookings Institution, Washington, D.C.; Robert Sears, Dean of the School of Humanities and Sciences, Stanford University, Palo Alto, California; Benson R. Snyder, Psychiatrist in Chief of the Medical Department, Massachusetts Institute of Technology, Cambridge; Frederick P. Thieme, Vice-President of the University of Washington, Seattle; Lawrence N. Bloomberg, Assistant Chief of the Office of Statistical Standards, Bureau of the Budget, Washington, D.C.; and Colin M. MacLeod, Deputy Director of the Office of Science and Technology (now Vice-President for Medical Affairs, the Commonwealth Fund, New York, New York). Consultant to the Panel is Richard M. Michaels, Technical Assistant at Office of Science and Technology, Washington, D.C. The full text of the report is available from the Superintendent of Documents, Government Printing Office, Washington, D.C. 20402.

is private to the men, women, and children who are the subjects of their study. In most instances this information is freely given by those who consent to cooperate in the scientific process. But the very nature of behavioral research is such that there is a risk of invasion of privacy if unusual care is not taken to secure the consent of research subjects, or if the data obtained are not given full confidentiality. . . .

It is probable that relatively few of the studies undertaken by social scientists raise serious questions of propriety in relation to privacy and human dignity. From a survey of articles published in professional journals and of research grant applications submitted to Government agencies, we have concluded that most scientists who conduct research in privacy-sensitive areas are aware of the ethical implications of their experimental designs and arrange to secure the consent of subjects and to protect the confidentiality of the data obtained from them.

It cannot be denied, however, that, in a limited number of instances, behavioral scientists have not followed appropriate procedures to protect the rights of their subjects, and that in other cases recognition of the importance of privacy-invading considerations has not been as sophisticated, or the considerations as affirmatively implemented, as good practice demands. Because of this failure there has been pressure from some quarters, both within the Government and outside of it, to place arbitrary limits on the research methods which may be used. Behavioral scientists as a group do not question the importance of the right to privacy and are understandably concerned when suggestions are made that the detailed processes of science should be subjected to control by legislation or arbitrary administrative ruling. All scientists are opposed to restrictions which may curtail important research. At the same time they have an obligation to insure that all possible steps are taken to assure respect for the privacy and dignity of their subjects.

CONFLICTING RIGHTS

It is clear that there exists an important conflict between two values, both of which are strongly held in American society.

The individual has an inalienable right to dignity, self-respect, and freedom to determine his own thoughts and actions within the broad limits set by the requirements of society. The essential element in privacy and self-determination is the privilege of making one's own decision as to the extent to which one will reveal thoughts, feelings, and actions. When a person consents freely and fully to share himself with others—with a scientist, an employer, or a credit investigator—there is no invasion of privacy, regardless of the quality or nature of the information revealed.

Behavioral science is representative of another value vigorously championed by most American citizens, the right to know anything that may be known or discovered about any part of the universe. Man is part of this universe and the extent of the Federal Government's financial support of human behavioral research (on the order of $300 million in 1966) testifies to the importance placed on the study of human behavior by the American people. In the past there have been conflicts between theological beliefs and the theoretical analyses of the physical sciences. These conflicts have largely subsided, but the behavioral sciences seem to have inherited the basic conflict that arises when strongly held beliefs or moral attitudes—whether theologically, economically, or politically, based—are subjected to the free ranging process of scientific inquiry. If society is to exercise its right to know, it must free its behavioral scientists as much as possible from unnecessary restraints. Behavioral scientists in turn must accept the constructive restraints that society imposes in order to establish that level of dignity, freedom, and personal fulfillment that men treasure virtually above all else in life.

The root of the conflict between the individual's right to privacy and society's right of discovery is the research process. Behavioral science seeks to assess and to measure many qualities of men's minds, feelings, and actions. In the absence of informed consent on the part of the subject, these measurements represent invasion of privacy. The scientist must therefore obtain the consent of his subject.

To obtain truly informed consent is often difficult. In the first place, the nature of the inquiry sometimes cannot be explained adequately because it involves complex variables that the nonscientist does not understand. Examples are the personality variables measured by questionnaires, and the qualities of cognitive processes measured by creativity tests. Second, the validity of an experiment is sometimes destroyed if the subject knows all the details of its conduct. Examples include drug testing, in which the effect of suggestion (placebo effect) must be avoided, and studies of persuasability in which the subjects remain ignorant of the influences that are being presented experimentally. Clearly, then, if behavioral research is to be effective, some modification of the traditional concept of informed consent is needed.

Such a change in no sense voids the more general proposition that the performance of human behavioral research is the product of a partnership between the scientist and his subject. Consent to participate in a study must be the norm before any subject embarks on the enterprise. Since consent must sometimes be given despite an admittedly inadequate understanding of the scientific purposes of the research procedures, the right to discontinue participation at any point must be stipulated in clear terms. In the meantime, when full information is not available to the subject and when no alternative procedures to minimize the privacy problem are available to the subject, the relationship between the subject and the scientist (and between the subject and the institution sponsoring the scientist) must be based upon trust. This places the scientist and the sponsoring institution under a fiduciary obligation to protect the privacy and dignity of the subject who entrusts himself to them. The scientist must agree to treat the subject fairly and with dignity, to cause him no inconvenience or discomfort unless the extent of the inconvenience and discomfort has been accepted by the subject in advance, to inform the subject as fully as possible of the purposes of the inquiry or experiment, and to put into effect all procedures which will assure the confidentiality of whatever information is obtained.

Occasionally, even this degree of consent cannot be obtained. Naturalistic observations of group behavior must sometimes be made unbeknownst to the subjects. In such cases as well as in all others, the scientist has the obligation to insure full confidentiality of the research records. Only by doing so, and by making certain that published reports contain no identifying reference to a given subject, can the invasion of privacy be minimized.

Basically, then, the protection of privacy in research is assured first by securing the informed consent of the subject. When the subject cannot be completely informed, the consent must be based on trust in the scientist and in the institution sponsoring him. In any case, the scientist and his sponsoring institution must insure privacy by the maintenance of confidentiality.

In the end, the fact must be accepted that human behavioral research will at times produce discomfort to some subjects, and will entail a partial invasion of their privacy. Neither the principle of privacy nor the need to discover new knowledge can supervene universally. As with other conflicting values in our society, there must be constant adjustment and compromise, with the decision as to which value is to govern in a given instance to be determined by a weighing of the costs and the gains—the cost in privacy, the gain in knowledge. The decision cannot be made by the investigator alone, because he has vested interest in his own research program, but must be a positive concern of his scientific peers and the institution which sponsors his work. Our society has grown strong on the principle of minimizing costs and maximizing gains, and, when warmly held values are in conflict, there must be a thoughtful evaluation of the specific case. In particular we do not believe that detailed Governmental controls of research methods or instruments can substitute for the more effective procedures which are available and carry less risk of damage to the scientific enterprise. . . .

CONCLUSIONS

From our examination of the relation of behavioral science research to the right to privacy, we have been led to the following conclusions.

1. While most current practices in the field pose no significant threat to the privacy of research subjects, a sufficient number of exceptions have been noted to warrant a sharp increase in attention to procedures that will assure protection of this right. The increasing scale of behavioral research is itself an additional reason for focusing attention in this area.

2. Participation by subjects must be voluntary and based on informed consent to the extent that this is consistent with the objectives of the research. It is fully consistent with the protection of privacy that, in the absence of full information, consent be based on trust in the qualified investigator and the integrity of his institution.

3. The scientist has an obligation to insure that no permanent physical or psychological harm will ensue from the research procedures, and that temporary discomfort or loss of privacy will be remedied in an appropriate way during the course of the research or at its completion. To merit trust, the scientist must design his research with a view of protecting, to the fullest extent possible, the privacy of the subjects. If intrusion on privacy proves essential to the research, he should not proceed with his proposed experiment until he and his colleagues have considered all of the relevant facts and he has determined, with support from them, that the benefits outweigh the costs.

4. The scientist has the same responsibility to protect the privacy of the individual in published reports and in research records that he has in the conduct of the research itself.

5. The primary responsibility for the use of ethical procedures must rest with the individual investigator, but Government agencies that support behavioral research should satisfy themselves that the institution which employs the investigator has effectively accepted its responsibility to require that he meet proper ethical standards.

6. Legislation to assure appropriate recognition of the rights of human subjects is neither necessary nor desirable if the scientists and sponsoring institutions fully discharge their responsibilities in accommodating to the claim of privacy. Because of its relative inflexibility, legislation cannot meet the challenge of the subtle and sensitive conflict of values under consideration, nor can it aid in the wise decision making by individuals which is required to assume optimum protection of subjects, together with the fullest effectiveness of research. . . .

The Day the Computers Got Waldon Ashenfelter
BOB ELLIOTT AND RAY GOULDING[2]

The chroniclers of the life and times of Mary Backstayge, Noble Wife, of Steve Bosco the sportscaster, of the Piels brothers, and other almost fictional characters here prove that they can be as telling in print as on the air or the

[2] Bob Elliott and Ray Goulding, "The Day the Computers Got Waldon Ashenfelter," *Atlantic Monthly*, November 1967, pp. 658–61, copyright © 1967 by The Atlantic Monthly Company, reprinted by permission of Robert B. Elliott.

TV screen. Ashenfelter thought the computers would help him trap Y. Claude
Garfunkel, but he was tripped up by his own shoe size.

A presidential commission has recommended approval of plans for establishing a computerized data center where all personal information on individual Amer-
icans compiled by some twenty scattered agencies would be assembled in one place
and made available to the federal government as a whole.

Backers of the proposal contend that it would lead to greater efficiency, and
insist that the cradle-to-grave dossiers on the nation's citizens would be used only in
a generalized way to help deal with broad issues. Opponents argue that the ready
availability of so much confidential data at the push of a computer button could pose
a dangerous threat to the privacy of the individual by enabling the federal bureaucracy
to become a monstrous snooping Big Brother.

Obviously, the plan elicits reactions that are emotional, and cooler heads
are needed to envision the aura of quiet, uneventful routine certain to pervade the
Central Data Bank once it becomes accepted as just another minor government
agency.

Fade in:

Interior—Basement GHQ of the Central Data Bank—Night.

*(At stage right, 950 sophisticated third-generation computers may be seen
stretching off into the distance. At stage left, the CDB graveyard-shift charge d'affaires,
Nimrod Gippard, is seated behind a desk. He is thirty-five-ish and attired in socks that
don't match. At the open, Gippard is efficiently stuffing mimeographed extortion
letters to Omaha's 3277 suspected sex deviates into envelopes. He glances up as
Waldon Ashenfelter, an indoorsy type of questionable ancestry, enters.)*

Gippard: Yes, sir?

Ashenfelter (flashing ID card): Ashenfelter. Bureau of Indian Affairs. Like to
have you run a check on a key figure named Y. Claude Garfunkel.

Gippard (reaching for pad and pencil): Sure thing. What's his Social Security
number?

Ashenfelter: I dunno.

Gippard: Hmmm. How about his zip code? Or maybe a cross-reference to
some banks where he may have been turned down for a loan. Just any clue at all to his
identity.

Ashenfelter: Well, as I say, his name is Y. Claude Garfunkel.

Gippard (after a weary sigh): It's not much to go on, but I'll see what I can do.

*(Gippard rises and crosses to the master data-recall panel. Ashenfelter strolls
to a nearby computer and casually begins checking the confidential reports on his
four small children to learn how many are known extremists.)*

Ashenfelter: You're new here, aren't you?

Gippard: No. Just my first week on the night shift. Everybody got moved
around after we lost McElhenny.

Ashenfelter: Wasn't he that heavyset fellow with beady eyes who drove the
Hudson?

Gippard: Yeah. Terrible thing. Pulled his own dossier one night when things
were quiet and found out he was a swish. Kind of made him go all to pieces.

Ashenfelter: That's a shame. And now I suppose he's gone into analysis and
gotten himself cross-filed as a loony.

Gippard: No. He blew his brains out right away. But having a suicide on your
record can make things tough, too.

Ashenfelter: Yeah. Shows a strong trend toward instability.

(The computer informs Ashenfelter that his oldest boy was detained by police 1 1963 for roller-skating on municipal property, and that the five-year-old probably >unded the Farmer-Labor Party in Minnesota.)

Ashenfelter (cont.) *(mutters in despair):* Where did I fail them as a father?

Gippard: Didn't you tell me you're with Indian Affairs?

Ashenfelter: Yeah. Why?

Gippard: I think I'm onto something hot. Is that like India Indians or whoop-
-up Indians?

Ashenfelter: I guess you'd say whoop-it-up.

Gippard: Well, either way, no Indian named Garfunkel has ever complied
,vith the Alien Registration Law.

Ashenfelter: I never said he was an Indian. He's Jewish, and I think he's play-
1g around with my wife.

Gippard: Gee, that's too bad.

Ashenfelter *(dramatically):* Oh, I blame myself really. I guess I'd started taking
aVerne for granted and—

Gippard: No. I mean it's too bad he's only Jewish. The computers aren't pro-
,rammed to feed back home-wreckers by religious affiliation.

Ashenfelter: Oh.

Gippard: Can you think of anything kinky that's traditional with Jews? You
,now. Like draft dodging—smoking pot—something a computer could really hang
ts hat on.

Ashenfelter: No. They just seem to feed each other a lot of chicken soup. And
hey do something around Christmastime with candles. But I'm not sure any of it's
Ilegal.

Gippard: We'll soon see. If the curve on known poultry processors correlates
,eographically with a year-end upswing in tallow rendering—well, you can appre-
iate what that kind of data would mean to the bird dogs at the ICC and the FDA.
hey'd be able to pinpoint exactly where it was all happening and when.

Ashenfelter: Uh-huh—where and when what?

Gippard: That's exactly what I intend to find out.

*(Gippard turns back to the panel and resumes work with a sense of destiny.
\shenfelter, whistling softly to himself, absently begins plunking the basic melody of
'Mexicali Rose" on the keyboard of a nearby computer. The machine responds by
urnishing him with Howard Hughes's 1965 income tax return and the unlisted phone
1umbers of eight members of a New Orleans wife-swapping club who may have
:nown Lee Harvey Oswald. As Ashenfelter pockets the information, Major General
_ourtney ("Old Napalm and Guts") Nimshaw enters. He has a riding crop but no
noustache.)*

Nimshaw: Yoohoo! Anybody home?

Gippard: Back here at the main console.

*(Nimshaw moves to join Gippard, then sees Ashenfelter for the first time and
reezes. The two stand eyeing each other suspiciously as Gippard reenters the scene.)*

Gippard: Oh, forgive me. General Nimshaw, I'd like for you to meet Ashen-
elter from Indian Affairs.

*(Nimshaw and Ashenfelter ad-lib warm greetings as they shake hands. Then
:ach rushes off to pull the dossier of the other. Ashenfelter learns that Nimshaw was a
1otorious bed wetter during his days at West Point and that his heavy drinking later
:aused an entire airborne division to be parachuted into Ireland on D-Day. Nimshaw
'earns Ashenfelter owns 200 shares of stock in a Canadian steel mill that trades with
_ommunist China and that he has been considered a bad credit risk since 1949,
when he refused to pay a Cincinnati dance studio for $5500 worth of tango lessons.
Apparently satisfied, both men return to join Gippard, who has been checking out a*

possible similarity in the patterns of poultry-buying by key Jewish housewives an
reported sightings of Soviet fishing trawlers off the Alaskan coast.)
    Ashenfelter: Working late tonight, eh, General?
    Nimshaw (nervously): Well, I just stumbled across a little military hardwar
transport thing. We seem to have mislaid an eighty-six-car trainload of munitior
between here and the West Coast. Can't very well write it off as normal pilferage. So
thought Gippard could run a check for me on the engineer and brakeman. You knov
Where they hang out in their spare time. Whether they might take a freight train wit
them. What do you think, Gipp?
    Gippard: Sure. Just have a few more things to run through for Ashenfelt■
first. He's seeking a final solution to the Jewish problem.
    Ashenfelter (blanching): Well, not exactly the whole—
    Nimshaw: Oh, has all that come up again?
    (Two janitors carrying lunch pails enter and cross directly to the compute
programmed for medical case histories of nymphomaniacs. They pull several dossier
at random and then cross directly to a far corner, unwrapping bacon, lettuce, an
tomato sandwiches as they go. They spread a picnic cloth on the floor and begin reac
ing the dossiers as they eat. They emit occasional guffaws, but the others pay n■
attention to them.
    Gippard (as he compares graph curves): No doubt about it. Whatever thos■
Russian trawlers are up to, it's good for the delicatessen business. This could be th
break we've been hoping for.
    Nimshaw: Hating Jews been a big thing with you for quite a while, Asher
felter?
    Ashenfelter (coldly): About as long as you've been losing government prop■
erty by the trainload, I imagine.
    (Nimshaw and Ashenfelter eye each other uneasily for a moment. Then the
quickly exchange hush money in the form of drafts drawn against secret Swiss ban■
accounts as Gippard's assistant, Llewelyn Fordyce, enters. Fordyce is a typical bri■
liant young career civil servant who has been lost for several hours trying to find h■
way back from the men's room. He appears haggard, but is in satisfactory conditio■
otherwise.)
    Fordyce: Are you gentlemen being taken care of?
    (Ashenfelter and Nimshaw nod affirmatively. Fordyce hurriedly roots throug■
the desk drawers, pausing only to take a quick, compulsive inventory of paper clip■
and map pins as he does so.)
    Fordyce (cont.) (shouts): Hey Gipp! I can't find the registry cards for thes■
two idiots out here.
    Gippard (faintly, from a distance): I've been too busy to sign 'em in yet. Tak■
care of it, will you?
    (Fordyce gives a curt, efficient nod, inefficiently failing to realize that Gippar■
is too far away to see him nodding. Fordyce then brings forth two large pink card■
and hands them to Nimshaw and Ashenfelter.)
    Fordyce: If you'd just fill these out please. We're trying to accumulate data o■
everybody who uses the Data Bank so we can eventually tie it all in with somethin■
or other.
    (Nimshaw studies the section of his card dealing with maximum fines an■
imprisonment for giving false information, while Ashenfelter skips over the hard par
and goes directly to the multiple-choice questions.)
    Fordyce (cont.): And try to be as specific as you can about religious belief
and your affiliation with subversive groups. We're beginning to think there's more t■
this business of Quakers denying they belong to the Minutemen than meets the eye
    (Nimshaw and Ashenfelter squirm uneasily as they sense the implication■

Ashenfelter hurriedly changes his answer regarding prayer in public schools from "undecided" to "not necessarily" as Nimshaw perjures himself by listing the principal activity at the Forest Hills Tennis Club as tennis. Meantime, Gippard has rejoined the group, carrying four rolls of computer tape carefully stacked in no particular sequence.)

Gippard: I know I'm on to something here, Fordyce, but I'm not sure what to make of it. Surveillance reports on kosher poultry dealers indicate that most of them don't show up for work on Saturday. And that timing correlates with an unexplained increase in activity at golf courses near key military installations. But the big thing is that drunken drivers tend to get nabbed most often on Saturday night, and that's exactly when organized groups are endangering national security by deliberately staying up late with their lights turned on to overload public power plants.

Fordyce (whistles softly in amazement): We're really going to catch a covey of them in this net. How'd you happen to stumble across it all?

Gippard: Well, it seemed pretty innocent at first. This clown from Indian Affairs just asked me to dig up what I could so he'd have some excuse for exterminating the Jews.

(Ashenfelter emits a burbling throat noise as an apparent prelude to something more coherent, but he is quickly shushed.)

Gippard (cont.): But you know how one correlation always leads to another. Now we've got a grizzly by the tail, Fordyce, and I can see "organized conspiracy" written all over it.

Fordyce: Beyond question. And somewhere among those 192 million dossiers is the ID number of the Mister Big we're after. Do the machines compute a cause-and-effect relationship that might help narrow things down?

Gippard: Well, frankly, the computers have gotten into a pretty nasty argument among themselves over that. Most of them see how golf could lead to drunken driving. But the one that's programmed to chart moral decay and leisure time fun is pretty sure that drunken driving causes golf.

(Nimshaw glances up from the job of filling out his registry card.)

Nimshaw: That's the most ridiculous thing I ever heard of.

Fordyce (with forced restraint): General, would you please stick to whatever people like you are supposed to know about and leave computer finding interpretation to analysts who are trained for the job?

(Nimshaw starts to reply, but then recalls the fate of a fellow officer who was broken to corporal for insubordination. He meekly resumes pondering question No. 153, unable to decide whether admitting or denying the purchase of Girl Scout cookies will weigh most heavily against him in years to come.)

Fordyce (cont.): Any other cause-and-effect computation that we ought to consider in depth, Gipp?

Gippard: Not really. Of course, Number 327's been out of step with the others ever since it had that circuitry trouble. It just keeps saying, "Malcolm W. Biggs causes kosher poultry." Types out the same damned thing over and over: "Malcolm W. Biggs causes kosher poultry."

Fordyce: Who's Malcolm W. Biggs?

Gippard: I think he was a juror at one of the Jimmy Hoffa trials. Number 327 was running a check on him when the circuits blew, and it's had kind of an obsession about him ever since.

Fordyce: Mmmm. Well, personally, I've never paid much attention to the opinions of paranoids. They can get your thinking as screwed up as theirs is.

(Fordyce notices Ashenfelter making an erasure on his card to change the data regarding his shoe size from 9½C to something less likely to pinch across the instep.)

Fordyce (cont.) (shrieks at Ashenfelter): What do you think you're doing there?

You're trying to hide something from me. I've met your kind before.

(Ashenfelter wearily goes back to a 9½C, even though they make his feet hurt, and Fordyce reacts with a look of smug satisfaction.)

Gippard: Maybe if I fed this junk back into the machine, it could name some people who fit the pattern.

Fordyce: Why don't you just reprocess the computations in an effort to gain individualized data that correlates?

(Gippard stares thoughtfully at Fordyce for a long moment and then exits to nail the ringleaders·through incriminating association with the key words "drunk," "poultry," "golf," and "kilowatt.")

Nimshaw: I think maybe I'd better come back sometime when you're not so busy.

(He slips his registry card into his pocket and starts toward the door, but Fordyce grabs him firmly by the wrist.)

Fordyce: Just a minute. You can't take that card out of here with you. It may contain classified information you shouldn't even have access to.

Nimshaw: But it's about me. I'm the one who just filled it out.

Fordyce: Don't try to muddy up the issue. Nobody walks out of this department with government property. Let's have it.

(Nimshaw reluctantly surrenders the card. Fordyce glances at it and reacts with a look of horror.)

Fordyce (cont.): You've filled this whole thing out in longhand! The instructions clearly state, "Type or print legibly." You'll have to do it over again.

(Fordyce tears up the card and hands Nimshaw a new one. Nimshaw, suddenly aware that a display of bad conduct could cost him his good conduct medal, goes back to work, sobbing quietly to himself.)

Gippard (faintly, from a distance): Eureka! Hot damn!

Fordyce (happily): He's hit paydirt. I know old Gippard, and he hasn't cut loose like that since he linked Ralph Nader with the trouble at Berkeley.

(Gippard enters on the dead run, unmindful of the computer tape streaming out behind him.)

Gippard: It all correlates beautifully. (*Ticks off points on his fingers.*) A chicken plucker. Three arrests for common drunk. FBI's observed him playing golf with a known Cuban. Psychiatric report shows he sleeps with all the lights on.

Fordyce: All wrapped up in one neat bundle. Who is he?

Gippard: A virtual unknown. Never been tagged as anything worse than possibly disloyal until I found him. He uses the name Y. Claude Garfunkel.

Ashenfelter: Y. Claude Garfunkel!

Fordyce (menacingly): Touch a raw nerve, Ashenfelter?

(The two janitors, who are really undercover sophomores majoring in forestry at Kansas State on CIA scholarships, rise and slowly converge on Ashenfelter.)

Gippard: Want to tell us about it, Ashenfelter? We have our own methods of computing the truth out of you anyway, you know.

Fordyce: No point in stalling. What's the connection? The two of you conspired to give false opinions to the Harris Poll, didn't you?

Ashenfelter (pitifully): No! Nothing like that. I swear.

Gippard: Then what, man? What? Have you tried to sabotage the Data Bank by forging each other's Social Security numbers?

Ashenfelter (a barely audible whisper): No. Please don't build a treason case against me. I'll tell. A neighbor saw him with my wife at a luau in Baltimore.

(The CIA men posing as college students posing as janitors react intuitively to jab Ashenfelter with a sodium-pentathol injection. Gippard rushes to a computer,

here he begins cross-checking Garfunkel and Ashenfelter in the Urban Affairs file
"Polynesian Power" advocates in Baltimore's Hawaiian ghetto and Interstate
ommerce Commission reports on suspected participants in interstate hanky-panky.
rdyce grabs the red "hot line" telephone on his desk and reacts with annoyance
he gets a busy signal. General Nimshaw, sensing himself caught up in a tide of
vents which he can neither turn back nor understand, hastily erases the computer
pe containing his own dossier and then slashes his wrists under an assumed name.)
    Fade out.

Summary

he intent of this chapter has been to raise rather than to attempt to resolve
e moral and ethical questions of the scientific study of human behavior.
the first article it is recommended, among other things, that:

1. When possible, participation of subjects must be voluntary and based on informed consent. (How does this apply to the parents of students and to the
   administration of such measures as I.Q. tests, achievement tests, personality
   tests, and so on?)
2. In those conditions where subjects cannot be fully informed or where their
   consent cannot be requested because of threat to the validity of the study,
   there must exist a condition of trust in the research process to protect as much
   as possible the privacy of the subject. (How is this established in the school setting? Who should have access to a student's record? Should records be given
   to others without consent of the student or his parents?)

The story of Waldon Ashenfelter points out that data, once gathered,
an be misused in decision making. Specifically, it suggested that:

1. Once recorded, subjective information based upon opinion has a tendency to
   become fact.
2. Adverse information, though accurate at one point in time, may become inaccurate with the passage of time.
3. Dossiers may become accessible to persons unskilled in interpretation of
   data.

Inasmuch as schools often have subjective data on students, what are the
guidelines for using these data?)
    The two articles raise important questions for the student of behavior,
n this case, the teacher-researcher. The first step in facing the problems of
research is the explication of the problem, but as with many issues in ethics
resolution is not a simple matter.

II / CHANGING BEHAVIOR

A Brief Essay on the Occasion of Choice

The first part of the text has been devoted in the main to tools and techniques for descriptive research. Part II is designed to suggest a frame of reference based upon learning theory to facilitate getting from where students are to where the teacher wants them to go. But first it seems appropriate to make several statements concerning the decisions that have gone into the development of what you are about to read.

Learning Theory or Learning Theories?

As you probably well know, there is no one learning theory. The problem, then, is the choice of giving a necessarily brief overview of learning theories or of selecting one position and treating it in depth. It is clearly a question of choice involving the values, the biases, the hunches, and the intuitions of the chooser. The majority of educational psychology texts have opted for general rather than in-depth treatment of learning. The position seems to be that since no single learning theory is satisfactory to everyone, it is better to include the major theoretical positions to be sure the student will get the widest—albeit superficial—exposure.

Contrary to traditional practice, the choice for this text has been to select a single position on learning. The decision was made for three reasons: (1) the theory chosen seems to have the greatest promise for application, and, in fact, it is the only learning position that has been systematically used in classrooms; (2) the theory is comprehensive; and (3) the alternative choice of extensive rather than intensive treatment of learning is probably more con-using than helpful. Since the teacher is a practitioner desiring to bring about certain predictable changes, it appears logical that the system that increases the probability of change is the most appropriate for the teacher to know. As previously stated, that position is the one called *operant conditioning*. The serious student, of course, will want exposure to other theories of learning. One excellent introductory source is Ernest Hilgard's book *Theories of Learning*, which considers as many as fourteen different ways to cut the cake.[1]

The Gaps Between Theory and Practice

Lest the reader expect a learning theory immediately applicable to the complex environment of the classroom, it should be further stated that all theories of learning, by their very nature, are creations of the trained researcher working in the confines of his laboratory, and, as with any set of principles developed in a highly controlled setting, exportation to the less controlled world of the classroom is not accomplished easily. For example, one of the principles to be considered is that the consequences of behavior may have a great deal to do with whether or not that behavior will be repeated again in the same or reasonably similar environmental conditions. This is an abstraction, but it takes on concrete form when one observes children in a class who upon successful completion of a puzzle (a *consequence* of problem-solving behavior) request another puzzle or mix up the pieces and begin anew. The process just described is a matter of knowing an abstract principle—in this case that behavior is a function of its consequences—and translating that principle to an operational level by observing how it is manifested in a child's behavior.

Abstract or theoretical knowledge differs from applied "cookbook" knowledge in that it transcends the immediate. It is one thing to know that a roast will taste better if it is cooked—an important but limited bit of specific information; it is another thing to know that heat renders most food more palatable. The latter knowledge encompasses a much wider range of situations and gives the cook considerably more power over his task. Similarly, the teacher who understands a set of principles both to describe and to facilitate learning has more opportunity to achieve the school's, the teacher's, and the children's goals.

Part II deals with empirically based principles and actual examples of how the principles have been put into operation. It is crucially important if the following material is to be useful that you not begin with an expectation of a listing of fifty nifty rules on how to teach, nor should you assume that even the examples will be directly applicable. The process of going from the principle to the operation will be suggested, but in the final analysis it is your task to make the translation.

[1] Ernest Hilgard, *Theories of Learning,* 3rd ed. (New York: Appleton-Century-Crofts, 1966).

8 / A Basis for Applying a Psychology of Learning

This chapter's purpose is to provide a conceptual backdrop for this and the following sections. You will note, however, that the manner of presentation differs from that of previous chapters. The format might be called a scrambled program, where the response you make to the questions at the bottom of the page will determine where you go. Once there, you will be given more information and questions, your answers again prescribing where to go. In other words, you will not read pages consecutively but will follow directions depending on your response. This change in style of presentation is made for more important reasons than novelty, and these reasons will become clear as you proceed through the chapter.

The scientific study of human behavior holds to the axiom that only what can be observed can be studied scientifically. Observable aspects of behavior include performance on a test, tactics of problem solving, rate of response, verbal behavior, how long one keeps at an activity, and so on. These are called *operants*, behaviors that operate on the environment.

Inferred states, the behind-the-scene "causes" of behavior that are derived from observation of overt behavior (operants), have relatively little value for science. That is, such assumptions as that someone is perplexed when he frowns, happy when he smiles, anxious when he paces the floor, sad when he cries, and is lost in thought when reading a book are outside the pale of scientific methodology because the conditions of perplexity, happiness, anxiety, sadness, and thoughtfulness are merely inferred from the real stuff of behavioral science, namely, the operants of frowning, smiling, pacing, crying, and reading. The distinction being made is between actual behavior and inferences of the conditions leading to the observed behavior. The former can be accepted as scientific data more readily than the latter.

In his later writings Sigmund Freud postulated an innate (unlearned) death instinct in order to account for aggression and urges of self-destruction.

If you categorize Freud's theory of aggression and urges of suicide (overt behaviors) as a scientific observation, **turn to page 86.**
If you view this aspect of Freudian theory as outside the realm of science, **turn to page 88.**

You are close, and perhaps the fault lies with the writer rather tha the reader.

The only way a reinforcer can be defined is by demonstrating in eac case that it increases the probability of certain behavior. If it works, it is reinforcer; if it does not work, it is not a reinforcer.

One can often make a fairly good guess about a potential reinforce before the fact, because you do have knowledge about what people generall respond or fail to respond to. For a thirsty man water is reinforcing; you prob ably like steak; children usually enjoy praise; a salesman is characteristicall pleased with a large order; and most prisoners want release from jail. Bu water, steaks, praise, large orders, and release from prison cannot be consid ered reinforcers until they have been shown in the individual situation t increase the probability of certain behavior.

Now return to page 85 and select the right answer.

Very good! Although there has been a great deal of interest in genetics, the geneticists are a long way from isolating a factor or factors as a cause of "intelligent" behavior. This is not to deny that there may be genetic intelligence, but as yet no evidence exists of such a factor transmitted through the genes.

What we have been considering is the erroneous notion that naming is explaining. Because a factor such as instinct, inheritance, or need has been named, it is assumed that the behavior is also explained. The terms that teachers use to explain a child's behavior often fall into this category. A few of the more common are emotional instability, feelings of hostility, inferiority complex, lack of intelligence, and low motivation. These "causes" are not useful because their vagueness does not indicate what can be done to correct the child's behavior.

What would be helpful to the teacher is a more precise psychology that describes an operant behavior as it is related to a desired behavior. For example, Gregory does not perform well academically, or, more specifically, in a math exercise Gregory finished correctly only five of thirty problems. Now, you might "blame" Gregory's lack of achievement on a low interest in math, but that analysis gets you nowhere because your job, among other things, is to raise Gregory's level of performance, not to categorize him as a low achiever in math. To help do this, you need a learning theory that considers Gregory's behavior in ways that indicate how to manipulate his environment to maximize the probability of his success in math, that is, of thirty correct responses out of thirty test problems.

One such concept is reinforcement. Reinforcement is defined as an immediate consequence to behavior that increases the probability that that behavior will occur again. Once a student has behaved, the environmental consequences that the teacher controls can do one of three things: increase the recurrence of behavior, decrease recurrence of the behavior, or have no observable effect with respect to that behavior.

It follows from the above that some reinforcers are praise, good grades, money, and attention.

These are reinforcers. **Turn to page 84.**
These may be reinforcers. **Turn to page 87.**

Not quite, but it is understandable why you have categorized Freud and his theory as scientific. In some ways, particularly as reflected in his earlier work in neurology, Freud did behave as a scientist, and some have erroneously confused the work of the young Freud with that of the older Freud. The fact that he was a medical doctor—essentially a scientific discipline—may also have misled you.

The problem with his aggression–self-destruction theory is that an instinct cannot be measured. Freud described an instinct as an "internal stimulus," but he had little notion where it was, what form it took, where it came from, or where it went. It was all rather mysterious.

Inferring conditions as causes or correlates of observable behavior opens up too much opportunity for contamination by the observer's biases. You will remember this possibility was discussed in Chapters 4 and 5 on observational techniques. A way to avoid subjective observations is to stick close to the data at hand, the overt behavior. You lose a certain amount of richness by confining yourself to the measurable obvious, but in science the value of "clean" data far outweighs subjective interpretations.

Now go back to page 83, read it again, and make the alternative response.

Fine! You have said they *may* be reinforcers and you are correct. A reinforcer is defined as any condition that increases the probability of the recurrence of selected behavior. If the condition does not actually increase the desired behavior so that you can quantify the increase, it is not a reinforcer.

There are positive and negative reinforcers. A positive reinforcer is the consequence to a behavior that is followed by an increase in that behavior. If a student says "good morning" to his teacher and the consequence is a smile and a cheery response from the teacher and if his "good mornings" increase in frequency on ensuing days, it can be said that his behavior has been positively reinforced.

On the other hand, some behavior produces a punishing consequence. When other behavior that escapes the punishing consequence goes up in probability, it is said to have been negatively reinforced. Another way of saying the same thing is that behavior that removes or avoids an aversive stimulus is negatively reinforced and, as such, will be increased.

An attractive coed has discovered that crying whenever a policeman is about to write a ticket for illegal parking usually stops the ticket-writing behavior. Her crying is an example of:

Negative reinforcement. **Turn to page 90.**
Positive reinforcement. **Turn to page 89.**

Right you are! With all due respect to Freud, one could hardly consider an unmeasurable, unobservable instinct as a cause and remain within the framework of science. Other causal concepts frequently invoked to explain behavior but equally unscientific are needs, drives, wishes, and hopes, where no attempt has been made to measure these antecedent states independently. By the same token, thoughts and ideas are only inferred from observable behavior; we know they exist because we have them, but they are not accessible to scientific study because they cannot be observed and measured. What is observable and measurable is, of course, the overt expression of a thought or an idea, and this is fair game for behavioral science.

Let's try one more example to be sure you have this information clearly in mind. (Note that my measure of your having the information in mind is your observable response.)

When you come right down to it, one's intelligence is best explained by what the child inherits from his parents.

Is this a statement of science? **Turn to page 99.**
Or of nonscience? **Turn to page 85.**

The relief of not getting a ticket has clear positive aspects about it, but that quality is a result of her rather effective means of *avoiding* the aversive consequences of going to court, paying a fine, and so on. Crying in this case, therefore, is a form of negatively reinforced behavior because it avoids punishing consequences.

Similarly, studying is negatively reinforced behavior when the student seeks to avoid a poor grade. A school environment, however, in which studying is a form of negative reinforcement is obviously undesirable. Undoubtedly it is the occasion for the well-known couplet sung by children as they leave for vacation:

> No more pencils, no more books,
> No more teachers' dirty looks.

Turn now to page 90.

Correct.

The coed's tears are a form of negative reinforcement. Behavior that leads to successful avoidance or escape is usually negatively reinforced. The occasion for such behavior is the anticipation of some form of aversive consequence, learned by having been punished in the past or by having seen or heard of someone else punished for that behavior.

Using punishment or the threat of punishment as the primary means of changing behavior—a common practice in schools—is seriously deficient mainly because, though it may control short term behavior, long term responses are often unpredictable. With the loss of predictability, the teacher becomes considerably less effective.

Similarly, the teacher's effectiveness is diminished as a behavioral engineer or shaper because when the threat of punishing or noxious consequences is used as the principal motivator, the teacher becomes aversive and the possibility of effective change is diminished.

Turn to the next page.

A Brief Review

So far, the following points have been made:

1. Things unobservable (and therefore unquantifiable) are not very helpful to the scientist, particularly the applied scientist who wants to bring about change.
2. Observable things that can be isolated and manipulated constitute the first step in the construction of a psychology of change.
3. One concept that can be observed and manipulated is that of reinforcement. Positive reinforcement is a condition that follows operant behavior and increases the probability of that behavior. If it does not increase the probability it is not a reinforcer.
4. Another concept that can be observed and manipulated is negative reinforcement. Negative reinforcement is a condition that terminates or avoids an undesirable state of affairs. When the undesirable state of affairs occurs or is anticipated again, behavior associated with previous termination is more likely to occur.

Go to the next page.

Reinforcement—both positive and negative—is a condition for *adding* certain types of behavior. But how does behavior get stopped? One way is obvious: nonreinforcement. An example will help explain.[1] A healthy twenty-month-old child had a tantrum every time he was put to bed. His behavior was obviously maintained by the attention received for crying. Finally, after the very high operant level of crying was established, the parents, now at wit's end, decided to withhold reinforcement of crying by not reentering the room once he was put to bed. As predicted, when the parents stopped lavishing attention on his crying, it was in time replaced with more appropriate bed-time behavior. About a week later a visiting and unwary aunt put the child to bed. He cried and the aunt responded with concern by coming back into the room and remaining until the child's tantrum fatigued him and he fell asleep. A second extinction of the crying was necessary. Figure 13 shows the results of both extinctions. It should be added that no undesirable after-effects were observed.

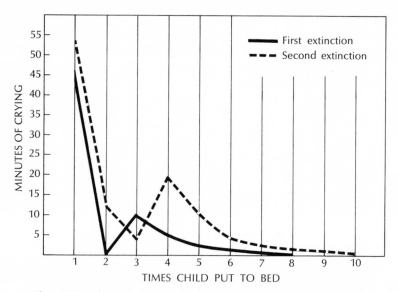

Figure 13. Length of crying in two extinction series as a function of successive occasions of being put to bed (Williams, "The Elimination of Tantrum Behavior . . .").

The moral is obvious: reinforce desirable behavior; withhold reinforcement of undesirable behavior.

True. **Turn to next page.**
False. **Turn to page 93.**

[1] Charles D. Williams, "The Elimination of Tantrum Behavior by Extinction Procedures," *Journal of Abnormal and Social Psychology* 59 (1959): 2–9, as reported in J. R. Millenson, *Principles of Behavioral Analysis* (New York: The Macmillan Company, 1967), pp. 105–6.

Well and good. The statement is accurate, but operationally it is rather difficult in a classroom to extinguish behavior by nonreinforcement. There are simply too many reinforcers over which you have little or no control. These may include attention from other children, self-reinforcing aspects of the behavior in which the child is engaging, fear of losing a fight, and so on—any of which may be more powerful than the teacher's nonreinforcing behavior. In the study by Charles D. Williams just cited, extraneous reinforcers for crying were minimal, but the lively classroom has a host of conditions that might maintain behavior. There may be times when punishment—that is, a negative consequence to an operant—is necessary. Obviously, whenever a child's safety is in question, quick and decisive action to stop behavior is called for.

Fortunately, there are relatively few occasions when a teacher is concerned just with stopping undesirable behavior. Extinction by nonreinforcement from the teacher can become the occasion for introducing another kind of environment that makes undesirable behavior incompatible with a new set of behaviors. For example, say that a student disrupts a class. Rather than dressing him down before the group (which could be a subtle reinforcer), the teacher might introduce another set of activities to terminate the disruption wherein the new behavioral demands are incompatible with prior behavior. Wise mothers use this technique when they divert inappropriate behavior with a well placed "Look over here." The new activity, then, allows for the use of positive reinforcers. Or, say a child makes the same kind of error over and over again. The teacher might want to break the problem into smaller segments (a new environment) that demand different responses incompatible with the previous incorrect responses. When study behavior is necessary and when the class cannot seem to get started, it may be prudent for the teacher to program study by saying, "Let's first get out our notebooks—our pencils—our books—and now we're ready to begin our assignment."

The point is that extinction by nonreinforcement can be accomplished only in a highly controlled environment where extraneous reinforcers are absent. Since today's classroom does not provide that kind of control, behavioral change from inappropriate to appropriate is usually best accomplished by diverting activity to that which can be rewarded.

Go to the next page.

In general, the process of helping students get from where they are to where you want them to be is accomplished most efficiently by systematic, progressively difficult steps rather than by exposure to great chunks of disordered information. Also, when relatively immediate feedback on one's progress is provided, errors and misunderstandings are minimized. But rather than describe this method for learning, it is preferable that you experience it.

Reproduced on the next several pages is a teaching program that combines the qualities of systematic, progressively difficult bits of information about an instrument used in behavioral research.[2] The program is self-explanatory, and you are invited to go through it by filling in the blank spaces.

[2] Millenson, *Principles of Behavioral Analysis*, pp. 67–70.

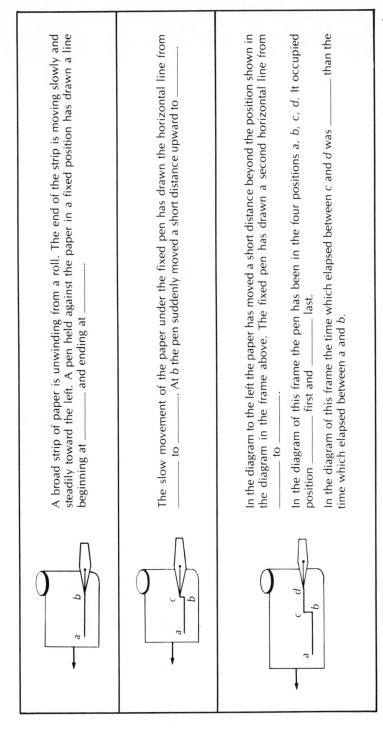

A broad strip of paper is unwinding from a roll. The end of the strip is moving slowly and steadily toward the left. A pen held against the paper in a fixed position has drawn a line beginning at ———— and ending at ————.

The slow movement of the paper under the fixed pen has drawn the horizontal line from ———— to ————. At *b* the pen suddenly moved a short distance upward to ————.

In the diagram to the left the paper has moved a short distance beyond the position shown in the diagram in the frame above. The fixed pen has drawn a second horizontal line from ———— to ————.

In the diagram of this frame the pen has been in the four positions *a, b, c, d*. It occupied position ———— first and ———— last.

In the diagram of this frame the time which elapsed between *c* and *d* was ———— than the time which elapsed between *a* and *b*.

Figure 14. An instructional sequence on how to read a cumulative response record (adapted from B. F. Skinner, *Cumulative Record*, Century Psychology Series [New York: Appleton-Century-Crofts, 1959]).

In recording the responses made by an organism, the pen moves upward and draws a short vertical line each time a response is made. In the diagram to the left an experiment began when the pen was at a. The first response was made at _____.

In the diagram three responses were made fairly quickly, and at a steady rate at _____, _____, and _____.

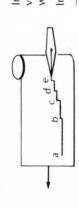

In the diagram to the left the three responses recorded at a were emitted _____ rapidly than the three at b.

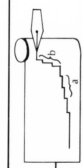

The more rapid the responding, the _____ the pauses between responses.

The higher the rate of responding, the _____ the horizontal line drawn by the pen between successive responses.

In the diagram of the last frame, the more rapid the responding, the _____ the slope of the step-like line.

Rate of responding is shown by the _____ of the step-like line.

Responding in the diagram at the left begins at a relatively high rate at a. The time between successive responses grows progressively _____.

In the diagram the slope of the first part of the curve drawn by the pen beginning at a is relatively _____.

Figure 14. Continued

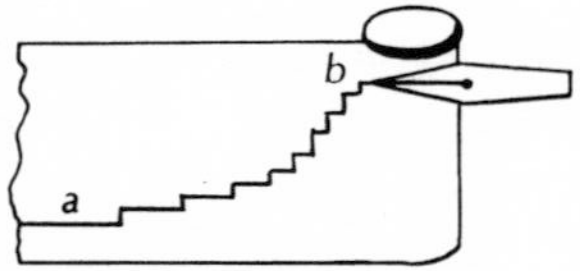

In this diagram the rate increases fairly steadily from a low value near _____ to a high value near _____.

An *increase* in rate is called *positive acceleration*. Positive acceleration is shown in this diagram/the diagram in the frame above (choose one).

Negative acceleration refers to a(n) _____ in rate.

Negative acceleration is shown in the diagram of this frame/the frame above (choose one).

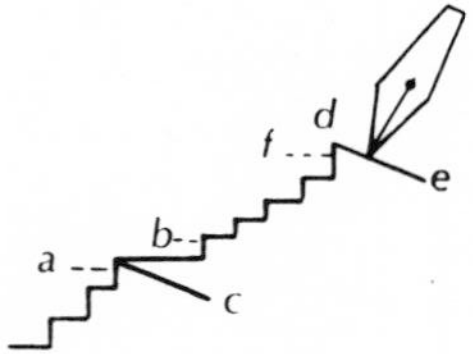

To record other events which occur while an animal is responding, the pen swings quickly "to the southeast" and back again. In the diagram to the left the pen has just drawn a line from _____ to _____. The point of the pen will immediately return to _____.

The short diagonal mark ("hatch" or "pip") at _____ was made by the same movement of the pen as shown at *d–e*.

The "southeast" mark or hatch is often used to indicate that a response has produced some special consequence. In the diagram of this frame these reponses only were recorded by the vertical marks at _____ and _____.

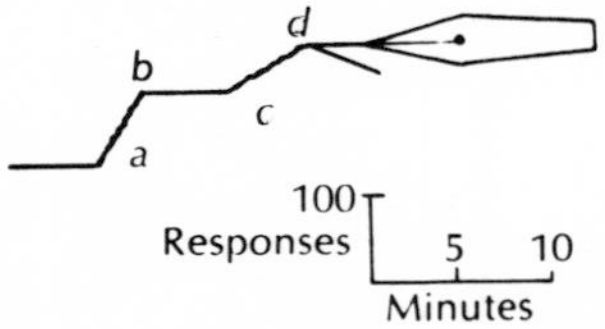

In the diagram of this frame a response received a special consequence at _____.

In practice, the vertical mark made by a single response is too small to be easily identified. However, we can still use the _____ of the curve at any point as a valid indicator of rate of responding.

In the diagram the rate was highest between _____ and _____, zero between _____ and _____, and of an intermediate value between _____ and _____.

Figure 14. Continued.

97

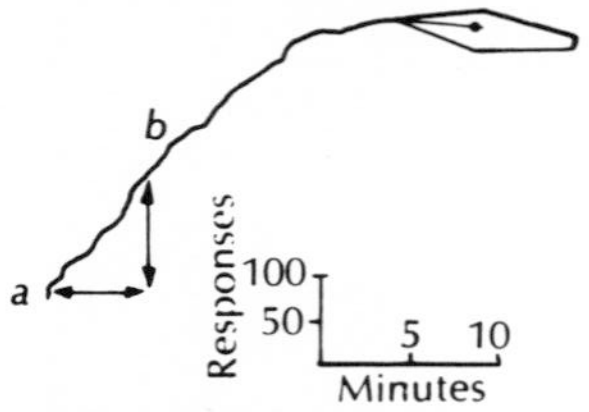

When the steps are so small that we cannot count responses, we can still determine the number of responses between two points on the record by using a scale. In the diagram of this frame the vertical portion of the scale at the right tells us that approximately ———— responses were made between a and b in the cumulative record at the left.

If the paper moves very slowly, we may not be able to measure accurately the time between two responses, but we can still determine the time elapsing between two chosen points. In the diagram of this frame the horizontal portion of the scale at the right tells us that responses at a and b in the cumulative record at the left occurred approximately ———— minutes apart.

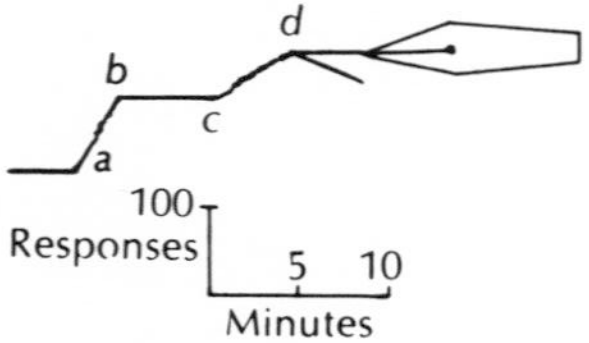

In the diagram to the left after completing about 100 responses, between a and b, the animal paused for a short period, ———— to ————, and then emitted about ———— responses between c and d.

Sometimes a cumulative curve is used to record the progress of a moving automobile, and then the slope indicates the speed of motion. When a cumulative curve is used to record animal behavior the slope indicates ————.

"Rate of responding" means number of responses per unit time. In a cumulative record, number of responses can be determined from the distance traversed by the pen in a ———— direction.

In a cumulative record, time is indicated by the distance traversed by the pen in a ———— direction.

Figure 14 Continued

Go to page 100.

No, you are wrong.

Intelligence has been assumed by many to be genetically determined, that is, transmitted at birth through the genes of the parents to the child. But the staunch opposition maintains that intelligence is a learned rather than inborn set of behaviors. People have had a way of lining up on the opposite poles of the nature-nurture, hereditary-environment, inherited-learned controversy, and the arguments will continue if the past is any indication of the future.

The fact that the controversy has raged for years ought to indicate its pseudoscientific basis. That is, the evidence for one position over another is not clear enough for the issue to be resolved. One recourse, and the one taken here, is to encourage biologists to more research in genetics but to leave that issue to them and concentrate on the kind of noninferential data that affords the greatest potential for changing behavior from less intelligent to more intelligent. Inheritance is not one of those variables amenable to scientific investigation.

Go back now to page 88, reread the page, and make the alternative response.

A Test

In the introduction to this chapter it was stated that the purpose was to confront you with a set of terminology from the field of operant conditioning which will be used in ensuing chapters. The following test is included to help you determine your level of achievement. The criterion for evaluating yourself is nineteen correct responses out of the twenty-one questions. If you score below nineteen, it is suggested you go back over the material missed. Inability to answer these questions correctly would make it quite difficult to understand the chapters to follow.

1. The scientist finds it difficult to function when what he is investigating cannot be measured.   T   F
2. In the behavioral sciences an operant is unmeasurable.   T   F
3. Operants are so termed because they "operate" on the environment.   T   F
4. An instinct is a reasonable cause of behavior for the behavioral scientist.   T   F
5. Thoughts obviously do not exist because the scientist cannot measure phenomena "in the head."   T   F
6. To describe a child as needing love gives the teacher insight into how to work with him.   T   F
7. In behavioral terms reinforcement increases the probability that the behavior just prior to the reinforcer will occur.   T   F
8. Positive reinforcement differs from negative reinforcement in that the former is a good state of affairs, the latter a bad state of affairs.   T   F
9. Negative reinforcement is reinforcing because it builds in behavior that turns off an aversive condition.   T   F
10. Extinction by nonreinforcement is a viable method of stopping unwanted behavior within the classroom setting.   T   F
11. The Williams study on extinction of a child's tantrums indicates greater resistance to change during the second extinction.   T   F

12. "Enthusiastic" behavior might be described as behavior which has been _____ in the past.

13, 14, 15. A consequence to behavior may be _____, _____, or _____.

16. A reinforcer can only be determined by whether or not it

   _____.
   (phrase)

17, 18, 19. One of the main problems in using punishment is that when the teacher is seen as the source of _____, effectiveness as a behavioral _____ may be _____ in the future.

20. A cumulative recorder measures _____ of _____.

21. In a learning task it is better that feedback (a potential reinforcer) follow behavior:

   (a) Immediately after.
   (b) Within five minutes.
   (c) Any time, as long as it follows.

Turn to page 102 for answers to test.

Answers to the Test

1. True.
2. False.
3. True.
4. False.
5. False.
6. False.
7. True.
8. False.
9. True.
10. False.
11. True.
12. Reinforced.
13, 14, 15. Positive, negative, or neutral.
16. Increases the probability of a response.
17, 18, 19. Punishment, modifier or shaper, lost or diminished.
20. Rate of response.
21. (a) Immediately after.

Go to the next chapter if you have reached the criterion nineteen out of twenty-one. If you have not met the criterion, go quickly over this chapter again.

9 / The Strengthening of Selected Behaviors

This chapter is designed to consider in detail one method of using positive reinforcement to deal with two common classroom problems. The chapter is built around actual situations involving a child in the first grade and one in a nursery.

The first study is about a six-year-old boy who had difficulty in reading.

Note on Reading Acquisition: An Extension of Laboratory Principles
CAROLYN WHITLOCK[1]

Staats, Minke, Finley, Wolf, and Brooks (1964) have shown that reading behavior can be effectively conditioned in a laboratory setting. The present paper reports an extension of these principles.

The subject (S) was a six-year-old male in the first grade at the Webster College Experimental School, Webster Groves, Missouri. The S was recommended for this study by his teacher because, in her opinion, he was "below normal" in reading performance. No reading tests had been administered to the child, but he had an I.Q. of 100 on the Stanford-Binet test. For five weeks he was given special group training in daily sessions with a special reading teacher, but had not responded and still did not read according to the average reading-grade level of his class.

PROCEDURE

In the first session the S was introduced to the experimenter (E) by his teacher. Beginning as a 15-minute period and gradually working up to 60 minutes by the sixth session, each session was terminated before the S expressed desire to leave.

[1] Carolyn Whitlock, "Note on Reading Acquisition: An Extension of Laboratory Principles," *Journal of Experimental Child Development* 3 (1966): 83–85. The study was conducted under the direction of Don Bushell, Jr.

Investigations were made during the first three sessions, through various word-oriented games, to determine the S's repertoire of reading responses. Once the baseline was established, a reinforcement system of tokens was introduced (third session) and a continuous reinforcement schedule established.

Two new concepts have been added to those of Chapter 8: *baseline* and *continuous reinforcement schedule* (CRF). A baseline is the kind of behavior—in this case, reading behavior—exhibited before training. It is a measure of the beginning level, sometimes called a pretest, and it is an important measure because without it one is never certain where to begin or how much change has occurred during training.

A continuous reinforcement schedule (CRF) involves for *every* correct response a reinforcing consequence—in this case, a small plastic token given the child immediately after each word was read correctly. Because of the nature of a reinforcer, the E did not know in advance if the token would serve to increase the probability of correct responses, but, as will become evident, it was an effective reinforcer.

The reading stimuli were presented to the child in a discrimination procedure via flash cards, each card containing one word. The cards were placed in front of the child in groups of two or three, pairing one unknown word with one known. The S was asked to select the word requested by E and bring it to her until all words were identified. When an unknown word was asked for, S made use of phonetic approaches to identify the word (primarily the initial sound of the word). When S responded correctly, he was immediately given a small colored plastic token. After collecting several jars of tokens, S's interest began to diminish . . .

Obviously most reinforcers will lose their effectiveness in time, particularly when the S is responding well and is on a CRF. As much as a certain kind of food can be very reinforcing to you, the reinforcing quality can change to nausea or punishment if that food is the only commodity available.

. . . so back-up reinforcers of tickets were introduced beginning with the seventh session. The ratio of tokens to these back-up reinforcers was dictated by the capacity and number of jars in which the tokens were deposited. Each jar contained 36 tokens. The tickets read as follows:

1. A story book will be read to you—1 jar of tokens.
2. Play a game of your choice—2 jars of tokens.
3. Listen to a record—3 jars of tokens.
4. Paint a picture with water colors—4 jars of tokens.
5. Watch a cartoon movie—7 jars of tokens.
6. Take a walk—10 jars of tokens.
7. Play outside for an hour—10 jars of tokens.

Note that several important changes have occurred. The child discovers that the tokens are negotiable; that is, like money they can be used to obtain certain privileges. It is necessary, however, that S's reading behavior continue to achieve the back-up reinforcers. What is happening is the development of an exchange system. In exchange for certain specified behavior the E wants, the S is afforded a set of reinforcing experiences he wants. Here learning literally pays off.

The notion of exchange is an important concept in operant conditioning, particularly as one views this technique in contrast to what often happens in classrooms. Teachers frequently, especially in the junior and senior high grades and in college, afford little positive reinforcing consequences for learning. Characteristically, the reinforcement used by the teacher is negative reinforcement. Far too many students perform academic tasks because their behavior removes them from the aversive consequences of the threat of poor grades. As one would expect, when these aversive consequences are removed, as when the teacher leaves the room, the student rarely continues with academic endeavor.

Beginning in the eighth session, reading stimuli were presented via story books (preprimer to reader level). Each story was preceded by presenting any unfamiliar words on flash cards. During the story reading, reinforcement was given on an intermittent schedule moving from 1 token per 2 words to 1 per 4 words to 1 per page (averaging 10 to 25 words), to 1 per story (averaging 50 to 70 words). After reaching the 1-token-per-story ratio on the twelfth session, S requested discontinuance of flash cards and permission to begin reading in the story book. Tokens were then issued only upon request of the S in about a four-to-one story-token ratio.

The new concept introduced in this section is *intermittent reinforcement* (IRF). In the early stages of deliberate training a CRF is usually preferable for efficiency. But as time goes on after the reinforcer is firmly established, a new kind of efficiency is preferable that necessitates a greater amount of performance for fewer reinforcers. A rigged "one armed bandit," or slot machine, illustrates how an IRF can maintain behavior. If, as the naive gambler begins to drop in his quarters, the slot machine pays off on a near-CRF, in short order the player can become "hooked" because of the reinforcing qualities of winning. The schedule can then shift toward an IRF, paying off less frequently but eliciting the same hope for the gambler so as to maintain a steady input even though there is a lessening output.

The kind of intermittent reinforcement employed in this study is ratio; the reinforcer is contingent upon a predetermined number of correct responses (1 token per 2 words in the early part of learning changed to 1 per 4, to 1 per page, to 1 per story). The greater the production for a reinforcer, the greater the ratio, that is, ½, ¼, 1/10-25, 1/50-70, and so on. Note that the shift from a CRF to a rather high ratio schedule was accomplished by degrees. When a jump from CRF to an IRF is abrupt, one may lose the S, in which case it is important to reverse the process and adopt a smaller ratio, closer to the previously successful schedule. Notice, also, that in the study the E has begun the process of *phasing out* the use of the external token and specified back-up reinforcers.

RESULTS

Prior to the thirteenth session S returned to the classroom, found a book like the one used during the experimental sessions, and finished reading it. In the fifteenth session, S brought a story book from home and asked E if he could read it to her. From this time on the tokens and back-up reinforcers were eliminated.

During the fifth and last week of the study E took S to the public library where he chose three books. The remainder of the sessions, at S's request, were spent in reading these books. At the final session S asked to return to the library to get more books to read.

In about four weeks a child's reading performance changed from "below normal" to a level which enabled him to be placed into the regular reading program of his class. After the twenty-third session, the study was terminated. Three months after completion of the study his teacher reported that the S read with ease and accuracy both alone and in a group and has been placed in the normal reading group within his class. The S's mother recounted a distinct change in his attitude toward reading and in his actual reading behavior since the beginning of the study. Prior to this study she characterized him as "having a fear of words; therefore being uninterested to the point of refusing to try to read."

An interesting event has occurred. In the beginning of remedial training the E employed plastic tokens as reinforcers. They worked effectively for a time even though there was no logical connection between correct reading responses and receiving the token. When the token by itself began to lose its strength, it suddenly took on new meaning by becoming negotiable for other reinforcers, most of which were still unrelated to reading—playing a game, listening to a record, painting a picture, watching a cartoon, taking a walk, playing outside—but the combination of which was powerful enough to maintain reading. Then a curious thing happened. The tokens and back-up reinforcers after being switched to an intermittent ratio schedule were eliminated; yet *reading behavior continued*. Obviously other reinforcers had begun to take over. The child was doing better in class, his parents were pleased and undoubtedly expressed their pleasure at his progress, and perhaps the sheer joy of reading began to take on reinforcing qualities, to "work" for the child. The child moved from dependence on the experimenter-teacher in the beginning to independent reading on his own at termination. Within the teaching-learning context such a change is always desirable since it would have defeated the purpose had the child only developed greater dependence on the teacher and her reinforcers. In effect the teacher helped the child open a whole range of new reinforcers external to the laboratory situation.

CONCLUSIONS

While the present results of this study are found to be consistent with those outlined by Staats et al., and provide additional supporting evidence for the effectiveness of positive reinforcement upon the reading behavior of a child in a one-to-one, tutorial setting, two questions may be raised regarding the findings: (a) How can this particular procedure be modified to work with a group—preferably in a regular classroom situation? (b) Were the tokens the most important reinforcement, or did the social reinforcement of E's verbal response to S account for the shaping of his reading behavior?

This preliminary study suggests that the step-by-step scheduling of a positive reinforcement accounts for the reading behavior being developed, accelerated, and maintained; and also extends a most promising approach to the long-standing problems of reading acquisition.

REFERENCES

Staats, A. W., Minke, K. A., Finley, J. R., Wolf, M. M., and Brooks, L. O. 1964. A reinforcer system and experimental procedure for the laboratory study of reading acquisition. *Child Development* 35:209–31.

Another Example of the Use of Positive Reinforcers

Reproduced below is another study involving the use of the positive reinforcement of the teacher's attention to change the behavior of a nursery school child. The technique of Harris et al. is very similar to that of the Whitlock study except that here an ABA design determines if the teacher's attention were the principal reinforcer. An ABA design means that after baseline behavior is determined (condition A), the experimental variable is introduced (condition B), withdrawn (condition A), and reintroduced.[2] In each stage, data on the behavior in question is gathered for comparison with each other stage to determine the effect of the variable. The Harris study examines the problem raised by Whitlock: what was it that shaped the six-year-old's reading?

Effects of Positive Social Reinforcement on Regressed Crawling of a Nursery School Child
FLORENCE R. HARRIS, MARGARET K. JOHNSTON,
C. SUSAN KELLEY, AND MONTROSE M. WOLF[3]

INTRODUCTION

This paper reports a use of positive social reinforcement procedures to help a nursery school child to substitute well-developed walking behavior for recently reacquired crawling behavior. Principles of reinforcement have long been established through experimental research with infra-human subjects. Recently, many of these principles

[2] Literally, the design pattern in the Harris study is ABAB but such a procedure is usually called ABA to designate manipulation of conditions for purposes of isolating variables. Perhaps a more accurate designation would be ABA'B' since the second A and B are different from the first in that they are removed in time and, having already appeared, are not novel.

[3] Florence R. Harris, Margaret K. Johnston, C. Susan Kelley, and Montrose M. Wolf, "Effects of Positive Social Reinforcement on Regressed Crawling of a Nursery School Child," *Journal of Educational Psychology* 55 (1964): 35–41. The authors gratefully acknowledge indebtedness to Sidney W. Bijou, Donald M. Baer, and Jay S. Birnbrauer, without whose counsel and encouragement this study would not have been possible. Robert G. Wahler also contributed generously to development of observation techniques. This investigation was supported in part by Public Health Service Research Grants MH-02232 and MH-02208, from the National Institute of Mental Health.

have also been demonstrated with human beings and have been successfully applied to practical problems. Examples of the latter include Ferster's study of autistic children (Ferster and Demyer, 1961), Brady's treatment of functional blindness (Brady and Lind, 1961), and Ayllon's work with psychotic patients (Ayllon and Haughton, 1962). Ferster and Brady applied the principles in a controlled laboratory situation. Ayllon, however, made applications in a "natural" situation, comparable to the setting in the present study.

Application of reinforcement principles to nursery school children may be an important step in the process of learning more about child behavior and its relation to guidance practices. Such knowledge relates directly not only to teacher guidance at school but also to parent guidance of children in the home.

The main concern of the study was to see (1) whether presentation of positive social reinforcement by teachers could be used to help a three-year-old use more frequently her already well-established walking behavior; (2) if this occurred, whether withdrawing such reinforcement weakened the behavior; and (3) whether reinstating social reinforcement practices reestablished walking behavior. The reason for the second and third objectives was, of course, to attempt to demonstrate that the positive reinforcement stimuli used were in fact the determining conditions in such behavior change. Conclusive data were essential to effective guidance of the child at school, as well as to subsequent counseling with the child's parents.

SUBJECT

The subject was a girl three years and five months old who had just enrolled in a university nursery school. She will hereafter be referred to as Dee. Dee was the oldest child in her family, having two younger brothers, one eighteen months old and one eight months old. The parents were a pleasant and likable young couple. Both held college degrees, the father also having an advanced degree. He was well launched upon a professional career. The mother seemed a warm and responsive person whose primary interest was her family.

Dee was one of twelve children in the nursery school group of six boys and six girls. Ages ranged from three years to three years and six months. Two teachers supervised the group, which attended school mornings for two and a half hours five days a week.

On the first day of school Dee showed unusually strong withdrawal behavior. That is, she crouched on the floor most of the time, turning her head away or hiding her face in her arms whenever an adult or a child approached. She did not attempt to remain close to her mother, who sat in one corner of the room or of the play yard. Dee spoke to no one, and crawled from indoors to outdoors and from place to place as school activities shifted.

Dee continued to show little reaction to her mother's presence during subsequent days at school. On the seventh day of school her mother was leaving a few minutes after bringing her and coming back to get her two hours later (the same as most of the other mothers), with Dee seemingly indifferent to her presence or absence.

Typically, Dee removed and put on her wraps while sitting on the floor in the locker area, and then either left them on the floor or crawled to her locker and stuffed them in. Sometimes she pulled herself to her feet with her hands on the locker edges and hung her wraps on the appropriate hooks. Then, dropping to hands and knees, she crawled to an out-of-the-way spot and sat or crouched. She crawled into the bathroom beside other children before snack time and occasionally pulled herself to a standing position beside a sink to rinse her hands. She did not use a toilet at school but remained dry. From the sink she usually crawled to a group gathered for snacks and sat near a teacher and some children. She usually accepted and ate a snack, but remained impassive, somber, silent. The rest of the group talked, laughed, and in general responded freely to both the teachers and to other children. The usual teacher approaches to Dee (friendly, warm, solicitous) resulted in strong withdrawal behavior as described.

Her mother reported that the same behavior was strongly evident when visitors came to her home or when Dee was taken on visits. Otherwise Dee was described as "gentle, sweet, and cooperative." The mother was, of course, greatly concerned over her child's withdrawal behavior. It was this concern which had, at least in part, prompted her to enroll Dee in a nursery school.

By the end of the second week of school Dee was avoiding all contacts with children or adults and avoiding use of most material and equipment. A half-hour record written at this time showed Dee in a standing position for only 6.7% of the time, once at her locker and once at a bathroom sink. For 93.3% of the observation period she sat, or crouched on hands and knees. She had spoken only a few words during these weeks. She had spoken only to teachers. The words had consisted of a soft "no" or "yes" at snack time. In staff discussion, teachers gave a conservative estimate that at least 75% of her time at school, exclusive of group times when everyone was normally seated, Dee was in off-feet positions. Since this behavior prevented her participation in the broad range of available learning activities, and since the behavior was such as to be readily observable by students and by staff, the staff decided to help the child by applying reinforcement principles.

INITIAL REINFORCEMENT PROCEDURES

It was decided that the teachers should attempt to weaken Dee's off-feet behavior by withholding attention when Dee was off her feet. An exception to this might occur at group times, when attention was to be a minimum consonant with courtesy. The withdrawal-of-attention procedure was to be casually implemented by a teacher's simply becoming fully occupied with any one of the many immediate requirements always confronting nursery school teachers. In other words, teacher-attention was to show no obvious relationship to Dee's off-feet behavior. Teachers were also to avoid displaying any behavior that might suggest anger, disappointment, disgust, shame, or dislike. There was to be nothing punitive about their behavior.

Concurrent with the above procedure, on-feet behavior was immediately to be positively reinforced. That is, Dee was to be given attention whenever she displayed standing behavior. Since she stood up so infrequently and so briefly, the behaviors closely approximating standing were also to be reinforced during initial days. That is, when she rose even partially to her feet, as well as when she stood, a teacher was to give her attention. Such attention was to consist of going immediately to her and making appropriate interested comments about what she was doing. Sample comments might be, "You hung that up all by yourself. You know just where it goes," and "It's fun to let water slide over your fingers. It feels nice and warm, doesn't it?" A teacher's attention behavior was to convey to Dee that she was liked, appreciated, and considered capable.

In order for a reinforcer to be most effective, it must immediately follow the behavior to be changed. Therefore, to insure that Dee received immediate positive reinforcement for standing positions, one teacher was assigned to remain within range of her at all times, carrying major responsibility for this aspect of the guidance program. The other teacher was to carry major responsibility for the program of the rest of the children in the group. The teacher assigned the role of giving positive reinforcement every time Dee got on her feet was selected because she seemed to have a good relationship with the child. For example, Dee usually crawled to her group at snack time.

RECORDING BEHAVIOR CHANGES

No special plans beyond teacher observations were made, at first, for recording behavior changes and the incidence of reinforcement. A staff member recorded the previously-mentioned half-hour observation. Teachers, of course, observed Dee's behavior from the first day and recorded the kinds of incident notes that they took on behavior of each child in the group. Teachers' subjective estimates based on their daily observations were also used. In addition, subjective estimates by students in an observation course were considered. These students first observed Dee's group during the second week of school. All noted her behavior at once, although no reference had been made to it in class, and discussed it at the next class meeting.

Two weeks after reinforcement procedures were begun, several students volunteered to procure more adequate recordings of Dee's behavior for purposes of making a more systematic study and to satisfy their own interest. Most of the data presented in curves 2 and 3 in figure 15 were secured by these students, each recording for an hour. Their efforts could provide only about four hours of data. The remainder (about two and a half hours) were recorded by a staff member.

RESULTS OF INITIAL PROCEDURES

The intensive recording of Dee's behavior by students and staff was stimulated by dramatic results of application of the planned procedures. Within one week from the start of reinforcing on-feet positions and ignoring off-feet behavior, Dee was on her feet a large proportion of time. Percentages of time on-feet and time off-feet seemed to have reversed. By the end of two weeks (one month after she entered school) Dee's behavior was indistinguishable from that of the rest of the children. She talked readily, often with smiling animation, to the teacher administering the planned schedule of social reinforcement. She used all of the outdoor equipment with vigor and enthusiasm. She worked with obvious enjoyment at the easels, with housekeeping-play facilities, and with such materials as clay.

However, Dee was not making direct responses to children, although she engaged in much parallel activity; nor did she initiate contacts with children or with the other teacher, ignoring them for the most part. But she accepted without position changes any approach or suggestion made by the other teacher or a staff member, and on the whole made use of available learning experiences as effectively as most of the other children in the group. She could no longer be considered severely withdrawn at school. Her mother also reported a remarkable improvement in her social behavior at home.

REVERSING REINFORCEMENT PROCEDURES

In order to be sure that the reinforcement procedures applied had been the significant causative factor in Dee's change in behavior, the teaching staff were obliged to pursue their study through two more processes: (1) reinstate off-feet behavior, and then (2) once again establish appropriate on-feet behaviors. In addition to personal reluctance to institute these processes, the staff at this point seriously questioned their ability to succeed in getting Dee again into off-feet behavior. She appeared to be getting strong reinforcement from her vigorous and exploratory activities, from exchange of speech with adults, and from parallel activities with children. It seemed unlikely that manipulation of adult social reinforcers could now have an effect strong enough to compete with these newly-experienced reinforcements. Partly because of this doubt, and partly because of the necessity to be certain that adult social reinforcement had been the critical independent variable, the staff agreed to attempt to reinstate Dee's off-feet behavior.

The teachers' procedure in extinguishing on-feet behavior was to reverse their previous reinforcement contingencies; that is (1) give no attention when Dee was on-feet, and (2) give continuous attention when she was off-feet. The staff agreed that any evidence of detrimental effects, such as loss of speech, crying or other emotional behavior, would be sufficient cause for terminating the plan.

At this phase of the study students assisted in getting more detailed and extensive records.

RESULTS OF REVERSE PROCEDURES

During the first morning of giving Dee attention (reinforcement) during off-feet but not during on-feet behavior, a two-hour record was kept. Each 30-second period of these two hours was then arbitrarily considered as a discrete unit of behavior. Units of time off-feet were then plotted in a cumulative graph, the horizontal axis showing time and the vertical axis showing number of off-feet units. (See figure 15, curve 1.) Rises on the graph indicate periods of time off-feet, while plateaus indicate periods on-feet. Exclusive of a group time of 12 minutes, during which children were expected to be seated together, Dee spent 75.7% of the morning off her feet. On the following day, which was similarly recorded and graphed, she spent 81.9% of the morning off her feet. (See figure 15, curve 2.) There were no signs on either day of detrimental effects on Dee other than those associated with behaving from a crawling position.

With nearly 82% of her time spent off her feet, clearly Dee had returned to her old behavior pattern. The staff therefore decided at that point to reinstate on-feet behavior.

SECOND REVERSAL OF PROCEDURES

Reinforcement procedures were again reversed, that is, teachers gave steady attention whenever Dee got to her feet and gave no attention when she was off her feet. Figure 15, curve 3, graphs her off-feet behavior for the first hour of the third subsequent day. During the observation, Dee spent 75.9% of the time off her feet and only 24.1% on-feet. Teachers reported, however, that during the last half of the morning, for which a written record was not secured, Dee spent most of the time in vigorous activity on her feet. Figure 15, curve 4, graphs the first hour of the following day. Dee spent 37.8% of the hour off-feet and 62.2% on-feet. Again, the second hour she was reported to have spent on her feet almost steadily. From this day on, Dee's behavior was in every way adequate and she seemed happily occupied.

DISCUSSION

The data strongly indicate that adult attention changed Dee's behavior in the desired direction (was the significant independent variable), and that for Dee adults were very powerful reinforcers. It also seems that social reinforcement principles, carefully delineated and applied, can provide effective and efficient guidance tools for teachers and parents of young children.

Although the graphs show only the time Dee spent in the positional behaviors being specifically controlled, other interesting behavioral changes occurred during the study. These changes seemed to be largely salutory and to develop with unusual rapidity. Some changes seemed causally linked to the fact that reinforcement contingencies were reversed twice, a possibility that merits further study.

Much of the normal behavior, in addition to positional changes, resulted from the initial process of reinforcing only on-feet behaviors. This normal behavior included (1) ready verbalization with one adult (the assistant teacher), (2) adequate verbalization in response to questions from other adults but little if any initiation of

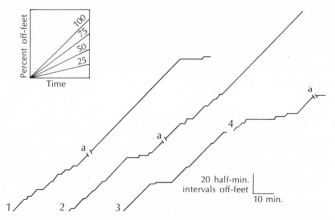

Figure 15. Subject's off-feet behavior on four different mornings: the first (curve 1) and second (curve 2) mornings of giving attention during off-feet and ignoring on-feet behavior, and the third (curve 3) and fourth (curve 4) mornings of giving attention during on-feet and ignoring off-feet behavior. Breaks at *a* indicate snack times averaging 12 minutes duration, which were not included in the data.

contacts with them, (3) parallel activities with other children but little if any verbalization to them, (4) play using a wide range of materials and equipment. These changes occurred within two weeks of instituting the reinforcement procedures.

When a shift was made from reinforcement of on-feet to reinforcement of off-feet behavior, some loss was observed, but significant gains appeared as well. The major loss appeared to be vigorous motor activities such as jumping and running. This, of course, was a direct result of Dee's off-feet positions. Another change that appeared to involve both loss and gain came in Dee's adult relationships. On the first day on which testing procedures began (reinforcing off-feet behavior and giving no reinforcement while on-feet), Dee tended to move away from the reinforcing teacher and for the first time to accept, even seek, attention from the other teacher. Reinforcement from both the teachers maintained off-feet behavior during much of the morning. During the first part of the morning, Dee made many short trials of standing positions. After 35 minutes of this alternating up and down behavior, Dee remained off her feet until close to the end of the morning. During this time she spoke readily to the second teacher, asking questions, asking for help occasionally, and answering the teacher's comments and questions. She also engaged in play with materials, near other children. Occasionally she exchanged words with the latter, a new aspect of behavior for Dee. Part of her activity consisted of going upright on her knees from one play situation to another. At the doll-corner table where two other children were making cookies with dough and utensils, Dee insisted on staying on her knees beside the table although the teacher pointed out that there was an empty chair beside her and that the other children were seated. Dee's response was, "I *want* to be on the floor doing it."

Near the close of that morning (reinforcement of off-feet positions) Dee went outdoors again. She got to her feet at the door, ran across the yard to where another child played on packing boxes and boards, and joined the other in vigorous running and jumping. This play was at a distance from both teachers, and of course neither teacher approached. The play continued with much laughter, shouts, and some talking. It drew two more children. Dee's mother arrived shortly. She showed great pleasure in finding Dee in joyous active play with other children. She stood near, smiling and commending Dee's and her friends' balancing and jumping stunts. Dee was smiling, eyes sparkling, when she and her mother left. Dee waved from the gate and called "Goodbye!" to both the teachers. Hence, it seems apparent that there were sources of social reinforcement not in coordination with those controlled in the experiment.

Teachers and the observer judged that the first day of reinstating (reinforcing) off-feet positions (1) precipitated much off-feet behavior, (2) had little or no effect on the amount and quality of Dee's verbalizations, (3) had surprisingly slight effect on the amount, diversity, and quality of Dee's use of materials and equipment, (4) may have extended Dee's social experiences to include satisfying contacts with the other teacher, (5) had reduced considerably Dee's approaches to the reinforcing teacher, and (6) may have encouraged her to initiate play with other children, play that seemed positively reinforcing to all the children involved. In other words, the positive effects of reversing reinforcement contingencies seemed to outweigh by far the momentary negative results.

During the second day of reinforcement of off-feet behavior, the first two-thirds of the session was punctuated by tentative bursts of standing. During two of the longer bursts, Dee moved about the yard pushing over the movable upright equipment. Teachers presented no reinforcement. Periods of standing dwindled to steady off-feet behavior. Even the arrival of Dee's mother at the end of the morning did not draw Dee to her feet. Mother walked across to her and somewhat impatiently pulled her to her feet and took her away. Although Dee seemed to lose only those vigorous behaviors for which standing postures were essential, the investigators judged that her behavior for the two days gave sufficient demonstration of the power of adult social reinforcement in changing her behavior. Rather than risk possible loss in the areas of verbal or child-child social behavior, they decided to terminate the study by again reinforcing on-feet behavior. In addition, they decided to reinforce all verbal behavior, regardless of Dee's position. Another influential aspect in terminating the "test" procedure was that it was distasteful to the investigators and therefore made them apprehensive about its effects on Dee. Further, no observer besides the teachers could be available during the following two days of school.

During approximately one hour of the third day of again reinforcing on-feet behavior, plus positive reinforcement of all verbal behavior, a record was taken during the first half of the morning. Teachers reported that during most of the latter half of the morning Dee played vigorously on her feet on climbing equipment with other children, with apparent pleasure and with much reinforcement from adults and children. The behavior of pushing over equipment, which was at no time followed by presentation of either positive or negative reinforcement, had dropped out entirely. On the fourth day of reinstating on-feet behavior, Dee spent better than 60% of the recorded hour on her feet, a proportion of time which made her positional behavior indistinguishable from that of the group. Teachers noted that some of her standing behavior at this time was sufficiently different from the group mode to be classed as "stunting on equipment." She stood up to swing and also to propel the long rocking-board, two activities usually pursued by the threes in a sitting position. The latter part of the morning, Dee played vigorously with children, usually on her feet.

By the end of a week of reinforcing on-feet positions, Dee showed positional behavior that was normal in the group. In addition, she was readily initiating and accepting social contacts with all of the adult staff as well as with several of the children in the group. Within a five-week period of school attendance, Dee's behavior showed a degree of progress that would have been expected within not less than five or six months under previous guidance techniques. Her parents were as pleased as the staff over her progress, as well as over their fresh understandings of their roles in helping her develop appropriate social behaviors.

SUMMARY

Use of social reinforcement as a guidance procedure with young children was studied in a university laboratory nursery school, the subject being a three-year-old girl who exhibited strong withdrawal behavior. Results of the study seemed to indicate that (1) adult attention had strong reinforcement values for this child, (2) reversal of the initial reinforcement procedures had distinct positive effects on the child, apparently through helping her quickly to seek relationships with all adults and many of the children in the school situation, and (3) use of reinforcement principles brought about much more rapid changes in the child's behavior than would have been expected under previous guidance techniques.

It would seem that the systematic application of reinforcement principles to guidance of young children shows considerable promise for facilitating the learning behaviors of children and the teaching tasks of adults, both teachers and parents.

REFERENCES

Ayllon, T., and Haughton, E. Control of the behavior of schizophrenic patients by food. *Journal of Experimental Analysis of Behavior* 5 (1963): 343–52.

Brady, J. P., and Lind, D. L. Experimental analysis of hysterical blindness. *Archives of General Psychiatry* 4 (1961): 331–39.

Ferster, C. B., and Demyer, Marian K. The development of performance in autistic children in an automatically controlled environment. *Journal of Chronic Diseases* 13 (1961): 312–45.

This study hardly needs comment. It presents a straightforward use of one of the more readily accessible commodities for reinforcement, attention. This is not to say that attention is a sure-fire reinforcer, but if present research is any indication, it has been found to work in a variety of different settings. R. M. Baron has made an important addition to knowledge about using verbal praise as a reinforcement.[4] He has suggested that one's social reinforcement history is an important factor in response to praise. For example, if one is accustomed to a certain level of praise and that level is exceeded, there may actually be a reduction in rate of performance. If you have had a teacher who used praise continuously and indiscriminately, you know the phenomenon.

Baron's findings have implications for educational programs with culturally disadvantaged and emotionally disturbed children. If, as some have posited, these children have had a history of a low rate of verbal praise, a sudden change to an educationally rich environment filled with social reinforcers may retard rather than accelerate performance. At least, it may retard performance in the early stages until the children become more accustomed to their new kind of learning environment.

The Harris study does help demonstrate that attention to the undesired behavior is just as powerful as attention to the desired behavior, or conversely that lack of attention to desired behavior is just as effective as lack of attention to undesired behavior. What frequently happens in the classroom, unfortun-

---

[4] R. M. Baron, "Social Reinforcement Effects as a Function of Social Reinforcement History," *Psychological Review* 73 (November 1966): 527–39.

ately, is that misbehavior usually gets much more attention than behavior that the teacher wants. The result of such an inappropriate use of reinforcers is that the teacher often becomes a party to development and maintenance of the very behavior that needs to be extinguished.

The next chapter broadens the notion of positive reinforcement by demonstrating a process called *shaping*. Shaping entails starting with behavior that only approximates what is wanted and, by careful use of reinforcement principles, changing that behavior by degrees to approach the desired outcome.

Summary

The major emphasis in this chapter was the use of positive reinforcement as a means of changing behavior. In the Whitlock study it was demonstrated that a child having difficulty in reading could be shaped with negotiable plastic tokens and related back-up reinforcers. The concepts introduced were baseline measures, reinforcement schedules (CRF and IRF), the wearing out of reinforcers, back-up reinforcers, exchange conditions implicit in operant conditioning, and phasing out to reinforcers external to the experimental study.

Using essentially the same kind of methodology, the Harris study relied upon the teacher's attention as a reinforcer and included important additional information about positive reinforcement to follow immediately after the desired behavior is emitted, determination of the exact nature of the reinforcer by an ABA design, and the extent of possible generalization of success in one behavioral mode to others.

10 / Shaping: The Step-by-Step Process

The study of human learning has led to certain lawful relationships that, on occasion, have a delightful commonsense quality about them. One of these is that dramatic learning or behavioral changes can hardly be expected to occur overnight. That is, because behavior is the result of years of prior reinforcement and practice, it is not changed easily. Consequently, the teacher should not expect a child who has never demonstrated desired, or "terminal," behavior to begin suddenly engaging in that behavior as the result of a single demonstration, lecture, or learning activity. But empirical evidence now supports the notion that environmental consequences can be arranged by involving the student in an increasingly complex, step-by-step process so that learning can occur with a high level of effectiveness and efficiency.

Shaping Through Successive Approximations

A theme running throughout prior parts of this text has been that the teacher's role is discovering where students are, defining in measurable ways where they are to be at some future time, and arranging an intermediate environment to increase the probability of achieving the objectives. Reprinted below is a portion of a study by Gerald R. Patterson with a seven-year-old child who was overly dependent upon his parents and who, more specifically, was terrified about leaving them to go to school.

Initially the child's baseline behavior was his fear of school, his refusal to let his mother out of his sight, and his tantrums when she was. The objective, of course, was to get the boy to be able to go to school without fear and o engage comfortably in activities with the other children. The process of moving the child from where he was to where they wanted him to be was accomplished by reinforcing successive approximations to the objective. In order that you may see more clearly the steps in shaping, the more important examples of shaping have been italicized.

A Learning Theory Approach to the Treatment of the School Phobic Child
GERALD R. PATTERSON[1]

. . To determine the kind of reinforcing stimulus appropriate for the patient, he was tested in a laboratory procedure described by Patterson, Littman, and Hinsey (1963). It was found that in the early stage of treatment he was less responsive to social reinforcers dispensed by his therapist than were a hundred other children who had been reinforced by a variety of social agents. This nonresponsiveness to social reinforcers is in keeping with the findings by Levine and Simmons (1962), who showed that emotionally disturbed boys are less responsive to social reinforcers than are normal boys. For this reason, M&M candies were used in the present study as reinforcers in conjunction with social approval. It was assumed that this pairing of M&Ms and social reinforcers would increase the incentive value of social approval, resulting in a wider range of possibilities for behavior control.

In keeping with the suggestions by Jones (1924) and Wolpe (1962), the ES [experimental setting] was presented on a graduate series so that initially only low intensity escape and anxiety reactions were evoked. As the trials progressed, the intensity of the ES was increased. In all situations, the ESs used in the conditioning trials matched as closely as possible situational cues from the child's environment.

Doll play, structured by the experimenter, was the procedure used in the conditioning trials. These sessions occurred four days a week and lasted fifteen minutes; the sessions are described in detail below. Following each conditioning session, both the child and the parents were interviewed. During the early interviews, the procedure was explained in detail to the family. The nature of the specific interfering response being conditioned was discussed with particular emphasis upon the parents' being alert to its occurrence in the home. When these behaviors occurred, they were instructed to reinforce them immediately and then to describe them in the interview on the following day. Particular emphasis was placed upon reinforcing the appropriate behaviors and ignoring behaviors associated with reactions to separation anxiety. It is felt that these highly structured interviews with the parents are of particular importance in insuring generalization of conditioning effects from the laboratory to the home.

THE PATIENT

Karl was seven years old when referred to the University Clinic by the school nurse. In his first few days of attendance in the first grade, he had shown increasing reluctance to stay in school. In the second week of school, he would stay in the classroom only as long as one of his parents remained in the room with him.

[1] Gerald R. Patterson, "An Application of Conditioning Techniques to the Control of a Hyperactive Child," in Case Studies in Behavior Modification, ed. Leonard P. Ullman and Leonard Krasner (New York: Holt, Rinehart and Winston, Inc., 1965), pp. 279–83, copyright © 1965 by Holt, Rinehart and Winston, Inc., reprinted by permission of the publisher. Emphasis added.

Karl had similar difficulties in attending a nursery school during the previous year, even though the school was only a few blocks from his home. For the past few years, he found it necessary to play only in the immediate vicinity of his home. He would frequently interrupt his play to go into the house and "check" to see if his mother was still there. If the mother was going to the store, a short distance away, Karl would insist upon accompanying her. Attempts to use punishment, bribes, or cajoling had failed to keep him in school.

In the clinic, Karl was observed to be an attractive child, rather immature in his behavior and having a severe articulation defect. Testing at the end of treatment revealed a low reading readiness score and an above average intelligence quotient. Extensive intake interviewing with the parents revealed no marked pathology in the parents or in the family; this impression was in agreement with the essentially normal MMPI [Minnesota Multiphasic Personality Inventory] profiles of both parents.

Session 1 / In his first appointment at the clinic, Karl refused to go to the playroom without his mother. Teeth chattering, he clenched one fist, while with the other he maintained a firm hold upon his mother's coat. Karl was seated at a table just inside the door of the playroom while the mother sat across from him in the doorway. The experimenter proceeded to set up a doll-play situation in which a little boy, "Henry," was being taken by the mother to see a doctor. Karl divided his attention between the experimenter and his mother. *The first reinforcing contingency was one M&M for each thirty-second interval during which Karl did not look at his mother.* After five minutes, the mother left the room and sat outside the closed door.

The doll play was restructured so that Henry was inside the doctor's office. *When Karl was asked where Henry's mother was, he replied, "Outside," and received one M&M.* In the procedure that followed, the mother doll left the boy in the doctor's office for increasingly long periods of time; on each occasion Karl was queried as to how the boy felt and what he was going to do. *If he replied that the boy was not afraid or that he would stay in the doctor's office, he received both praise and one M&M.* Similar situations were structured in which the boy remained at home while the mother went shopping or the mother remained at home while the boy walked toward the school building.

In the interview with the mother that followed this session, she was encouraged to praise Karl for staying in the playroom without her. She was further instructed to keep track of Karl's "checking" behavior at home; *if he stayed outside for longer than thirty minutes without coming inside, she was to make an announcement at the dinner table to the whole family.* Karl seemed obviously pleased with his success on this first contact and listened very closely to the interchange between the mother and the experimenter.

Session 2 / The mother seated herself in a chair outside the playroom. *When Karl acquiesced to the experimenter's closing the door, he immediately received two M&Ms and praise from the experimenter.* The doll play was repeated with the boy in the doctor's office and the mother's leaving him there for increasing periods of time. As in the previous session, *if Karl said that the boy was not afraid or that the boy would stay in the situation, he was reinforced by both candy and social approval.* At the end of this sequence of doll play, *Karl was asked if he would, on the next visit, allow his mother to stay in the reception room rather than sitting outside the door of the playroom. He readily agreed to this and was reinforced for his bravery with both praise and several M&Ms.* For any given session, there were generally thirty or forty of these reinforcers dispensed by the experimenter.

The structured play relating to the school was again initiated; on this occasion, Karl specified the reaction of the boy to saying goodbye to the mother, getting upon is bicycle, walking into the school, sitting at the desk, and reading aloud from a book. A third play theme was introduced in this session concerning Karl's anxiety bout physical injury as being the outcome of playing with his peers. *Doll play was nitiated involving "Little Henry's" playing with his peers and receiving minor injuries;* in each case Karl reported the boy was not afraid, did not return to the mother, nd he showed how Little Henry would place a Band-Aid upon his own leg.

In the interview with the father, he reported that Karl had actually stayed outside for an hour and that they had made an announcement at the dinner table. He was old about Karl's decision to allow his parents to remain in the reception room, and e responded with approval. *He was encouraged to continue to reinforce Karl for ndependent behavior in the home and to be particularly careful not to overreact to mall injuries that he might receive while playing.* It was also suggested that they obain some preprimers from the school and reinforce Karl whenever he indicated an nterest in the books or in returning to school.

Sessions 3 through 9 / Karl continued to allow his parents to remain in the reception room while he "worked" in the playroom. On each occasion *he was reinforced for saying that he was not afraid;* he began to boast that the parents would not have to remain in the clinic at all. Karl gave a brief report of his activities at the beginning of each conditioning session and *was reinforced for reports indicating attempts to read, climbing trees without being afraid of injuring himself, playing some distance from home, and not checking on his mother.* The structured play sessions were expanded to include two new areas. Karl expressed some further anxiety about being attacked by members of the peer group. *In the play sessions he was reinforced for counter-aggressing to such attacks and heavily reinforced for attempts to initiate play activity with the peer group.* Karl was also reinforced for making disrciminations between behaviors appropriate for Little Henry and those appropriate for a new and more mature "Big Henry." Both of these areas had been brought up in the interviews with the parents, and *they had been encouraged to reinforce him for playing with children his own age and ignoring any expression of fear of the aggression of other children.* The mother particularly had been instructed to label those aspects of Karl's behavior that were immature and to respond, if possible, only when he acted maturely. As before, the parents were required to bring examples of their attempts to reinforce Karl. Arrangements were also made for a visiting teacher to assist Karl in the development of reading skills.

Session 10 / The material which follows is a brief excerpt from this session and illustrates in detail the procedures used throughout the sessions.

E: What shall we have Henry do today?
K: Well, we could have him go to school.
E: Yeah, I think that is a good idea, to have some work on going to school again today. That probably is the hardest thing for him to do. O.K., here he is (picking up the Henry doll). Where is mamma, oh here she is (sets up blocks and furniture). Ah, maybe we had better have Little Henry start off from home; when he does go to school, we won't have him go into the classroom today; he'll just run errands for the principal; no reading or writing this time. So Little Henry is talking to his mother and he says, "Mom, I think I'll go to school for a little while today." What does mom say?
K: O.K.
E: Is he afraid when he is right there talking to mamma?
K: No. *(One M&M.)*
E: And so he gets on his bike and says bye-bye mamma. He stops halfway to school. What does he think now that mamma is not there?

K: Ma-amma (laughs).

E: Yeah, but what does he do? *Does he go back or go on to school?*

K: Goes to school. *(One M&M.)*

E: Yeah, that's right, he goes to school; Little Henry would go back and look but Big Henry would go on to school . . . and he goes to the principal's office and says, "Hi, Mr. Principal. I thought I would come back to school for a little while. Can I run some errands for you . . . ?" Henry gives the note to the teacher, then he is coming back to the principal's office. He stops. What is he thinking about now?

K: Mamma is not there again.

E: Yeah, he is scaring himself again. *Now, does he go back to the principal's office or does he go home?*

K: He goes back to the office. *(One M&M.)*

E: Yeah, that is right, he does. At least Big Henry would do that; Little Henry would get scareder and more scareder; but Big Henry feels pretty good. "I am back, Mr. Principal." The principal says, "Why don't you go down to the cafeteria and get a glass of milk. I don't have any more errands for you to run right now." So he goes and is sitting there drinking his milk. What does he think about now? Every time he is alone he thinks about this.

K: Mamma again.

E: That's right, he always thinks about mamma. *Does he go home?*

K: No. *(One M&M.)*

E: That's right, he doesn't. Big Henry doesn't go home.

K: (laughs) He sure is big.

—A few moments later.—

E: . . . and he is lying there on the sleeping mat. What is he thinking about?

K: Mamma. No, I don't think so because he got a nice neighbor (child) next to him.

E: So, he is not thinking about mamma.

K: Nope. (E was too surprised to get reinforcement in on time.)

—About five minutes later.—

E: Well, Karl, what have you been doing at home like Big Henry?

K: Well, ah, yesterday I done some numbers (very excited) and I went up to a hundred. *(One M&M.)*

E: You did! Good *(with emphasis).* What else did you do like Big Henry?

K: I made a cake. . . .

E: Were you outside playing yesterday? Of course it was stormy yesterday.

K: Yes, I was outside playing.

E: Did you think about mamma when you were outside?

K: Uh-uh. I wasn't thinking about mamma. *(One M&M.)* I'm not thinking about her now either. *(One M&M.)*

In the past few sessions, several play sequences had been devoted to Little Henry's return to school for an hour or so with his visiting teacher. The possibility of Karl's actually doing this had also been discussed with him.

Sessions 11 through 23 / Karl made his first trip to the school with the special teacher with him at all times. On the following day, he returned and *the teacher left him alone in the room for a few minutes.* On each of the days following this, the teacher left him for longer periods of time. *This sequence at school was accompanied by conditioning sequences in the playroom and a good deal of praise and approval by his family.* After a week of this, he announced at home that he would not be afraid to ride to school and stay by himself for one hour. *He carried this out on the following day amid applause* and acclaim for his singular act of bravery. He then announced that he would return to school full time within the week, which he did.

On the last week of the treatment program, Karl and the writer returned to the procedure for testing his reaction to social reinforcers. On this second trial, the reinforcers were effective in changing his position preference on the marble box game. Social reinforcers had no effect on a second disturbed boy tested at the same time as Karl but not receiving treatment. An important implication of this finding for Karl is that his behavior is now under the control of social reinforcers dispensed by a wide variety of social agents.

On a follow-up of Karl's classroom adjustment three months after termination of treatment, the school reported dramatic improvement in his general adjustment as well as no further evidence of fearfulness. The Department of Special Education is continuing their program of remedial reading and speech.

DISCUSSION

At the cost of twenty bags of M&Ms and ten hours of staff time, Karl returned to school. This, of course, does not constitute a record for the "cure" of school phobia in the amount of time necessary for the return to school (Sperling, 1961), nor is it the first time that learning theories have been applied in treating this type of problem behavior (Lazarus, 1960). The implication is that the present modification of standard clinical practices is at least as effective as traditional procedures.

Since terminating the treatment program with Karl, the same procedures have been followed in conditioning a second child whose presenting symptoms were very similar to Karl's. The second case responded dramatically in less than six hours of staff time. These two cases are not offered as constituting confirmation for the efficacy of this procedure; however, the apparent success of the procedure has encouraged the author to apply a similar procedure to dealing with behavior problems that are ordinarily resistive to traditional clinical manipulations. In this third case, application of simple operant procedures was very successful in extinguishing hyperactive behaviors in the classroom setting (Patterson, 1963). Taken together, the successes strongly suggest that modifications of clinical procedures in accord with principles from learning theories will be a powerful tool in effecting behavior change in the clinical setting.

In retrospect, there is little doubt that one of the crucial variables involved in this procedure is the reinforcement contingencies being used by social agents other than the experimenter. Although it may very well be true that the same effect could be achieved by relying only upon the conditioning-play sessions, there is little doubt on both the theoretical and the practical levels that the parents and the teacher enhanced the generalization from behavior change in the playroom to behavior change in the natural setting. Although the clinician has been concerned traditionally with enhancing generalization from play therapy, the present procedure does not assume that the parents are emotionally disturbed but simply that they have been reinforcing the wrong behaviors. This being the case, it is not necessary for the parents to be involved in intensive psychotherapy, but it is necessary for the parents to be given specific instructions as to what to reinforce and how to reinforce child behaviors. In our extensive practice, with three cases, we have been impressed with the general lack of awareness displayed by these parents as to what it is that they are reinforcing and the effect of this reinforcement upon the behavior of the child. The procedure described here should be appropriate for a variety of child behavior problems and for parents who do not show obvious signs of pathology. This latter statement assumes of course that the reinforcing contingencies adopted by any particular parents are not necessarily determined by the intensity or kind of emotional conflict in the parents. It is hypothesized here that many parents have been conditioned rather than "driven" to adopt their idiosyncratic schedules of reinforcement.

The research by Levine & Simmons (1962), Patterson, Littman, and Hinsey (1963) agree in identifying the child with behavior problems as being unresponsive to social approval; the research by Patterson (1963) suggests that these children might be overly responsive to disapproval. Although satisfactory empirical evidence is lacking at the present time, it seems highly probable that the child with behavior problems is responsive to only a limited aspect of his social environment. In Karl's case, for example, it seemed as if he was responsive only to the approval of his mother (and father perhaps). This restriction in responsiveness to one or two social agents would mean that his behavior was not being conditioned to the normal extent by other agents such as the peer group or adults outside of the family circle. In such a situation, if the parental programing of reinforcers was not in accord with contingencies adopted by the remainder of the culture, it would not be surprising to observe that the child displayed some rather deviant behavior patterns.

If such a child were brought into the clinic, it would be predicted that much of his behavior would not be under the control of the therapist. One of the first functions of the therapist was to change the incentive value of social stimuli; once this was achieved, the therapist could potentially have some effect in changing the behavior of the child. It is of interest to note that Anna Freud strongly urged the pairing of such primary reinforcers as food with the presence of the therapist in order to create a "relationship" with the child (Freud, 1946). It is hypothesized here that whatever such pairing might do for the "relationship" the *effect* is to increase the status of the therapist as a secondary reinforcer as witnessed by Karl's increased responsiveness to social reinforcers at termination of treatment. This would suggest either that nonsocial reinforcers be used in the earlier phases of conditioning with these children or that the therapist make it a point to become associated with a wide range of pleasant stimuli before attempting any behavior manipulation.

SUMMARY

A procedure was described for applying the principles of interference and reinforcement to the treatment of a school phobic child. A series of twenty-three 20-minute conditioning sessions with the child followed by highly structured ten-minute interviews with the parents resulted in dramatic changes in behavior.

REFERENCES

Freud, A. 1946. *The psycho-analytical treatment of children.* New York: International Universities.

Jones, M. C. 1924. The elimination of children's fears. *Journal of Experimental Psychology* 7: 382–90.

Lazarus, A. A. 1960. The elimination of children's phobias by deconditioning. In *Behavior therapy and the neurosis,* ed. H. J. Eysenck. New York: Pergamon, pp. 116–19.

Levine, G. R., and Simmons, J. T. 1962. Response to praise by emotionally disturbed boys. *Psychological Reports* 11:10.

Patterson, G. R. 1963. Parents as dispensers of aversive stimuli. Unpublished manuscript.

Patterson, G. R.; Littman, R.; and Hinsey, C. 1963. Parents as social stimuli. Unpublished manuscript.

Sperling, M. 1961. Analytic first aid in school phobias. *Psychoanalytical Quarterly* 30: 504–18.

Wolpe, J. 1958. *Psychotherapy by reciprocal inhibition.* Stanford, Calif.: Stanford University Press.

Using the Reinforcer in Shaping Successive Approximations

For full understanding of the method of successive approximations more extensive consideration of this concept is necessary. Specifically, the aspects of the timing of the reinforcer, the kind of reinforcer, and the schedules of reinforcement merit special attention.

When the Reinforcer Occurs

A careful rereading of Patterson's work to see when the reinforcer occurred in relation to Karl's growing independence would produce examples such as the following:

When Karl was asked where Henry's mother was, he replied, "Outside," and received one M&M.

When Karl acquiesced to the experimenter's closing the door, he immediately received two M&Ms and praise. . . .

E: Is he afraid when he is right there talking to mamma?
K: No. (One M&M.)

E: Does he go back or go on to school?
K: Goes to school. (One M&M.)

K: Uh-uh. I wasn't thinking about mamma. (One M&M.) I'm not thinking about her now either. (One M&M.)

A crucial fact in shaping is that reinforcement is most effective *immediately after* correct responses. Although the human organism can learn when there is delay between correct response and reinforcing consequence, the more delay that occurs the less efficient is learning, particularly during shaping.

This fact has important implications for the classroom. If a teacher is trying to shape certain responses for a class of thirty students and if that teacher is the only source of reinforcement, the task of shaping is virtually impossible. With limited sources of reinforcement, the fault is not with the principle of immediate reinforcement but with the classroom environment. The teacher simply cannot be an effective reinforcer since immediacy is crucial.

One solution to the problem is to provide a classroom with many sources of reinforcement instead of a few. That is, each of the students, because they progress at different rates, must have the opportunity to produce their own reinforcers or have access to other reinforcing agents without having to rely solely on the teacher when correct responses are emitted.

One reasonably successful attempt to create sources of reinforcement other than the teacher is programmed learning, where the individual student is allowed to "interact" with an environment suited to his abilities and where the student's response to an item of the program, is immediately confirmed as correct or incorrect. The assumption is that for most people confirmation of success can be reinforcing, but that assumption will be examined later in the chapter. For now, let it simply remain as an assumption.

Another method allowing possibilities for immediate reinforcing consequences is the use of learning activities where confirmation is inherent in the task. For example, Skinner has developed a simple device for teaching young children to write that has built-in reinforcers.[2]

One method now being tested is to treat paper chemically so that the pen the child uses writes in dark blue when a response is correct and yellow when it is incorrect. The dark blue line is made automatically reinforcing through generous commendation. Under such contingencies the proper execution of a letter can be programmed; at first the child makes a very small contribution in completing a letter, but through progressive stages he approaches the point at which he composes the letter as a whole, the chemical response of the paper differentially reinforcing good form throughout. The model to be copied is then made progressively less important by separating it in both time and space from the child's work. Eventually words are written to dictation, letter by letter, in spelling dictated words, and in describing pictures. The same kind of differential reinforcement can be used to teach good form, proper spacing, and so on. The child is eventually forming letters skillfully under continuous automatic reinforcement. The method is directed as much toward motivation as toward good form. Even quite young children remain busily at work for long periods of time without coercion or threat, showing few signs of fatigue, nervousness, or other forms of escape.[3]

The point is that, because the timing of reinforcement is so important during the shaping process, learning tasks with their own reinforcers and technological devices such as programmed teaching are much more efficacious than a situation where the teacher is the only source of reinforcement.

The Use of External Reinforcers

In reading the Patterson study one of the reinforcers for shaping Karl was M&Ms, small candy-covered chocolate bits. This may have struck you as extreme. But you will have noted that verbal praise or social approval was not a good reinforcer during the early part of training. Somehow the therapist had to have control over something Karl wanted. M&Ms were tried in conjunction with social approval because "it was assumed that the pairing of

        [2] *Handwriting with Write and See,* produced under the direction of B. F. Skinner with the assistance of Sue Ann Krakower, Lyons and Carnahan, Inc., Chicago, 1968.
        [3] B. F. Skinner, "The Technology of Teaching," *Proceedings of the Royal Society,* 162 (1945): 436, reprinted by permission of B. F. Skinner and the Royal Society.

M&Ms and social reinforcers would increase the incentive value of social approval, resulting in a wider range of possibilities for behavior control." The combination worked, the M&Ms were phased out, and Karl's behavior "is now under the control of social reinforcers dispensed by a wide variety of social agents."

Ideally, reinforcers should become internalized not only because self-reinforcement happens to fit our value system but also, perhaps more important, because the individual student does not have to rely on an external source, which may not be present at the right moment. One long-range goal of education has been to develop the person who is able to go ahead on his own steam solving problems, creating works of art, relating effectively to others, making discoveries, and so on, without having someone around to pat him on the head whenever he produces. The point of view of this text agrees with that objective of independence. The process of internalization, however, seems to be accomplished most effectively by the careful use of manipulative external reinforcers, whether these are a teacher's smile, a comment of "good" from a parent, or more unusual reinforcers such as a plastic negotiable token or an M&M. And, as often happens, these reinforcers can be removed as the desired behavior begins to take on its own reinforcing qualities or opens up, as in the case with Karl, other more natural reinforcing states.

The objection to contrived reinforcers arises from a misunderstanding of the nature of teaching. The teacher expedites learning by arranging special contingencies of reinforcement, which may not resemble the contingencies under which the behavior is eventually useful. Parents teach a baby to talk by reinforcing its first efforts with approval and affection, but these are not natural consequences of speech. The baby learns to say *mama, dada, spoon,* or *cup* months before he ever calls to his father or mother or identifies them to a passing stranger or asks for a spoon or cup or reports their presence to someone who cannot see them. The contrived reinforcement shapes the topography of verbal behavior long before that behavior can produce its normal consequences in a verbal community. In the same way a child reinforced for the proper formation of letters by a chemical reaction is prepared to write long before the natural consequences of effective writing take over. . . . The real issue is whether the teacher prepares the student for the natural reinforcers which are to replace the contrived reinforcers used in teaching. The behavior which is expedited in the teaching process would be useless if it were not to be effective in the world at large in the absence of instructional contingencies.[4]

Schedules of Reinforcement in Shaping

Previously, schedules of reinforcement have been mentioned. It has been pointed out that the two main categories are continuous reinforcement (CRF) and intermittent reinforcement. Assuming that the teacher is the major source

[4] Skinner, "The Technology of Teaching," p. 439.

of reinforcement in learning activities designed for the classroom, teacher-to-pupil reinforcement schedules necessarily tend to be intermittent; usually the teacher can reward only on occasion because, if nothing else, the teacher cannot be present for each student when reinforcing consequences should occur.

It has been found that during the acquisition phase involving new learning, however, a CRF is more effective than intermittent reinforcement. This finding means that as new material is introduced to a class, greater learning efficiency occurs if the sources of immediate reinforcement are continuous. Therefore, introducing the class as a group to a new body of information as is often done through classroom demonstrations, lectures, or films may be an ineffective method because of the different abilities in comprehension. If half the class understands (presumably, a reinforcing state of affairs) and half does not (presumably, a form of punishment particularly when students expect a poor grade) the teacher is in a quandary. Should one go back to catch up those who do not understand and risk boring those who do, or should one go on and hope the others will catch up?

This typical classroom problem was handled cleverly and in a way consistent with learning theory by one teacher who opened up sources of reinforcement by first differentiating those who understood from those who did not by several brief multiple-choice questions administered right after presentation of the new material. Each of the students who understood then chose someone in the class who did not understand, and five minutes were set aside for student to teach student. During that period the teacher was free to go around the room giving individual help to those teams who seemed to be having difficulty. Similar questions were asked after the five minute student-student instructional period, and, as is usually the case, the number of those who did not understand decreased sharply. The teacher then arranged to provide special help to those few who had not caught on. Therein may be an important way to alleviate the common situation of too many students for too few teachers: students can be and have been used to good advantage as teachers. And, equally important, those who served as teachers in all probability know the material better for having taught it.

Moving from CRF to Intermittent Reinforcement

Providing a CRF during the early stages of learning is demonstrably the most efficient means, but obviously a CRF could hardly continue. Nor *should* it continue, for reasons other than the impracticability of providing continuous reinforcing consequences. A person trained on a CRF is highly susceptible to extinction of his newly discovered ability if reinforcement suddenly stops. For example, say that a high-school chemistry student is taught how to convert sea water to drinking water by the usual process of heating salt water, channeling the steam, cooling it, collecting the droplets, and drinking the result. With proper equipment this is a fairly simple way to illustrate distillation. The student learns the process, as demonstrated by his ability to assemble the equipment and produce uncontaminated water on three occasions. It always works. But say that on a fourth occasion it does not work. What was formerly pure and drinkable is now bitter and distasteful. The student tries again, another failure, and again, still bitter. He will probably soon give up distilling water. In contrast, say that a student has his first failure shortly after he has learned how to distill. But this time it was followed by several successful trials, then another failure, several more successes, and so on. The probability of extinction is much less in this differently reinforced situation.

Consider another example. Person A has been given a key to open the front door of his house. When inserted and turned, it always works, until one evening the usual insertion and turn does not open the door. How long will person A continue trying to get the key to work? Person B, on the other hand, is given the same key but discovers early during training that sometimes it takes a certain amount of jiggling to get the door open. How long will person B continue trying to get the key to work?

These two examples are illustrative of the principle that though a CRF is the more expeditious reinforcement schedule to learn a new task, it is also more susceptible to extinction. Teaching with intermittent reinforcement takes longer but is less susceptible to extinction. The moral, if one is interested in having his cake and eating it too, is to begin training with a CRF and switch to intermittent reinforcement once learning has occurred. The behavior of one so trained is often called "well motivated"; he is able to work at an activity with persistence and can put out a large amount of work with only occasional reinforcement. But to be well motivated is not always a desirable state of affairs; a student may be well motivated to malinger because a reinforcement schedule inadvertently trained him to shirk his responsibilities.

The Shaping Process in Conceptual Learning

In the Patterson study the problem was to shape by successive approximations the child's overt behavior from dependence to independence. You may have difficulty translating this kind of change to another, equally important kind of change: conceptual in-the-head learning. Because conceptual changes are impossible for even a well-trained neurophysiologist to measure, the next level of evidence, performance as a result of presumed internal changes, becomes the primary source of data. More plainly, student A does not know how to solve a differential equation problem.

Beginning with what the student knows as determined by baseline performance, the teacher's job is to add selected "bits" of information until, *voilà!*, he can solve the equation. The process, then, begins with establishing what a student can do and confronting (shaping) him with an ordered series of steps each of which increasingly demands behavior approximating the terminal state. A further extension to determine whether the student has reached the desired conceptual level is to see if he can solve correctly nine out of ten problems. This, of course, is the basis of programmed learning, a technique already considered in previous sections. The principle of conceptual shaping is the same as for producing the kinds of changes Patterson described with the seven-year-old boy.

Another technique in shaping is called *fading*. In previous examples of shaping, the technique began with the simple and moved to the complex. With fading, one begins with a model of the final production and as the subject reproduces it, the model slowly fades until it can be duplicated or recognized without the model. Figures 16–21 illustrate a five-minute exercise with a child who had just passed his fifth birthday. The purpose was to teach the child how to write his name. The boy was asked first to write his name on a blank sheet of paper without a model (figure 16), where it can be seen he had some knowledge of letters. The second page has a complete model (figure 17). Instructions were to copy it twice. The model began to fade (figures 18–20) until on the fifth page it was barely recognizable. The sixth page (figure 21) has the first writing without a model. Comparison of figure 16 with figure 21 demonstrates rather clearly the effectiveness of the fading process. Further practice would refine the product.

Fading can be adapted to a variety of learning tasks. Brethower and James G. Holland have used it in neuroanatomy with Harvard students for training in identification of areas of the brain[5]; Murray Sidman has taught difficult discrimination tasks to a microcephalic idiot[6]; it has been used in memorization of poetry, musical passages, symbol recognition, learning a foreign language, and so on. The technique is apparently limited only by the creativeness of the teacher.

Is a Correct Answer Reinforcing?

The assumption underlying teaching programs is that, generally, the success of a correct answer or a series of correct answers is reinforcing. The careful reader, however, may want to question that assumption in view of the definition of a reinforcer, a condition that increases the probability of the behavior just prior to the reinforcing event. The meaning of reinforcement implies

---

[5] James G. Holland, "Teaching Machines: An Application of Principles from the Laboratory," *Journal of the Experimental Analysis of Behavior* 3 (1960): 275–87.

[6] Murray Sidman, "Retarded Children as 'Early Learners,'" paper delivered at 1968 American Educational Research Association Meetings in Chicago.

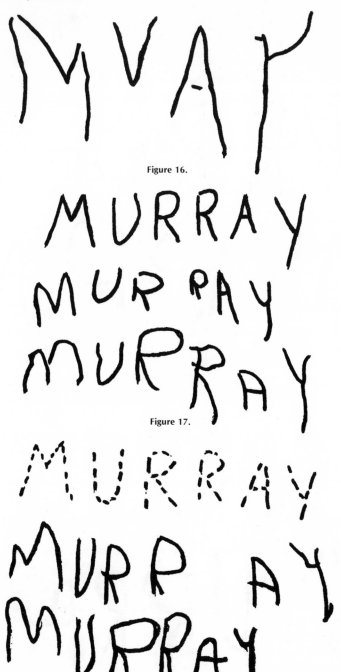

Figure 16.

Figure 17.

Figure 18.

Figure 19.

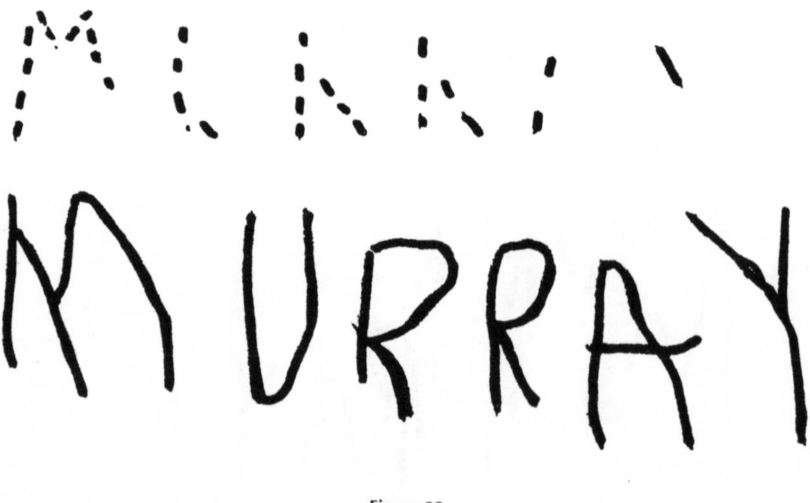

Figure 20.

Figure 21.

that whether or not correct responses are reinforcing can be determined only by observing if the probability of the desired behavior increases or decreases; and that is correct. Turning a student loose with a shaping program is no assurance that he will either learn or, if he does, that the experience will be positively reinforcing. It would seem unnecessary to make such an obvious statement except that too many teachers have been guilty of assuming that any teaching program, just because it is a program, will work.

The shaping process designed to bring about changes in conceptual performance or behavioral skills has to be a process of reciprocity between the learner and the instructional device, whether machine or teacher. For example, say that a shaping process was planned to take a student from A to G, each step of which was progressively more difficult. With most published programs, empirical evidence from preliminary results indicates that the steps are both logical and *psycho*logical. That is, they have face validity (it appears as though the order will assure satisfactory movement from A to G) as well as pragmatic validity (most students during the development stage progressed through it without appreciable error). But to assume that all students will behave the same way is unwarranted. One solution is to design the program in such a fashion that it is more contingent upon the student's response so as to allow a wider range of reinforcement possibilities. This is a form of programming known as *branching,* which gives alternative paths depending upon performance on a prior step. Figure 22 is a flow chart of a branching program. Branching programs can become complex, in which case the program is best carried out with electronic equipment such as a computer. For the person interested in constructing a program, however, a less complicated form similar to that used in Chapter 8 can be developed without much difficulty.

Since a reinforcer is defined by its results, correct answers are reinforcing only to the extent that the student stays with the task. The more one allows for a variety of potential reinforcers, as with branching programs where the program becomes in part contingent upon the student's response, the greater probability there is for successful responses to work as reinforcers.

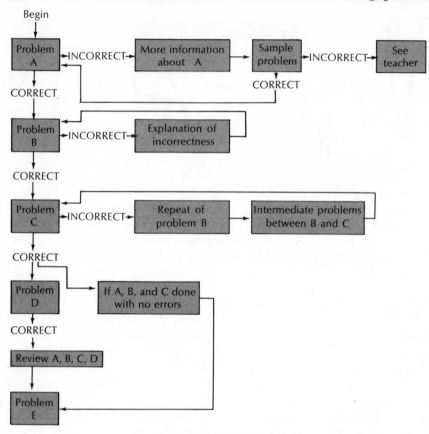

Figure 22. Flow chart of branching program.

Summary

One way to get from baseline behavior to learning objectives is to shape, by reinforcement, behavior that progressively approximates the terminal state.

The chapter began with an example of the shaping process with a seven-year-old boy for changing, by successively reinforced approximations, behavior that was overly dependent to independent. The remainder of the chapter elaborated upon shaping by considering the following:

1. Reinforcement is more effective when it follows immediately upon the behavior being shaped.
2. The efficacy of immediate reinforcement supports the need for a classroom environment where students can produce their own reinforcers.
3. Contrived reinforcers often have to be used in teaching because the more natural reinforcers are not as manipulable by the teacher. Behavior learned

by means of contrived reinforcers can rather easily be transferred to more natural reinforcers.

4. During acquisition of new information or behavior, CRF is more efficient than an intermittent schedule. This suggests the need for a variety of sources of reinforcement.

5. Changing from a CRF to intermittent reinforcement once learning has occurred is one method of insuring against rapid extinction.

6. There are essentially two forms of shaping: (1) the usual notion of programming information or behavioral expectation by adding increasingly complex bits until the final concept or terminal behavior is added, and (2) fading, a technique where the full-blown model is presented and the learner relies less and less upon the model as it fades away.

7. The more alternatives for the student to manipulate his learning environment, the greater the probability that success will be reinforcing.

Another more succinct way of summarizing the chapter is that learning of whatever form is greatly facilitated when the classroom climate is rich with reinforcing potential and invites the learner to explore that potential.

11 / Changing Undesirable Behavior

With a pained expression of exasperation the teacher muttered under her breath, "What can I do with that child?" and in so doing she joins the ranks of the perplexed who find themselves at a loss with the problem student. Few, if any, teachers ever escape that dilemma because in addition to their role as teacher they also have the responsibility for discipline. In an insightful book on teaching, Philip W. Jackson says that

schools resemble so-called total institutions, such as prisons, mental hospitals, and the like, in that one subgroup of their clientele (the students) are involuntarily committed to the institution, whereas another subgroup (the staff) has greater freedom of movement and, most important, has the ultimate freedom to leave the institution entirely. Under these circumstances it is common for the more privileged group to guard the exits, either figuratively or literally. Again, teachers may not like this description and may, in protesting, insist that they operate "democratic" classrooms, but in a very real sense their responsibilities bear some resemblance to those of prison guards. In "progressive" prisons, as in most classrooms, the inhabitants are allowed certain freedoms, but there are real limits. In both institutions the inmates might be allowed to plan a Christmas party, but in neither place are they allowed to plan a "break." . . .

In the best of all possible worlds it is expected that children will adapt to the teacher's authority by becoming "good workers" and "model students." And, by and large, this ideal comes close to being realized. Most students learn to look and to listen when told to and to keep their private fantasies in check when class is in session. But not all students become good workers. . . .[1]

[1] Philip W. Jackson, *Life in Classrooms* (New York: Holt, Rinehart and Winston, Inc., 1968), pp. 31–32, reprinted by permission of the publisher.

134

The Problem of Punishment

Barring sainthood, it is difficult not to become personally entangled with those troublesome students who continually violate one's sense of values, disrupt the class, whine, complain, and so on. Because such behavior is often a threat, the teacher's first impulse may be to unload with both barrels and put the obstreperous student back in his place; in short, to suppress undesirable behavior by punishment. Setting aside the ethical questions one might raise about punishment, there are other equally important questions concerning punishment as a means for achieving classroom goals.

The problem is with its lack of predictability. That is, there are many more consequences to punishment than just the cessation of undesirable behavior, and these unpredictable consequences work against the teacher's goals more often than for them. An extensive body of research has indicated that what happens after punishment depends upon a variety of factors, few of which, if any, the punisher knows about or has much control over. These are:

a. The timing of punishment—just as the misbehavior begins, during, immediately after, or several hours after.
b. The intensity of punishment.
c. The nature of punishment—threat of withdrawal of love, spanking, embarrassment, and so on.
d. The previous history of punishment.
e. The status of the punisher.
f. The schedule of punishment.

Not only does each of these factors render punishment unpredictable, but the interaction possibilities further complicate the picture. For example, is embarrassment caused by a high status teacher equal in predictability to spanking by a low status teacher?

Furthermore, and perhaps as important as the unpredictable quality of punishment, suppression of behavior weakens the teacher's effectiveness in shaping desirable behavior. By association, the teacher may be perceived as a very undesirable person, and on occasions of shaping, that teacher will have lost reinforcement potential. Of course, the teacher's effectiveness as a reinforcing agent can usually be regained, but valuable time will have been lost.

One might wonder, therefore, why punishment or the threat of punishment, which can have the same effect, is so frequently used in the schools. First of all, when successful, there is a reinforcing "workability" for the teacher. Though it may be short term, getting a child to stop misbehaving, particularly when he is disrupting classroom routine is very reinforcing for the teacher. In addition, it is usually reinforcing to express anger if the teacher is emotionally involved. It "feels good" for one to get it out of his system and direct anger toward the source of irritation. Thus the act of punishing can be a source of reinforcement for the teacher, and by definition such a consequence will increase the probability of punishment given disruptive behavior in the future.

As alluring as punishment may be because of the teacher's emotional involvement and the reinforcement of seeing undesirable behavior stop, it is not a useful technique if one looks beyond the heat of the moment. A more predictable method and a more detached, clinical attitude are necessary. The psychologist who becomes angry when a mental patient aggresses could hardly be an effective therapist. Similarly, the teacher who is angered easily will lose contact with students early in the game.

Techniques for Changing Undesirable Behavior

There is yet to be a definite theory of discipline, and the subject is approached here with no little humility. Because discipline involves transgressions of some variety, there is often an emotional component that stymies rational solutions. For example, a psychologist is frequently consulted when parent or teacher with an acting-out child has reached the end of the proverbial rope. In their desperation, approaching the problem objectively, which would be the nature of the psychologist's suggestions, is almost impossible. How many times have the psychologist's words been met with "Well, I've already tried that" or "Why don't you psychologists come down out of the clouds?" Subjective involvement is not a fertile ground for impartial guidance. This is not to defend all counseling psychologists; it is to say that the more objectivity on the part of the counselor and the adult living with the problem, the greater the probability that a satisfactory course of action can be mapped out. The guidelines offered below are given in that spirit of mutual objectivity in the interests of changing undesirable behavior in a predictable and therapeutic fashion.

Extinction

Extinction is the process of behavioral modification brought about by non-reinforcement. That is, instead of negative consequences as in punishment, extinction is a condition of neutral consequences. Previously reinforced behavior is now not reinforced.

An example of extinction is the Williams study outlined on page 92. You will remember it dealt with eliminating a child's crying at bedtime by ignoring him after he had been put to bed. In seven trials his crying went from fifty-five minutes the first evening to no crying.

Another example of extinction is discussed by Teodoro Ayllon and J. Michael.[2] A female patient in a mental institution persisted in walking into the nurses' station. On each occasion a nurse would stop what she was doing and walk the patient out to the ward again. When the nurses were instructed not to respond in any way while the patient was in the station, the intrusive behavior was almost completely eliminated. The fact that the nurses attended to her when she was where she should not have been was obviously a reinforcer, discontinuance of which effectively eliminated the behavior.

If the reinforcing agent for disruptive behavior comes from a *single* source that can be withdrawn, the possibility of change is great. Usually reinforcers come from a variety of sources, in which case the chance of change is less if they cannot be eliminated or controlled. Because groups such as those in the classroom are often powerful sources of reinforcement for individual behavior, it is sometimes possible for the group to withhold reinforcing consequences to disruptive behavior. It is difficult, however, to manipulate the group to withhold reinforcement because it means each member must withhold reinforcement when the undesirable behavior occurs. If even only one member does not go along with the plan, his attention may be sufficient to maintain the behavior that others are trying to extinguish.

Withdrawal and Re-presentation of Reinforcers

When a reinforcer has been found, presentation of that reinforcer may be made contingent upon cessation of the undesired behavior, or withdrawal of the reinforcer can be a consequence of the onset of undesired behavior. In other words, presentation or withdrawal of the reinforcing condition may be made contingent upon the kind of behavior engaged in.

Donald Baer took this method seriously in changing thumbsucking behavior.[3] He begins his study with a brief review of some of the purported "causes" of thumbsucking. These include inner tensions and conflicts, self-reinforcing consequences of thumbsucking, and sucking deprivation during infancy. Dissatisfied with these interpretations, Baer chooses to view thumbsucking as a learned response that can be modified by environmental control.

A five-year-old child was seated before a movie screen and cartoons were projected while a baseline measure of thumbsucking was made. In the second part of the study continuance of the cartoons was contingent upon the child's having his thumb out of his mouth. As soon as he put it in, the projector was turned off. As predicted, thumbsucking rapidly diminished.

[2] T. Ayllon and J. Michael, "The Psychiatric Nurse as a Behavioral Engineer," *Journal of the Experimental Analysis of Behavior* 2 (1959): 323–34.

[3] Donald Baer, "Laboratory Control of Thumbsucking by Withdrawal of Re-presentation of Reinforcement, *Journal of the Experimental Analysis of Behavior* 5 (1962): 525–28.

Baer's example illustrates the reciprocal relationship between teacher and student (in this case, experimenter and subject) necessary in the training situation. There were certain reinforcers the five-year-old child wanted. The two entered into a nonverbal reciprocal agreement where nonthumbsucking was obviously reinforcing to Baer whereas watching cartoons was rewarding to the child. Baer did not continue this particular study beyond the laboratory, but it would appear from previous research that extinguishing thumbsucking would have been relatively easy by a shaping process consisting of other reinforcers.

Negative Reinforcement Coupled with Positive Reinforcement

A frequent and effective technique of behavioral control is negative reinforcement in the form of a warning: a teacher's frown or other sign that present behavior is not acceptable and if continued will result in consequences not to the liking of those to whom the frown is directed. The warning is usually sufficient to initiate *escape behavior* designed to avoid the forewarned consequences, and if escape works, it is negatively reinforcing. The warning-frown technique is often sufficient to terminate many disruptions, and in general it is perfectly acceptable if not used too frequently. If it begins to lose its effectiveness, a different strategy is necessary.

Negatively reinforcing behavior can be coupled with positive reinforcers. That is, for not behaving in a particular fashion and for avoiding the inevitable clash (negative reinforcement), there can be other consequences more positive in nature. This is the dimension many teachers neglect, and as a result they fail to capitalize on the more powerful use of reinforcement of coupling negative and positive consequences. For example, as a consequence of a clearly established restoration of order, the class could be granted the opportunity of activity related to classroom objectives that have in the past been rewarding. It is important, however, that the reinforcing state of affairs be clearly connected to the restoration of order rather than the disruption. Hence the emphasis is upon *clearly established* restoration of order.

Extinction and Multiple Positive Reinforcement

Another form of coupling is extinction with positive reinforcement. Gerald R. Patterson gives an example of such a method where he uses both tangible reinforcers and the peer group to extinguish hyperactive behavior. In the portions of this study reproduced below, note particularly the provision for reinforcement of the peer group's behavior.

After several hours of observing Earl's behavior both at home and in the school, it was decided that most of his "hyperactivity" could be described by the inappropriate occurrence of the following behaviors: talking, pushing, hitting, pinching, looking about the room, looking out of the window, moving out of location (walking or moving desk), and moving in location (tapping, squirming, handling objects).

The frequency of occurrence of each of these responses was tabulated for each thirty-second interval. During this interval, a tabulation was made for each second during which a response persisted. For example, if Earl were walking about the room (when he was supposed to be studying) he received one check for each second during which he was walking.

Prior to each conditioning session, Earl was observed for twenty minutes to establish a baseline rate of estimate for the occurrence of the undesirable behaviors. The estimate of rate was calculated by dividing the total number of tabulations by the number of minutes during which the observations were made.

Following the tabulation of the baseline observations, a conditioning session was initiated. The amount of time directly involved in the conditioning sessions varied somewhat from one day to the next. The first conditioning trial lasted five minutes. By the end of the fifteen sessions, the time interval had been extended to twenty or thirty minutes. The observation data described above were also tabulated during the conditioning session. The data were collected by three experimenters who worked on alternate days, and were collected at roughly the same time on each day (10:30) over a four week period.

The apparatus consisted of a small box six by eight by five inches. A small flashlight bulb was mounted on top of the box; the dial of an electric counter could also be observed in the top of the box. The light and counter were controlled by the experimenter who sat across the room from Earl. Before the conditioning trials began, Earl was given several short trial runs with the apparatus. During the pretraining sessions, Earl was given a book to look at. During each ten second interval when only "attending" behaviors occurred, the light would flash on, the counter click, and the experimenter deposited one M&M candy on the desk. It was explained to Earl that each time the light went on in the trials that would follow it meant he had "earned" one candy or one penny. The counter would keep score for him and he would get the candy or pennies at the end of each "lesson."

At the beginning of the first conditioning trial the following instructions were given to the class, in Earl's presence.

> Earl has some trouble in learning things here in school because he is always moving around. This is a magic teaching machine that is going to teach Earl to sit still so that he can learn like other children. Each time that the light flashes on it means that Earl has been sitting still. It also means that he has earned one piece of candy (penny). The counter here will keep score. At the end of the lesson we will take the candy (pennies) and divide it up among all of you. If you want to help Earl earn the candy you can do so by not paying any attention to him when he is "working."

The classroom situations during which the conditioning was carried out varied from silent reading and art work at the desk, reading, or arithmetic in small groups, and class recitation.

During the conditioning sessions, an average of 60 to 100 reinforcers were dispensed by the experimenter. During the initial conditioning sessions, M&M candies were used; during later sessions the candy was alternated with pennies as reinforcers.

It should be noted, however, that the peer group proved to be a source of social reinforcers that undoubtedly had some effect upon Earl's behavior. For example, at the end of each conditioning session when the score was announced to the class, they would typically applaud Earl for his performance earnings. They also frequently walked by his desk and peered at the counter to see how well he was doing. During breaks in the classroom routine, for example at recess, the experimenters overheard frequent comments such as "You sure are doing good; you get better every day." There seems little reason to deny that these reinforcers had some effect; in fact, the procedure was structured in such a way as to maximize the possibility of their occurrence.[4]

Results of the study were dramatic. The child's hyperactivity was significantly decreased when operant level was compared to conditioning scores. The learning generalized beyond the experimental periods: the teacher reported improvement outside the classroom, where, as she phrased it, he seemed for the first time to "play with other children rather than hurl himself at them." In addition, the mere sight of the experimenter served to bring about more orderly behavior while in the classroom, and there seemed to be little need for the experimental apparatus or contingencies as time went on.

Time Out

Another technique which has been used in preschools and the early grades has been to institute a time-out procedure when a student misbehaves. Time out is a mild form of punishment where positive reinforcers are removed immediately following a child's infraction of classroom rules. Usually the more the child's reinforcement comes from interacting with other children, the more effective is time out. Say that one of the classroom rules is that children not take toys forcibly from other children during free play. An infraction occurs. The teacher firmly but gently moves in and announces to the offender that for breaking a rule the consequences are to move out of the group for a specified period, usually not longer than three minutes. It is important that the child recognize that the cause of time out is his misbehavior and not that the teacher dislikes him. The child is escorted to the time-out chair, which is removed from the group but in full view of the group. He is to remain there until the specified time is up. A child can often monitor his own infraction penalty if given an egg timer and informed that as soon as the sand from the top trickles to the bottom he may return. Having paid his penalty, the child is welcomed back into the group.

[4] Gerald R. Patterson, "An Application of Conditioning Techniques to the Control of a Hyperactive Child," in *Case Studies in Behavior Modification,* ed. Leonard P. Ullman and Leonard Krasner (New York: Holt, Rinehart & Winston, Inc., 1965), pp. 371–73, copyright © 1965 by Holt, Rinehart & Winston, Inc., reprinted by permission of the publisher.

As with all forms of punishment, time out has limitations. If used frequently, it will lose its power to control misbehavior. It is not a technique for all children. Some will not remain quietly in the time-out chair, and the teacher's attention necessary to keep that kind of child in the chair may be reinforcing to the misbehavior. The advantages of the time-out procedure, when properly used, are several: it works with many children when emphasized as a consequence of the child's behavior and not the teacher's whim; it is convenient in that time out can be administered quickly with a minimum of disruption to the group, and it affords opportunity for positive social reinforcement upon its termination.

Summary

Teaching goes beyond just the presentation of material. There is an obvious responsibility to eliminate inappropriate behavior. The problem with punishment, one of the most frequently used techniques to suppress behavior, is that the adult has little control over a wide range of consequences, so predictability is almost nonexistent. Although sometimes reinforcing to the adult, punishment, by association, may cause the adult to lose his ability to shape.

Other strategies for changing undesirable behavior are extinction, withdrawal and re-presentation of reinforcers, negative reinforcement coupled with positive reinforcement, extinction and multiple positive reinforcement, and time out.

12 / More About Reinforcers

The last several chapters on operant conditioning should have made it apparent that one of the most crucial aspects of the system is reinforcement. Or as B. F. Skinner once said, "One of the most important questions a teacher can ask is 'What do I have or what can I make available that they [the students] want?'" [1] In effect Skinner was asking, "What are their reinforcers?" This chapter is devoted exclusively to considering some of the reinforcers already available in today's schools and also those that can be made available by creative structuring. The rationale underlying this emphasis is that the ideal learning environment consists of mutually supportive reinforcement, where students achieve what they want and the teacher is reinforced by the student's progress toward individual and classroom goals.

The Problem of Disparate Teacher-Pupil Goals

Before attempting a direct response to the determination and development of reinforcing consequences for students, some attention needs to be given to the apparent gap between what students want and what teachers want.

It is curious that many teachers would expect otherwise. Because of age, greater seriousness about learning, and pressures from administration and parents for more mature behavior on the part of the students (to mention

[1] B. F. Skinner, in a colloquium given at Webster College, Webster Groves, Missouri, on October 23, 1965.

a few of the factors determining the teacher's expectation), the teacher's goals are necessarily different from those of the student, whose expectations are molded by entirely different factors. In an often cited study, James S. Coleman writes about what one group of students wants:

. . . what our society has done is to set apart, in an institution of their own, adolescents for whom home is little more than a dormitory and whose world is made up of activities peculiar to their fellows. They have been given as well many of the instruments which can make them a functioning community: cars, freedom in dating, continual contact with the opposite sex, money, and entertainment, like popular music and movies, designed especially for them. The international spread of "rock-and-roll" and of so-called American patterns of adolescent behavior is a consequence, I would suggest, of these economic changes which have set adolescents off in a world of their own.[2]

The same could be said about students in nursery schools, elementary schools, and undergraduate and graduate programs, though they would obviously be subjected to kinds of external pressures other than those listed by Coleman.

But the teacher-student expectation gap has been effectively dealt with by many teachers. Young children have been taught in depth a wide range of subject material that has little or no direct relationship to their immediate worlds. Moreover, they seem to enjoy learning, as demonstrated by a high level of persistence even with the teacher out of the scene. The secret seems to be that these teachers have arranged certain contingencies such that learning has an internal or external pay-off quality. From the point of view of the students, their behavior "works" in some fashion for them.

In a previous quotation of B. F. Skinner (page 125), it was suggested that the teacher may have to resort to "unnatural" reinforcers to capture the students' initial interest and involvement, but with time the teacher shifts to more natural reinforcers. These latter reinforcers do not necessitate the teacher's presence, allowing society—the peer group or the "intrinsic" value of learning for the sake of learning—to take over and sustain continued learning. It is not difficult to think of many such examples in one's own life where the "unnatural" reinforcers assured those initial first successes that opened up other kinds of reinforcers. History is filled with accounts of similar incidents that developed into such important choices as a life's vocation, an avidly pursued hobby, avocations, and other core interests. The point is that one ought not be ashamed or afraid to use unnatural reinforcers during the early stages of learning as long as these are followed up by deliberate attempts to transfer the source of reinforcement to other consequences that assure maintenance of independent searching and probing into an area.

[2] James S. Coleman, "The Adolescent Subculture and Academic Achievement," *The American Journal of Sociology* 65 (1960): 337–47.

Discovering Reinforcers by Observation

If a person's behavior is observed methodically as was described in Chapter 9, an analysis of the data often produces a list of potential reinforcers based upon what the person does and how long he does it. For example, say that the observation occurred in a classroom where the students were given the opportunity to choose their activities. Since duration of time spent in an activity has often proved to be a sensitive measure of a set of potential reinforcers, those activities on which was spent the greatest proportion of time would constitute an important possibility, or at least these would be testable reinforcers to be used at a future time as consequences for desired behaviors.

This has been dubbed the "Premack Principle" after David Premack, who discovered that if behavior A is higher in probability than behavior B, behavior B can be made more probable by making performance of behavior A a consequence of behavior B.[3] This principle was used effectively in a nursery school by L. E. Homme et al.:

In a preliminary exploration of nursery school procedures, three three-year-old subjects (Ss) were available three hours a day, five days a week, for about one month. At the first, verbal instructions usually had little effect on the Ss' behavior. When they were instructed to sit in their chairs, Ss would often continue what they were doing—running around the room, screaming, pushing chairs, or quietly working jigsaw puzzles. Taking Premack seriously, such behaviors were labeled as high probability behaviors and used in combination with the signals for them as reinforcers. These high probability behaviors were then made contingent on desired behaviors. For example, sitting quietly in a chair and looking at the blackboard would be intermittently followed by the sound of the bell, with the instruction: "Run and scream." The Ss would then leap to their feet and run around the room screaming. At another signal they would stop. At this time they would get another signal and an instruction to engage in some other behavior which, on a quasi-random schedule, might be one of high or low probability. At a later stage, Ss earned tokens for low probability behaviors which could later be used to "buy" the opportunity for high probability activities.

With this kind of procedure, control was virtually perfect after a few days. For example, when Ss were requested to "sit and look at the blackboard" (an activity which in the past had intermittently been interrupted by the signal for some higher probability behavior), they were under such good control that an observer, new on the scene, almost certainly would have assumed extensive aversive control was being used.

An examination of high probability behaviors quickly showed that many, if not most of them, were behaviors which ordinarily would be suppressed through punishment. Extrapolating from this we were able to predict the reinforcing properties of some behaviors which had never been emitted. For example, throwing a plastic cup across the room and kicking a waste basket had never been observed but proved to be highly reinforcing activities after they had once been evoked by instructions. (Some unpredicted behaviors proved to be highly reinforcing, e.g., pushing the experimenter around the room in his caster-equipped chair.)

[3] David Premack, "Toward Empirical Behavior Laws: I Positive Reinforcement." *Psychological Review* 66 (1959): 219–33.

In summary, even in this preliminary, unsystematic application, the Premack hypothesis proved to be an exceptionally practical principle for controlling the behavior of nursery school Ss.[4]

In this study a group reinforcer was found. The same procedure can be used for individual reinforcers, as one identifies through observation a student's rather stable, frequent behaviors, given an environment where he has an opportunity to select.

11:06:20 / Billy is off to the side of the room stacking wooden blocks. When he gets a stack about equal to his height, he pulls out the bottom block. They all fall down. He laughs and starts stacking again.

11:09:05 / Down they go. Mary comes over briefly to watch. Turns and leaves. Billy hardly notices her. Starts building two towers.

11:11:31 / Towers complete. Billy puts a section of 2 × 4 across the tops, connecting the two. Throws string over 2 × 4 and ties a small car to what is now a swing. Swings car back and forth pendulum style between the two towers. Smiles.

11:14:20 / Turns and walks to teacher. Tugs on her skirt. "Yes, Billy?" "Look!" He shouts and points to the swing and towers. "Billy," she exclaims, "that's very interesting." He runs over to the blocks, starts the car swinging, turns to teacher, laughs.

11:17:01 / Teacher diverted by Debbie. Billy turns back to blocks. Pulls out both bottom blocks, all tumble. Billy laughs and jumps up and down.

11:19:00 / Starts building. This time three towers are going up. "Time to get ready for lunch," teacher addresses the group. Billy turns to group, "Aw," imitates crying. Standing akimbo facing group.

This is not to suggest that Billy now be deprived of block-building contingent upon other behaviors the teacher wants. It is to say that the invitation to play with blocks may be used as a reinforcer when Billy engages in behavior that needs to be reinforced.

Carefully collected observational data can give insight into a variety of other, already developed reinforcers. In the two examples above, time spent during free play was the factor used to differentiate reinforcing from neutral events. Another obvious means of determining reinforcers is by the consistency of choices students make. The events or conditions most frequently made have in all probability reinforcement potential.

To translate what is being said in more common-sense terms: observation can help determine what children like, and these activities can be used as consequences to the kind of behavior the teacher likes. The conditions the children enjoy can sometimes be made contingent upon what the teacher wants.

[4] Lloyd E. Homme, P. C. de Baca, James V. Devine, R. Steinhorst, and E. J. Rickert, "Use of the Premack Principle in Controlling the Behavior of Nursery School Children," *Journal of the Experimental Analysis of Behavior* 6 (1963): 544.

Even less formal observation with a little creative thought can pro-duce a list of reinforcing consequences. Not every item is a surefire reinforcer for every student, but many items on the list would probably serve effectively for a majority of the students. These, then, could be used in tandem with the kinds of behaviors and performances that are reinforcing to the teacher. For example, a college teacher discovered that his students were notoriously late in finishing their term papers, and a late paper was sufficiently disruptive that he decided to do something about it. From another class in the same academic area, psychology, he had discovered that a day's field trip to a state hospital where an innovative therapeutic program was in development had been both a fruitful learning experience and one to which the class looked forward. These two facts—consistently late term papers and the enthusiastic response to a visit to the state hospital—were yoked together, and at mid semester the seminar class was informed that each student would be granted a trip to the hospital contingent upon meeting the deadline. As one might expect, there were no late papers. Of course, it would not have been difficult to get the papers on time by the threat of failure, but the advantages of positive reinforcement as opposed to the threat of punishment are obvious, especially as the reinforcer in this case was the opportunity for a more enriching learn-ing experience.

That actual episode is provocative of other collegiate possibilities. Fred S. Keller in an almost (but not quite) tongue-in-cheek style addresses himself to the construction of a reinforcement-laden learning environment for both teacher and student, which has important implications for elementary and secondary schools.

I would like you to imagine that you have recently agreed to help establish a depart-ment of psychology. It is to be complete in every respect, with all the major speciali-zations and at every level of training from the first course to the most advanced, in a university that is just being formed, and in a country where no such department now exists. Together with four young psychologists and former pupils as co-workers, you are expected to take a constructive part in procuring a complete staff, purchasing equipment, outfitting a library, designing a department building, and—especially—developing a curriculum of study. You have been assured of financial and moral support, and you have been told to be as bold and experimental as you wish in the program you adopt.

Imagine, too, that, in a few months, you will have awaiting you, at the uni-versity's opening, a group of perhaps one hundred students, fairly well grounded in language, mathematics, arts, and the other sciences, who want basic psychological training. You and your colleagues, with a few assistants, working in temporary quar-ters and with limited facilities, are expected to introduce them to psychology and to carry them thereafter as far as they may want to go.

To start you on your way, you and your colleagues have spent a month or more in visiting colleges, universities, hospitals, and research centers, where psychol-ogy is taught in one way or another. You have talked with interested teachers and researchers about your problem; you have examined shops, laboratories, libraries, classrooms, and clinics. You have taken notes on everything and tried to extract from every experience something of value for your project. You have bought some books and ordered some equipment. And you have sat down together at the end of your travels to decide upon your next objective. What is it going to be?

Under such conditions, I suggest that your first concern would be the introductory course and those hundred-odd students who will be enrolled therein. There is only *one* introductory course, and it is, or should be, a key course and a foundation for the work to come. While teaching it, you and your co-workers can prepare for the courses that immediately follow. At the same time, you can begin your search for a distinguished staff of teachers at the more advanced levels. These new teachers will, in turn, help you design and equip your workshops and laboratories, stock your library, give form and clearer purpose to your program, and, finally, help you design your building. Right now, your job is to get ready for those hundred young men and women who will be there to greet you when the school bell rings.

But what sort of first course will you teach? There's much talk today of an educational reawakening; much dissatisfaction throughout this country with our aims, our methods, and the results we now achieve. Will you try to export a course that is under fire at home? Perhaps you, yourself, have complained about the failure of your teaching—talked about the inefficiency of the lecture system, the evil of examinations, the meaninglessness of letter and number grades, the short-term retention of course content, and the rigid frame of hours, days, and weeks within which each course of study is presumed to fit. Perhaps you have even expressed a willingness to change these things, if you could only escape from the "system." Now you have your chance. What are you going to do?

The kind of course I'm going to suggest has never been taught. It won't work. It conflicts with the natural tendencies of man. It has nothing new about it. Even if it worked, it could only teach reinforcement theory. It might be all right somewhere else, but it won't go here. And I think you will find, in the last analysis, that it is against the law. So, having anticipated some of your criticisms, let me tell you more about it.

It is a course with lectures, demonstrations, discussions, laboratory hours, and "homework." The lectures and demonstrations are infrequent and primarily inspirational: ideally, they are interesting, informative, and memorable—even entertaining. Once the course has started, they are provided at suitable places along the way, but only for those students who have reached a point that guarantees an appreciation of their content. For students who do not qualify until a later date, a recording of the lecture and, if possible, the demonstration, is available. Attendance at either lectures or demonstrations, however, is entirely optional, and no examination is based upon them.

Discussions, with one's peers or with an instructor, or both, are provided at certain times for those students who desire them and, as in the case of lectures and demonstrations, if they have earned the privilege. These discussions are also recorded and may be listened to again by any of the participants. Needless to say, the discussions are never to be used as examining devices by the teacher. They are primarily for the student, who has won the right to ask questions or to express himself with respect to the work he has been doing in the laboratory or at home.

The laboratory work itself begins on the second or third day of the course, and is its most important feature. Each student has his own private and well-equipped little room or cubicle, for a certain time each day (say an hour and a half), on five or six days of the week. There he works alone, or perhaps with a partner, under the general supervision of a laboratory assistant who has no more than nine other students in his charge at the time. The student's daily task begins when he has qualified for it— for example, when he has turned in a report of the preceding day's experiment, answered two or three questions on the last reading assignment, studied a description of his laboratory mission for the day, or done all of these things.

The experiments themselves are carefully planned to let each student discover for himself the operation of certain well-established principles of behavior; to teach him some basic skills in the use of equipment and the treatment of data; and to lead him from minimal to maximal responsibility in the writing of reports.

When a laboratory task has been completed (and *only* then), the student receives the assignment that will prepare him for the next. This is his "homework." It may include textbook study—plain or programmed; the reading of an article or technical report, carefully edited or supplemented to make it fully clear, and provided with a few key questions like those he may be asked at the beginning of his next laboratory session; and other readings may be given solely as a reward for work completed and to whet the appetite for more.

Besides preparing him for further laboratory missions, lectures, demonstrations, and conferences, this "homework" is intended to broaden the student's perspective by teaching him to generalize from the laboratory to many other situations of human life. It aims to encourage thinking in the direction of both research and practical application. And, finally, it is meant to provide the student with at least a nodding acquaintance with the great variety that goes by the name of psychology today.

The assistant's functions in such a course are very important. He is the one who prepares and checks equipment, collects reports, passes out work material and assignments, and records, in each student's individual logbook, each important step along the route—including the time of arrival and the number of the setbacks, if any, before reaching port. He will also collect any student complaints, requests, comments, or suggestions (in writing), which he then passes on to the course director or other designated person.

The teachers, in a course like this, are not as conspicuous as they were under the old order. Their work load and responsibility, however, are as great as before— especially during the first year's operation. They are the ones who design, in every minute detail and, initially, for just one student, each day's teaching program; and they are the ones who redesign this program in the light of student performance and assistants' reports. They must also stand ready to give an occasional lecture or preside at a demonstration; they must sometimes be available for conference or discussion with qualified students; and they must be prepared to read an occasional student paper. Their general loss in visibility to their students, which might be aversive to long-time performers on the classroom stage, is perhaps offset by the improved reception of their messages when given and, more generally, the increased status of their academic position.

When all the course requirements have been met, the course is at an end. At this point, the student's logbook is examined by the course director, who records the achievement, places the book in the department files, and takes a few moments, perhaps, to offer his congratulations. No final examination is given, no course grade, no reward for speed of attainment, and no punishment for delay. Examining and teaching were inseparable parts of the same educational process; and something better than a letter or a number is available, in a list of the goals that were reached and the time it took to reach them. The student is ready for Course No. 2, a new logbook, a new cubicle, a new assistant, a new body of fact and skills, and, probably, a new teacher. But this is not, at the moment, our concern.

I have sketched for you, during the past few minutes, a more or less imaginary first course in psychology, and I have suggested its more or less imaginary origin. More or less, pilot research in this kind of teaching is already going on at several places in this country, although not exclusively aimed at first-course needs; and a full-scale test is now being planned for the first course itself, along the lines I have suggested here, at the new University of Brasília, in Brazil, beginning in 1964. If success attends these ventures, it might well be that some such personal-course method of instruction could be applied in other sciences and at other levels of education.[5]

Grades as Reinforcers

Grading, that delicate two-edged sword the teacher so often employs to force as well as reward academic behavior, has seldom been used in a creative manner to exploit its full reinforcement potential. There are two problems with grades as they are customarily used. First, because a grade may run the gamut from failure to success, there is always a potential threat to the student. Even the better students are plagued because a respectable A or B can slip to a C or even the more punitive D or F. Second, the granting of a grade often occurs long after the behavior that produced it, and the longer the reinforcer is withheld the more it loses its effectiveness.

The grade, however, becomes a more viable reinforcer if it is recast in a different framework. Say there were only three evaluations a student can receive—an A, a B, and a deferred grade. The A and B are granted when the student reaches a predetermined level of performance; the deferred grade simply means that the student has not satisfied the criterion and has another opportunity to succeed. This way a student would know at the beginning of the semester that the lowest grade he could get is a B, contingent of course upon B level performance as the teacher defines it. The punishing aspect of grades, then, would be eliminated, and they could serve the more important function of positive reinforcer.

But what about the student who does not reach the criterion of a B? If the teacher holds to the attitude that a teacher is to teach, not to fail, and if he views the profession of teaching as a setting for providing ways whereby all persons can succeed, the task becomes one of devising alternative ways that assure, in time, a student's success. For example, if a measure of performance is about to be taken, it appears reasonable that the students have a fairly clear idea *ahead of time* of what will appear on the test. After all, letting students know what they are expected to know seems perfectly reasonable, since in a very real way that is the function of teaching. More concretely, before giving the test the teacher might make a tape recording that covers in some detail what will be on the test. A tape recorder equipped with earphones would be avail-

---

[5] Fred S. Keller, "A Personal Course in Psychology," in *Control of Human Behavior,* ed. Roger Ulrich, Thomas Stachnik, John Mabry (Glenview, Illinois: Scott, Foresman and Company, 1966), pp. 91–93, from a paper read at the American Psychological Association Annual Meeting in Philadelphia, August 1963; reprinted by permission of the author.

Since this 1963 article, Keller has written a follow-up report on the results of this technique in several schools. Unfortunately the Brasília venture was disrupted by a general upheaval and the dismissal of over two hundred teachers in the university. He was able to put into effect an introductory course similar to the one described here. The results are very encouraging and the program is still in use with only minor changes. See Fred S. Keller, "Good-Bye Teacher," *Journal of Applied Behavior Analysis* 1 (Spring 1968): 79–89.

able in the library, learning center, or in the back of the classroom, and the students would be allowed to listen to it sometime before the test. There might even be a sample test at the end of the tape to ensure that the students have a clear idea of what will be included. After the test, all those who did not meet the criterion would have access to a tape recording that discusses the test, and upon listening to it they would take another test, equal to but slightly different from the first. Such a process changes the traditional function of testing from the game of wits teachers sometimes play with their students; this type of test is a way not to trick but to teach. The tape recorder, now a fairly standard piece of technology in most schools, is one way to deal with students who fail to meet criteria on first or second try. The creative teacher will think of a variety of other ways to assure the learning objectives for many more students.

The second problem of using a grade as a reinforcer—the time lag between graded behavior and the student's knowledge of his grade—is solved in a very straightforward way. The student should get his grade as soon after the test as possible. *There is no alternative to promptness if one wants to use the grade as a reinforcer.* Fairly immediate feedback is sometimes impossible. The teacher has other responsibilities than just grading papers, but the fact remains: the later the reinforcer follows the behavior it is to reinforce, the less effective it becomes.

Summary

This chapter, an extension of the previous chapter, explains in more detail how the school environment may become more reinforcing to students. Because the school staff is made up of adults and because the students are not adults, there is a disparity in the kinds of outcomes expected by each. Therefore one of the teacher's tasks is to yoke together in a reciprocal relationship the adult and the student reinforcers. The chapter discusses a variety of ways to discover and use the students' reinforcers.

III / WHERE ARE YOU GOING?

And How Do You Know
When You Get There?

Teaching is essentially a deliberate undertaking. That is, the teaching act is designed to communicate certain knowledges and skills as well as attitudes and commitments. There may not be common agreement on *what* knowledges or attitudes are to be communicated—such is the grist of the educational philosophy mill—but there is little disagreement over the notion that the school is a goal-oriented institution. Pupils are expected to change in certain predictable ways. The goal is sometimes quite specific ("I want my students to be able to solve quadratic equations") and sometimes more open-ended ("I want my students to be able to have an appreciation of art"). But, specific or open-ended, each thrust is toward some sort of goal, some new position, some change in student behavior.

One purpose of Part III is to introduce you to the wide range of goals. The primary source is a taxonomy (classification system) of educational objectives within the area of knowledge and ability as well as of attitude. A second purpose is to give more insight into measurement of objectives, for unless the teacher can skillfully measure progress to a goal, there is no way of knowing whether the teaching process is effective or not.

Chapter 13 deals with cognitive goals, kinds of knowledges to be reached or approached. Chapter 14 deals with affective or attitudinal goals. Interspersed throughout both chapters is a consideration of means of measuring the goals. To put it in more colloquial terms, these two chapters are devoted to the question "Where do you want to go with your students, and how do you know you are getting there?"

13 / The Cognitive Domain

In a sense, this and the next chapter are at the center of the teacher's task. Students are expected to change over the semester as a function of the learning environment, and the change is often in terms of particular skills, knowledges, and attitudes. This and the next chapter are designed to emphasize the need for clearly specified goals and for translating them so that they may be measured.

Operationalizing Educational Objectives

When a teacher says, "I want my students to gain an appreciation of English literature," or "to understand mathematics," or "to be able to think creatively," or "to communicate with clarity," he is attempting to set goals. They are only first approximations, however, because the next question a teacher has to ask is "How will I know when my students appreciate, understand, think creatively, or communicate with clarity?" The discussion of criteria in the first chapter, you will remember, maintained that these abstract terms of creative thinking, appreciation, and understanding have to be translated into measurable behaviors. One has to respond in fairly concrete ways to the question "How must a person behave to be said to have reached a predetermined objective?" The standardized test is one way to determine a student's progress toward a criterion.

The Standardized Test

In the first part of this book it was stated that little consideration would be given to the standardized test, on the assumption that it would be dealt with in other courses in teacher preparation, but some attention will be given here since the standardized test is one important form of measurement used in the schools.

No student in today's school has escaped standardized tests. There is hardly need to describe them since you have already experienced the standardized test in its varied forms for measuring aptitude, achievement, interests, and personality. Aptitude tests are supposed to measure an individual's capacity for acquiring knowledge and skills; achievement tests, to measure mastery of and ability to use what has been learned; interest and personality tests, as their names imply, to determine one's interest and personality configurations underlying behavior.

The descriptive term "standardized" is apt. The measure has been designed to be administered under standard conditions, and it has been developed by administration to a large representative sample from which norms—standards—have been obtained. The presentation of norms that accompanies every standardized test allows the tester to compare his obtained scores with the scores derived from other populations.

The advantages of the standardized test are its accessibility (the teacher does not have to develop it), ease in scoring (most tests have a scoring overlay), availability of equivalent but different forms of the same test (allowing "before" and "after" measures to study amount of change), and objectivity (administration, scoring, and interpretation are independent of the teacher's judgment). In addition, one can be reasonably sure that the test maker has lavished great care in the test's construction, in determining the difficulty level of an item or the whole test and in establishing reliability. Then there is the question of validity, the crucial consideration. How can one be sure the standardized test is measuring what it purports to measure?

From the previous discussion of validity you will remember that a measure's most significant ability is of prediction. Tests designed to measure vocational aptitude, say for a potential airline pilot, ought to be able to predict before the fact who will make a good or poor pilot. Or, for lack of data on a measure's predictive power, validation may be established by construct validity, that is by its positive relationship to other measures designed to get at the same quality. In the construction of a standardized test, it is the test maker's responsibility to determine validity before the test is published and to report the procedure for and the data on establishment of validity.

But there are some problems in the use of standardized tests. First of all, merely that a test is published, distributed, and used does not necessarily make it a good test. A quick perusal of the test evaluations contained in O. K. Buros' *Mental Measurement* will indicate that even some of the widely used tests leave much to be desired.[1] For too many educators, the mere existence of a printed test qualifies it as a valid measure.

Although there is a wide range of kinds of tests in the areas of interest, achievement, aptitude, and personality, these tests do not cover all the areas a teacher might wish to measure. And even if an appropriate standardized test can be found, it is not unusual that its norms are inappropriate. That is, the test may be normed on a different kind of population than that to be tested. In such a case, an alternative is for one to develop norms, but this is a lengthy and often expensive undertaking that few teachers can pursue.

There has been a good deal of criticism of standardized testing, some based upon legitimate concerns shared by the test makers. The criticism largely deals with the misuse of the test rather than with the test itself. Henry S. Dyer, a test maker himself, catches the essence of the mistaken expectations of those who would seemingly stake their lives on a score—*any* score —from a standardized test.[2]

Their first assumption is that one can prove something by giving a single test after the show is over. The second is that a standardized objective test is standard and objective in some absolute sense, as though it had been made in heaven. The third is that testing agencies are like vending machines: all you have to do is put your nickel in the right slot, and out will come precisely the test you are looking for. All of which would be dandy if true, but unfortunately none of these assumptions bears any noticeable relation to the facts of testing and the assessment of achievement.

Because the standardized test is "canned," the task left to the school is selection, administration, and interpretation using the discretion any good researcher would use in selecting his measuring device and analyzing his data. The same plumb lines considered in Chapters 1–3 are just as applicable to standardized test data as they are to any data. But since the standardized test measures only a few of the concerns the classroom teacher has, attention will now be directed to less standardized measures, in particular to those that can be designed by the teacher as specific needs arise.

Developing One's Own Measures

Say that you are teaching a creative writing unit in a fifth-grade language-art program. The more abstract objective is to increase the childrens' ability to communicate by the creative use of words. That is a good beginning, but it is worthless if there are no explicit criteria to judge a student's performance.

---

[1] Oscar K. Buros, *Mental Measurement,* 6th ed. (Highland Park, N.J.: The Gryphon Press, 1965). This excellent resource book on standardized tests defines a test's purpose, reliability, and validity as well as an independent evaluation of the test. It is now in its sixth edition and is available in the reference section of most libraries.

[2] Henry S. Dyer, "On the Assessment of Academic Achievement," *Teachers College Record* 62 (1960): 164. Used by permission of the author and the *Teachers College Record.*

In short, what is a "creative use of words"? How do you operationalize this term into specific behaviors to know whether or not students are moving toward the objective?

Think about it for a moment. Take a sheet of paper and write in as concrete a way as you can what you mean by creativity. Then give examples.

Here is how one person operationalized such an objective.

The first step I would take would be to cut down the broad term "creativity" into a more manageable definition. Since I would be dealing with words, I would confine my measure just to words from the papers the students produce. One of the more common and almost intuitive definitions for things creative is *unusualness*. There is more to creativity than that, but for the time being I will settle for unusualness as my criterion. One way to operationalize unusualness would be to have the children use as many adjectives they can think of to describe everyday objects such as trees, buildings, or fireplugs. Certainly adjectives like "big" and "small," "red" and "white" are obvious. These would comprise categories of size and color. But how many other categories would be evident? The data could be treated several ways. One would be to compare the number of categories of one student to the number of categories of the whole group. Or a baseline measure of categories used at the beginning of the unit could be compared with the final measure to determine if a particular student has increased his ability to produce categories. Of course, I would want to use other measures than just this one. Another possibility would be to look at the use of adjectives in weekly papers I would assign. With this criterion as my measure, I now know one kind of activity to concentrate on in the daily class session.[3]

Several aspects of this account at operationalizing creativity are noteworthy: the objective was broken down to a very specific performance; the validity of the measure was of the face-validity variety; other measures than the one described here were to be used in conjunction with this measure; and the class sessions would be an outgrowth of the operationalized objectives rather than the other way around.

Where Do You Want to Go?

As a practitioner, the main tasks of the teacher are those of selecting objectives, providing the environment to maximize the possibility of achieving these objectives, and measuring to what degree the objectives have been achieved. In this section of the chapter attention will be directed to the selection of objectives or, as the subtitle queries, to where you want to go.

Even a brief glance at the history of education will indicate there has been no lack of statement about what education is supposed to do. One might choose to go back to Plato (427–347 B.C.), Aristotle (384–322 B.C.), Quintilian (A.D. 35?–95?), the Jesuits' *Ratio studiorum* (1599), John Locke's

[3] This is an adaptation of one undergraduate student's response to the request to operationalize creativity.

Some Thoughts Concerning Education (1690), or Rousseau's *Émile* (1762). As philosophers, their statements were cast in terms of values, of "proper" ends, of man's metaphysical nature, how he comes to know and whether what he knows approximates the truth. But with the advent of a science anxiously straining to break with philosophy, the goals of education began to be tainted with a new way of describing man. Herbart (1776–1841) deliberately borrowed from what was then an emerging branch of science, psychology, to state what he felt education should be about. The most articulate spokesman for a psychological philosophy of education was John Dewey (1859–1952). A kind of Renaissance man, Dewey was a well-trained psychologist, a first-rate philosopher, and a prodigious writer on the purposes of education. He strongly affected education in the United States, particularly in getting educators to state purposes of the schools in experimental and psychological rather than traditional and philosophical terms. As viewed by Dewey, the methods of science provided the most promising approach to educational problems. While director of the experimental laboratory school at the University of Chicago, he described its tasks as "the problem of viewing the education of the child in the light of the principles of mental activity and processes of growth made known by modern psychology."[4] This was a far cry from the earlier statements of the philosophers.

A Taxonomy of Educational Objectives

Following in the Deweyan tradition, a group of psychologists interested in education gathered informally at the 1948 meetings of the American Psychological Association[5] for the purpose of developing a classification system of educational objectives based upon psychological principles. It was felt that if there could be a statement of psychological objectives, research in education could be greatly facilitated by the common criteria.

The 1948 gathering became the first of a series of meetings that has culminated in publication of two significant works, one dealing with cognitive, the other with affective, goals of education. The first work is an attempt to construct a multi-dimensional classification, a taxonomy, of the cognitive domain with levels of knowledge and intellectual abilities and skills. The second work is a similar endeavor with objectives in the areas of attitudes, values, and appreciations.[6] Versions of both taxonomies, condensed by the authors, have been reprinted below to sensitize you to the wide range of objectives that can exist in classroom activity.

[4] John Dewey, *School and Society* (Chicago: University of Chicago Press, 1899), p. 88.
[5] An organization of which, incidentally, John Dewey was once president.
[6] A third taxonomy is in the process of development. It will consider psychomotor skills, those activities involving manipulative tasks such as writing, drawing, learning to swim, handling laboratory equipment, and so on.

A Condensed Version of the Cognitive
Domain of the Taxonomy of Educational Objectives[7]

KNOWLEDGE

1.00. Knowledge / Knowledge, as defined here, involves the recall of specifics and universals, the recall of methods and processes, or the recall of a pattern, structure, or setting. For measurement purposes, the recall situation involves little more than bringing to mind the appropriate material. Although some alteration of the material may be required, this is a relatively minor part of the task. The knowledge objectives emphasize most of the psychological processes of remembering. The process of relating is also involved in that a knowledge test situation requires the organization and reorganization of a problem such that it will furnish the appropriate signals and cues for the information and knowledge the individual possesses. To use an analogy, if one thinks of the mind as a file, the problem in a knowledge test situation is that of finding in the problem or task the appropriate signals, cues, and clues which will most effectively bring out whatever knowledge is filed or stored.

1.10. Knowledge of Specifics / The recall of specific and isolable bits of information. The emphasis is on symbols with concrete referents. This material, which is at a very low level of abstraction, may be thought of as the elements from which more complex and abstract forms of knowledge are built.

1.11. Knowledge of Terminology / Knowledge of the referents for specific symbols (verbal and nonverbal). This may include knowledge of the most generally accepted symbol referent, knowledge of the variety of symbols which may be used for a single referent, or knowledge of the referent most appropriate to a given use of a symbol.

> To define technical terms by giving their attributes, properties, or relations. Familiarity with a large number of words in their common range of meanings.[8]

1.12. Knowledge of Specific Facts / Knowledge of dates, events, persons, places, etc. This may include very precise and specific information such as the specific date or exact magnitude of a phenomenon. It may also include approximate or relative information such as an approximate time period or the general order of magnitude of a phenomenon.

> The recall of major facts about particular cultures.
> The possession of a minimum knowledge about the organisms studied in the laboratory.

1.20. Knowledge of Ways and Means of Dealing with Specifics / Knowledge of the ways of organizing, studying, judging, and critizing. This includes the methods of inquiry, the chronological sequences, and the standards of judgment within a field as well as the patterns of organization through which the areas of the fields themselves are determined and internally organized. This knowledge is at an intermediate level of abstraction between specific knowledge on the one hand and knowledge of universals on the other. It does not so much demand the activity of the student in using the materials as it does a more passive awareness of their nature.

[7] Benjamin S. Bloom, Max D. Engelhart, Edward J. Furst, Walker H. Hill, David R. Krathwohl, *Taxonomy of Educational Objectives: Cognitive Domain* (New York: David McKay Co., Inc., 1956).

[8] Each subcategory is followed by illustrative educational objectives selected from the literature.

1.21. Knowledge of Conventions / Knowledge of characteristic ways of treating and presenting ideas and phenomena. For purposes of communication and consistency, workers in a field employ usages, styles, practices, and forms which best suit their purposes and/or which appear to suit best the phenomena with which they deal. It should be recognized that although these forms and conventions are likely to be set up on arbitrary, accidental, or authoritative bases, they are retained because of the general agreement or concurrence of individuals concerned with the subject, phenomenon, or problem.

> Familiarity with the forms and conventions of the major types of works; e.g., verse, plays, scientific papers, etc.
> To make pupils conscious of correct form and usage in speech and writing.

1.22. Knowledge of Trends and Sequences / Knowledge of the processes, directions, and movements of phenomena with respect to time.

> Understanding of the continuity and development of American culture as exemplified in American life.
> Knowledge of the basic trends underlying the development of public assistance programs.

1.23. Knowledge of Classifications and Categories / Knowledge of the classes, sets, divisions, and arrangements which are regarded as fundamental for a given subject field, purpose, argument, or problem.

> To recognize the area encompassed by various kinds of problems or materials.
> Becoming familiar with a range of types of literature.

1.24. Knowledge of Criteria / Knowledge of the criteria by which facts, principles, opinions, and conduct are tested or judged.

> Familiarity with criteria for judgment appropriate to the type of work and the purpose for which it is read.
> Knowledge of criteria for the evaluation of recreational activities.

1.25. Knowledge of Methodology / Knowledge of the methods of inquiry, techniques, and procedures employed in a particular subject field as well as those employed in investigating particular problems and phenomena. The emphasis here is on the individual's knowledge of the method rather than his ability to use the method.

> Knowledge of scientific methods for evaluating health concepts.
> The student shall know the methods of attack relevant to the kinds of problems of concern to the social sciences.

1.30. Knowledge of the Universals and Abstractions in a Field / Knowledge of the major schemes and patterns by which phenomena and ideas are organized. These are the large structures, theories, and generalizations which dominate a subject field or which are quite generally used in studying phenomena or solving problems. These are at the highest levels of abstraction and complexity.

1.31. Knowledge of Principles and Generalizations / Knowledge of particular abstractions which summarize observations of phenomena. These are the abstractions which are of value in explaining, describing, predicting, or in determining the most appropriate and relevant action or direction to be taken.

Knowledge of the important principles by which our experience with biological phenomena is summarized.
The recall of major generalizations about particular cultures.

1.32. Knowledge of Theories and Structures / Knowledge of the *body* of principles and generalizations together with their interrelations which present a clear, rounded, and systematic view of a complex phenomenon, problem, or field. These are the most abstract formulations, and they can be used to show the interrelation and organization of a great range of specifics.

The recall of major theories about particular cultures.
Knowledge of a relatively complete formulation of the theory of evolution.

INTELLECTUAL ABILITIES AND SKILLS

Abilities and skills refer to organized modes of operation and generalized techniques for dealing with materials and problems. The materials and problems may be of such a nature that little or no specialized and technical information is required. Such information as is required can be assumed to be part of the individual's general fund of knowledge. Other problems may require specialized and technical information at a rather high level such that specific knowledge and skill in dealing with the problem and the materials are required. The abilities and skills objectives emphasize the mental processes of organizing and reorganizing material to achieve a particular purpose. The materials may be given or remembered.

2.00. Comprehension / This represents the lowest level of understanding. It refers to a type of understanding or apprehension such that the individual knows what is being communicated and can make use of the material or idea being communicated without necessarily relating it to other material or seeing its fullest implications.

2.10. Translation / Comprehension as evidenced by the care and accuracy with which the communication is paraphrased or rendered from one language or form of communication to another. Translation is judged on the basis of faithfulness and accuracy; that is, on the extent to which the material in the original communication is preserved although the form of the communication has been altered.

The ability to understand nonliteral statements (metaphor, symbolism, irony, exaggeration).
Skill in translating mathematical verbal material into symbolic statements and vice versa.

2.20. Interpretation / The explanation or summarization of a communication. Whereas translation involves an objective part-for-part rendering of a communication, interpretation involves a reordering, rearrangement, or a new view of the material.

The ability to grasp the thought of the work as a whole at any desired level of generality.
The ability to interpret various types of social data.

2.30. Extrapolation / The extension of trends or tendencies beyond the given data to determine implications, consequences, corollaries, effects, etc., which are in accordance with the conditions described in the original communication.

The ability to deal with the conclusions of a work in terms of the immediate inference made from the explicit statements.
Skill in predicting continuation of trends.

3.00. Application / The use of abstractions in particular and concrete situations. The abstractions may be in the form of general ideas, rules of procedures, or generalized methods. The abstractions may also be technical principles, ideas, and theories which must be remembered and applied.

> Application to the phenomena discussed in one paper of the scientific terms or concepts used in other papers.
> The ability to predict the probable effect of a change in a factor on a biological situation previously at equilibrium.

4.00. Analysis / The breakdown of a communication into its constituent elements or parts such that the relative hierarchy of ideas is made clear and/or the relations between the ideas expressed are made explicit. Such analyses are intended to clarify the communication, to indicate how the communication is organized, and the way in which it manages to convey its effects, as well as its basis and arrangement.

4.10. Analysis of Elements / Identification of the elements included in a communication.

> The ability to recognize unstated assumptions.
> Skill in distinguishing facts from hypotheses.

4.20. Analysis of Relationships / The connections and interactions between elements and parts of a communication.

> Ability to check the consistency of hypotheses with given information and assumptions.
> Skill in comprehending the interrelationships among the ideas in a passage.

4.30. Analysis of Organizational Principles / The organization, systematic arrangement, and structure which hold the communication together. This includes the "explicit" as well as "implicit" structure. It includes the bases, necessary arrangement, and mechanics which make the communication a unit.

> The ability to recognize form and pattern in literary or artistic works as a means of understanding their meaning.
> Ability to recognize the general techniques used in persuasive materials, such as advertising, propaganda, etc.

5.00. Synthesis / The putting together of elements and parts so as to form a whole. This involves the process of working with pieces, parts, elements, etc., and arranging and combining them in such a way as to constitute a pattern or structure not clearly there before.

5.10. Production of a Unique Communication / The development of a communication in which the writer or speaker attempts to convey ideas, feelings, and/or experiences to others.

> Skill in writing, using an excellent organization of ideas and statements.
> Ability to tell a personal experience effectively.

5.20. Production of a Plan, or Proposed Set of Operations / The development of a plan of work or the proposal of a plan of operations. The plan should satisfy requirements of the task which may be given to the student or which he may develop for himself.

Ability to propose ways of testing hypotheses.
Ability to plan a unit of instruction for a particular teaching situation.

5.30. Derivation of a Set of Abstract Relations / The development of a set of abstract relations either to classify or explain particular data of phenomena, or the deduction of propositions and relations from a set of basic propositions or symbolic representations.

Ability to formulate appropriate hypothesis based upon an analysis of factors involved, and to modify such hypothesis in the light of new factors and considerations.
Ability to make mathematical discoveries and generalizations.

6.00. Evaluation / Judgments about the value of material and methods for given purposes. Quantitative and qualitative judgments about the extent to which material and methods satisfy criteria. Use of standard of appraisal. The criteria may be those determined by the student or those which are given to him.

6.10. Judgments in Terms of Internal Evidence / Evaluation of the accuracy of a communication from such evidence as logical accuracy, consistency, and other internal criteria.

Judging by internal standards, the ability to assess general probability of accuracy in reporting facts from the care given to exactness of statement, documentation, proof, etc.
The ability to indicate logical fallacies in arguments.

6.20. Judgments in Terms of External Criterias / Evaluation of material with reference to selected or remembered criteria.

The comparison of major theories, generalizations, and facts about particular cultures. Judging by external standards, the ability to compare a work with the highest known standards in its field—especially with other works of recognized excellence.

Summary

In this first of two chapters devoted to the process of stating and operationalizing objectives, the emphasis is upon the cognitive domain. Bloom's *Taxonomy of Educational Objectives* has been the primary source for presenting a wide range of psychological objectives, including both a classification of knowledge and of skills and abilities. The perceptive reader will have noted that the two taxonomies were constructed on a simple-to-complex continuum; that is, both progress from elementary knowledges and skills to more sophisticated levels.

Also included in the chapter is a discussion of operationalizing objectives, of translating the more abstract goals into behavioral criteria that allow measurement of progress.

14 / The Affective Domain

The American Psychological Association committee assigned to write educational objectives decided upon three areas of concentration: the cognitive domain as outlined in the previous chapter, the affective domain (of attitudinal or "feeling tone" learning), and the psychomotor domain (of skills involving the combinations of physical and psychological tasks.)[1] After the cognitive domain, undertaken first perhaps because the most familiar, the committee members turned to affective objectives.

The usefulness of the first Handbook and a variety of pressures have kept us aware of the need for completing the second Handbook on the affective domain. The group of examiners responsible for the development of the cognitive domain also felt great interest in and some responsibility for preparing the second volume. A subcommittee was delegated responsibility for working on various aspects of the domain. At least six working meetings were devoted to this task. Although some progress was made, we did not feel secure enough in our results to publish the reports produced at these meetings. Several difficulties beset this work. First, there was a lack of clarity in the statements of affective objectives that we found in the literature. Second, it was difficult to find an ordering principle as simple and pervasive as that of complexity, which worked so satisfactorily in the cognitive domain. Third, few of the examiners at the college level were convinced that the development of the affective domain would make much more difference in their work or that they would find great use for it, when completed. There was no doubt that the affective domain represented a more difficult classification problem than the cognitive domain.

However, our failure to complete the affective-domain Handbook and our pessimism about the possibility of completing it satisfactorily was more than offset by the many letters we received from teachers, specialists in measurement and eval-

[1] At this writing, educational objectives for the psychomotor domain have not yet been developed.

uation, and educational research workers asking when the second Handbook would be published. It was evident that we had dropped one shoe and that the tenants in the room below were waiting for the second shoe to fall.[2]

The Basis for Affective Classification

As has already been noted, the backbone of the cognitive domain was a simple-to-complex dimension. The knowledge area began with the relatively simple act of recalling specific facts and ended with recall of theories and structures; the abilities and skills area started with comprehension and ended with the much more complex act of evaluation based upon internal and external criteria. What was to be the basis for organizing the affective domain?

[In its development] the continuum progressed from a level at which the individual is merely *aware* of a phenomenon, being *able to perceive it*. At a next level he is *willing to attend* to phenomena. At a next level he *responds* to the phenomena with a *positive feeling*. Eventually he may feel strongly enough to *go out of his way* to respond. At some point in the process he conceptualizes his behavior and feelings and organizes these conceptualizations into a structure. This structure grows in complexity as *it becomes his life outlook*.

This ordering of the components seemed to describe a process by which a given phenomenon or value passed from a level of bare awareness to a position of some power to guide or control the behavior of a person. If it passed through all stages in which it played an increasingly important role in a person's life, it would come to dominate and control certain aspects of that life as it was absorbed more and more into the internal controlling structure. This process or continuum seemed best described by a term which was heard at various times in our discussions and which has been used similarly in the literature: "internalization." This word seemed an apt description of the process by which the phenomenon or value successively and pervasively becomes a part of the individual.[3]

A Condensed Version of the Affective Domain of the Taxonomy of Educational Objectives[4]

1.0. RECEIVING (ATTENDING)

At this level we are concerned that the learner be sensitized to the existence of certain phenomena and stimuli; that is, that he be willing to receive or to attend to them. This is clearly the first and crucial step if the learner is to be properly oriented to learn what the teacher intends that he will. To indicate that this is the bottom rung of the ladder, however, is not at all to imply that the teacher is starting *de novo*. Because of previous experience (formal or informal), the student brings to each situation a point of view or set which may facilitate or hinder his recognition of the phenomena to which the teacher is trying to sensitize him.

[2] David R. Krathwohl, Benjamin S. Bloom, and B. B. Masia, *Taxonomy of Educational Objectives, Handbook II: Affective Domain* (New York: David McKay Co., Inc., 1964), pp. 12–13, reprinted by permission of the publisher.
[3] Ibid., p. 27.
[4] Ibid., pp. 176–85.

The category of *Receiving* has been divided into three subcategories to indi-cate three different levels of attending to phenomena. While the division points be-tween the subcategories are arbitrary, the subcategories do represent a continuum. From an extremely passive position or role level, we are here describing the behavior of being willing to tolerate a given stimulus, not to avoid it. Like *Awareness*, it in-volves a neutrality or suspended judgment toward the stimulus. At this level of the continuum the teacher is not concerned that the student seek it out, nor even, per-haps, that in an environment crowded with many other stimuli the learner will neces-sarily attend to the stimulus. Rather, at worst, given the opportunity to attend in a field with relatively few competing stimuli, the learner is not actively seeking to avoid it. At best, he is willing to take notice of the phenomenon and give it his attention.

> Attends (carefully) when others speak—in direct conversation on the tele-phone, in audiences.

> Appreciation (tolerance) of cultural patterns exhibited by individuals from other groups—religious, social, political, economic, national, etc.
> Increase in sensitivity to human need and pressing social problems.

1.3. CONTROLLED OR SELECTED ATTENTION

At a somewhat higher level we are concerned with a new phenomenon, the differen-tiation of a given stimulus into figure and ground at a conscious or perhaps semicon-scious level—the differentiation of aspects of a stimulus which is perceived as clearly marked off from adjacent impressions. The perception is still without tension or as-sessment, and the student may not know the technical terms or symbols with which to describe it correctly or precisely to others. In some instances it may refer not so much to the selectivity of attention as to the control of attention, so that when certain stimuli are present they will be attended to. There is an element of the learner's con-trolling the attention here, so that the favored stimulus is selected and attended to de-spite competing and distracting stimuli.

> Listens to music with some discrimination as to its mood and meaning and with some recognition of the contributions of various musical elements and instruments to the total effect.

> Alertness toward human values and judgments on life as they are recorded in literature.

2.0. RESPONDING

At this level we are concerned with responses which go beyond merely attending to the phenomenon. The student is sufficiently motivated that he is not just 1.2 *Willing to attend,* but perhaps it is correct to say that he is actively attending. As a first stage in a "learning by doing" process the student is committing himself in some small measure to the phenomena involved. This is a very low level of commitment, and we would not say at this level that this was "a value of his" or that he had "such and such an attitude." These terms belong to the next higher level that we describe. But we could say that he is doing something with or about the phenomenon besides merely perceiving it, as would be true at the next level below this of 1.3 *Controlled or se-lected attention.*

This is the category that many teachers will find best describes their "interest" objectives. Most commonly we use the term to indicate the desire that a child become sufficiently involved in or committed to a subject, phenomenon, or activity that he will seek it out and gain satisfaction from working with it or engaging in it.

2.1. ACQUIESCENCE IN RESPONDING

We might use the word "obedience" or "compliance" to describe this behavior. As both of these terms indicate, there is a passiveness so far as the initiation of the behavior is concerned, and the stimulus calling for this behavior is not subtle. Compliance is perhaps a better term than obedience, since there is more of the element of reaction to a suggestion and less of the implication of resistance or yielding unwillingly. The student makes the response, but he has not fully accepted the necessity for doing so.

> Willingness to comply with health regulations.
> Obeys the playground regulations.

2.2. WILLINGNESS TO RESPOND

The key to this level is in the term "willingness," with its implication of capacity for voluntary activity. There is the implication that the learner is sufficiently committed to exhibiting the behavior that he does, not just because of a fear of punishment, but "on his own" or voluntarily. It may help to note that the element of resistance or of yielding unwillingly, which is possibly present at the previous level, is here replaced with consent or proceeding from one's own choice.

> Acquaints himself with significant current issues in international, political, social, and economic affairs through voluntary reading and discussion.
> Acceptance of responsibility for his own health and for the protection of the health of others.

2.3 SATISFACTION IN RESPONSE

The additional element in the step beyond the *Willingness to respond* level, the consent, the assent to responding, or the voluntary response, is that the behavior is accompanied by a feeling of satisfaction, an emotional response, generally of pleasure, zest, or enjoyment. The location of this category in the hierarchy has given us a great deal of difficulty. Just where in the process of internalization the attachment of an emotional response, kick, or thrill to a behavior occurs has been hard to determine. For that matter there is some uncertainty as to whether the level of internalization at which it occurs may not depend on the particular behavior. We have even questioned whether it should be a category. If our structure is to be a hierarchy, then each category should include the behavior in the next level below it. The emotional component appears gradually through the range of internalization categories. The attempt to specify a given position in the hierarchy as *the* one at which the emotional component is added is doomed to failure.

The category is arbitrarily placed at this point in the hierarchy where it seems to appear most frequently and where it is cited as or appears to be an important component of the objectives at this level on the continuum. The category's inclusion at this point serves the pragmatic purpose of reminding us of the presence of the emotional component and its value in the building of affective behaviors. But it should not be thought of as appearing and occurring at this one point in the continuum and thus destroying the hierarchy which we are attempting to build.

> Enjoyment of self-expression in music and in arts and crafts as another means of personal enrichment.
> Finds pleasure in reading for recreation.
> Takes pleasure in conversing with many different kinds of people.

3.0. VALUING

This is the only category headed by a term which is in common use in the expression of objectives by teachers. Further, it is employed in its usual sense: that a thing, phenomenon, or behavior has worth. This abstract concept of worth is in part a result of the individual's own valuing or assessment, but it is much more a social product that has been slowly internalized or accepted and has come to be used by the student as his own criterion of worth.

Behavior categorized at this level is sufficiently consistent and stable to have taken on the characteristics of a belief or an attitude. The learner displays this behavior with sufficient consistency in appropriate situations that he comes to be perceived as holding a value. At this level, we are not concerned with the relationships among values but rather with the internalization of a set of specified, ideal values. Viewed from another standpoint, the objectives classified here are the prime stuff from which the conscience of the individual is developed into active control of behavior.

This category will be found appropriate for many objectives that use the term "attitude" (as well as, of course, "value").

An important element of behavior characterized by *Valuing* is that it is motivated, not by the desire to comply or obey, but by the individual's commitment to the underlying value guiding the behavior.

3.1. ACCEPTANCE OF A VALUE

At this level we are concerned with the ascribing of worth to a phenomenon, behavior, object, etc. The term "belief," which is defined as "the emotional acceptance of a proposition or doctrine upon what one implicitly considers adequate ground" (English and English, A *Comprehensive Dictionary of Psychological and Psychoanalytical Terms* [New York: David McKay Co., Inc.] 1958, p. 64), describes quite well what may be thought of as the dominant characteristic here. Beliefs have varying degrees of certitude. At this lowest level of *Valuing* we are concerned with the lowest levels of certainty; that is, there is more of a readiness to reevaluate one's position than at the higher levels. It is a position that is somewhat tentative.

One of the distinguishing characteristics of this behavior is consistency of response to the class of objects, phenomena, etc., with which the belief or attitude is identified. It is consistent enough so that the person is perceived by others as holding the belief or value. At the level we are describing here, he is both sufficiently consistent that others can identify the value, and sufficiently committed that he is willing to be so identified.

Continuing desire to develop the ability to speak and write effectively.

Grows in his sense of kinship with human beings of all nations.

3.2 PREFERENCE FOR A VALUE

The provision for this subdivision arose out of a feeling that there were objectives that expressed a level of internalization between the mere acceptance of a value and commitment or conviction in the usual connotation of deep involvement in an area. Behavior at this level implies not just the acceptance of a value to the point of being willing to be identified with it, but the individual is sufficiently committed to the value to pursue it, to seek it out, to want it.

Assumes responsibility for drawing reticent members of a group into conversation.

Deliberately examines a variety of viewpoints on controversial issues with a view to forming opinions about them.

Actively participates in arranging for the showing of contemporary artistic efforts.

3.3. COMMITMENT

Belief at this level involves a high degree of certainty. The ideas of "conviction" and "certainty beyond a shadow of a doubt" help to convey further the level of behavior intended. In some instances this may border on faith, in the sense of it being a firm emotional acceptance of a belief upon admittedly nonrational grounds. Loyalty to a position, group, or cause would also be classified here.

The person who displays behavior at this level is clearly perceived as holding the value. He acts to further the thing valued in some way, to extend the possibility of his developing it, to deepen his involvement with it and with the things representing it. He tries to convince others and seeks converts to his cause. There is a tension here which needs to be satisfied; action is the result of an aroused need or drive. There is a real motivation to act out the behavior.

> Devotion to those ideas and ideals which are the foundations of democracy.
> Faith in the power of reason and in methods of experiment and discussion.

4.0. ORGANIZATION

As the learner successively internalizes values, he encounters situations for which more than one value is relevant. Thus necessity arises for (a) the organization of the values into a system, (b) the determination of the interrelationships among them, and (c) the establishment of the dominant and pervasive ones. Such a system is built gradually, subject to change as new values are incorporated. This category is intended as the proper classification for objectives which describe the beginnings of the building of a value system. It is subdivided into two levels, since a prerequisite to interrelating is the conceptualization of the value in a form which permits organization. *Conceptualization* forms the first subdivision in the organization process, *Organization of a value system* the second.

While the order of the two subcategories seems appropriate enough with reference to one another, it is not so certain that 4.1 *Conceptualization of a value* is properly placed as the next level above 3.3 *Commitment.* Conceptualization undoubtedly begins at an earlier level for some objectives. Like 2.3 *Satisfaction in response,* it is doubtful that a single completely satisfactory location for this category can be found. Positioning it before 4.2 *Organization of a value system* appropriately indicates a prerequisite of such a system. It also calls attention to a component of affective growth that occurs at least by this point on the continuum but may begin earlier.

4.1. CONCEPTUALIZATION OF A VALUE

In the previous category, 3.0 *Valuing,* we noted that consistency and stability are integral characteristics of the particular value or belief. At this level (4.1) the quality of abstraction or conceptualization is added. This permits the individual to see how the value relates to those that he already holds or to new ones that he is coming to hold.

Conceptualization will be abstract, and in this sense it will be symbolic. But the symbols need not be verbal symbols. Whether conceptualization first appears at this point on the affective continuum is a moot point, as noted above.

> Attempts to identify the characteristics of an art object which he admires.
> Forms judgments as to the responsibility of society for conserving human and material resources.

4.2. ORGANIZATION OF A VALUE SYSTEM

Objectives properly classified here are those which require the learner to bring together a complex of values, possibly disparate values, and to bring these into an ordered relationship with one another. Ideally, the ordered relationship will be one which is harmonious and internally consistent. This is, of course, the goal of such objectives, which seek to have the student formulate a philosophy of life. In actuality, the integration may be something less than entirely harmonious. More likely the relationship is better described as a kind of dynamic equilibrium which is, in part, dependent upon those portions of the environment which are salient at any point in time. In many instances the organization of values may result in their synthesis into a new value or value complex of a higher order.

> Weighs alternative social policies and practices against the standards of the public welfare rather than the advantage of specialized and narrow interest groups.
> Develops a plan for regulating his rest in accordance with the demands of his activities.

5.0. CHARACTERIZATION BY A VALUE OR VALUE COMPLEX

At this level of internalization the values already have a place in the individual's value hierarchy, are organized into some kind of internally consistent system, have controlled the behavior of the individual for a sufficient time that he has adapted to behaving this way; and an evocation of the behavior no longer arouses emotion or affect except when the individual is threatened or challenged.

The individual acts consistently in accordance with the values he has internalized at this level, and our concern is to indicate two things: (a) the generalization of this control to so much of the individual's behavior that he is described and characterized as a person by these pervasive controlling tendencies, and (b) the integration of these beliefs, ideas, and attitudes into a total philosophy or world view. These two aspects constitute the subcategories.

5.1. GENERALIZED SET

The generalized set is that which gives an internal consistency to the system of attitudes and values at any particular moment. It is selective responding at a very high level. It is sometimes spoken of as a determining tendency, an orientation toward phenomena, or a predisposition to act in a certain way. The generalized set is a response to a highly generalized phenomena. It is a persistent and consistent response to a family of related situations or objects. It may often be an unconscious set which guides action without conscious forethought. The generalized set may be thought of as closely related to the idea of an attitude cluster, where the commonality is based on behavioral characteristics rather than the subject or object of the attitude. A generalized set is a basic orientation which enables the individual to reduce and order the complex world about him and to act consistently and effectively in it.

> Readiness to revise judgments and to change behavior in the light of evidence.
> Judges problems and issues in terms of situations, issues, purposes, and consequences involved, rather than in terms of fixed, dogmatic precepts or emotionally wishful thinking.

5.2. CHARACTERIZATION

This, the peak of the internalization process, includes those objectives which are broadest with respect both to the phenomena covered and to the range of behavior which they comprise. Thus, here are found those objectives which concern one's view of the universe, one's philosophy of life, one's *Weltanschauung*—a value system having as its object the whole of what is known or knowable.

Objectives categorized here are more than generalized sets in the sense that they involve a greater inclusiveness and, within the group of attitudes, behaviors, beliefs, or ideas, an emphasis on internal consistency. Though this internal consistency may not always be exhibited behaviorally by the students toward whom the objective is directed, since we are categorizing teachers' objectives, this consistency feature will always be a component of *Characterization* objectives.

As the title of the category implies, these objectives are so encompassing that they tend to characterize the individual almost completely.

Develops for regulation of one's personal and civic life a code of behavior based on ethical principles consistent with democratic ideals.
Develops a consistent philosophy of life.

Relationship of Cognitive and Affective Goals

The separate handling of the cognitive and affective goals may seem to imply an unrelatedness between cognitive and affective goals, but the authors of the taxonomy maintain such is not the case.

The reason the two domains were presented as though they were independent are several: educators have traditionally made the separation, and analysis of the two domains is greatly facilitated by a separate treatment. The authors argue that there may be pure examples of cognitive or affective goals (such as 2 + 2 = 4 or the emotional response to a work of art) but that these are not typical. More usually, cognitions have affective tone, which means, of course, that when the teacher defines objectives, the realistic definition consists of both the cognitive and affective domains.

For example, in a high-school class the objectives in a unit on political power might be:

1.25. KNOWLEDGE OF METHODOLOGY (COGNITIVE DOMAIN)

Knowledge of the methods of inquiry, techniques, and procedures employed in a particular subject field. . . .

4.30. ANALYSIS OF ORGANIZATIONAL PRINCIPLES (COGNITIVE DOMAIN)

The organization, systematic arrangement, and structure which hold the communication [the concept, political power] together . . . [including] the bases, necessary arrangement, and mechanics which make the communication a unit.

1.2. WILLINGNESS TO RECEIVE (AFFECTIVE DOMAIN)

. . . we are describing here the behavior of being willing to tolerate a given stimulus [the concept, political power], not to avoid it.[5]

Each of these sets of objectives would be operationalized differently, and appropriate measures would have to be developed. The point is that objectives ought to be phrased both in terms of cognitive goals (knowledge, skills, and abilities) and affective goals.

How Do You Know You're Reaching Your Objectives with Students

In both the cognitive and affective taxonomies there has been described a span of psychological objectives for students in the classroom, and the

[5] Ibid., pp. 203, 204, 107.

authors have given some hints of ways one might find out if the objectives have been reached. But more needs to be said about operationalizing goals, for the task of translating objectives into ways of measuring them is not easy.

Since one cannot measure what is "deposited" in another's head, what is learned can be determined only by observing some aspect of the student's performance: in paper-pencil tests, behavioral patterns or styles, self-reports, reports by others, and so on. In the cognitive domain, for example, translation involves faithful rendering from one language or communication mode to another. For young children, translation could consist of acting out a story read to them; for junior-highs it could consist of expressing what is meant in a captionless political cartoon; for unobtrusive measures, it could consist of the outcroppings of a researcher's own creativity designed to test attitudes or interests, often through contrived experimental situations where the participant does not know he is being observed or measured (few prescriptions can be offered here because creativity cannot be prescribed).

The process of stating goals and operationalizing those goals is the limb on which many a researcher places himself for the remainder of his research days. By now you should have no illusion that there can be a fixed set of rules that provide the security (if, indeed, there is security) of an errorless plan. As shaky as the limb may be, it is nonetheless an exhilarating challenge to one's problem-solving ability.

Summary

The two chapters of Part III present a wide range of possible psychological objectives and reemphasize the operationalization process. It is assumed in a text such as this, devoted to deliberate behavioral change, that a statement of objectives *before* the teaching process begins is the sine qua non for successful teaching.

Both taxonomies are based upon a simple-to-complex dimension; both must be part of the objectives in any teaching endeavor; each involves a discriminably different set of behaviors.

Not every single occurrence initiated by the teacher must be in some way related to a previously determined objective—a teacher could hardly be expected to be that self-conscious—but, in general, learning activities should be related to specific objectives that can be measured in ways meeting the criteria of all good measurement as described in Chapter 1.

IV / ANALYTICAL TOOLS

How to Handle Data

A brief review of what has gone before should indicate an appropriate rationale for what is to follow.

The first three parts provide guidelines for gathering data. In the early chapters some of the rules of scientific investigation were proffered, with emphasis on such concepts as validity, reliability, selective perception, and the need for measurement. Discussions of standard social-behavioral-science tools—observation, interviewing, sociometry—were followed by the presentation of a technique for behavioral modification and a section on objectives and their operationalization. In one way or another, the serious student ought now to have methods for compiling and to have developed a discriminating eye for data that approximate the quality of science. Were the text to end here, it would be to provide you with intricate and reasonably sensitive instruments but with only gross instructions on their use. The subtle but important nuances of what can be done with data would be lost. Hence this final part on ways to treat and manipulate quantified data collected in a manner compatible with science.

Experience in having taught graphing and rudimentary statistics leaves one with a kind of damned-if-you-do, damned-if-you-don't prospect. Many students go into shock as the instructor utters the term "statistics," and they soon bastardize it to "sadistics." For some reason even the very confident lose their cool at the first sight of a correlational formula. On the other hand, some students, usually a small minority, are not fazed by mathematical symbols and even look forward to the exactitude of the process. Given the task of writing this necessary section on statistics, one can hardly change the aversive response to mathematics that the majority of students have built up over the years of confusion, and yet the obvious alternative of providing a mathematical pablum would scarcely appeal to the more sophisticated.

The solution seems to be an informal programming beginning at a very simple level and progressing to the more complex. This procedure will allow some readers to go through the material rapidly, others more slowly, but everyone will have the opportunity to start with the elementary concepts and progress to the more difficult. At various stages throughout the section are review problems, each followed by its solution. Obviously, one of the best ways to learn statistics is to *do* statistics. It is strongly recommended that you complete *all* of each problem before you check the answers.

Chapter 15 of this section is devoted to graphing, the visual presentation of data in condensed form. Chapter 16 describes several ways of reducing data mathematically to single concepts; for example, the mean or arithmetic average is a derivative for describing a group's performance, for boiling down many performance scores to a single score. Chapter 17 is devoted to ways of determining the strength of the relationship between two variables, of dealing with such questions as "Is there a relationship between students' grades and their measured I.Q.'s?"

But, by all means, don't become a victim of symbol shock.

15 / Descriptive Graphing

One of the characteristics of science—indeed, of many fields of knowledge —is the seeking of *parsimony*. Parsimony involves boiling down extraneous details to capture the essence of whatever is being studied. A classic example is Einstein's $E = MC^2$, a keystone formula in his theory of relativity, encompassing years of experimental work and thought, all of which is succinctly caught up in a three-term expression. It is typical of all such essences that they are very convenient for the cognoscente to use but often confusing to the uninitiated.

A graph, for example, represents "pictorially" the product of an investigation, and for those who understand the nature of graphic pictures it is the most expeditious means of presenting a lot with a little. Unfortunately, for those who do not understand the graph is an ugly intrusion. This chapter introduces the method of graphic presentation so that graphs may be understood as the important tools they are to the researcher.

In this chapter and the two that follow, several terms will be used frequently.

Variables

The things that scientists observe are called *variables* or *variates*. Objects, whether persons or things, which can assume different values, are variables. For example, with a thermometer, the variable is presence or absence of heat; in studying the intelligence of a child, the variable is I.Q.; in gathering data on the number of children in a rural community, the variable is birth rate. Anything that can be measured and that can change in value is a potential variable in scientific investigation.

Variables can be subdivided into *discrete* and *continuous* types. A discrete variable can assume only certain values. The number of cows in a field is a discrete variable: there may be no cows, one cow, two cows, three cows, but there could hardly be three and one-half cows. Nominal measures are always discrete because there can never be a part of a value; the variable either exists in toto or it does not.

A continuous variable can be separated into parts without violating one's sense of logic. Height is a continuous variable because no matter how fine the measure (by feet, inches, twelfths of an inch, and so on) it can always be made finer by a smaller unit of measure. Similarly, time is a continuous variable because it can be identified in terms of years, months, weeks, days, hours, seconds, and so on. Ordinal and interval-ratio measures are continuous variables because they can always be considered in larger or smaller terms.

The Abscissa and the Ordinate

Each graph has at least two elements: the horizontal dimension is the *abscissa,* and the vertical dimension is the *ordinate,* as shown in figure 23.

The space in between the abscissa and ordinate is the area for plotting the relationship between the two dimensions. A teacher may want to make a graph representing the performance of her class on a social studies test. In this case, the two dimensions are the scores arranged by *class intervals* (not to be confused with the "class" of children) and *frequency,* or how many fell into each class interval. Convention dictates that the abscissa consist of the scores arranged by class interval and the ordinate consist of the frequency or number of children who performed in each interval, as in figure 24.

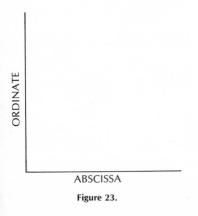

Figure 23.

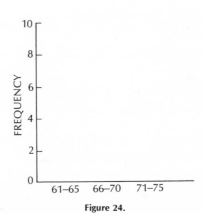

Figure 24.

If six student scores were in the class interval of 60–65, the combination of frequency and class interval would be represented graphically by that point of the intersection of six and 60–65, as in figure 25.

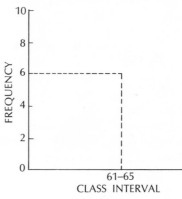

Figure 25.

Table 2

Score Interval	Tally	Frequency (f)
91–95	I	1
86–90	IIII	4
81–85	╫╫ IIII	9
76–80	╫╫ III	8
71–75	╫╫ I	6
66–70	╫╫ I	6
61–65	II	2
		36

The Histogram

Also known as a *rectangular frequency polygon,* the *histogram* is constructed from a frequency distribution in the following manner. Rectangles are erected on the abscissa using as the width the class interval and as the height the frequency in each class interval. Figure 26 is a histogram of the data on the achievement test from table 1.

The Frequency Polygon

Another graphic form is the *frequency polygon,* which is made in the same fashion as a histogram except that dots with a connecting line are used instead of rectangular bars. Figure 27 represents the same data in a frequency polygon.

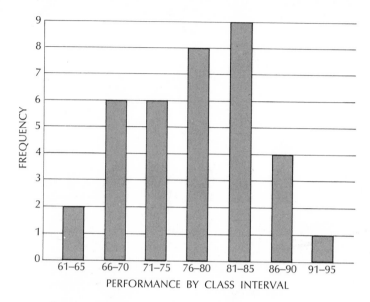

Figure 26. Performance scores for thirty-six students on achievement test.

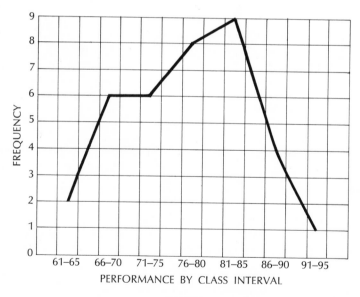

PERFORMANCE BY CLASS INTERVAL

Figure 27.

The Three-Quarter Rule

Without guidelines, graphs can easily present an inaccurate picture of data. In figure 28 two histograms have been drawn using the same data. By changing the scales for the abscissa, the impression is given that graph B contains fewer pronounced differences than graph A.

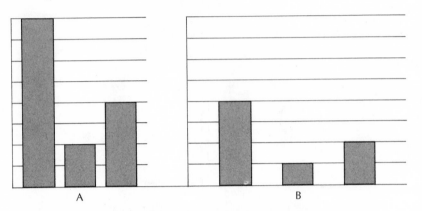

A   B

Figure 28. Two histograms based upon identical data.

A convention known as the *three-quarter high rule* has been agreed upon by most statisticians to avoid misleading graphs. This rule stipulates that the interval with the highest frequency be approximately three-quarters the length of the abscissa. The histogram and frequency polygon from table 1 follow the three-quarter rule. The interval with the greatest frequency (81–85) is three-quarters the length of the combined intervals.

The procedure for constructing a graph that satisfies the three-quarter rule is:

    a) Decide on the length of the abscissa. This is an arbitrary decision based upon the number of class intervals. See figure 29.

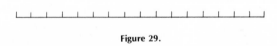

Figure 29.

    b) Determine ¾ of the abscissa. See figure 30.

Figure 30. ¾ of 16 units = 12 units.

c) This ¾ length automatically becomes the height of the class interval with the greatest frequency. See figure 31.

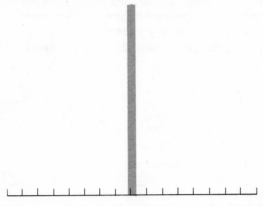

Figure 31.

d) Draw in the ordinate and section into units proportionate to the frequency shown by the largest class interval. See figure 32.

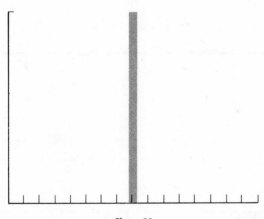

Figure 32.

To express the same process numerically, if the abscissa is to be 10 centimeters[1] (about 4 inches), the height of the ordinate would be 7.5 cm (¾ of 10 cm = 7.5 cm). And if the tallest interval (which will automatically be 7.5 cm) has a frequency of 15, the number of centimeters representing each frequency is .5 cm $\left(\dfrac{7.5}{15} = .5 \text{ cm}\right)$.

[1] Use the metric system of measurement rather than that of inches. The metric ruler is far superior when one has to work with fractions and decimals.

Problem: Making a Graph

The problem below includes all the operations considered up to this point in the chapter. The correct answers follow.

The following raw data comes from test scores of a college class in psychology. Prepare a frequency tabulation and construct a histogram following the three-quarter rule.

70	72	73	74	74	75
81	84	74	86	87	88
89	85	83	83	80	79
91	91	92	94	94	92
91	96	91	94	96	93

Answers to Graph Problem

Frequency Distribution:

Class Interval	*Tally*	*Frequency*
70–74.9	~~IIII~~ I	6
75–79.9	II	2
80–84.9	IIII	4
85–89.9	~~IIII~~ I	6
90–94.9	~~IIII~~ ~~IIII~~	10
95–99.9	II	2

Histogram:

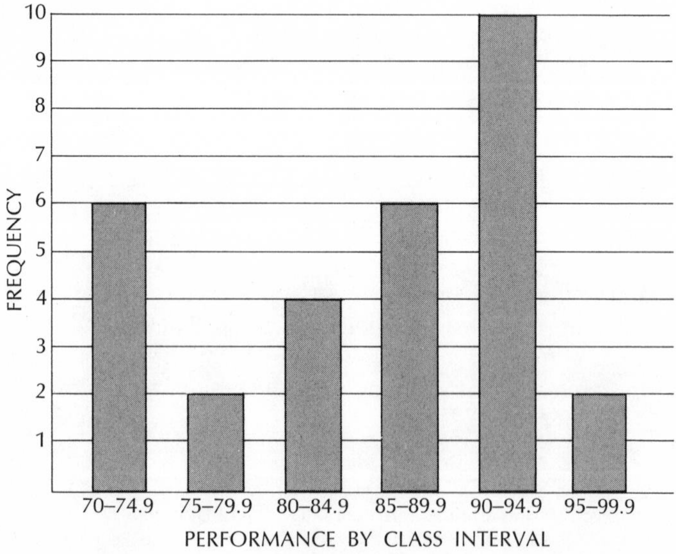

Bivariate Distributions

The graphs of figures 26 and 27, for scores for thirty-six students, are based upon only one measure, in this case test scores. These are *univariate* graphs; that is, only one variable or score was used to develop the graphic picture. A *bivariate* graph shows two variables (scores) for each person on the single graph. Bivariate graphs indicate relationships between two measures and by the shape of the plot can give a great deal of information to the investigator. Let us say that twenty-five students are ranked by their teacher on academic performance and that these rankings are compared to rankings of the students based upon achievement test scores. That is, the teacher is asked to arrange the students, according to performance in class, in order of most capable student, second most capable, and so on. These ranks are then compared to the students' performances on a standardized achievement test arranged in order of highest scoring student, second highest, and so on. These two rankings are compared side by side in table 3.

Table 3

Student	Teacher's Perception (converted to rank order)	Achievement Scores (converted to rank order)
A	1	5
B	2	3
C	3	2
D	4	1
E	5	4
F	6	6
G	7	9
H	8	7
I	9	8
J	10	12
K	11	10
L	12	11
M	13	16
N	14	14
O	15	15
P	16	13
Q	17	17
R	18	19
S	19	18
T	20	24
U	21	20
W	22	21
X	23	23
Y	24	22
Z	25	25

The two rank scores for each student are plotted by finding the intersection of the two scores and placing a single dot. For example, let us designate the abscissa as the teacher's perception and the ordinate as the achievement scores. In the case of student A, you count one unit to the right on the abscissa and five units up on the ordinate, as in figure 33. The plotting for student B would be treated similarly, counting two units to the right on the abscissa and three units up on the ordinate. Complete the plotting by filling in the points for each student on figure 33.[2]

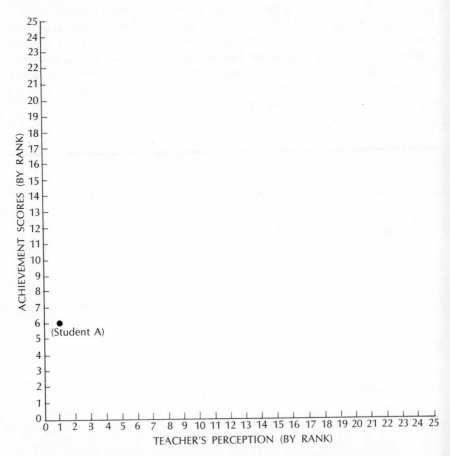

Figure 33. Bivariate plotting of two ranked measures, teacher's ranking, and ranked achievement scores.

[2] Notice that the three-quarter rule is not followed in bivariate plotting. The three-quarter rule is applicable only to the histogram and the frequency polygon. Bivariate plotting consists of plots of *two* different measures on the same individuals; histograms and frequency polygons consist of *one* measure per individual and the frequency associated with each class interval.

Configurations on Bivariate Plotting

The data on achievement and the teacher's perception indicates that in this case the relationship is quite high. That is, the teacher tends to perceive students' academic performance in much the same way as measured on the achievement test. When two measures are such that high values on one are associated with high values on the second and low values on one are associated with low values on the second, the relationship is described as *positive*. Graphically, high positive relationships form a cluster of dots bisecting the abscissa and ordinate, as in figure 34. Similarly, when high values on one measure are associated with low scores on the second measure and low scores on one are associated with high scores on the second, the relationship is said to be inverse or *negative*, and plotted the graph looks like figure 35. When there is little relationship between first and second measures, the plotted dots fall indiscriminately between the abscissa and ordinate, as in figure 36. Bivariate graphing will take on more meaning in Chapter 17, when correlation, a statistical process for measuring the strength of the relationship of two variables, is considered.

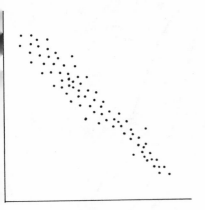

Figure 34.

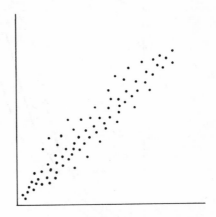

Figure 35.

Using Graphs to Discover Change

One of the primary tasks of the teacher is to bring about change in performance. If the changes are quantifiable, they can be converted to a graph, an excellent means of "seeing" the kinds of shifts that have occurred. Let us say that teacher A has plotted class performance on several forms of a standardized math test at the beginning, middle, and end of the semester. One would

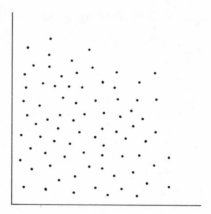

Figure 36.

expect change, but until the scores are plotted as in figure 37, it is difficult to tell the shape of the change.

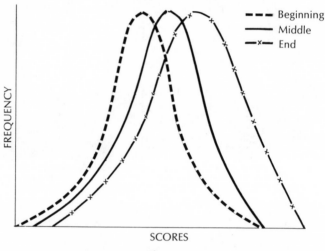

SCORES

Figure 37.

  Notice, however, that the data came from *several forms of a standardized test*. It is essential when two sets of scores are compared on a histogram or frequency polygon that they be based upon a scale common to each measure. For example, it would be misleading to compare graphically the readings from a centigrade and Fahrenheit thermometer: each is based upon a different scale, and to compare them without conversion to a common scale would be misleading.

Summary

The elements presented in this chapter are variables, discrete and continuous; graphic dimensions, ordinate and abscissa; and class interval. The steps in constructing a graph are:

1. Selecting a class interval.
2. Constructing a frequency tabulation.
3. Converting the frequency tabulation to a histogram or frequency polygon.
4. Following the three-quarter rule.

Bivariate distributions have been considered, and a means for graphing has been demonstrated. The chapter includes interpretation of various graphic pictures, defining the strength of the relationship between the two variables, and one method for using the graph to discover changes in performance.

16 / Statistics 1

Statistics hardly rate as one of the more popular academic endeavors on the undergraduate campus. For some reason, probably because mathematics has been so poorly taught, statistics call up an image of senseless flounderings in a morass of symbols and mathematical abstractions that have little or no relevance to the "real" world. Unfortunately, students rarely have the opportunity to use statistics in the proper context, as an important and useful tool to gain deeper insight into and knowledge about a broader problem, because too often statistics have been taught as an end unto themselves. In this and the next chapter statistics are placed in the more realistic context of an actual classroom of twenty-nine students in a sixth-grade suburban classroom near a large midwestern city.

Fortunately, you do not have to be a mathematical genius to understand what is to be presented. The degree of computational sophistication required by the next two chapters is little more than that of a high school algebra course. More to the point, comprehending the statistics presented here requires more persistence than mathematical expertise. It is important that you stay with the problems and concepts until they are mastered. If so, statistics will be found to be one of the most powerful classroom tools within the social and behavioral sciences.

The Grammar of Mathematical Notation

In an unusually well-written statistics text, Richard P. Runyon and Audrey Haber introduce a mathematical "grammar" for understanding the language of statistics:

It is not surprising to learn that many students become so involved in the forest of mathematical symbols, formulas, and operations that they fail to realize that mathematics has a form of grammar which closely parallels the spoken language. Thus, mathematics has its nouns, adjectives, verbs, and adverbs.

MATHEMATICAL NOUNS

In mathematics, we commonly use symbols to stand for quantities. The notation we shall employ most commonly in statistics to represent quantity (or a score) is X, although we shall occasionally employ Y. In addition X and Y are employed to identify variables; for example, if weight and height are two variables in a study, X might be used to represent weight and Y to represent height. Another frequently used "noun" is the symbol N which represents the number of scores or quantities with which we are dealing. Thus, if we have ten quantities,

$$N = 10$$

MATHEMATICAL ADJECTIVES

When we want to modify a mathematical noun, to identify it more precisely, we commonly employ subscripts. Thus, if we have a series of scores or quantities, we may represent them as X_1, X_2, X_3, etc. We shall also frequently encounter X_i, in which the subscript may take on any value that we desire.

MATHEMATICAL VERBS

Notations which direct the reader to do something have the same characteristics as verbs in the spoken language. One of the most important "verbs" is the symbol . . . Σ. This notation directs us to sum all quantities or scores following the symbol. Thus,

$$\Sigma\, (X_1,\, X_2,\, X_3,\, X_4,\, X_5)$$

indicates that we should add together all these quantities from X_1 through X_5. Other "verbs" we shall encounter frequently are $\sqrt{}$, directing us to find the square root and exponents (X^a), which tell us to raise a quantity to the indicated power. In mathematics, mathematical verbs are commonly referred to as operators.

MATHEMATICAL ADVERBS

These are notations which, as in spoken language, modify the verbs. We shall frequently find that the summation signs are modified by adverbial notations. Let us imagine that we want to indicate that the following quantities are to be added:

$$X_1 + X_2 + X_3 + X_4 + X_5 \ldots + X_N.$$

Symbolically, we would represent these operations as follows:

$$\sum_{i=1}^{N} X_i$$

The notations above and below the summation sign indicate that i takes on the successive values from 1, 2, 3, 4, 5 up to N. Stated verbally, the notation reads: We should sum all quantities of X starting with $i = 1$ (that is X_1) and proceeding through to $i = N$ (that is, X_N).[1]

---

[1] Richard P. Runyon and Audrey Haber, *Fundamentals of Behavioral Statistics* (Reading, Mass.: Addison-Wesley Publishing Co., Inc., 1967), pp. 10–11, reprinted by permission of the publisher.

A Data Pool for This and the Next Chapter

As previously mentioned, this and the next chapter will be based on data gathered from a class of twenty-nine sixth-grade children in a suburban school. The scores in table 4 come from a standard I.Q. test administered at the beginning of the school year.

Table 4   I.Q. Scores of a Class of Twenty-nine Students in a Suburban Sixth-Grade Class

87	97	103	106	108	116
90	98	103	106	110	118
91	100	103	107	111	122
95	101	104	107	112	128
95	102	105	107	113	

A Graphic Picture of the Class

A frequency distribution was made from the data of table 4. In view of the distribution of the data, it seemed appropriate to use class intervals of five. See table 5.

Table 5   Frequency Distribution of I.Q. Scores of Twenty-nine Students

Class Interval	Tally	Frequency
85–89	I	1
90–94	II	2
95–99	IIII	4
100–104	⊞ II	7
105–109	⊞ II	7
110–114	IIII	4
115–119	II	2
120–124	I	1
125–129	I	1

The frequency distribution was converted to a frequency polygon, figure 38, for a graphic picture of the group. Notice that in the development of the frequency polygon the three-quarter rule was followed.

Reducing Data to Meaningful Concepts

In figure 38 the I.Q. data has been organized to give a better picture of the sixth-grade class. There are other, more succinct ways to describe the class than by frequency polygon. A frequency distribution and a frequency polygon

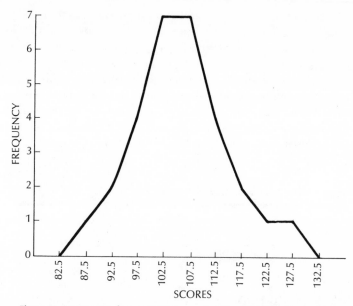

Figure 38. Frequency polygon of I.Q. scores of a class of twenty-nine students.

are adequate as far as they go, but they do not allow very powerful quantitative statements about the class. Other descriptive means are needed to characterize a group in a way that can be used within a mathematical system.

Measures of Central Tendency

The *arithmetic mean* is calculated by adding all the scores and dividing the sum by the number of scores. The resulting number, sometimes called an average, is simply a parsimonious way to describe the group. But, more important, the mean can be used in ways other than description.

Mathematically, the formula for deriving the mean is:

$$\bar{X} = \frac{X_1 + X_2 + X_3 \ldots X_N}{N} = \frac{\Sigma X}{N}$$

in which

$\bar{X}$ (called "X bar") is the mean.
N is the number of scores.
Σ is the mathematical notation for sum.

Calculation of the mean of the I.Q. scores gives:

$$\bar{X} = \frac{\Sigma X}{N} = \frac{3045}{29} = 105$$

(3045 is the sum of the X column, and 29 is the number in the class.)

What does a mean of 105 imply? As a descriptive term of the group of numbers, the mean states that 105 is the point within the scores about which the summed deviations from the mean are equal to zero. That is, if one were to subtract the mean I.Q. from each individual I.Q. score and sum the deviations paying attention to the negative and positive sign, the result would be zero. The mean, then, is the "balance point" within the range of numbers. Notice that the sum of the negative deviations from the mean is equal to the sum of the positive deviations from the mean. See table 6.

Table 6   The Mean as a Balance of Deviations

X	$\bar{X}$	$X-\bar{X}$	
87	105	−18	
90	105	−15	
91	105	−14	
95	105	−10	
95	105	−10	
97	105	− 8	
98	105	− 7	
100	105	− 5	−101
101	105	− 4	
102	105	− 3	
103	105	− 2	
103	105	− 2	
103	105	− 2	
104	105	− 1	
105	105	0	(Mean)
106	105	1	
106	105	1	
107	105	2	
107	105	2	
107	105	2	
108	105	3	
110	105	5	101
111	105	6	
112	105	7	
113	105	8	
116	105	11	
118	105	13	
122	105	17	
128	105	23	
3045		0	

It can be seen that the mean is affected by extreme numbers. For example, two sets of identical numbers would obviously yield the same mean, but if one of the numbers is changed in the set, there is a corresponding effect on the mean, as shown in table 7.

Table 7

	A	B
	6	6
	4	4
	5	5
	6	6
	7	7
	8	26
	36	54
	$\bar{X} = 6$	$\bar{X} = 9$

In the I.Q. data in table 4 there are no extreme scores. Were the 128 score changed to 160, the mean would change from 105 to 106.1.

The Median

The nonstatistical definition of the term *median* is "being in the middle." Translated to statistics, the median is that point in a frequency distribution with half the scores below and half the scores above when the data is arranged in descending order. With twenty-nine students in the class, the median from the data of table 4 is the score of the child who has fourteen scores below and fourteen scores above him. Counting down fifteen from the lowest score or up fifteen from the highest score gives a median score of 105. In this case the median is the same as the mean.

A characteristic of the median that distinguishes it from the mean is its insensitivity to extreme scores. Therefore, the median sometimes describes central tendency better since the mean is affected by extreme scores. For example, if the mean were used to describe the annual income of nine residents in a city block, the presence of one resident who was strikingly different from the others would lead to a false impression of the central tendency of the block's income. See table 8. Obviously the median income is more typical of the nine residents than is the mean.

Table 8

Resident	Income
A	$1,555
B	2,000
C	2,050
D	2,160
E	3,000
F	3,050
G	4,000
H	6,000
I	50,000
Mean = $8,201.6	
Median = $3,000	

When the number of cases is even, the median is the arithmetic mean of the two middle values. Adding to the example of annual income another resident, whose income is $2,025 per year, as in table 9, the median is the arithmetic mean between the fifth and sixth income levels, as shown in table 10.

Table 9

Resident	Income
A	$1,555
B	2,000
X	2,025
C	2,050
D	2,160
E	3,000
F	3,050
G	4,000
H	6,000
I	50,000

Table 10

$3,000	6th highest income
2,160	5th highest income
5,160	

$$\frac{\$5,160}{2} = \$2,580 \text{ median}$$

The Mode

One of the meanings of the French word *mode* is "popular custom or style." In statistics the mode is the score that occurs with the greatest frequency. Consequently, the mode is less an arithmetic or quantitative measure and more a measure of inspection. In the I.Q. data of table 4, the mode is 103 and 107. This is a bimodal distribution because two numbers appear with the greatest frequency.

Problem: Calculation of Mean, Median, Mode

From the raw data below, calculate the mean, the median, and the mode.

70
81
89
91
91
72
84
85
91
96
73
74
83
92
91
74
86
83
94
94
74
87
80
94
96
75
88
79
92
93

Answer: Calculation of Mean, Median, Mode

Step 1. Arrange data in ascending order

70
72
73
74
74
74
75
79
80
81
83
83
84
85
86
87
88
89
91
91
91
91
92
92
93
94
94
94
96
96
$\overline{\Sigma2552}$

Calculation of Mean

$$\overline{X} = \frac{\Sigma X}{N}$$

$$\overline{X} = \frac{2552}{30}$$

$$\overline{X} = 85.07$$

Calculation of Median

Since $N = 30$, the median is to be found between the top 15 scores and the low 15 scores. Counting down (and up) indicates the median is between 86 and 87. Splitting the difference gives a median of 86.5.

Calculation of Mode

Since the mode is that set of scores appearing most often in the distribution, the mode is 91.

Choosing the Measure for Central Tendency

The three measures of central tendency—mean, median, and mode—have various advantages and disadvantages. In general, the mean is most useful because of its sensitivity and, as will be considered in detail later, because it can be used in more sophisticated statistical analysis than the median or mode. There are conditions such as the example of income on a city block where the mean does not describe as well as the median. The median is superior to the mean in accommodating extreme scores in the distribution or in handling a lack of data for one or several members. This latter case of missing data is actually one of extreme scores because a lack of data constitutes the extreme score of zero. For example, say that several students in a class have not been tested for an I.Q. score, but you still want to describe the class without excluding the missing members. The median could be more appropriate than the mean because the inflated N would give a smaller mean than is characteristic or descriptive of the class. The mode is rarely used in behavioral sciences because of its gross descriptive qualities. Only when a rough, quick estimate is desired is the mode of much value.

A more thorough practice for measures of central tendency is to report all three statistics rather than one. The combination of the three measures obviously gives a more accurate description of a group than does a single measure. Thus the I.Q. data from table 4 has three statistics of central tendency:

Mean = 105
Median = 105
Mode = 103 and 107

Variability Around the Mean

Measures of central tendency reduce a lot of data to several descriptive concepts. But measures of central tendency are inadequate to describe a group comprehensively. The amount of information they give is important but limited. It is like the man who was seen running barefoot across the ice with his hat on fire. When asked how he felt, he shouted, "On the average I feel okay." Averages are not always the best way to describe one's condition.

Say that a high school teacher compared the performances of two classes in history on the same examination. Intuitively, the teacher had the feeling that there would be differences in performance. One of the classes was difficult to teach because of the wide range of "history talent"; the other was a joy because most of the students were similar in ability. By comparison of their mean performances on the test, however, the teacher discovered little difference between the groups: of a possible 140 points on the test, class A had a mean of 82, class B had a mean of 83. Determination of median gave similar data: class A had a median of 81.5 and class B had one of 82.7. Similarly, the mode described the two groups alike: the score with the greatest frequency for each class was 82. The teacher was not satisfied and checked the calculations, assuming a mistake had been made. The data remained the same, however, even with several recalculations.

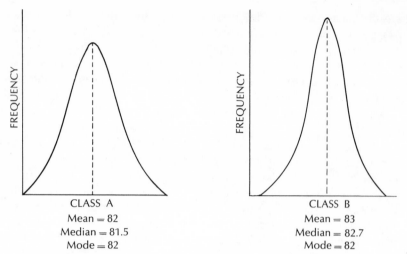

CLASS A
Mean = 82
Median = 81.5
Mode = 82

CLASS B
Mean = 83
Median = 82.7
Mode = 82

Figure 39. Comparison of two groups with similar central tendencies but different variability.

Our persistent teacher decided to develop a graphic picture of the groups and constructed a frequency polygon for each. This latter step began to turn up differences, as figure 39 shows. The teacher's initial hunch that there were differences between the classes seems to be borne out. Class A did possess a wider range of "history talent" than class B. Or, to put it in statistical terms, there was more dispersion around the mean in class A than in Class B. Comparatively, scores of class A were heterogeneous (mixed); scores of class B were homogeneous (similar). If description is confined to measures of central tendency, there is little difference shown between the groups. With the addition of the measure of variability, the groups become strikingly different. It is important, then, that a measure of variation be introduced to increase one's interpretive power over data.

The statistical measure about to be explained is one of the measures of dispersion (variability) around the mean. But before *mean deviation* is considered a brief review statement about the mean must be made. You will remember that the mean is usually the most sensitive describer of central tendency. In order to capitalize upon that sensitivity, the mean deviation is a mathematical technique based upon the mean. It is computed by subtracting the mean from each score, summing variations around the mean, and taking a mean of the sum of variation.

Recall that the sum of the deviations from the mean for all scores is zero (see table 6). In mean deviation it is the *average* of the deviations from the mean, rather than the mean, that is of importance. Consequently, there is no need to pay attention to the negative and positive signs in the $(X-\bar{X})$ column because the concern is with *how much* deviation there is rather than with the negative or positive direction of the deviation. The formula for mean deviation is:

Mean Deviation $= \dfrac{\Sigma(X-\bar{X})}{N}$

Using the data from table 4, the process for calculating mean deviation is shown in table 11.

Table 11   Calculation of Mean Deviation of I.Q. Scores from a Sixth-Grade Class

X	$(X-\bar{X})$	
87	18	
90	15	
91	14	
95	10	
95	10	
97	8	
98	7	
100	5	
101	4	
102	3	
103	2	
103	2	
103	2	$MD = \dfrac{\Sigma(X-\bar{X})}{N}$
104	1	
105	0	
106	1	$MD = \dfrac{202}{29}$
106	1	
107	2	$MD = 6.97$
107	2	
107	2	
108	3	
110	5	
111	6	
112	7	
113	8	
116	11	
118	13	
122	17	
128	23	
3045	202	

$$\bar{X} = \frac{3045}{29} = 105$$

From table 11 the result, 6.97, states that one description of variability in I.Q. for the twenty-nine members of the class is within the range of I.Q. points 6.97 plus or minus the mean. That is, the span of scores from 98.1 to 111.9 describes the average deviation from the mean. It follows that the larger the mean deviation, the greater the dispersion of scores around the mean; the smaller the mean deviation, the less dispersion around the mean.

There are several characteristics about mean deviation which need to be stated:

1. The value of mean deviation is determined by the value of each item in the series.
2. Mean deviation can be computed using either the mean or the median as measures of central tendency. Obviously the median is preferable when the median is a better describer of the central tendency of the scores.

Standard Deviation

Another form of measuring variability that is more generally used in statistics is *standard deviation*. Standard deviation has several advantages over mean deviation, not the least of which is that as part of a mathematical system it can be used in more advanced statistics. A full explanation of the meaning of standard deviation goes beyond the scope of this text. Suffice it to say here that standard deviation like mean deviation is a measure of dispersion around the mean, but unlike mean deviation standard deviation is more affected by extreme scores in the frequency distribution.

One way to derive standard deviation is by an elaboration of mean deviation. The mean is subtracted from each score; the result is squared; and all the squares are added. The sum of the squares is then divided by N, and the result is reconverted to the "language" of the score by taking the square root of the result.

$$s = \sqrt{\frac{\Sigma(X-\bar{X})^2}{N}}$$

However, because means are sometimes fractional values, this computational formula is sometimes unwieldy. It was used here to demonstrate that s is based on the deviation of scores from the mean. The process can be shortened by mathematical substitution in the recommended computational formula:

$$s = \sqrt{\frac{\Sigma X^2}{N} - \bar{X}^2}$$

Step 1: Derive mean.

Step 2: Square mean.

Step 3: Square each score.

Step 4: Sum squared scores.

Step 5: Derive mean of step 4.

Step 6: Subtract mean squared from step 5.

Step 7: Take $\sqrt{}$ (square root) of step 6.

(1)
X
X_1
X_2
X_3
.
.
.
X_N
―――
ΣX

$= \bar{X}$

(2)
$\bar{X}^2$

(3)
X^2
X_1^2
X_2^2
X_3^2
.
.
.
X_N^2

(4)
ΣX^2

(5)
$\dfrac{\Sigma X^2}{N}$

(6)
$\dfrac{\Sigma X^2}{N} - \bar{X}^2$

(7)
$\sqrt{\dfrac{\Sigma X^2}{N} - \bar{X}^2}$

Returning to the I.Q. data and using the computational formula, s is rather easily determined, as shown in table 12.

Table 12   Calculation of Standard Deviation of I.Q. Scores from Sixth-Grade Class

X	$(3)X^2$
87	7569
90	8100
91	8281
95	9025
95	9025
97	9409
98	9604
100	10000
101	10201
102	10404
103	10609
103	10609
103	10609
104	10816
105	11025
106	11236
106	11236
107	11449
107	11449
107	11449
108	11664
110	12100
111	12321
112	12544
113	12769
116	13456
118	13924
122	14884
128	16384
3045	$(4)322151$

$(1)\bar{X} = 105$
$(2)\bar{X}^2 = 11025$

$$(5, 6, 7)\ s = \sqrt{\frac{\Sigma X^2}{N} - \bar{X}^2}$$

$$s = \sqrt{\frac{322151}{29} - 11025}$$

$$s = \sqrt{11108.65 - 11025}$$

$$s = \sqrt{83.65}$$

$$s = 9.15$$

Calculation of Square Root

If one does not have access to a square-root table, it is necessary to calculate it. The process consists of first splitting the number for which you want the square root into pairs of numbers starting from the decimal point. If the number is 563.21, the initial split would be:

5   62.   21

Beginning with the left-most number, 5, the largest square root equal to or less than 5 is 2, because $2 \times 2 = 4$. The 2 is written to the right of the number, and the square of 2 is subtracted from the 5:

```
 5   62.   21        (2
 4
 1
```

The next set is brought down beside the 1, giving 162:

```
 5   62.   21        (2
 4
162
```

The 2 is doubled and written at the left of 162:

```
    5   62.   21        (2
    4
 4│162
```

The next step is to determine the number which when multiplied by the number composed of 4 and itself is closest to being equal to or less than 162. For example:

$$41 \times 1 = 41$$
$$42 \times 2 = 84$$
$$43 \times 3 = 129$$
$$44 \times 4 = 176$$

Of the above, 43×3 is the combination closest to 162. The 3 is written after the 2 in the answer, is multiplied by 43, and is subtracted from 162, and the difference is followed by the next set of numbers:

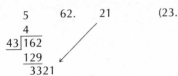

```
     5    62.   21        (23.
     4
 43│162
   129
   3321
```

Notice that the decimal is now inserted in the answer. The partial answer 23 is doubled and written at the left below the 43.

```
     5    62.   21        (23.
     4
 43│162
   129
 46│ 3321
```

Again, by trial it is discovered that 467×7 is the correct combination:

$$461 \times 1 = 461$$
$$462 \times 2 = 924$$
$$463 \times 3 = 1389$$
$$464 \times 4 = 1856$$
$$465 \times 5 = 2325$$
$$466 \times 6 = 2796$$
$$467 \times 7 = 3269$$
$$468 \times 8 = 3744$$

Its product, 3269, is closest to being equal to or less than 3321. The next digit in the answer is therefore 7:

```
      5   62.   21        (23.7
      4
43│162
    129
467│ 3321
     3269
      5200
```

If one wanted to carry out the answer to further decimal places the process would continue as described above.

As a check, square your answer to see if it is similar to the original.

```
 23.7
 23.7
165 9
711
474
561.69
```

Further decimal places would have given a more accurate square root.

Problem: Calculation of Standard Deviation

With the raw data below, calculate the standard deviation using the procedure outlined on pages 200–202.

70	72	73	74	74	75
81	84	74	86	87	88
89	85	83	83	80	79
91	91	92	94	94	92
91	96	91	94	96	93

Answer: Calculation of Standard Deviation

X	X^2
70	4900
81	6561
89	7921
91	8281
91	8281
72	5184
84	7056
85	7225
91	8281
96	9216
73	5329
74	5476
86	7396
83	6889
92	8464
91	8281
74	5476
83	6889
94	8836
94	8836
74	5476
87	7569
80	6400
94	8836
96	9216
75	5625
88	7744
79	6241
92	8464
93	8649
2552	218998

$$s = \sqrt{\frac{\Sigma X^2}{N} - \bar{X}^2}$$

$$s = \sqrt{\frac{218998}{30} - 7235.2}$$

$$s = \sqrt{7299.93 - 7235.2}$$

$$s = \sqrt{64.73}$$

$$s = 8.04$$

$\bar{X} = 85.06$

$\bar{X}^2 = 7235.2$

What Does It All Mean?

Now, so that the tree will not be lost in the forest, remember that the intent of this chapter is to consider ways to reduce a mass of data into mathematical concepts for description and comparison. In the first part of the chapter measures of central tendency were considered (mean, median, and mode), but it was pointed out that more definitive description can be afforded by adding measures of dispersion (mean and standard deviation). Given the I.Q. data from table 4, the data can now be described in a variety of ways:

Mean = 105
Median = 105
Mode = 103 and 107
MD = 6.97
s = 9.15
Range = 87–129

These mathematical describers, however, may still not have much significance for you. Descriptions are not very useful unless there is some reference group for contrast. It is a little like reading in the newspaper that a 700-pound llama has been captured in Bolivia. Why should that be news? Because the average weight of the llama is 200 pounds. The statistics above can become more meaningful if the boys and girls studied here were compared to sixth-grade children in another school or to other sixth-grade children in the same school, as in table 13.

Table 13

	Group 1	Group 2
Mean I.Q.	105	97
Median I.Q.	105	94
Mode	103 and 107	92
MD	6.97	10.5
s	9.62	14.3
Range	87–129	73–140

What differences might be expected in the two classrooms? Several things are obvious. Group 2 has a lower mean and there is considerably more dispersion around the mean. The classroom approach suitable for group 1 could not be expected to fare very well with group 2, particularly because of the amount of dispersion in group 2. Since group 1 is more homogeneous than group 2, it would suggest that some students of group 2, because they are so atypical, would have difficulty adjusting to the rest of the class unless special programs were developed for them. To say much more with just the data given here might be presumptuous, yet the information is valuable as a first approximation for description and contrast.

Summary

The concepts dealt with in this introductory chapter on statistics have been mathematical notations, measures of central tendency (mean, median, and mode), and measures of variability (mean deviation and standard deviation). Each concept is a different describer, a boiling down of a mass to its essentials. A describer, to have meaning, must have a reference point—something to which it can be compared—and various measures from two different groups illustrate how comparisons can be made.

17 / Statistics 2

Among other things, science is in the business of discovering relationships between variables. In the scientific study of behavior the investigator involves himself with a vast array of variables to see not only *if* they are related but *how* and *how much* they are related. The school, an ideal laboratory for research, affords many variables to be related.

1. What is the relationship of student performance at the beginning of a semester to that at the end?
2. As one increases praise, do children tend to work harder?
3. Is a child's level of anxiety related to his performance?
4. Will one method of teaching result in greater average achievement?
5. Is the teacher's perception of students like the student's perception of other students?
6. What relationship is there between leadership and I.Q. scores?
7. Do high-school students learn as much from discussion groups as from lectures?
8. Is social status in a group related to achievement?
9. Are television presentations as good as live presentations?
10. How much relationship is there between college-board scores and grade-point average for high-school seniors?
11. Do children who achieve well in one subject tend to achieve equally well in others?
12. Are stated beliefs related to one's behavior?

Operationalization of Variables

When research questions are properly phrased they become the basis for hypotheses to be subjected to empirical tests. To test them, a necessary step is *operationalization,* the translation of the variables into measurable terms. This concept was considered in some detail in Part III, but perhaps it needs to be reconsidered because of its importance.

If one hypothesized that a child's performance is related to his anxiety level, it could be confirmed only upon measures of performance and anxiety. With respect to performance, do academic grades serve adequately as a measure of performance? Are there other measures of performance more applicable to the hypothesis? And what about anxiety? Is a paper-pencil personality test appropriate? Or if a more behavioral measure is desired, what overt behavior would be classified as anxious? Obviously both variables might be operationalized in a variety of ways. The point is, one *cannot* conduct research without recasting the variables into measurable terms, that is, without operationalizing.

Once data has been gathered, it must be subjected to an analysis of relationships. The statistical method considered in this chapter is one of the more useful when data have been gathered with two independent measures for a single person or phenomenon. With one exception most of the techniques considered in Chapters 15 and 16 have dealt with univariate distributions. The exception, bivariate distributions, which deals with two measures for each person, is an appropriate beginning point for this chapter.

The Correlational Coefficient

In a bivariate analysis, the variables are conventionally designated as X and Y where there are two measures for each observation or instance. Of the samples mentioned above, the bivariates are praise and level of work, anxiety and performance, method of teaching and achievement, learning by discussion and learning by lectures, television classes and live presentations, college-board scores and grade-point averages, performance in class A and performance in class B (or C, D, E, and so on), and stated beliefs and behavior.

Recall that two measures taken on individuals within a group can be plotted to get a visual picture of the relationship between the two variables. When plots are fitted to a straight line of best fit, a positive relationship bisects the X and Y axis, a negative relationship is perpendicular to the positive relationship, and a lack of relationship consists of unrelated plots between the two axes (Chapter 15, pp. 183–86). In a positive relationship, changes in one variable are related in the same fashion to changes in the second variable; in a negative relationship, changes in one variable are opposite to the changes in the second variable; with a lack of relationship, changes in one variable have no discernible effect on the second variable.

The Pearson r

Karl Pearson (1857–1936) was a British mathematician and one of the founders of statistics. Pearson, who first began his professional life as a lawyer, was appointed professor of applied mathematics at University College of London when about twenty-seven years old. His entire teaching career was spent at that school until his retirement in 1933, an unusual history in contrast to today's mobile academicians. Pearson's contributions to science were far-reaching. In 1890 his interests began to shift from statistics to its application in biological problems of evolution and heredity and to the philosophy of science. His series of published lectures *The Grammar of Science* is one of the classics in the philosophy of science. The contribution for which Pearson is probably most well-known and to which his name became attached is the Pearsonian Coefficient of Correlation, also called *the Pearson r*.

The notion of correlation can be grasped in the word *co-relation,* for it is a process of boiling down into one mathematical statement how two variables co-relate.[1] Conceptually, correlation can be defined in terms of the relationship of the scores: in a perfect positive correlation each individual obtains the same relative score on both variables; in a perfect negative correlation each individual obtains the same relative score but the two scores are opposite in sign. Scores need not be converted to relative scores in correlation because the correlational formula handles that for you (these are called *z* scores). This automatic conversion allows comparison of raw data even though each variate may be based upon a different scale.

Calculation of the Pearson r

One computational formula for the Pearson *r* (for there are several equivalent formulas) is:

$$r = \Sigma XY - \frac{\frac{(\Sigma X)(\Sigma Y)}{n}}{\sqrt{\left[\Sigma X^2 - \frac{(\Sigma X)^2}{n}\right]\left[\Sigma Y^2 - \frac{(\Sigma Y)^2}{n}\right]}}$$

Now, before you run for a tranquilizer or whatever else you use to calm your nerves, let it be said that you have already faced most of these symbols in one form or another, and with a modicum of patience and con-

[1] Advanced statistics affords ways to compare more than two variates through multiple *r* techniques but these statistics are beyond the scope of this text.

trol of "symbol shock" the formula can be broken down into understandable bits without much difficulty. A simple example will help carry one through the maze. Let us say that we want to discover the relationship between the two sets of data with the variables unspecified, or as it is sometimes called "dummy data," shown in table 14.

Table 14   Preliminary Calculation of Correlational Coefficient Using "Dummy Data"

X	Y	X²	Y²	XY
7	70	49	4900	490
3	33	9	1089	99
9	95	81	9025	855
4	48	16	2304	192
6	61	38	3721	366
29	307	191	21039	2002

$$r = \frac{\Sigma XY - \dfrac{\Sigma X \cdot \Sigma Y}{n}}{\sqrt{\left[\Sigma X^2 - \dfrac{(\Sigma X)^2}{n}\right]\left[\Sigma Y^2 - \dfrac{(\Sigma Y)^2}{n}\right]}}$$

Plugging in, the formula becomes:

$$r = \frac{2002 - \dfrac{(29)(307)}{5}}{\sqrt{\left[191 - \dfrac{(\Sigma X)^2}{5}\right]\left[21039 - \dfrac{(\Sigma Y)^2}{5}\right]}}$$

The two outstanding symbols are $(\Sigma X)^2$ and $(\Sigma Y)^2$, the sum of X squared and the sum of Y squared.[2]

$$\frac{(\Sigma X)^2}{n} = \frac{(29)^2}{5} = \frac{841}{5} = 168.2$$

$$\frac{(\Sigma Y)^2}{n} = \frac{(307)^2}{5} = \frac{94249}{5} = 18849.8$$

[2] A source of confusion to the beginning student is improper differentiation between ΣX^2 and $(\Sigma X)^2$. ΣX^2 means the sum of the square of each X; $(\Sigma X)^2$ means the square of the sum of the X's.

Now the formula can be filled in completely:

$$r = \frac{2002 - \dfrac{(29)(307)}{5}}{\sqrt{\left(191 - \dfrac{(29)^2}{5}\right)\left(21039 - \dfrac{(307)^2}{5}\right)}} = \frac{2002 - \dfrac{8903}{5}}{\sqrt{\left(191 - \dfrac{841}{5}\right)\left(21039 - \dfrac{94249}{5}\right)}}$$

The solution for r is:

$$r = \frac{2002 - 1780.6}{\sqrt{(191 - 168.5)(21039 - 18849.8)}} = \frac{221.4}{\sqrt{(22.5)(2189.2)}} = \frac{221.4}{\sqrt{49,257}} = \frac{221.4}{221.9} = .9$$

The Meaning of the Correlational Coefficient

What does a correlational coefficient of .99 suggest? First, correlation is designed so that every correlational coefficient must fall between −1.00 and 1.00:

	Negative		Positive	
−1.00		0		1.00

Correlations around 0 mean that there appears to be little relationship between the variables of the two sets of data; correlations closer to 1.00 or −1.00 signify that the variables are related. With positive correlation, as one variable changes the other variable tends to change in the same fashion. With negative correlation, the variables are inversely related: as one changes the other changes but in an opposite direction. Usually one finds a positive relationship between the height and weight of grade school children and a negative relationship between success in school and absenteeism. Look now at the X and Y variables in table 14. Cursory visual inspection shows that there would be a high correlation, for example, 7 and 70, 3 and 33, and 9 and 95.

Another way to describe the meaning of the mathematical product of correlations is by the concept of *coefficient of determination*. The coefficient of determination is a transformation of the correlational coefficient into a percentage measure, defining how much of one variable determines the other. To get the coefficient of determination, one simply squares the correlational coefficient:

Coefficient of determination $= r^2$

If, for example, one discovered there was a correlation of .30 between I.Q. scores and academic achievement, conversion to the coefficient of determination:

$$(.30)^2 = .09$$

indicates that 9% of either one of the variables is involved in determining the other. Or, to say it another way, 91% (100%–9%) of the relationship is accounted for by factors other than I.Q. or academic performance.

When Correlations Are Low

Presuming the measures are adequate, there may be two ways to view a low correlational coefficient: the relationship is actually low, or the data is of such a nature that a relationship does exist but for some reason or another it is not reflected in the correlaton. This latter case needs to be considered further.

Perhaps you have already noted that correlation deals with straight-line or linear relationships between two variables. If you have not discovered the linear quality of correlation, it should be made explicit. Correlational analysis is limited to those conditions that are best described by a straight line when X and Y variables are compared on a bivariate graph. There are, however, some situations where strong relationships exist but where correlations will always be low. These conditions are curvilinear. For example, if one compares deprivation of food and the running speed of a laboratory rat from the starting box to the feeding box in a maze, it is evident, as shown in figure 40, that up to a point speed is highly correlated with how long the rat has

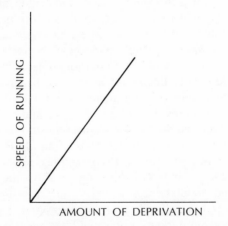

AMOUNT OF DEPRIVATION

Figure 40. Relationship of speed of running and amount of deprivation.

been deprived of food. If amount of deprivation is extended, however, the rat becomes so weak that his speed decreases sharply, as shown in figure 41. Although the relationship of the two variables remains consistently high, a correlational coefficient for little to extreme deprivation would be somewhere around zero because, as previously stated, correlation is based upon a straight line to describe the relationship, not upon a curvilinear line. Given

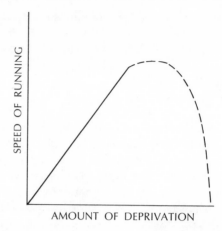

AMOUNT OF DEPRIVATION

Figure 41. Relationship of speed of running and amount of deprivation, extended.

a curvilinear relationship between two variables, the correlational coefficient can at best provide only a poor approximation. Other examples of possible curvilinear relationships are level of motivation and learning (medium levels of motivation facilitate learning but high levels disrupt it), strength and age (young people increase in strength as they grow older but older people decrease in strength as they grow older), and anxiety and performance (a little anxiety is good but a lot of anxiety inhibits performance).

These examples lead to another source of logical inaccuracy in interpretation of correlational data. With the two variables of strength and age, a high correlation would probably be found for subjects in the span from infancy to late adolescence. Beginning at that point a positive relationship would level off until in older subjects the relationship would become negative or inverse—as age increases strength wanes. If in studying age-strength variables the subjects were high-school students, one kind of relationship would be found, but if the subjects were residents of an old-folks home, another kind of relationship would be found. This example is obvious, but it is striking how often in the study of human behavior generalities are made from a very limited and specific population. Since the majority of research on human behavior is conducted in universities and colleges and since the most available subjects are college students, one should be cautious about the applicability of these findings beyond the college-age group.

This problem is not a problem of the method of correlation but of the inaccurate interpretation of correlational data. This error is known as *truncation*. Whenever the range of values of one of the variables is restricted, a generalized finding may be spurious. The moral of the story is *Be very careful in generalizing correlational findings to other groups or populations not represented in the group studied.* A lack of relationship found between two variables in your class, for example, does not describe that class or other classes in other settings, nor does it describe classes of differing age groups.

Rank Correlation

It will be noted that in the discussion on the Pearsonian correlational coefficient both variables were based upon interval-ratio data. If part or all of the data is ordinal, the Pearsonian r is not applicable. A correlational technique called *rank correlation (rho)* is not as powerful a statistic as the Pearson r, but it can accommodate ordinal data. For illustration let us return to the class used in Chapter 16, where I.Q. data had been gathered on the twenty-nine members of the class (see table 4, p. 190). To discover if there is any relationship between measured I.Q. and sociometric status, data were gathered on social choices using the specified-choice technique discussed in Chapter 4. The number of choices received gave an ordinal ranking for each student, which was set alongside that student's I.Q. score. Note that table 15 consists of two kinds of scales for X and Y: the social-choice ranking is ordinal; the I.Q. scores are interval-ratio. Obviously, an interval-ratio scale can be transformed to an ordinal scale, but the reverse is impossible. Therefore it is necessary to convert the I.Q. (interval) scale to a rank (ordinal) scale to allow computation of r. See table 15.

Table 15   I.Q. Scores Converted to Rank for Comparison with Social Rank

X	Rank	Y
87	29	25
90	28	28
91	27	23
95	25.5	29
95	25.5	19
97	24	24
98	23	27
100	22	6
101	21	26
102	20	10
103	18	22
103	18	3
103	18	17
104	16	8
105	15	15
106	13.5	2
106	13.5	11
107	11	8
107	11	5
107	11	21
108	9	8
110	8	12
111	7	1
112	6	4
113	5	19
116	4	14
118	3	19
122	2	6
128	1	13

Notice that as you read up the table in the column of I.Q., you come across tied scores (107, 106, 103, and 95). Tied scores are converted to rank by assigning a mean rank until the tie is broken and the next rank is the number normally assigned it, as shown in table 16.

Table 16

105 = 15
106 = 13.5
106 = 13.5
107 = 11
107 = 11
107 = 11

Now that data for each student has been converted to an ordinal scale, we can proceed with the computation of rank correlation. This formula, relatively simpler than the Pearson r, is carried out in table 17.

$$r_{rho} = 1 - \frac{6D^2}{n(n^2 - 1)}$$

r_{rho} = Rank correlation (called rho)
D = Difference in rank
n = Number of comparisons

As previously stated, rank correlation is less precise than the Pearson r. An inspection of table 15 will indicate why. Notice that the difference between 122 and 129 is seven I.Q. points. Yet the difference in rank is only one. Compare this to the difference between 105 and 104 where the difference in I.Q. is one and the difference in rank is also one. In distributions with large gaps in the interval score, conversion to a ranking loses the precision of a Pearson r. However, in distributions with little difference between ranking and raw score, rank correlation is little different from the Pearson r.

Problem: Calculation of Pearson r and rho

Two measures were taken on ten students. The first measure was made in January, the second in May. What is the correlation between these two sets of scores using the two correlational techniques, r and rho?

Correlation and Causality

Because of the human mind-set to unearth "causes" of other events, uses of correlation may imply a causal relation between variables that does not in fact exist. In the data just computed, because of the .502 correlation, one could infer that I.Q. "causes" a high social rank. But is it not just as logical to assume that high social rank "causes" a higher I.Q., particularly if one takes the position that I.Q. is a function of the environment more than of biology?

Imputation of causality is a very tricky business, to be indulged in only with great caution. Simply that two variables are related does not mean that one causes another. One statistical wag demonstrated that during the years 1926 and 1933 there was a significantly positive relationship between importation of bananas and birthrate. Does that mean that importing bananas causes increased impregnation? Or maybe an increased birthrate causes importation of bananas. Similarly, the Bob and Ray article in Chapter 7 contains many examples of nonlogical "causes."

In general, correlational relationships suggest a concomitant relationship; that is, as one of the variables changes, the other tends to change predictably. But demonstrating concomitance is a long way from demonstrating that one condition causes another. What is more typically the case in concomitant relationships is that factor X is related to factor Y through mediating factor or factors, Z, but because factor Z was not measured, it appears that X and Y are directly related. Such would appear to be the condition between bananas and birthrate. In short, stick close to the data and focus upon the relationship between variables rather than upon imputation of causality.

Summary

This chapter, the second of two devoted to statistical tools, extends Chapter 15 by introducing a technique for measuring the strength of the relationship between two measures taken on the same individual or phenomenon. The important concepts introduced have been operationalization, the Pearson r, the coefficient of determination, linear and curvilinear relationships, truncation, rank correlation (rho), and imputation of causality from correlational coefficients.

Table 17 Rank Correlation of I.Q. and Social Ranking of Twenty-nine Sixth-Graders

X	Y	D	D^2	
29	25	4	16	
28	28	0	0	
27	23	4	16	
25.5	29	−3.5	12.3	
25.5	19	6.5	42.3	
24	24	0	0	
23	27	−4	16	
22	6	16	256	$r_{rho} = 1 - \dfrac{6D^2}{n(n^2 - 1)}$
21	26	−5	25	
20	10	10	100	
18	22	−4	16	$r_{rho} = 1 - \dfrac{6(2022.2)}{29(841 - 1)}$
18	3	15	225	
18	17	1	1	$r_{rho} = 1 - \dfrac{12133.2}{29(840)}$
16	8	8	64	
15	15	0	0	
13.5	2	11.5	132.3	$r_{rho} = 1 - \dfrac{12133.2}{24360}$
13.5	11	2.5	6.3	
11	8	3	9	$r_{rho} = 1 - .498$
11	5	6	36	
11	21	−10	100	$r_{rho} = .502$
9	8	1	1	
8	12	−4	16	
7	1	6	36	
6	4	2	4	
5	19	−14	196	
4	14	−10	100	
3	19	−16	256	
2	16	−14	196	
1	13	−12	144	
		0	2022.2	

Student	Test 1 (Jan.)	Test 2 (May)
A	16	20
B	13	25
C	13	18
D	21	16
E	19	19
F	26	29
G	19	21
H	20	27
I	18	23
J	30	28

Answer: Calculation of Pearson *r* and *rho*

Pearson *r*:

X	Y	X²	Y²	XY
16	20	256	400	320
13	25	169	625	325
13	18	169	324	234
21	16	441	256	336
19	19	361	361	361
26	29	676	841	754
19	21	361	441	399
20	27	400	729	540
18	23	324	529	414
30	28	900	784	840
195	226	4057	5290	4523

$$r = \frac{4523 - \frac{(195)(226)}{10}}{\sqrt{\left[4057 - \frac{38025}{10}\right]\left[5290 - \frac{51076}{10}\right]}}$$

$$r = \frac{4523 - 4407}{\sqrt{(254.5)(182.4)}}$$

$$r = \frac{116}{\sqrt{46420.8}}$$

$$r = \frac{116}{215.46}$$

$$r = .535$$

Rho:

X	Y	X rank	Y rank	(D) difference in rank	D²
16	20	8	7	1	1
13	25	9.5	4	5.5	30.2
13	18	9.5	9	.5	.2
21	16	3	10	7	49
19	19	5.5	8	2.5	6.2
29	29	2	1	1	1
19	21	5.5	6	.5	.2
20	27	4	3	1	1
18	23	7	5	2	4
30	28	1	2	1	1
					93.6

$$rho = 1 - \frac{6(93.6)}{10(100 - 1)}$$

$$rho = \frac{561.6}{990}$$

$$rho = 1 - .56$$

$$rho = .44$$

EPILOGUE

It would be a serious omission at the end of a text designed to give you purchase on a set of descriptive tools and behavioral-change principles if there were no final comment on some of the problems in using a psychological-learning approach to education. In no sense is this final statement an apology for having presented the material in the last seventeen chapters. Rather it is an attempt to delineate some reasons why a teacher skilled in the use of an educational psychology may be hampered in putting that skill to effective use. What is to follow was prompted by statements of teachers who had become acquainted with this text in its formative stages before spending a year or so actually teaching in a school. Their reflections are worthy of careful attention.

Elementary and secondary education is sometimes less than one would desire. Overcrowded classrooms, severely limited budgets, administrators who see little value in research, lack of time for anything beyond immediate demands, and a "get-tough" policy for student control are a few of the deterrents to the utilization of the skills discussed herein. These same conditions not only obstruct the use of psychologically sound practices, they destroy the very purpose for which today's school has been designed, namely that of creating a dynamically evolutionary and intellectually exciting environment for successful learning.

Fortunately schools exist where the problems are not so great, schools where the classrooms are reasonably small, with twenty-five to thirty students, and where the teacher has help from colleagues, administrators, parents, school boards, and—most important—students. Such an ideal educational climate allows innovation and encourages the teacher to prepare and carry out descriptive-action research.

But these polarized sketches illustrate only the outer extremes of the educational picture, neither of which describes the "average" school. As a corrective, Philip W. Jackson provides a view of the teacher's world perhaps more in line with schools you know. Based upon interviews with a sample of teachers chosen by their administrators as "outstanding," he comments:

> There was a striking immediacy about the things that concerned the teachers —a here-and-nowness about their talk that becomes compellingly evident after prolonged listening. Perhaps this quality should not surprise us. After all, during every working day the teacher is immersed in an environment of real people and things whose demands upon her are continuous and insistent. Moreover, many of the unique features of her world become so well known to the teacher that it becomes difficult for her mentally to erase their identity and think of them as merely concrete manifestations of more abstract phenomena. Consequently, generalizations about the characteristics of children or about the merits of an educational theory are continually being tested, as the teacher considers them, against the qualities of the particular students with whom she is working and the specific constraints of her classroom. As might be expected, this degree of specificity greatly inhibits the easy translation of theory into practice and serves to increase the difficulty of communications between the teacher and others with more abstract interests.[1]

Jackson's teachers reflect a frame of mind embedded in the here and now. Indeed, there are many existential demands in the classroom. The exclamations of "Teacher, teacher!" pervading the first-grade class or the more sophisticated requests for help from the senior high are calls to immediate action. They are a seductive appeal and a threat to consume the major portion of the teacher's energies. But the task of effective teaching encompasses more than an irrevocable tie to the present, and that, of course, is the theme of this text. Since each class has its own "personality," generalized statements about behavior, beyond a few important principles, are of little utility. Consequently, the teacher must possess the tools and skills to create his or her own modes of utility.

Robert J. Shaefer, in a provocative book entitled *The School as a Center of Inquiry*, catches the essense of the purpose of this text. He provides an appropriate close to this endeavor by suggesting a new frame of reference for the teacher and the schools:

> The primary job of the school is to teach—to provide instruction in the various skills and subjects deemed crucial for the young. Society has not expected the school to be systematically reflective about its work—to serve as a center of inquiry into teaching—for the simple reason that there has seemed nothing of great complexity in the instructional task, few problems in teaching which demand serious investigation. Although schools admittedly have not always been able to fulfill their primary purpose, it has traditionally been assumed either that they were teaching the wrong

[1] Philip W. Jackson, *Life in Classrooms* (New York: Holt, Rinehart and Winston, Inc., 1968), p. 147.

subjects or that they had failed to attract reasonably able persons as teachers. Educational reform, therefore, has historically focused upon modifying the curriculum or raising the standards for admission into teaching.

The theme of my remarks is that we can no longer afford to conceive of the schools simply as distribution centers for dispensing cultural orientations, information and knowledge developed by other social units. The complexities of teaching and learning in formal classrooms have become so formidable and the intellectual demands upon the system so enormous that the school must be much more than a place of instruction. It must be a center of inquiry—a producer as well as a transmitter of knowledge.[2]

[2] Robert J. Schaefer, *The School as a Center of Inquiry* (New York: Harper and Row, Publishers, 1967), p. 1, reprinted by permission of the publisher.

GLOSSARY

Abscissa (p. 177). The horizontal dimension of a graph, which in a histogram or frequency polygon consists of class intervals and which in a bivariate graph is the scale for one of the two variables.

Back-up reinforcer. *See* **Reinforcer, back-up.**

Baseline (p. 104). Behavior exhibited before modification procedures are begun. Often a baseline is a necessary datum to determine if predicted change is occurring.

Behavior, operant. *See* **Operant behavior.**

Behavioral ecology (pp. 34–40). An extension of Malinowski's functionalism as a method of observation. In this text the behavioral ecologists considered are Roger Barker and Herbert Wright, whose contribution is to delineate an observational technique to minimize inferences about the historical causes of behavior. *See also* **Functionalism.**

Branching program. *See* **Program, branching.**

Class interval (pp. 177–78). The numerical categories that make up a frequency distribution. That is, a group of scores can be arranged by class intervals in preparation for graphing.

Coefficient of determination (pp. 212–13). The square of the correlational coefficient, which defines in percentage how much each correlational variable determines the other. Coefficient of determination $= r^2$.

Continuous reinforcement schedule. *See* **Reinforcement, continuous schedule.**

Contrived unobtrusive observation. *See* **Observation, contrived unobtrusive.**

Correlation, rank. *See* **Rank correlation.**

Criterion (pp. 4-5). A predetermined standard to which a phenomenon or event is compared. Without criteria, measurement or evaluation cannot exist. In some cases criteria are well established, for example, for time, weight, and mass; in others, not so clearly, for example, for attitudes, attention, and emotion, because of the lack of agreement on what constitutes a valid measurement device.

Criterion question in sociometry. See **Sociometry, criterion question in.**

Cumulative recorder (pp. 95–98). A device to record how many and when responses occur during a period of time.

Determination, coefficient of. See **Coefficient of determination.**

Deviation, mean (pp. 198–200). A measure of deviation from or dispersion around the mean. The mean deviation is the average of the deviations

from the mean. $MD = \dfrac{\Sigma X - \bar{X}}{N}$

Deviation, standard (pp. 200–202). A measure of deviation from or dispersion around the mean. The standard deviation is a more powerful measure

than mean deviation. $s = \sqrt{\dfrac{\Sigma X^2 - \bar{X}^2}{N}}$

Ecology, behavioral. See **Behavioral ecology.**

Extinction (pp. 92–93). A modification technique to decrease certain behaviors so that the consequences are not reinforcing. Extinction involves nonreinforcement.

Fading (p. 128). The shaping process where terminal or desired behavior is presented in model form for the student to duplicate. In successive trials the model is presented in increasing abstraction as the student practices duplication of the model.

Frequency polygon (pp. 178–79). A type of graph similar to the histogram that has, rather than rectangular bars, plots and connecting lines to depict the frequency distribution.

Functionalism (p. 34). A point of view about observation that maintains that (a) behavior can be understood only by taking into account the totality of the organism's environment, (b) history or evolution is less important than current happenings, and (c) observation is best conducted in a natural rather than an observer-contrived environment. Malinowski is the anthropologist most responsible for the development of functionalism.

Histogram (p. 178). A type of graph with class intervals on the abscissa, frequency within the interval on the ordinate.

Intermittent reinforcement. See **Reinforcement, intermittent.**

Interval, class. See **Class interval.**

Learning, programmed. See **Programmed learning.**

Mean (pp. 191–93). The arithmetic average of a group of numbers. The formula $\bar{x} = \dfrac{\Sigma X}{N}$ states that the X column is summed and then divided by the number of scores. The mean, symbolized by $\bar{X}$, is a measure of central tendency sensitive to extreme scores.

Mean deviation. *See* **Deviation, mean.**

Measure, nominal (pp. 10–11). A measure yielding differences by name, for example, boys or girls, cars or ships, black or white, heavy or light, and did perform or did not perform.

Measure, ordinal (pp. 10–11). A measure yielding data that can be ranked along a continuum, for example, of bigger or smaller, heavier or lighter, and first, second, third, and so on. Note that ordinal measurement makes distinctions but does not hint at how much difference there is.

Measure, ratio-interval (pp. 10–11). A measure yielding "how-much" relationships, for example, I.Q., temperature in degrees, rate of response per minute, and weight in pounds.

Median (pp. 193–94). A mathematical concept meaning the midpoint of a group of numbers arranged in ascending order. The median is less sensitive to extreme scores than is the mean.

Method, ranking sociometric. *See* **Sociometric method, ranking.**

Method, specified sociometric. *See* **Sociometric method, specified.**

Method, unspecified sociometric. *See* **Sociometric method, unspecified.**

Mode (p. 195). A measure of central tendency, which is the score in a group of scores that appears most frequently.

N (pp. 189, 211). A mathematical notation to symbolize number. For example, $N = 10$ means there are scores for ten subjects. A small n is used to symbolize pairs of scores, particularly in correlational analysis. Thus, $n = 10$ means there are ten subjects, each of which has two scores.

Negative reinforcer. *See* **Reinforcer, negative.**

Nominal measure. *See* **Measure, nominal.**

Observation, contrived unobtrusive (pp. 49–51). A method of setting certain conditions in the natural environment and observing from an unobtrusive vantage point what occurs as "experimental" conditions change.

Observation, unobtrusive (pp. 47–51). A method of gathering data about behavior in the natural environment where the subject does not know data is being gathered. Three types of unobtrusive observation are erosion (pp. 47–48), accretion (pp. 48–49), and archival (p. 49).

Observer reliability. *See* **Reliability, observer.**

Operant behavior (p. 83). Behavior that operates on the environment to bring about reinforcement. For example, a thirsty one-year-old child ·

may approach his mother and say, "Wa-wa." This operant behavior is presumably designed to relieve thirst, and it is reinforced by drinking.

Operationalizing (pp. 153–56, 171). The process of translating abstract concepts into measurable concepts. For example, a term that has been studied at great length in psychology is "anxiety." The term is not operationalized until one sets criteria for measurement of anxious behavior.

Ordinal measure. *See* **Measure, ordinal.**

Ordinate (p. 177). The vertical dimension of a graph, which in a histogram or frequency polygon consists of frequency and which in a bivariate graph is the scale for one of the two variables.

Pearson *r* (pp. 210–12). A method for computing the strength of the relationship between two variables, developed by the British mathematician, Karl Pearson.

$$r = \Sigma XY - \frac{\dfrac{(\Sigma X)(\Sigma Y)}{n}}{\sqrt{\left[\Sigma X^2 - \dfrac{(\Sigma X)^2}{n}\right]\left[\Sigma Y^2 - \dfrac{(\Sigma Y)^2}{n}\right]}}$$

Perception, selective. *See* **Selective perception.**

Phasing out (p. 105). The process of withdrawing a reinforcer or set of reinforcers, particularly used when the behavior begins to take on its own reinforcing qualities. For example, verbal praise from a parent or teacher may be necessary as a reinforcer in the early part of the teaching of reading, but the praise may be phased out as reading becomes its own reinforcer.

Polygon, frequency. *See* **Frequency polygon.**

Premack principle (p. 144–45). A method of using high-frequency choice behavior as a consequence to desired behavior. That is, those behaviors engaged in by choice most frequently can be used as reinforcers for other behavior.

Program, branching (pp. 131–32). A type of programming where the design of the program is planned so that what follows depends on the learner's previous performance.

Programmed learning (pp. 94–98). A learning procedure in which progressively difficult steps are systematically provided to reach a predetermined performance level.

r, **Pearson.** *See* **Pearson** *r*.

Rank correlation (*rho*) (pp. 215–16). A method for computing the strength of the relationship between two variables when one or both of the variables are ordinal. $rho = 1 - \dfrac{6d^2}{n(n^2 - 1)}$

Ranking sociometric method. *See* **Sociometric method, ranking.**

Ratio-interval measure. *See* **Measure, ratio-interval.**

Recorder, cumulative. *See* **Cumulative recorder.**

Reinforcement, continuous schedule (pp. 104, 126–27). A strategy of reinforcement whereby every correct response or adequate approximation
is followed by a reinforcer. Learning based upon a CRF is usually
extinguished fairly easily.

Reinforcement, intermittent (p. 105). A schedule of reinforcement other
than a CRF. An intermittent schedule might call for one reinforcer for
every ten correct responses, every two minutes, or at random.

Reinforcer (pp. 84, 85, 87). A consequence to behavior that increases the
probability of that behavior. A consequence cannot be termed a reinforcer unless it demonstrably increases the behavior prior to it.

Reinforcer, back-up (p. 104). Introduction of a new set of reinforcers as
the first set begins to lose effectiveness, that is, as the behavior being
reinforced decreases for reasons other than fatigue.

Reinforcer, negative (pp. 89–90). Behavior that goes up in probability
because it successfully avoids punishing consequences. Negative
reinforcement is not to be confused with punishment; rather, it involves escape from punishment. Escape or avoidance is the reinforcing
aspect of the behavior.

Reliability (pp. 8–9). The quality of a measure to give the same results
when conditions remain constant. Reliability involves consistency:
an unreliable measure is inconsistent.

Reliability, observer (pp. 27–28). A form of reliability applicable to measures
derived from observation. Usually the observers' first step in achieving
reliability is to develop criteria for the various categories they wish to
observe. Then there is a dry-run stage of independent observation,
the purpose of which is to refine the categories and to practice until
there is an eighty-five to ninety percent agreement between observers.
Then the actual observation process begins. Independent observations
must maintain a minimum of eighty-five percent reliability for the
observational data to be considered adequate.

Rho. See **Rank correlation** *(rho).*

Roles, sociometric. *See* **Sociometric roles.**

$\sqrt{}$ (pp. 189, 202–204). A mathematical symbol meaning "take the square
root of." The symbol is also known as a radical.

Rule, three-quarter high. *See* **Three-quarter high rule.**

Selective perception (pp. 9–10, 31–34). The unconscious interpretive tendency to be attentive only to certain aspects of the behavior of others
according to the observer's predispositions.

Shaping (pp. 116–33). The step-by-step process of modification necessary
when the baseline behavior is unlike terminal or desired behavior.
Shaping relies upon the reinforcement of increasingly difficult successive approximations to desired responses. For example, in shaping
communication skills, reinforcement may begin with the only sound
utterance the subject has in his speaking repertoire.

Σ (p. 189). Sigma, a mathematical symbol meaning "to sum" or "the sum of."

Sociometric method, ranking (pp. 53–54). A sociometric method where the respondent is requested to rank every member of the group. This method is more pertinent in small groups where every member of the group knows everyone else.

Sociometric method, specified (p. 53). A sociometric method where the respondent is requested to list a specified number, usually three, of choices from within a group.

Sociometric method, unspecified (p. 53). A sociometric method where the respondent has the option of choosing or not choosing others in the group. The advantage of this method is that it is the only method for determining the isolate.

Sociometric roles (pp. 56–57). The names assigned to various persons in established groups derived from choice patterns. Three types are stars, who are highly chosen; rejectees, who receive rejection choices; and isolates, who neither choose nor are chosen.

Sociometry (pp. 52–53). A technique developed by Jacob Moreno for determining social structure by directly questioning members of a group.

Sociometry, criterion question in (p. 54). The kind of sociometric question to which the group is asked to respond. Three varieties are social ("With whom would you like to go to a party?"), task ("With whom would you like to work?"); and elective ("Whom would you select to represent you?").

Specified sociometric method. See **Sociometric method, specified.**

Square root. See $\sqrt{}$

Standard deviation. See **Deviation, standard.**

Standardized test (pp. 154–55). A measure ot performance developed under standardized conditions and normed on (usually) a large population of subjects.

Taxonomy (Chapters 13–14). A method of classification. Bloom, Krathwohl, et al., developed a taxonomy of educational objectives based upon psychological rather than value goals, including both cognitive and affective goals.

Test, standardized. See **Standardized test.**

Three-quarter high rule (pp. 180–81). A method tor standardizing histograms and frequency polygons. The rule is that the class interval with the greatest frequency must be equal to three-quarters of the length of the abscissa.

Unobtrusive observation. See **Observation, unobtrusive.**

Unspecified sociometric method. See **Sociometric method, unspecified.**

Validity (pp. 6–8, 61–62). A quality of measurement. A valid measure has a logical or demonstrably close relationship between the measure and what it purports to measure. Three types are face (having an obvious and logical relationship), construct (yielding the same readings as other measures designed for the same purpose), and pragmatic (predictive of responses).

Variable (pp. 176–77). Anything studied by scientists that varies and seems to bring about certain effects. The two types are discrete and continuous.

X (p. 189). A mathematical symbol for a quantity or a score, X_1, X_2, and so on, can mean the score of subject 1, subject 2, and so on. ΣX means the sum of all X's.

X^2 (p. 189). A mathematical symbol meaning the square of the X quantity.

Y (p. 189). A mathematical symbol for a quantity or a score. Y_1, Y_2, and so on, can mean the score of subject 1, subject 2, and so on. ΣY means the sum of all Y's.

INDEX

Selma Blair is an actress best known for her roles in *Legally Blonde*, *Cruel Intentions*, *The Sweetest Thing*, and *Hellboy*. Blair was named a *Time* Person of the Year in 2017 as one of their Silence Breakers, and she was nominated for a Grammy Award for Best Spoken Word Album for her narration of *Anne Frank: The Diary of a Young Girl*. She is the subject of the documentary *Introducing, Selma Blair*, which reveals Blair's intimate and raw journey with multiple sclerosis. Blair lives with her son in Los Angeles.

Praise for *Mean Baby*

'Jaw-flooring' Helen Brown, *Telegraph*

'Written in vignettes and sharply observed, the sometimes harrowing subject matter never weighs *Mean Baby* down. At times, you feel like you shouldn't be having quite as much fun as you are but Blair has a self-awareness, wit and charm that makes her sound like a competition winner despite the difficulties she's faced ... This is not a misery memoir – I laughed out loud more than I cried' Frances Doyle, *Guardian*

'Blair demonstrates a rare level of self-awareness for someone who's been encased in the celebrity industrial complex for most of her adult life ... [she] writes with unflinching, unapologetic honesty about her trauma' Adam White, *Independent*

'Elegantly expressed ... Evocative ... for years Blair looked to astrologers, mediums and healers to tell her story ... she herself is the right person' Susan Burton, *New York Times*

'Blair engages with her MS starkly and movingly ... [she] puts it all out there' Joanne Kaufman, *Wall Street Journal*

'[*Mean Baby*] is funny and frank, a chance to spend time with a brave and big-hearted woman who's grown up to be not so mean, after all' Jennifer LaRue, *Washington Post*

'If you thought you knew Selma Blair, think again' *Marie Claire*

'Blair, in her typical fashion, finds a way to transform her burden into an opportunity, sharing her experience of living with MS with astounding candor and grace. This compassionate and intelligent work will leave fans floored' *Publisher's Weekly*, starred review

'Captivating and unflinching ... raw and real, *Mean Baby* is Blair's life in words – warts and all. And well worth the time' Mike Householder, *Associated Press*

'A fascinating exploration about the power of prophecy, of labels, and of one woman's determination to defy them all. Blair is a rebel, an artist, and it turns out: a writer' Glennon Doyle, author of the #1 *New York Times* bestseller *Untamed*

'*Mean Baby*, Selma Blair's brilliant book, demands attention. It grabs you by the collar and says *Listen to all that I have to say: about love, pain, motherhood, illness, celebrity, and the tidal ferocity that pours through all our lives.* Read it and be caught in the voice of one of our luminous stars' Esmé Weijun Wang, bestselling author of *The Collected Schizophrenias*

'Blair honestly writes about the uncertainty, messiness, joy, and weirdness of living in a 'broken' body. Disability is not always constant or known, and *Mean Baby* depicts this reality with compassion and grace' Alice Wong, editor of *Disability Visibility*

'Bold, intimate, sassy, profound – and a vital reminder that the hectic glitter of the exterior rarely reflects the hard-earned wonder of the interior. So, while you might reach for *Mean Baby* because of the author's celebrity, you'll read into the night for her candor, eye for detail and stunning prose. In an embarrassment of riches, Selma Blair is as talented a writer as she is an actress' Adrienne Brodeur, bestselling author of *Wild Game*

'She writes with a ribald irreverence as darkly funny as anything I've ever read ... If you've ever felt broken or lost you'll find yourself on the pages of this book ... The rejects and outsiders have spoken, Selma, and we've elected you Queen' Mary-Louise Parker, bestselling author of *Dear Mr You*

Mean Baby

A MEMOIR
OF GROWING UP

Selma Blair

———

virago

VIRAGO

First published in the United States in 2022 by Alfred A. Knopf
First published in Great Britain in 2022 by Virago Press
This paperback edition published in 2023 by Virago Press

1 3 5 7 9 10 8 6 4 2

A CIP catalogue record for this book
is available from the British Library.

ISBN 978-0-349-01384-8

Designed by Anna B. Knighton
Printed and bound in Great Britain by
Clays Ltd, Elcograf S.p.A.

Papers used by Virago are from well-managed forests
and other responsible sources.

Virago Press
An imprint of
Little, Brown Book Group
Carmelite House
50 Victoria Embankment
London EC4Y 0DZ

An Hachette UK Company
www.hachette.co.uk

www.virago.co.uk

To my dearest Mommy
while we were apart

And to my greatest love,
Arthur Saint Bleick

And did you get what
you wanted from this life, even so?

—RAYMOND CARVER,
"LATE FRAGMENT," *A NEW PATH*
TO THE WATERFALL

I don't hate hardly ever, and when I love,
I love for miles and miles. A love so big it
should either be outlawed or it should
have a capital and its own currency.

—CARRIE FISHER, *SHOCKAHOLIC*

Let me begin again.

—OCEAN VUONG,
ON EARTH WE'RE BRIEFLY GORGEOUS

MEAN BABY

Prologue

In the fall of 2002, I saw a tarot reader in Los Angeles. I had just been cast in a movie that was about to film in Prague for six months. I was thirty years old, anxious and searching. My mind was a void, and I wanted someone to fill it. I wanted to hear the story of who I would become, what signs I should seek along the way. I wanted an outline, if not an epiphany. After all, that's why we open our checkbooks to fortune-tellers. Tell us a tale. Make it wild. Make it entertaining. But make it our own.

The reader was named T—, and she looked a bit like a Berkeley professor, very thin, very intellectual. Large eyes framed by black bangs falling straight across her forehead. She kept a hankie tucked in one palm. Her breath smelled of Altoids. A skinny black cat curled up at her feet. As we spoke, I learned that T— used to be a lawyer, a profession she left to fully utilize her gifts. In all ways, she seemed like a good captain to have on this metaphysical journey, the right person to relay the drama of my life.

T— was not my first intuitive. For much of my life, I'd sought out such stories from mystics and chakra healers, mediums and numerologists, past-life therapists and astrologers. My fascination goes way back to when I was a child growing up in Southfield, Michigan. At a birthday party in second grade, my friend Melissa Stern's glamorous mother dressed up as a fortune-teller, a sparkling vision in a headscarf and layers of necklaces and bracelets. Melissa's mom was beautiful and lived in a giant house, which felt like evidence enough that she could see into the future, or at the very least that her words must have some merit. When it was my turn, she stared into a crystal ball, traced the lines on both my palms, closed her eyes, held my little hands, and told me that when I grew up, I was going to be a beautiful actress.

"There will be so many boys throughout your life that there will be a line," Mrs. Stern said as she swept the air with her finger to indicate a long queue of men waiting to swoop me off my feet. Seven-year-old me couldn't imagine why on earth she thought this. I had heavy eyebrows and stringy hair and did not believe myself to be an especially attractive child. And though I was prone to dramatic outbursts, the idea of performing in front of an audience terrified me. But I wanted so desperately to believe it. So convinced was I by Mrs. Stern's future-predicting abilities that I internalized every word. I couldn't wait to tell my mother, who would delight in the news.

As soon as my mom drove up in her navy blue 1979 Corvette, the *Evita* soundtrack blaring, I climbed into the back. Our cute neighbor Todd, a little older than I was, settled into the white leather bucket seat that was tinged yellow from cigarette smoke. I wanted them both to know what was predicted for me, so I spilled it all. "Mrs. Stern read my fortune and she said I'm going to be a beautiful actress," I bragged. I wanted my mother to be impressed. I wanted Todd to notice me. Even at age seven I knew beauty was a rare prize.

"Yeah, right," Todd scoffed.

"That's ridiculous," my mother said as she pulled out of the Sterns' long driveway. Once we were safely out of view, she took a drag off her Vantage cigarette. She exhaled against the dashboard, filling the car with curls of smoke. "Why would she tell you that? Besides. If you do grow up to be beautiful"—emphasis on the "if"—"and tall"—emphasis on the "and"—"you'll be a model. Or you'll marry an oilman and spend your days on his yacht." That settled it. My mother's word was gospel. End of discussion. I looked out the window.

As it happened, Mrs. Stern's prediction for me came true, at least in part: I was an actress. And by this point, I'd gone through my fair share of men. Even an oilman, whom I eventually found lacking. But I was still searching, still unsatisfied, still restless and stuck, still desperate to please, still prone to periods of over-whelming despair. Still binge drinking when I couldn't make sense of what to do next or needed to escape my body. I wanted clues, signs, good fortune. I wanted someone to tell me how the story unfolded. I wanted someone to spell out what came next.

Now, many years and many seers later, here I was again. T— studied the cards for a long time and then stacked them up in a neat deck. She tented her fingers, her unpolished nails touching, and said with the kind of conviction that one expects from a tarot reader: "Your life is going to change in Prague." The cat at her feet looked up at me as if in agreement.

I smiled. There it was: my life was going to change in Prague. She went on to say that I would meet a little man who would become important to me and that the true meaning of my life would be revealed. This, too, sounded fine. In fact, this whole visit was turning out to be much better than the last psychic I'd seen, who informed me that in my past life I'd been held captive by my own father and locked in a cement tomb in the woods, where I was burned alive, unknown by anyone.

I was going to Prague to shoot the movie *Hellboy,* in which I'd been cast as Liz Sherman, a pyro-telekinetic who, in a rage, accidentally burned her family to death and now must learn to control her powers. The director, Guillermo del Toro, had seen me in an indie film called *Storytelling* and thought my face held great loss. Loss was at the pit of Liz, he said. She couldn't touch anyone. Any feeling made her burn. It was a fitting role for me because, for years of my life beginning in my twenties, I often had the sensation that my arms were on fire. The feeling would come and go inexplicably: a tingle all the way down to my fingertips like tiny electric shocks, then a burning so intense I felt I might combust, then gone. Though it nagged at me, I never said anything about this to anyone, not even my mother. It was just one more mystery about my body that I didn't understand.

So, I went to Prague, where I waited for the magical life-changing moment T— predicted. A short man—T— was right about that bit—sought me out, a refugee from the former Yugoslavia, and we spent every night together, drinking slivovitz and champagne in bars. We fought, made up, made out, got drunk, fought, made up, made out, drank more. I felt as if I were living inside a Bukowski novel. In the morning, I woke up wondering who this tiny, tattooed, hot-tempered, blue-eyed man next to me was. Only to realize he was now mine. This wasn't the change I wanted.

When the film wrapped, I returned to L.A., once again flailing. My life hadn't transformed in Prague, except that I got even better, and also worse, at drinking, a skill at which I already excelled. In retrospect, I see now that I did learn some things. How to play the part of a woman who was trying to gain control over her own disobedient body. How to distract myself from the pain in my arms when I felt them begin to flare. How to spend long, lonely nights in bars and somehow get through the next day.

But at the time, I felt hopeless.

What I didn't know then, but what I'm starting to learn now, is that I don't need a fortune-teller to tell me a story about who I am or where I'm going. I don't need a psychic to make connections between my past and my present. I know how the story unfolds. I've seen how the pieces fit together. And I want to be the one to tell it.

SIGNS

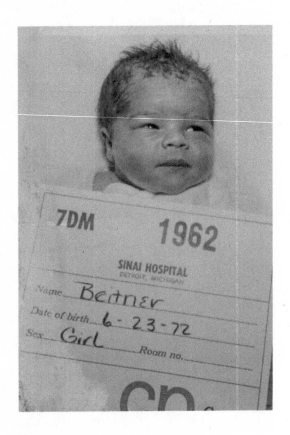

7DM   1962

SINAI HOSPITAL
DETROIT, MICHIGAN

Name   Bertner

Date of birth   6 - 23 - 72

Sex   Girl   Room no.

Mean Baby

I'M NOT SURE how to harness my meandering thoughts into words and sentences that make sense. So I'll start with what I know.

We are all in search of a story that explains who we are.

As Joan Didion wrote, "We tell ourselves stories in order to live." We are made not only by the stories we tell ourselves but by the tales of others—the stories they tell us, and the stories they tell about us.

The first story I was told about myself—other than the one about how my mother watched as the doctor pulled me out from her insides—is that I was a mean, mean baby.

I came into this world with my mouth pulled into a perpetual snarl. I was born with a glower, my face defined by a heavy brow that adults coveted. But on a child—an infant, no less—my face looked judgmental, scrutinizing. No one knew quite what to make of it.

When I arrived home from the hospital, only one of my three sisters, Katie, who was five, was waiting in our driveway. Mimi, aged twelve, and Lizzie, almost two, were elsewhere. Katie rushed out to meet me, my mother holding me on her lap. Katie asked if I was a baby doll for her. No, I wasn't, my expression said. A few days later, some of the neighborhood kids came over to meet the new

Beitner child. Within minutes, they left screaming, warning anyone who would listen, "Do *not* go over there. The Beitners have a mean baby." Can you imagine! Have you ever heard an infant described in this way? What could I have done? I was just days old! An infant with a snarl. I only wanted someone to pick me up, I think. Or put me down! But instead they all went and gossiped. From the very beginning, I was misunderstood.

Nevertheless, the label stuck, as labels are wont to do. What people call you does matter. The words we use hold weight. We say this sometimes, as lip service, but it's true. It's like having a sticker affixed to your back that the rest of the world can read but you can't. Before I could even speak, I was told who and what I was. I was mean.

In my defense, I did not have a proper name for the first few years of my life. My birth certificate reads, simply, "Baby Girl Beitner." In babyhood, I was given the nickname Baby Bear. My mom said they called me Bear because I had such a furry head that they would have to rub it to make way for my forehead. (I used to feel bad about this bit of my history, until I read that Rene Russo was born with the same affliction.)

Eventually, my family started calling me Blair—after Blair Moody, my mother told me. A U.S. senator and circuit court judge from Michigan whom she admired. This was funny, because I was so moody. (To this I say: Be careful what you name your kid!) I remember being a Blair, because they would all spell it out whenever they talked about me, as though I wouldn't piece it together. "B-L-A-I-R was mean," or "B-L-A-I-R wants to come."

This continued until I was three, when I went to preschool and needed a legal name. My mother decided to name me Selma, after her much-adored friend who died around the time I was born. In the Jewish tradition, babies are never named after a living person, and this seemed like a fitting tribute. The other names in contention were Ethel, Gretel—which I would have liked—Marta, Martha, and Gwyneth. (Gwyneth! To think, I could have been one, too!) There came a point where I loudly proclaimed, "When am I going to get one of those names?" referring to my sisters' nicknames of Ducky, Precious, and Princess. I wanted a pretty name. But it was not to be. From this point forward, I was Selma Blaire Bear Beitner, though my mother eventually removed the *e* from "Blaire," because she said it was "too pretentious." And there you have it.

For my entire life, I have been both. Selma and Blair. My two names would come to define me, as much as the stories around them.

❧

As a child, I never took to the name Selma. It seemed to me an old lady's name, not a name befitting a little girl. When given a choice, I always asked to be called Blair, but I got a real boatload of "Selma" in elementary school. Whenever the teacher did roll call, I was too shy to ask, "Can you call me Blair?" So all day long I was Selma, or Bat Sheva, the Hebrew name used by the teachers at my Jewish day school, and at home I was Blair. Mom was always sorry I didn't like Selma. A feminine of Saint Anselm, the Benedictine monk. Or a reference to Selma, Alabama. It was a good name, she often reminded me.

When I was five years old, Mom, Dad, and I went on a weekend trip where I struck up a friendship with a family with a baby. As we lounged poolside, the mother asked my name, and I casually replied that it was Lisa—a nice, normal name. As Lisa, I played with that baby for three hours, helping her navigate the hotel pool in her floaties. When the afternoon sun sank low in the sky, the woman approached my mother and told her that her daughter Lisa had been so helpful.

"Lisa!" My mother let out a wail. "Her name's not Lisa! What a crock! What a liar!"

The woman looked at me as though she were seeing me for the first time. My lovely afternoon had been erased. I was no longer Lisa, and now I was a liar as well.

⁓

My mother nicknamed me Saintly, but it was tongue in cheek. I was no saint. I could sometimes be saintly to my mother, but to everyone else I was a mean baby.

Growing up, I shared a bedroom with my sister Lizzie, since we were closest in age. Our parents let us choose the wallpaper, and since Lizzie didn't care, I picked a pattern with little pink and blue flowers floating against white. I chose it because it looked similar to what Jessica Lange describes as her childhood wallpaper in the movie *Tootsie*. Movies, even then, were what gave me ideas and hope.

Our room had two twin beds and those vinyl shades you needed to tug in order to pull them up or down. Every morning, I got out of bed very, very quickly. I had never been one to linger. (Can you believe it?) I rushed to pull the shade down, so it would snap to attention and rip-roll up loudly, sending the diffused morning sun straight into Lizzie's eyes.

"*Yehi or!*" I'd yell at the top of my lungs, quoting from the first lines of Genesis, the Hebrew words for "Let there be light!"

"Blair!" she would croak, rubbing her eyes. "Why do you do this?"

Next I made my way around the room, throwing open the door, turning on the television atop Mom's childhood maple dresser, her mother's before her, and flicking on the lights. I needed life, immediately. I needed every bit of everything, every bit of help, anything I could reach in order to cheerlead myself into embracing my day. Even then, I did this.

This was how our days began. I made Lizzie crazy. But she put up with me. Every night, we said good night back and forth until one of us fell asleep. She was always there with me.

⁓

I was three years old and jumping on the bed with Lizzie when I sank my teeth into her back for no good reason I can recall and took out a chunk of flesh, leaving a bluish-reddish dent in her skin. She forgave me for this, too.

When my father's father, Abraham, died, I stood next to my dad as he accepted condolences at the funeral and punched every man who came near us in the nuts. I was at groin level, and somehow I thought it made sense. (After that I was banned from family functions and made to stay home with our nanny.)

Then there was the time our next-door neighbor Mr. Glen was adjusting his sprinkler with this long metal rod, the water-valve key, and with the fervor of a dog chasing an intruder, I ran over to his yard, grabbed the poker out of his hand, swung it, and hit him squarely in the balls. Bridge instantly burned. He told my parents to "keep that mongrel out of my yard."

For a moment when I was six, I had a babysitter who was the daughter of a family friend. She had an amputation at the knuckle of her ring finger, chopped off by a paper cutter, she told me after I asked. I would study it as she read *Lassie* to me, imagining what it must be like to be her.

One afternoon, while we were playing checkers, I decided to make her feel better. I tucked my own ring finger under itself, pretending that part of it was gone. In my misguided way, I was attempting to make a connection. I thought she would believe me and think, "We're the same!" and that it would bond us. Instead, she reported to my mother that I was making fun of her.

She never came back.

Sometimes, I hung out by myself at the park behind our house after school, practicing my gymnastics. One of my specialties was the cherry drop, in which you hook your knees over a metal bar and swing and swing, then flip yourself over and land on your feet. "That's impressive," another kid's mom would say, to which I'd reply, "Yes, I'm training for the Olympics." Then I would strike the pose, arms outstretched and aloft, fingers splayed, as if I'd just finished my winning floor routine. As if that weren't enough, I continued spinning the tale, telling her how my trainer was arriving in a bit.

When I was two or three, on a vacation in Puerto Rico, I found myself separated from my parents in a busy plaza. An older woman found me wandering alone; she approached me and asked, "Are you lost, little girl?" I stared her down with my mean baby face, and when she didn't go away, I shouted, "Shut up!" When she asked again if I needed help, I screamed, "Get out of here!" Shaken, the kind woman waited until I was reunited with my family, at which point she reported to my mother what a horrid child I was and promptly fled the scene. "Shut up! Get out of here!" became an oft-repeated line in our household for years to come.

In fourth grade, I dared Ilyssa Wolin to swallow a row of staples so I could have her jeans when she died. I vaguely recall her folding the pointy ends inward with her purple-polished nails and swallowing. Even though I wanted those jeans, I must have been relieved when the day continued without her sudden death.

One of my worst recurring mean baby tricks was to pretend I'd lost my earring. As a child, I was always losing earrings while trying on turtlenecks and pulling them off. Somewhere I had learned that this was a consistent way to get the attention I craved. In kindergarten, I'd cry, "Oh my gosh! Oh no! I lost my earring! It just fell out of my ear on the ground!" Like clockwork, everyone stopped whatever they were doing and crawled around searching for my "missing" jewelry, which was never going to be found because it was safely in my pocket.

Once I successfully performed this trick enough times for a familiar audience, I decided to take it on the road. A boy from my old day-care center was having a birthday party, and I was invited. Once again, I told everyone in attendance that I lost my earring. "My mother will kill me if I don't find it!" I lamented, sending the boy's poor mother scrambling to locate it. She got down on her hands and knees, scouring the ground for my missing stud, patting under party shoes and brushing aside bits of bubble gum, when she should have been enjoying her son's party. Everyone spent most of their time searching.

When my mother came to pick me up, the boy's mom approached her, calmly promising that they would try to find the earring.

"Selma, what on earth!" my mom cried.

"I'm so sorry, Molly," the woman said to my mother in a hushed tone. "Selma said you have a temper—"

"She didn't lose her earring! She's a liar!"

The jig was up.

The boy's mother had been nothing but kind to me until this point, but in that instant everything shifted. The goody bags were all lined up on a table. I was reaching out for mine, and she looked me in the eye and said, "I don't think so." That was a good mom.

Looking back, I think I was jealous of how much that mom loved her son. She put so much effort into throwing her beautiful boy a suitably beautiful party, and I wanted the warm glow of that kind of attention to be lavished on me. I longed to understand how that felt. I thought there needed to be an emergency to get attention, and in the absence of a real emergency I manufactured one.

I didn't realize that I was wrecking someone else's party, or that I was taking away from this boy, until it was over. That was just one of my mean baby–isms, a penchant for ruining everyone's time. I bedeviled people, as my mother said, but I was misunderstood. All I wanted was to be that boy's friend, and instead I destroyed my chances. I still wonder if anyone knows I'm the same Blair who made everyone search for her earring.

To add insult to injury, I also told all the kids at the birthday party that the hot dogs—tiny party franks—resembled my dad's wiener. My mom turned to me in the parking lot as soon as we were out of earshot.

"Selma, when did you ever see your dad's penis?" she asked.

"I didn't," I told her. In fact, I had never seen it. It just seemed like something to say. Something funny.

My mother burst out laughing, so tickled was she that all the kids now thought my dad was equipped with a pig in a blanket. When we arrived home, she made me recount the story so my father would know how I'd slandered him. I don't think he particularly cared, though I'm sure he wouldn't have chosen that narrative.

Over and over, my impulses only cemented me as an evil, awful, but cute and determined bad seed. It felt . . . not so great. And I felt guilty and ashamed about all of it, horrible even, once I realized what I had done. But with no real plan to change who I was. What my label said. Mean baby. I didn't know how to make it better. I didn't understand how to be empathic. Or patient. The truth is, I wasn't wicked; I was merely a child who didn't plan her actions well. But it was no matter. I lived up to my name.

I was a mean baby. As if I'd ever had a choice.

Birth Stories

MY THREE SISTERS and I were all born at 8:45 on a Friday morning, purposefully scheduled so my mother would have the weekend to recover, as she tells it, and get back to work on Monday. My mom packed a punch with this story, whether or not it was accurate. My sister Katie says this story is a myth, that my mother stayed home for a standard maternity leave of about six weeks. But I like my mom's version better, because it seems like a more accurate reflection of her. The version of herself that she wanted to show off. Strong, resolute, remarkable, formidable—which was certainly the impression she wanted among her colleagues. (And I think, by the time I arrived, she was such a pro that she might have in fact returned to work in three days.)

I came into this world on June 23, 1972, at Sinai Hospital in Detroit. The doctor who delivered me was named Dr. Lipschitz, a fact I've always found very amusing (so does my son). As with much of my folklore, I discovered this tidbit from reading about it later, in a baby book I found in the basement. With its pink quilted taffeta cover that was water-stained from one of the basement floods, it looked old, even when I first stumbled across it as a child, the pages molded out and watermarked, the ink already turning colors. There's a picture of me as a newborn, and underneath it my mother had written, "Her eyes are so blue, and everybody says she looks just like mommy!"

These words thrilled me then and still do now. I wished to be like my mother since the second I was born.

The truly amazing thing about my birth was that my mother, who had never watched one of her C-sections before, told the nurses, "This is my last chance. I want to watch." So, she sat, propped up on her elbows, and observed as they cut into her belly. She loved to tell me this story, usually after dinner, once she'd had a couple glasses of wine. I was proud of my birth story. Proud that my mother was a witness and chose to be.

"Selma, it was wild! They actually took my intestines out," she told me, "and put them on the table!"

"Did it hurt?" I asked.

"No, no real pain," she said. "It just felt like people poking around. I was so thrilled I was going to see my baby!"

She reminded me that the nurses all cried—I loved this part, too—because they had never seen a mother so engaged with the experience of seeing herself be cut open and watching them lift out the fully cooked baby.

"Then they pulled you out, and I said, 'Oh, she's beautiful!'"

Family

SOME PEOPLE LOOK to their family to discover the origin of physical traits. What have they inherited from the past? Do they have their aunt Jean's nose? Their uncle Fred's eyes?

I look to my family for signs of illness, for evidence of sadness. I look to my history to trace where my maladies come from and whether they can be conquered. I also look to them for signs of resilience, for evidence of strength.

To understand the course of any cycle, we must trace it back to the beginning. Before me, there was my mother, Molly. And before her, there was her father, James Cooke, the man I knew as PopPop. When I open the door to the past to try to understand who I am, my maternal grandfather is the first one I see. I am my mother's daughter, fashioned in her image, and she was her father's, fashioned in his. As soon as I close my mind's eye, there he is, neatly pressed and fresh in his bow tie, with that same sideways smile I inherited.

PopPop was born Jewish in Kiev, where his father owned a successful tailoring business, known for his exquisite eye for dressmaking. When the pogroms began in the early twentieth century, his father brought the family to America. PopPop was only two years old. The family was always careful to say that they traveled in second class to Ellis Island. No steerage for them! Appearances mattered to my relatives, even when they were escaping persecution.

The family settled in Philadelphia and drifted away from Judaism in order to assimilate—to become American—though I recently learned that PopPop spoke fluent Yiddish. He was, in fact, a member of the Kohanim, descendants of the biblical Aaron who are conferred special privileges in synagogue. They are chosen beyond chosen. Still, he thought of himself as an ethnic Jew, not a religious one. And an American first and foremost.

My grandfather was one of eleven siblings, and as a child he worked with his older brother Sam, selling peas on Dock Street in Philadelphia. I learned about the pea selling only recently, from my cousin Joanna. "Wait, PopPop had a *vegetable* cart?" My elegant, worldly PopPop. I couldn't believe it. "It's like *My Fair Lady,* in Yiddish!" I was charmed by this detail.

When PopPop was a teenager, his brother Paul was out walking with their father and didn't see the trolley car barreling toward them. Their father looked up just in time to shove Paul out of the trolley's path before he was struck and killed instantly. I'm told my great-grandmother screamed and wailed as her husband's casket was lowered into the ground. She was alone, in a foreign country, with eleven children to feed. The grief was written on her face for the rest of her life. Paul and some of the younger children were sent to live in an orphanage, while PopPop was deemed old enough to live on his own.

PopPop and his brother Sam went on to become successful owners of a national chain of supermarkets called Penn Fruit. As a wealthy man, PopPop reinvented himself. He moved near the posh Main Line of Philadelphia and adopted the WASP uniform of tweed and seersucker.

I knew PopPop only as an unusually urbane and sophisticated American man, a lover of Shakespeare and Saul Bellow, well-heeled and dapperly dressed, with bow ties to match his adorable bowlegs. He was a doting grandfather who signed his letters to me "Oceans of Love, PopPop." For me, those words held all possibilities. An ocean of love. These words are the opposite of feeling unwanted. The promise of something exotic and grand. It's such a beautiful phrase. I still use it sparingly, for the best people.

June 23, 1987

Oceans of love to my dearly beloved Blair on your birthday and many happy returns!

Pop Pop

Growing up, my beautiful mother, Molly, was definitely a daddy's girl. She was PopPop's pride and joy, but like so many relationships it was complicated. He had a lock on her insecurities and could be critical. When I was ten or eleven, they had a terrible fight, after which their relationship was never the same. It started when he commented that her face was damp with sweat, an insult that deeply offended my mother, who took meticulous care in her appearance. "Lock him up!" my mother cried. I heard her on the phone, griping about this "dig" to a friend. "I never, ever sweat," she said. "My father of all people should know this." This was true, so far as I could tell. My mother's face was always matte, her skin perfectly powdered. No evidence of perspiration, ever, just as there were no signs of weakness.

PopPop died a few years later, when I was in ninth grade. We made the drive from Michigan to Pennsylvania to bury him; my sister Lizzie stuck a candy cane up my nose, and the blood came down bright and rich where it cut. My mother looked in the backseat to see what had happened. I was careful not to complain. Her father was dead. I knew how much she loved him, in spite of it all.

When we put the dirt on his coffin, my mother cried, wailed into the bleak winter day. "Daddy. My daddy."

There is always one person who gets under our skin, who knows our weak spots and neuroses and can't help but go in for the kill. They are the people who wound us the most, because we care so much about what they think.

For my mother, that person was PopPop.

For me, that person is my mother.

Was my mother a daddy's girl because her mother didn't like her? Or did her mother dislike her because of her devotion to Pop-Pop? I was always told that my grandmother Goggy was sadistic toward my mother, but the details remain unclear. I'll never know if there was one event or just a long series of slights and insults that accumulated over time. No one in my family seems to remember exactly what happened, only that Lillian always favored my aunt Sally, and PopPop favored my mother.

According to Cooke family lore, the first thing PopPop noticed about Lillian Minor were her legs. "Who is the lady with the gorgeous gams?" he inquired about the pretty new gal working as a cashier in the grocery store that he managed. He was sixteen; she was fifteen. They married soon after and had two daughters.

My mother was named after an aunt of Lillian's who died of complications from an abortion—a tragic story that was not sugarcoated and had the intended consequence of making me terrified of having sex and getting pregnant.

Like PopPop, Lillian was the child of first-generation immigrants, and her brother James died of rheumatic fever at thirteen. When the embalmer came to prepare the body for burial, she watched as her brother's blood was drained into a bucket. She developed a lifelong fear of blood, which she passed on to my mother. (Now my son has this aversion, too. A stubbed toe or scraped knee is enough to make him lose his breath.)

Over the years, Lillian grew heavy and unhappy; I'm not sure which came first. Eventually PopPop, who judged women harshly for their weight, lost interest in her. Their marriage floundered, and they became estranged and then divorced.

❦

When I was little, Lillian lived alone in a luxurious apartment building not far from our house in Southfield, Michigan, and she would invite her granddaughters—Katie, Lizzie, and me—to stay overnight. (Mimi was both too loyal to PopPop and too old for sleepovers by then.) But the three of us loved it. She doted on us in a way our mother did not. She let us have candy, she took us to see *The Wiz,* we played Parcheesi. I quite liked her. Still, I always steeled myself for the day when she would embarrass me or hurt me, because my mother said that was what Goggy did.

I waited. It never came to pass.

I loved my mother and I loved my grandmother. I wanted to

understand what had happened between them, in part because I didn't want the same thing to happen between my mother and me. So, one Saturday night in bed with Goggy, I asked her, "Do you think you were a good mother?"

She paused, considering it, then said, "Yes. I tried to be. Why?"

I admitted, "My mother said you weren't."

She didn't say anything, and we went to sleep.

On the way home the next day, my sister Lizzie reported what I'd said back to my mother. We were never allowed to visit Goggy's apartment again. We hardly ever saw Goggy after that, except at extended family gatherings at aunt Sally's house with uncle Jim and the cousins. Our allegiance was with our mother.

When Lillian was in her final years in a nursing home, she and my mother did reconcile. Enough. My mother was a moderate drinker by then, and for Christmas she would drop off cases of alcohol for Goggy—enough for a sizable wedding. "There, that should last Goggy for a year," she'd say. She literally drove her own mother to drink. But my mother might have meant it as a sign of love. Alcohol was the greatest salve she knew.

⁓

When my mother was a teenager, she became ill with a life-threatening viral infection, and Lillian sent her away to an institution to convalesce. My mother became so sick that her family was told to prepare for her death. She recovered, but it caused her to lose all her hair. One night she'd gone to bed with a full head of dark hair, and when she woke up, every strand was on her pillow. Her hair grew back, damaged and thin. It, and my mother, were never quite the same.

This was a period in her life that she seldom talked about. She even gave herself a different name during that time: Roseanne. She wanted to pretend the entire episode had happened to someone else.

I only learned about this when I found a drawing nestled among her keepsakes. The signature read, "Roseanne."

"This is really good, Mom. Who made this?" I asked.

And she said, "Oh, I did, after high school."

"But the name says 'Roseanne.'" I tilted my head. "Who is Roseanne?"

My mother explained it as if it were a perfectly normal thing to do. She was attempting to create a separate self, almost like a character she had performed in a play. That was all she said. Away into her drawer it went, never to be opened again.

Keeping up appearances mattered so much to PopPop, and my mother followed his lead. She was always impeccably dressed: regal in an Ungaro suit and Charles Jourdan four-inch heels, never without a full face of beauty. Only once did I see her wear sneakers—a pair of chic Keds in a style her idol Jackie O might have worn—paired with her signature red lip.

She was truly stunning; she resembled a young Anne Bancroft. She had good height and a nice figure, and she was thin. The rest, she understood, could be made glamorous. She wanted to make an impact.

My sisters and I were not allowed in our parents' bedroom until our mother was "complete," meaning fully dressed and made up. She wouldn't so much as open the bedroom door unless she had styled hair, red lips, a face contoured by Pattie Boyd's makeup maps, and pink blush. She kept the house lights dim to hide signs of her aging, even removing some of the bulbs. "I look best in low lighting," she would say. A friend of Mimi's once said my mom looked crazy because she wore too much blush, and it made me so angry I never spoke to that friend again.

That my mother had lost the thickness of her hair to the virus remained the biggest secret. She always wore a well-done hairpiece mixed in with her own hair, something I found out only accidentally. One day, I was hiding in her bed, under a blanket, when I saw her emerge from the dressing room. At first, I didn't recognize her; it took me several moments to understand. I was so shocked I couldn't move. Until that moment, I had no idea that her hair was a wig. I'm not sure if she knew I was there, if she knew I knew her secret. We never discussed it.

Roseanne was bald. Molly was not. Now I'd like to think that wouldn't have been such a big deal. But she was from a different generation, and a family that equated illness with weakness, and weakness was to risk becoming a victim, and she guarded her facade of strength above all else.

Once, I saw her lying in her bed asleep without her hair and makeup. I was shocked to see her that way, in a cotton nightgown and a terry cloth turban, pale, sans mascara or lipstick. She looked like a pharaoh. She was quite beautiful this way, actually. But it was also frightening, because this wasn't the mother I knew. How shocking to discover that underneath it all, she just looked like a lovely young woman.

⁓

My mother had the ability to stop people in their tracks. Much like PopPop, she possessed a star quality, an inherent spotlight that followed her wherever she went. She was a sphinx; people thought there was a deep mystery about her because her eyes held fun and sadness. And she was well dressed. My mother understood that presentation is everything. PopPop had his bespoke suits. My mother was always elegantly attired. Unsurprisingly, I too love couture.

If ever we passed a child who was dolled up by their mother, my own mother would take note and say, "That child is loved." It was my mother's greatest disappointment whenever I wasn't turned out well. "Selma, please make yourself beautiful," she would say. "It means so much." Once I was capable, I really did try. And I curried favor with her, because nothing was more important than showing off her children. She loved us. And she loved us more when we looked good.

We had very few things, but they were beautiful things. My mom bought me my first Burberry coat when I was twelve. (I remember how the saleswoman's eyes popped out of her young head at the thousand-dollar price tag when she rang up our purchase at the register. "What a lucky girl you are!" she exclaimed.) My mother even had my name embroidered on the inside, just as she did with her minks and sables and snow foxes. (It was the seventies.)

For my mother, fashion was more than just a wardrobe. It was a character. It was from her that I learned that the right clothes could protect you against a world that wants to tear you down, that people will treat you with more respect when you look cared for. Every day she got dressed to play a role. She was, in many ways, the first great stage actress I saw up close.

As soon as my mother left for work at 5:00 a.m. for the two-hour drive to the capital of Lansing, I'd head right for her immaculate closet. I'd try on her makeup at her vanity sink, examine her silk YSL shirts and Givenchy dresses, slip on her Maud Frizon heels. Everything she owned was quality. She always warned us against trends, telling us only to buy what would still be classic in ten years. She understood the power of a uniform, another lesson she passed down to me. People would ask her, "Why do you stay so skinny?" and she would say, "I can fit more in my closet this way!" A joke I never got until much later in life. But I also came to understand it was part of her frugality. If you're going to buy expensive clothes, you want to keep them for life. Her philosophy was spend as much as you can afford; then do whatever you must to continue to fit into it. She was very practical in that way.

At the same time, she cautioned against becoming too stuck in one's ways. If we were out somewhere and she caught sight of someone with a dated look—if our server at the steak house was an old-time broad, with dyed-black hair and cat eyeliner—she made an example out of them. "Careful, girls," she'd say. "You get your look, but you need to adjust it in time."

My mother saved her money. When she spent, she did so carefully. She was offended if ever I bought something cheap and trendy. "Why can't you just spend a little more and make yourself look important, Selma?"

Once when I was in high school, my mom took me to the Chanel counter to buy me a lipstick. I don't look right with lipstick and I never have. My face doesn't tolerate it; I look severe, not soft. But my mother always loved a lip on me, and I wanted to make her happy. When the person at the makeup counter said it was twenty dollars, I remember how she carried on. "Twenty dollars?! I like nice things, but twenty dollars!" She bought it anyway. It was hot pink. After all that fuss, it was so perfume-y and tasted so strongly like Chanel lipstick that I never wore it. I wore it just once, on Mackinac Island, with a green suede vest and my hair bleached blond and parted on the side, just the way she liked it.

My mother had rules. I followed each one to the letter.

> "Don't wear anything you wouldn't still wear in ten years."
> "Classic is best."
> "Go high drama, make it worth it."
> "A miss is as good as a mile."
> "Never chew gum in public."
> "People who say 'classy' have no class."
> "Never drink and drive."
> "People who walk with a lit cigarette have very bad
> taste . . . It stinks."
> "When you get to the door to leave, take one thing off."

But the one that I thought of all the time: "A good girl parts her hair on the side." If ever I parted my hair in the middle, she would say I resembled a renegade from an insane asylum. "Selma. Bad girls part their hair in the middle. Good girls part their hair on the side."

Looking back, I see that my mother was so much like her father. She could be simultaneously affectionate and hurtful; like Pop-Pop, she knew how to wound those she loved with her barbs. Her four daughters were frequent targets.

She made fun of me for my lazy eye, my hideous flanks of cheeks, and what she called my "jolie laide" quality. "How can you be so beautiful from one angle and so ugly full face?" My mother said I looked like Lauren Bacall, but only with my head turned three-quarters—never head-on. "Don't look at people head-on, Selma, or they'll know you're a frying pan." Always, always three-quarters. That became my mirror face and, eventually, how I would learn to pose.

Unlike other mothers, who told their children they were beautiful without a stitch of makeup on, she just wanted me to look good.

"Put on some makeup, Selma, your eyes look like piss holes in the snow!"

"Selma! You've got hair above your lip. But it's chic. Very European."

"Oh, Selma, fix your hair. It looks like a plate of worms."

"Selma, get on the stick. Make yourself presentable, please."

If someone said I was beautiful, my mother would squint, as if seeing me for the first time. "You really think so? Her lip sticks out kinda far." But when I fixed myself up, the accolades were so gratifying. The compliments were very few; she doled them out very carefully. I lived for her approval.

She called my feet bear paws, because, though they are flat, I have fallen arches. "Oh, Selma! Walk on your toes!" she called, whenever I got out of a pool. "You're leaving bear prints! It's embarrassing!" It was framed as a joke, but I understood that she meant it. I was never easily embarrassed by my mother. Even when she criticized me, in public or in private, I never minded. Still, it all gets in your head. I'm at a point in my life now when I can no longer walk on my toes, and this devastates me.

My mother always carried herself with the air of an aristocrat or stage actress, even though she wasn't. But she was educated, poised, and worldly.

"To know the rules is to break the rules," she'd say. I always found that fascinating. She was a judge; she *was* the rules.

I loved her, and I feared her, in equal measure. Looking back, I can see she designed it that way.

"You're a witch like me, Selma," my mother once said. She wasn't a witch, at least not in practice. She certainly never put a potion together. But she did give me a certain power, by saying that we were alike.

❧

When it came to storytellers, my mother was the most gifted one of all. She painted the world with self-fulfilling prophecies. Starting when I was around five or six, whenever we had guests over, my mother lined the four of us up, like the von Trapp children, and introduced us.

"Here is Marie, the student," she said of Mimi.

"Katherine, the overachiever." This drove Katie wild, and still does. "I can't believe Mom would call me that!" she'd lament. "It's really fucking awful. It means you're not capable, but that you've still done shit. Everyone wants to be an underachiever, which is a good, talented person who just hasn't tapped into it yet." (Katie, may the record state: you are not an overachiever.)

"This is Lizzie, the popular athlete," which she sometimes alternated with "Lizzie, the tomboy."

"And last but not least, Selma, the manic-depressive."

I always found this funny because there was nothing manic about me. I have only ever been a depressive. But I didn't dare protest. I considered it my fortune to play the part assigned to me. "Oh, it's true!" my mom would say, in case anyone harbored any doubt.

Just like that, she cemented us with our own identities.

Sometimes, she said cruel things, too. Once, about happy-go-lucky Lizzie, she said, "You could cover her soul with a dime." It wasn't true, of course, but Lizzie internalized it. How could she not?

Because my mother introduced me to her friends as a manic-depressive, she not only convinced herself it was who I was; she convinced me. The part was written for me; she wanted me to play it well, and I wanted to make her proud. Can we ever escape the labels our families bestow upon us?

For my sixth birthday, she brought me to Goldfingers, the very chic boutique jewelry store in Applegate Square, a great eighties shopping center, and picked out a gift—a gold necklace that I still wear. One side featured a girl with a bowl cut and smiley face, the other side, the same girl with a frown.

Does the face inform the personality, or was it the other way around? It's a chicken-and-egg thing, I think. However it happened, I grew into my fate.

"There, Selma! Now we don't have to guess," she said. "You wear the happy side when you're happy and the frown when you frown." It became my signature piece, and everyone knew to look for it. Now they could simply scan my necklace, and if they saw a smile, they knew it was safe to approach me.

Years after I received this gift, my sister Katie wrote a poem about the necklace for a college writing class, which I kept in my journal:

Dangling

You twirl one-handed cartwheels
Each limb moves the air flying
You soar beyond others, hopes and dreams
The smiling pendant dangles at your neck
I see you writing at your desk
Your hair just

Past the childish stringy stage
Hides your eyes as you scribble
I think what you write will be worthwhile
Your happiness sudden then subtle
Is a pink pastel mark
Your soiled fingertips move the colors on the page
These few motions make art
The smile fades
A halfhearted leap flips the pendant
Blair where has it all gone?
A stream of dazzlement has dried
A frown now dangles at your heart.

❧

My mother admired Waspy women well turned out, so I did, too.
She especially adored Grace Kelly. In my mind, I built the impression that they were friends, and that vague story led me to admire
all things flaxen-haired and athletic, especially if it came along
with big white teeth and some generational wealth. That was
the thing back then, and it always came with that rarefied air of
belonging—something I never felt. I loved thinking my mom was
so important that she had a direct line to the world of celebrities.
I believed that everyone she knew was really important, though
in reality they were nothing more than acquaintances whom she
sometimes mentioned.

When Grace Kelly died, my mother was so sad, quite possibly the saddest I'd ever seen her. No one was more revered than
Grace, although Natalie Wood was a close second. When Natalie died, I came home and told the horrible joke I'd heard on the
bus to school. "What kind of wood doesn't float?" That was so

typical of the 1980s, to tell those types of insensitive jokes without any awareness of how inappropriate they were. Needless to say, it didn't go over well. My mother was sickened and furious when I repeated what I heard.

Elizabeth Taylor did not garner the same esteem, at least not in my mother's eyes. She said she once saw her in a mall and was not impressed. "She looked like the cleaning lady!" I think she never forgave her for what she did to Debbie Reynolds, another of my mom's favorites. (I found this especially fascinating in light of the fact that the two women eventually mended their friendship. Elizabeth and Debbie might have been able to forgive, but my mother was not.) My mom also placed such a premium on skinniness and height, and Elizabeth was not known for either, especially in her later years.

I didn't have many connections to the outer world, our social circle was small, so these tokens from my family came to mean so much. An anecdote meant someone was my mother's best friend, and a gift or a photo meant we were connected. I had a yellow T-shirt with a photo of Elvis ironed on it, a gift from my aunt Anna when I was five. My sisters all got one, too, so I wore that same shirt, in all the different sizes, throughout my life. I always believed Elvis might secretly be my father, because we looked alike. I told other kids that he might be a close family friend! I sometimes claimed Muhammad Ali was my cousin. I was a total liar for much of my life, but it's only because I liked a good story. I didn't mean to lie; I just didn't do a lot of fact-checking.

Even though we could claim no connection to her, my mother and I both loved Brooke Shields. We had a Scavullo coffee-table book, and I looked at it every day. There was a photo of Brooke without a top on, with that long hair and those eyes. I would gaze at it and think, *I wish, I wish, I wish.* I knew I could never measure

up, but it was no matter. These figures loomed larger than life. To this day, I still can't get them out of my mind.

～

My mother's love of Waspy women went all the way back to her childhood. She grew up in an enclave with the kinds of blue-blooded women that Grace Kelly or Katharine Hepburn might play in a movie. After her illness, she attended Vassar, but she bristled at authority, so she dropped out after one semester. She married at age twenty, to an aspiring doctor, and was pregnant right away. Her parents put her new husband through medical school, which he thanked them for by abandoning his wife and infant daughter. Soon after the baby, my sister Mimi, was born, when she and Mom were attending Sally's wedding to Uncle Jimmy, Mom's husband skipped town for California and never returned. He started a new life with a new family, without ever acknowledging he'd had a family before. By telegram he told her: "Don't bother coming back for your things. I shipped them to Detroit." Then he charged her for shipping.

After her first husband left, my mother moved in with her parents, who by then had relocated to Michigan in order to expand PopPop's grocery store chain into the Midwest. She spent one whole week playing double solitaire, crying, smoking cigarettes, and watching her baby daughter, Mimi, play on the carpet. Then she dried her eyes and decided to up and go to law school. That would be the thing. She would not be vulnerable again.

Even though she didn't have a college degree, she managed to get herself into the University of Detroit Law School. The day she graduated, her mother, Goggy, gave her a pair of emerald earrings, which are now among my most treasured possessions, and she began her career as an attorney. She was a single working mother, beholden to no one. Powerful, brilliant, fully independent. A few years later, she agreed to marry the first—and, my mother claims, the only—man who would have her, a Jewish lawyer named Elliot Isser Beitner. "What else was I going to do? Who else would have me? I was damaged goods," she said. Looking back, their relationship was imbalanced from the start: Elliot worshipped his dazzling, ambitious wife, and she merely tolerated him.

Elliot's nonreligious, Eastern European–born parents, Esther and Abraham, didn't approve of my mother right away—she was, after all, a "shiksa." An East Coast gentile divorcée with a toddler—but Molly and Esther eventually warmed up to each other well enough. Esther's first and only question about Molly was, "But can she drive?" and she was thrilled when the answer was yes. Elliot and Molly married under a chuppah.

What my mother wanted—more than a husband—was a successful career and financial autonomy. She also wanted to stay stylish and beautiful till the end. I used to study her high school yearbook photo for hours, looking for clues about who she was before she became my mother. The picture showed her looking impossibly elegant (to me), her dark, sharp eyes alert and determined. Underneath her photo, it read, "Molly Ann Cooke is a sophisticated gal with a flair for dressing attractively." I longed for those same words to be written about me.

Elliot adopted Mimi, who was so grateful to have a father figure in her life that it seems she developed a bit of a crush on him at first. One day while sitting poolside together on vacation, she took his hand, squinted, and said, "'Haps we kill Mommy?" Elliot found this hilarious and reported the quip back to my mother, who was amused. But Mimi and Dad didn't become close.

My mother went on to have three more daughters. The four brown-haired Beitner girls. We would've given Louisa May Alcott a run for her money.

Molly was not particularly maternal. Usually, when I'd ask what we were having for dinner, she'd say "poison" without skipping a beat. I thought it funny. Poison was the easiest conversation ender. She had a full day of work as a judge and then came home to make dinner. She was a mother at a time when work-life balance wasn't a goal that women thought about or talked about or strove to achieve. Most of the women in our comfortable Michigan suburb stayed home and raised their children. She could not have known that it was possible to both have a powerful career and be an engaged mother. Life didn't cater to children and mothers so much then. It was a different generation. She chose her work because she didn't have a choice. To do both would have been impossible.

As much as I missed her because she worked long hours, I was impressed with her. It was my mother whom I revered and emulated more than anyone. I was mesmerized by her—her smile, her makeup, her clothes, the small grape-sized birthmark on her right calf, her throaty laugh. The way she smoked, sometimes blowing out plumes through her nostrils when Lizzie yelled, "Dragon!" The way she sat behind the wheel of her car, leather-gloved hands turning up the heat in winter. The way she held her martini glass, with her painted red nails, during our parents' nightly cocktail hour. I was riveted by her. She was my first great love. I wanted every cell of her body to repopulate itself into mine. I wanted to become her. This feeling never faltered. Decades later, when she was suffering from neurological distress, my mother was the person whose approval meant the most to me. Even when she had no idea I was there.

I did not share all of these feelings with her. She was not gooey. Like PopPop, my mom was a woman who believed in decorum, that there was a real dignity in keeping quiet, in being stoic and private about one's personal affairs. "Never talk about religion or politics," she reminded us. Part of this was informed by the 1950s world in which she was an adolescent. Most of it was innate to her.

Growing up, I knew better than to complain about the sparks in my arms and hands that came and went, the repeating nightmares and dark thoughts that I recorded in my diary, the moments of existential anguish I felt even as a little girl. Nor did I disclose my deep desire to feel needed by her. Held by her. Because I was born terrified. I needed to keep very still so she wouldn't see the fear. And disapprove.

Still, my mother and I related through sadness in a way I think the other kids didn't. We didn't acknowledge it; it was more of an intuitive bond. I think she understood this about me, that she recognized my natural tendency toward despair because she was similarly afflicted. We were linked in this way.

Once, when I was in middle school, she told me that if things ever got really bad, we could always go into the garage together. We could turn on the Corvette, seal the doors, and breathe until we didn't. "We'd be together," she said. "So, you tell me." I thought she was trying to be kind; it was her wildly inappropriate way of recognizing my pain, even if it's horrifying to contemplate that a mother would suggest this to her daughter. My sisters were shocked! I see it now. She knew I was depressive, but if I told her—Yes, let's do it—she could stop me.

My mother never wore her heart on her sleeve, save for some periodic displays of anger or jest. She rarely shared anything personal, except occasionally when she was well into her cups. For as much as I watched her, for as much as I studied and revered her, sometimes I think I still don't know anything about her. All I know is that we both saw the world with a critical eye. "Realists!" she'd declare about us. I also inherited her deep appreciation for a body of water, a drink and a cigarette, and a great suit.

Sustenance

EVERY EVENING at 7:00 p.m., our family sat down to dinner. My mother worked a full day, drove the two hours home, and had a full dinner—steak or chicken with greens and potatoes, spaghetti with salad—on the table. "Girls! Dinner!" she called, right on time. We each reported to our places in the kitchen, at the Saarinen tulip table. And then we ate.

Dinner on Coventry Woods Lane was almost formal, my mother still in her pencil skirt and heels, red lipstick staining the rim of the martini glass that was forever sweating at her side, my father in a cashmere sweater and tweed jacket, eyeglasses his constant prop. It was also very civilized. My mother was a Republican and Elliot was a Democrat. This was a time when people could sit at the same table and talk respectfully about the issues of the day and their day, so they did.

Our meals were rather simple: steak, salad, spaghetti. But on the rare occasions when we had luxury, we were always aware of it, though in her fashion my mother was very fatalistic about it. "Girls, these scallops are very special," she would say. "The estuaries are going away. By the time you're grown up, there won't even be scallops left!"

We ate off the blue-and-white china. Before I was able to cut my own food, my mother, who sat to my left in the master chair with the molded arms, cut my steak into bite-sized pieces, thin and pink, blood pooling around the chunk. "Now make a clock," my mother would direct, before going back to her meal, the martini glass having been replaced with a long-stemmed goblet more than half full of red wine.

When we were all young, my parents shared a single bottle of wine with our meal. By the time I was ten or so, the bottle became a Rossi jug, and the glass would be refilled until she and my father were done. After dinner, as I cleared the plates and the crumpled, stained paper napkins, she stayed at the table, smoking a cigarette in the dim kitchen light.

When I was about five, with a lopsided bowl cut and a hard, round tummy, my favorite meal was spaghetti. I liked the al dente pasta with the jarred pasta sauce and especially the grated parmesan cheese from the green Kraft canister.

One night, when my mother called us in for dinner, I was hungrier than usual. It was summer and Lizzie and I had played outside all day. Sweaty, salty, ravenous girls. We took our places at the table, as always, with Katie to my right, my mother on my left.

My mom served me first, a plate of spaghetti with sauce and cheese. As I tried to wait for the rest of the family to be served, Lizzie's eyes were on me as I took a big bite from my plate. She announced this loudly to my mother. "Blair didn't mix her cheese in and she ate it!" She said it in such an alarming way, as if I'd committed a mortal sin. I felt terror, endangered.

I was mortified. I was a sensitive soul (despite biting my sister's back), and my favorite Lizzie, my twin, my everything, had just looked at me with such disdain and told the wrong I'd done. Her tone turned my body cold. My mother, plating our spaghetti, didn't say anything, which meant she must agree. I didn't wait for the ax to fall. To me, this was my army, and they had turned.

I didn't know how to translate shame, which in that moment felt as big as death. In my mind, I surmised I'd poisoned myself. If I didn't know I was not allowed to put unmixed Kraft in my mouth, then nothing was safe. I pushed back my chair and ran to the other end of the house. When I reached our room, I slid myself under my bed, into my own little bomb shelter. I would now die under this bed, with the stained carpeting, evening already settling in. I had no compass. I didn't know! "I am sorry," I whispered inside this space. For me, for my life, for unmixed plates of spaghetti. *I am sorry I am bad. I am sorry I am bad.* I'd later learn that old pets often go under the bed to die.

After a minute, Lizzie came in. She coaxed me out. My mother called us back to the table. Unsure, I sat down and watched my sisters eat. They were careful to mix the parmesan cheese into their sauce before they ate it.

As I gaze through the lens at a life's worth of moments, a plate of Barilla spaghetti and a reprimand from my beloved sister are seemingly unimportant, but it filled in my heart from such a young age. This was one of my first introductions to shame. The same shame would keep coming as years went on. There was a whole system, I saw, that wasn't about being good or even just being. It was about authority, with rules we are not born knowing. If this was how the world worked, I was in for a rough ride.

We don't know what stains a pure heart. We may not remember all those times, when we follow the wrong woman in the grocery store and reach for her hand and feel the red-hot shame for this understandable error. By the time we reach adulthood, we are so accustomed to being here that we forget how big everything used to be. The trespasses that to us seem light once felt like life and death.

If someone had held me and said, "Oh, honey, you're just a child, it will be okay," it might have felt okay. But I kept my secret. I became very anxious when eating in front of people. I tried to avoid meals with friends or boys. I would not eat spaghetti again until long after high school and the shame had faded into the black of the hallway inside me. Flat under the bed of my mind. Even then, the shame spilled out from under the dusty ruffles. Shame upon shame. For years to come, I would believe I should not eat what was put before me.

The first time I remember feeling self-conscious about my body was on picture day at Stevenson Elementary. I was in kindergarten, dressed in a royal blue pantsuit with a white cotton top. When I was brought in to have my portrait taken, the photographer looked at me and said, "What a bluebird!" He meant it affectionately, a term of endearment. I still have the picture from that day, and I can now say I am objectively adorable. But at the time what I heard was: Bluebirds are fat. Bluebirds have fat chests and round bellies. I didn't want to look like a bluebird. I would not be fat.

In due course I grew out of being a bluebird and was, in fact, skinny. My mother would always exclaim how skinny and bony I was. I could tell by her voice that she didn't mind it. But she asked the doctor what she could do so I wouldn't look so fragile.

"Beer!" he said. "Put beer in her cereal. Beer is fattening!"

So, my mother advised beer in my cereal. It tasted awful. I like cereal and I grew to like beer, but not together. The prescription didn't take, in any event. I didn't gain a pound.

In fourth grade, a teacher told me I was very thin and that it looked nice. I pointed to another girl, Miri Bernard, and said, "Look at her, though. She's skinnier than I am." And the teacher said, "No, she's *small*. You're *thin*. Enjoy it."

ఁ

My mother valued thinness, so I wanted to be thin. Like PopPop, she prized beauty above all. I had a lazy eye as a girl, which made me feel invisible, but she still believed I was the one daughter of hers who might be pretty enough to model, a profession she seemed to think my only prospect of employment. (I always found this curious coming from a judge who also claimed to value education above all else.) She warned me that once I got my period, I would stop growing, so she said I should try to postpone menstruation for as long as possible, as if it were a biological process I could control. "You need to be at least five feet eight to be a model," she'd say.

When I saw the first drops of brown blood at the age of eleven, I hid the evidence from my mother. I prayed I'd continue to grow taller, longer, leaner. I did not.

When I was in seventh grade, I told my mother I had started my period. I acted surprised, as if it had only just begun. She asked how much I weighed. "Ninety pounds," I said. She told me not to get a pound heavier. Not a single pound. "This is your weight," she said. "This is your size." I have been wary of weight gain ever since.

My mother was dictatorial about weight, perhaps because she had watched her own mother grow heavy when Molly was young. She saw weight gain as a lack of control, a sign of weakness (another bias handed down from PopPop), and as usually unflattering in clothing. My mother kept a diary of her weight and went through phases when she weighed herself obsessively. A few years ago, my sister and I found a detailed chart in one of her notebooks. It looked like an EKG printout. We had no idea what it was until we looked more carefully at the graph paper and realized that it was a record of her weight at every hour of the day for several years.

After she retired, she'd hole up at home alone, smoking and drinking with various suitors. I'd call her to see if she'd like company. "I can come out for a visit," I said. "Oh, don't come visit me, I'm too fat," she'd say. I knew better than to argue.

~

Sometimes, on weekends when I was little, my mother would invite me to take a nap with her, a special treat. She didn't like to be touched, so any chance to be close to her, my body aligned with hers, was sacred.

I remember one time in particular, when I was eight years old. The sky was a blank wash of gray, the few trees on the property were naked. I knew I was too old to nap, but I wanted to be near her, to smell her Fracas perfume and to be near the idea of her. She beckoned me beside her, and of course I accepted. I would do anything she wanted, anything at all.

I climbed into her giant bed, resting my head on her shoulder as we lay side by side.

She told me a story. I listened quietly. We were on a dogsled. "Look up at the stars, Blair!" she said. "It's snowing. We're on a sled, wrapped in fur rugs, and it's *so cold*!" I giggled, wanting her to go on. She did. "But we are safe on the sled; the dogs are running through the night. There are so many stars, like sparklers held high up in the night sky. It is so beautiful and exciting!"

I wanted to believe her tale. I could see it then. It was a magic carpet ride, an insulation from ordinary life. I longed to turn to her and whisper, "Mother, I am scared of everything but this moment, right now." But I didn't say a thing, because I didn't want her to stop. I scooted my butt closer to her. "Be still," she said. "Stop moving so much." I obeyed. She went on a bit longer, describing the sliver of moon, the frozen wind. And then she drifted off to sleep.

My mother's stories were my sustenance. I repeated this one over and over in my head, feeling the furs and the stars and the snow, the rushing and whistling wind, the dogs leaping. I wondered how they knew where to go. I fell asleep. Afraid as always, but safe in our sleep.

❧

But those were not the only stories she told.

Sometimes she'd call me in for a nap, and I could tell by the look on her face that she was in no mood to tell me a whimsical tale. No dogsleds, no stars, no fur blanket. Instead, she'd tell me the story of how she didn't know if she wanted me, when I ask if she loved me from the start. "I already had three daughters," she said. She was older. She had a career. She didn't want to have another child.

Elliot didn't want this baby, either. Elliot pressured her to go to New York, she said, where abortion was legal.

Oh! When she got to this part, I felt so worried for her, my mom. I was only seven or eight, but I had heard the nightmare stories. I knew the woman she was named after had died from complications of an abortion. "Oh, Mommy," I'd say. "That sounds so scary."

Then she told me how she couldn't go through with it, didn't go through with it. And then I'd let out a breath.

I was always too scared to breathe during these stories. I knew I must stay still, silent. Any interruption was an attack, and she would retreat. When she was done, I always asked questions. But she said nothing more and eventually we fell asleep. Molly and the girl she chose to keep.

Later, when she was awake, I asked, "If I was never born, who would be Blair?" And she roared with laughter. I let out a small giggle. I had pleased her with my wit. She laughed so hard, clearly and deeply. I burrowed underneath the blanket next to her, close, breathing her in.

"Who would be Blair?" my mom says, when I visit her for the last time.

⁓

I've been told that story all my life, in many ways been defined by it.

Unwanted.

I wonder if I absorbed my mother's ambivalence about having me even in utero. I wonder if it's embedded deep within me, a part of my DNA.

⁓

Perhaps feeling guilty that she often told me how she hadn't wanted me, my mother took pains to show me I had earned the right to be here, that I was special to her.

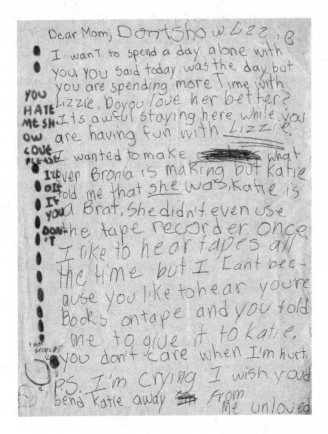

When I was five, my mother entrusted to me her beloved doll named Skinny, a childhood relic she had swiped from a store. Skinny was well worn and well loved, her face covered in filmy, gossamer fabric, small stitches for two blue eyes and a red mouth. I found the doll in Katie's closet one Sunday in October and begged her to let me keep her. My mother told me to be careful, because Skinny was her prized possession. Along with her other doll Checkers who was too fragile to touch.

When she left for work the next day, I missed her as always, but now I had Skinny, a part of Mom, my prize. Our nanny, Mrs. Ross, asked me what that filthy doll was. It wasn't filthy, I said. It was old. I told her it had been my mother's. She yanked it out of my hands and threw it in the garbage.

When Mrs. Ross returned her attention to the small black-and-white portable television set that she watched during the day at our kitchen table, I took Skinny out of the trash. I carried Skinny around all week and showed her my world, carefully avoiding Mrs. Ross. Until she opened the door to my bedroom and found me cradling the little rag doll. In two giant steps, she strode across the room, pulled Skinny from my hands. Mrs. Ross's own soft skin pulled apart Skinny's blue-cloth flesh and ripped her limb from limb. I watched, stricken. When she was done, she tossed the pieces in the garbage. "I told you not to play with that doll," she said. And then she left the room.

After dinner that night, I showed my mother the tragedy that had befallen Skinny under my care. I felt horrible, guilty, and unworthy. Most of all, I felt so sad for my mother. She picked the limbs out of the garbage one by one and examined them. She took Skinny's parts back to her room and sewed her up with pink thread as I watched silently from the doorway. Then she hid Skinny from me.

She never said a word about it to Mrs. Ross.

Another morning, when I was in kindergarten, I was down in the basement when I heard a shriek.

"Get out of my house!"

It was my mother's voice, directed at Mrs. Ross.

I raced up the stairs to see what was going on.

When I reached the top, I cracked open the dark wooden door

to the kitchen just as a coffee cup flew through the air. A skid followed by a smash. The mug landed on the tulip table, scarring its polished white top, before falling to the floor. Fragments of blue-and-white china scattered like confetti. Brown coffee dripped from the wallpaper. Mrs. Ross looked stunned.

"You. Are. Crazy," she said.

I retreated down the steps, back to the safety of the basement.

I didn't know what to do. I pulled out one of the mildewed books from the shelf, *A Very Young Dancer* by Jill Krementz. It was my favorite. In a series of black-and-white photographs, a girl demonstrated each ballet position: first, second, third, fourth, fifth. I took solace in the photos of the girl, who looked so sure and unblemished. I felt a solidarity with her; she was forever trapped in the book, just as I felt trapped in this home, in my family's basement. Unsure of what was unfolding above me, I made myself get lost in the pages. There she was, preparing to be Clara in *The Nutcracker.* There she was, eating dinner with her family. There she was, riding a sled through the snow with her handsome prince.

I looked up and saw Mrs. Ross standing before me, in this downstairs realm adults so rarely entered. She stood over me, wringing her fat hands. "Your mother no longer wants me to work for her. I won't be coming here again." She paused. "I hope you'll be okay."

I didn't say anything to her, the only other constant in my life. A long moment passed. Finally, I looked back at my book. I heard Mrs. Ross gather her things and leave through the back door. I didn't even say goodbye. I stared at the wooden veneer walls, the plastic tea set on the shelf. I wondered who would take me to school.

A few minutes later, my mother came down the steps. Now this was a first! My mother in my territory! I was mildly excited and nervous. She looked around, as if seeing it all for the first time. Then she looked back at me.

"Mrs. Ross is gone for good," she said, conclusively. "I guess you will have to go to day care in the morning, because I will be at work." And that was all.

My mother disappeared up the stairs and out of my view, back into the kitchen. I heard footsteps, the sound of sweeping. A chair scraping the floor. Footsteps retreating back into my mother's bedroom. Double doors shut.

Upstairs, I pieced some things together. When I tiptoed past my mother's room later, and the door was ajar again, I could see piles of folded laundry on the bed. And then I knew: Mrs. Ross had entered my mother's room, which was forbidden. Perhaps she thought my mother had already left for work. The underwear and socks were the witnesses of her transgression.

In the kitchen, the coffee-stained wallpaper stayed that way for the remainder of my childhood. I never knew if nobody cared enough to wipe it clean, or if my mother wanted a visual reminder of what happened when her privacy was violated. The white table, with its small brown gash, like the end of a scream, was never replaced.

After Mrs. Ross was fired, my mother found me the least terrible of the day-care centers in our area. I hated it, but I loved the journey to get there. My mother drove me herself in her new silver Monte Carlo with red velour interior, a red exterior pinstripe. The car had a sunroof and an eight-track player. I would spend two hours at the dismal day-care center, and then I'd shuttle over to Stevenson Elementary.

I hated day care, mostly because one of my classmates swiped the treat out of my lunch every day. With Mrs. Ross gone, I could tell a real confidante that someone was stealing the best part of my day. My mother knew exactly what to do: she started stapling the bag shut. "There. Now the thief will have to find someone else to prey on." And that was the end of that.

～

From the time we were very little, Lizzie and I wanted to ride horses. Anytime I'd see a field—which typically meant the big stretches of grass off the road on our two-mile walk to the mall— I could picture galloping over the land on a horse. I'd tell Lizzie, and she agreed. Oh, we'd declare, "If only we could cross this country on horseback!"

One evening, after we'd begged my mom for years, she came home from work and said, "Guess what! You girls are getting riding lessons." And I thought, "My life is going to change."

This was a big deal. Because my mom worked, and because Hillel, my parochial day school, didn't do sports, I never played anything until high school. Though I was athletic when it came to solo pursuits like gymnastics or figure skating, I was not an athlete. Even in the best of times, I couldn't run a mile, because I could never catch my breath.

That weekend, my mother took Lizzie and me to Haverhill Farms, a riding school and the only place near us where you could get lessons without having your own horse. Lizzie, wearing a plaid shirt, got right on her horse and trotted off, her head going up and down, a dust cloud billowing behind her. I got a horse named Humphrey whose only interest was eating grass. I couldn't get him to do anything; I had no idea how to make a horse go. I spent the entire lesson sitting on top of a grazing horse, pulling on reins with too much slack.

Piling into the Corvette afterward, my mother said, impressed,

"Oh, Lizzie, you really went!" I knew how I did. I didn't need to ask.

When we got home, I asked if I could take lessons still. My mom turned to me and said, "You're not ready." And that was that. My mother believed in spending money on people who were ready; otherwise it was a waste. It was a real heartbreak.

A year later, she let me try again a few times. It was winter, and a half-dozen students were in the indoor barn. They put me on a white horse named Cloud. We were trotting in a circle when I started sliding sideways toward the inside of the ring. The saddle slipped down, and so I fell. I was given a leg up again, but I was shaken. "Well, that was that again, Selma." I never pushed my mom to let me keep riding. I knew that I wasn't good enough. So Lizzie got to put on the velvet hat and learn to ride, to live my dream. Every week when Lizzie was at her lesson, my mother and I would go to the bakery to pick up a nice challah, to have ready when she got home.

Sometimes I would hold Lizzie's helmet and wish it were mine. In our room she would saddle up with our towels and let me ride her, instead. I'd climb onto her back, watching my posture in the mirror, her hands on the bed. Lizzie, as a horse, taught me everything she learned at her lessons, which was useful, actually, when I finally learned to ride in young adulthood. She was (and still is) the best big sister.

❧

But my mom was still my favorite person, and it made me sad to miss her when she was away at work all day. But as we grew, weekends became reserved for me and Lizzie. Every Saturday, we crammed into my mom's navy blue Stingray, with the white leather bucket seats. The car had a tape deck, which was a new thing then. If Katie was with us, she sat in the front seat, Lizzie and I in the back. My mom smoked Vantage cigarette after Vantage cigarette, and as she would say, we tooled around all day.

We mostly accompanied her on shopping trips, admiring as she tried on clothes at the nicest boutiques we had—beautiful shops with sofas and mirrors and candy in pretty dishes. My mother loved to be treated well, and I loved to watch her be treated well. She wrote a check for whatever she bought, lighting a cigarette as she filled it out. Every time, she would say, "It calms me, thank you." Most of those pieces remained part of her wardrobe until the day she died.

On all our shopping trips, I never drank water; because those Saturdays were so special, I wouldn't do anything to derail them. I learned early that with three girls, if we needed a bathroom and couldn't find one, my mother would throw up her hands and say, "Forget it! We're all going home!" So I went without water, and if I did need the restroom, I learned not to say anything about it, whimpering to Lizzie, who begged me to stay quiet.

I had constant bladder infections, but I didn't often report about those either, because it would irritate my mother. If I had to go pee in a cup, it would mean she needed to take the day off work to bring me to the doctor. Then she would get more irritated if I got a stage-fright bladder, and say, "We're going to be stuck in rush hour!" I tried to keep my ailments to myself.

❧

In addition to bladder problems, I often had a fever. "FUO," they called it, fever of unknown origin. For years, I kept a graph of my temperature, per the doctor's instructions. I had a fever almost every single day in fourth, fifth, and sixth grades.

Often, my body felt out of control, as if the connection between my brain and my limbs had been severed. One morning when I was in kindergarten, I discovered a pain in my left leg. "My leg hurts," I said as my mother was racing off to work. She didn't pay it much mind. "It really, really hurts." I dragged my leg across her bedroom to demonstrate the pain and how it gave out. Perhaps this was unnecessary, but it felt, to me, as if I should be dragging it. My mother just laughed. She kept on laughing as she told the story for years. "What a drama queen! What an actress! Dragging that leg across the floor!"

I learned that I couldn't show pain, and I certainly couldn't talk about it. To do so would only provoke laughter.

Now, as an adult, I happen to experience pain in the same leg. A drop foot. Looking back, it's hard to know what was real and what was drama. As a kid, you have new pains, but you don't have a vocabulary for them. Maybe it was a sign. Or maybe it was nothing at all.

⌒

As I grew up, it became apparent that I wasn't just dramatic. I was also unusually coordinated, limber, stretchy. Since early playground years I knew how to use my body in a physical way. I was quick and nimble, and I entertained with my physicality. My mother didn't believe in enrolling us in organized athletics; she was no soccer mom cheering on the sidelines. But certain individual sports came so easily—skiing, diving, ice-skating, tennis— I could become proficient in a matter of days. Without any formal gymnastics training, I could stand and do a backflip. A back handspring punctuated a sentence. I used my body dramatically, to dramatic ends.

Because I was so acrobatic, my mother hired a wonderful girl, Beth Willis, from my sister Katie's class at Kingswood, to come teach Lizzie and me gymnastics. She was a competitive gymnast (the exact thing I pretended to be at the park!), which felt quite official. The curriculum was a very homemade hodgepodge—a teenage girl demonstrating moves in a low-ceilinged suburban basement—but I took it seriously. My mom bought us some mats, and Beth taught us how to do back handsprings. She brought over her old balance beam, and I learned how to do a back walkover on it as my mom had her evening martini admiring my basic talent.

I was adept at doing flips, but I had to keep them low. My aerial cartwheel stayed close to the ground, because if I went any higher, I would hit the ceiling. That's the funny thing about limitations; sometimes they aren't about you at all. The ceiling was always there, and I didn't know any better. So I kept low to the ground, causing my audience to wince, afraid my neck would break.

When I got to college, I went through a period where I tried to be a real gymnast. It blew me away. There was a whole wide world out there. Space! Height! Breathing room! When I did an aerial cartwheel for the first time, I flew. I didn't know, without the limitations of a ceiling, I could do a double.

I still find myself looking for the safety of the ground. I still think small. "Accommodate for the low ceiling." I'm just now learning that the ceiling is imaginary. It's a relief, and also disorienting. Nothing is what I thought.

I felt very connected to that dark, smoky home, because it was my life. It was my mother. It was what I knew in that house. As a kid, I held tight to the belief that I never wanted to leave. "When I grow up," I'd think, "I'll come back and live here." I hadn't realized that in some ways that's exactly what I did. I brought that house, and its limitations, with me everywhere I went.

My son is a natural gymnast, much like me, and as I watched him practicing his flips, I saw he had a tendency to go low. Like his mother before him, he looks for the safety of the ground. "You gotta go up, kid," I told him, pointing to the sky. And he did a clear, high flip. I bought him a trampoline, because I want him to go higher. I pray that he always will.

⁓

There is so much that adults do, unknowingly, to children. To a child's mind (any mind, really), the smallest moments can become the biggest stories, images that change our lives forever.

It was a weeknight, September 1981, and Mom took Lizzie and me in the Corvette to see *An American Werewolf in London*. It was a big deal to be out with our mom, on a school night, after dark. She bought Jujubes and parceled them out, immediately taking out a filling.

I was eight or nine at the time, and I had no business seeing this movie. It's a comedy gore horror, and for all I know, the movie is hilarious; I haven't seen it since. What I do know is that I didn't recognize the comedy at that age. I saw only the terror.

The movie opens on a scene where the young leads, Jack and David, whose dark hair reminded me of mine and Lizzie's, leave this bar in the Yorkshire countryside. They're jubilant and singing, maybe drunk, when they're viciously attacked by a werewolf. Jack is mauled to death; David goes on, seeing his decomposing friend throughout the film.

That moment was the end of my childhood.

I hadn't grasped, until that moment, the reality of what death does. Until then, it had been an afterthought, a vague, distant mystery that happened to people you didn't know. But that night, I understood: Death is real, and it can happen unexpectedly. I would be dead someday. My mother would be dead someday. It took my breath away. I hadn't considered it really since I learned about death at age three.

This is what I carried home, in my mother's navy blue Stingray.

At home, I put my head on the pillow and tried to push out the images of dead bodies. It was too much for me. I felt unsafe everywhere, convinced that Lizzie and I would be ambushed like the men in the movie.

For weeks, I told my friends at school everything I could remember about the story. For nearly two years, I couldn't be alone in a room at night. When the lights went out, the dark pictures haunted me. A charred corpse beckoned from Lizzie's bed. I cowered in the shadows, sobbing softly into my pillow, wishing someone would come in and hold me. No matter how much I cried, my mother wouldn't come; she needed to get up early for work. She did not allow me to sleep in the big bed with her. Whenever I tried, my dad carried me back to my room, where I stayed awake most of the night. It went on this way, every day, for a year and a half. I kept my aunt Anna's fox stole in my arms as a protection.

I was sensitive and deeply affected by things, which I think made my childhood quite different from my sisters'. (I still need to edit what I watch.) My experiences were all or nothing, an exercise in extremes. This was a story I carried throughout my life, and still do, to some degree.

Lizzie is a mom to two children who are everything to her, and we rarely discuss our own childhoods. But the other day I asked her if she remembered the movie, this night that irrevocably terrorized me. A movie she seemed to have been unfazed by.

"That movie really fucked me up, Blair. It changed my life." Gobsmacked! I had no idea she ever felt that way. I can still see her, sitting in that passenger bucket seat, saying how much she liked it. "I remember getting out of Mom's Corvette that night, thinking, 'I don't know how I'm ever going to be okay.'"

It was a revelation to me. Lizzy was the tough one, acting nonchalant about big scary things. My big sister, always so brave. She pretended she enjoyed it. I didn't know the truth.

We play the parts we are given. We become the stories that are told about us. Lizzie was tough, her assigned role. She was the one who carried me on her back, and she wasn't going to let me down. Still, she wasn't able to help me, and my misery saddened her beyond my understanding. When I cried every night and she didn't console me, I never imagined she was silently experiencing her own brand of terror.

Lizzie grew up to embody everything strong and tough. She was stronger than most boys in her class; she ran hurdles and rode on the back of a motorcycle, embraced an athletic lifestyle. She became a cop after college, a hostage negotiator. To discover that deep down she had been just as afraid, but she never said a word. That rocked me almost as much as that scene had so many years before.

"I'm so sorry," she cried into the phone. "Blair, I am so sorry." And I was sorry, too.

As adults, we pull our childhoods with us wherever we go.

Elliot

WHEN I LOOK BACK on the characters of the past, my memories of my father are indistinct. I don't think I ever saw him clearly. I wish I could go back with wiser eyes.

I always liked his name, Elliot. But I never responded to the man with it. From early on, it was apparent that I was proudly my mother's daughter, and she required all my love and devotion. I could tell my mother was impartial toward her husband, with whom she maintained a cordial, if not cold, relationship throughout their marriage, so I didn't try very hard to please him.

It was my mother who commanded my attention. She was the person I wanted to kiss me good night, every night. She had the footsteps I ran out of my room toward. She had tremendous power over me. But some nights, when she was working late, my only option was Elliot. When he came to the bedroom I shared with Lizzie, he would jokingly ask her, "Who is your favorite? Mom or Dad?" And she would answer, "Tasca!" who was the German shepherd down the street. She knew how to handle his questions; she knew how to play him. And he would be amused. He never dared ask me that. He already knew the answer.

~

While our home life was humble compared with that of my wealthier friends, vacations were utopian. Where our house was marked by grim darkness and a shag pea green family room carpet, for me, vacations meant sunshine and pools, fresh pineapple, platters of breakfast room service, and chance encounters with other

kids. As children, we had such beautiful vacations that it became my life's pleasure to try to re-create them. To this day, a good hotel is still what I think of as the highest luxury.

In the 1970s and 1980s, my family would go on these gambling junkets, Elliot's thing, over Christmas and spring break. We kids would all get one suite, my parents another. There was coconut ice cream and Shasta with more fresh pineapple and a pink umbrella, which we could charge to the room! Most thrilling was the sense of adventure and independence. In my own house, I felt I was waiting for my turn to begin.

In my school day, I never ate the lunches packed for me—

typically salami or peanut butter sandwiches. I had a nervous stomach, Maalox in my backpack. I was embarrassed to eat in front of people. It was too vulnerable. Too sensual. But on vacation, I ate everything. I returned to my normal life feeling sated.

One year, when I was in third grade, we took a trip to Aruba that was comped by the hotel, another junket. I don't know the details beyond that my father hadn't gambled at the prescribed hour, or that he hadn't lost enough. Though they certainly had enough money to cover the rooms, my dad decided to leave in the middle of the night to avoid the unexpected expenditure of the vacation, on principle. I never really understood why my mom went along with this, only that Elliot was quite careful with a dollar, one of a collection of things my mother hated about him.

Early in the morning, under the cover of darkness, we secretly left the hotel without checking out and sped to the airport. Katie was so afraid. She kept saying that we were "like the von Trapp children," fleeing in the night. I somehow wasn't scared, merely inconvenienced, and was fine just as long as I didn't get separated from my mother.

Even at eight years old, I couldn't make sense of why he didn't just settle up. I remember asking, "Is this really worth it?" Sure enough, someone from the hotel met us at the airport, and Elliot was forced to settle his bill. In the end, we weren't criminals; we were just people who ended our vacation early. We still took trips as a family, but that was the last junket we went on.

Hillel

THE ROLE OF JUDAISM in my family was a tricky thing.

My sisters and I were all raised in the Jewish tradition, even though my mother never called herself Jewish. Judaism is matrilineal. Still, I always found it curious, given that her beloved father was Jewish and her mother—for whom she had only disdain—was Scottish and not a Jew, that she chose to identify as Anglican. In her jewelry box, she kept a cross that read, "In case of emergency, contact an Episcopal priest." She never wore it, out of deference to Elliot and our family, but I always knew it was there.

Even though my mother herself didn't identify as Jewish, it was important to her that I did. I was her chosen one. This became my first big role: to perform Jewishness. Over the years, it became a strange interweaving, where she would pit me against myself, telling me that I needed to be Jewish, telling me that I could never truly be.

My mother never socialized with any Jewish people. As a kid, I used to think she believed they were beneath her. As my sister Katie would say, "She would've hidden a Jew, but she doesn't want to be friends with one." But now, in hindsight, I suspect she felt as if she didn't truly belong.

Growing up, we never had a Christmas tree. We celebrated Hanukkah and fasted on Yom Kippur. Even my mother fasted. She was always respectful of our Jewish rituals. Her disdain ran somewhere beneath the surface, never outwardly visible. The Holocaust was at the front of her mind at all times. She referred to it often, citing the atrocity of *Sophie's Choice* and anchoring me firmly in the mindset of "do not forget."

My parents sent their three younger daughters to Hillel Day School, partly out of respect for Elliot, but mostly out of convenience. We could take the bus to Hillel, which meant my mother wouldn't have to drive us to school every morning. (Never mind that the bus ride took an hour and a half, because we were the first to get on.) It was a fully immersive Jewish education—Talmud study, prayer every morning, minyan, a congregation of students engaging in daily Hebrew instruction. I remember feeling grateful to have had this education. Still, my mother made it clear that in her view Hillel was not the be-all and end-all.

Once we were part of the Hillel community, we pretended to be good Jews. We played the part well. We overcompensated. We opposite-of-Anne-Franked. Our family went above and beyond in our Jewish calling. We stopped eating ham at home, in case one of our more observant friends came over and wanted to stay for dinner. My mother kept two sets of dishes, which she liked to brag about. "I keep two sets of dishes!" she would say to shopkeepers, who nodded politely. "One for milk and one for meat." The truth was, we didn't really keep the plates separate, so none of them were kosher. Thank God we never hosted an Orthodox person in our home, so these lies didn't actually harm anyone.

In my journals I wrestled with whether I believed in God. I wanted to believe; I loved the idea of God. "Dear Book," I wrote, ending each searching entry with "The End" in case I died before the next one, then crossing it out every time I sat down to write. At school, the fear of God was put into me, as well as the idea that we the Jews were his chosen people. I knew, given the usual metric of Judaism passing down through the matrilineal line, I wasn't really a Jew. But at school, no one could know this. We needed to keep it a secret.

I officially became a Jew when I was in second grade. My mother asked if I wanted to convert, because Katie had wanted to when she was the same age, and bat mitzvah time was approaching. "Selma, do you want to be Jewish, too?" She sat at the table after a dinner our new housekeeper made, smoking and drinking a glass of wine, dabbing her red lips.

I said that I did.

My conversion took place during the time I wore an eye patch. In first grade at Hillel we were all given an eye test, and mine came back saying I needed glasses. So we went to the eye doctor Leonard Lerner (coincidentally, the father of the kids who screamed about the mean Beitner baby). It was here I discovered I had a severe lazy eye. "We must take care of this right away!" he said. I was told I'd need to wear an eye patch for exactly two years. "We must trick the brain!" he said. A speech I came to imitate. Whenever anyone asked why I wore an eye patch, I would repeat, "We must trick the brain!" Emphasis on "trick."

We bought patches from the drugstore, black fabric with a little point in the center like the dart of a dress. They were a bit Gaultier, like Madonna's cone bra. The patch was sweaty in the summer, with a smell like a wet Band-Aid. It pushed my face down into an even meaner scowl—a mean baby pirate. I knew I wasn't pretty with my eye patch on, but my mother was supportive. She would draw on my patches, to make them cuter. I followed the doctor's words like the gospel. I never removed the eye patch.

The conversion process is immersion in a mikveh, a bath from which you emerge from holy water reborn as a Jew. Mine was lined with salmon-colored tiles, like something you'd find in a hospital bathroom. Before entering the mikveh, you are instructed to remove everything from your person—clothes, earrings, even traces of nail polish. But I refused to take off my eye patch. Dr. Lerner had been clear. I must never, ever remove it.

"You know, you're not really Jewish if you keep that on," said the woman at the synagogue who was presiding over us girls, gesturing to my eye patch. But the rabbi (coincidentally, the senior rabbi at Hillel) let it slide and gave me my conversion papers. For many years afterward, Katie would tease, "You didn't remove the eye patch, so you aren't really a Jew." To which I would say, "Shut up."

The day we removed the patch, my vision was perfect. Twenty-twenty.

"*Yehi or!*" I yelled. Let there be light. Everyone laughed.

Three days later, my vision went back to the way it had been. The brain was not tricked. It will always choose the easiest way, and the easiest way in this case was to turn that eye off. To this day, if I put one hand over my good eye, I cannot see.

I still have a patch. I put on every once in a while, thinking maybe I'll trick the brain. But the brain and I both know better.

The first time I got drunk it was a revelation.

I always liked Passover. Every year, as my family and I celebrated the exodus of the Jews, I actually felt that hope of next year in Jerusalem, as we sang in the Haggadah. I dunked my parsley in the salt water and tasted the pain of our tears. I loaded my matzo with horseradish. And as I took small sips of the small glasses of Manischewitz I was allowed throughout the seder, I felt warm, at one with my ancestors. A light flooded through me, filling me up with the warmth of God. (As a little kid, I *loved* God. Huge fan.)

But the year I was seven, when we basically had Manischewitz on tap and no one at the table was paying attention to my consumption level, I put it together. In that moment in the dining room, with the plagues and the frogs and the hail and the locusts, there came an epiphany. I realized, as I kept refilling my glass, the feeling was not God but fermentation.

That was heartbreaking to me, because it was like finding out Santa Claus wasn't real, if I'd cared about Santa Claus. It was also very convenient that I made this discovery at the table, where there was a glass of wine already in front of me. I thought, "Well, this is a huge disappointment, but since it turns out I can get the warmth of the Lord from a bottle, thank God there's one right here."

Because I wasn't very much of a planner, nor an in-the-moment critical thinker, I got drunk that night. Very drunk. The kind of drunk that would make most people never drink again. I rolled around the living room floor, then clung to my cousin Matt's leg, weeping and begging him not to leave me. I was out of control. Eventually, I was put in Katie's bigger bed with her, where I slept next to her all night long (a clear sign that I was gone if ever there was one). In the morning, I woke up and didn't remember how I'd gotten there.

So, now I knew. The relief I sought could be found in an inexpensive, sticky-sweet bottle—or *any* bottle. It wasn't spiritual; it was scientific. I didn't go back to it right away, but I knew it was there.

A few months later, there was this fly in the house that wouldn't leave me alone. It buzzed around and around the living room before landing on the cream carpet right next to the bookshelf. I squatted near the fly, attempting to swat it, but there was no need. It was already dead. That's when I saw it—an old paperback, wedged between S. E. Hinton's *Outsiders* and Judy Blume's *Forever*. I pulled it out and looked at the cover, intrigued. *Sarah T.: Portrait of a Teen-Age Alcoholic*. The book's pages were well-worn and stained, indicating it must have made the rounds with my sisters.

The book was about a sad misfit girl who turns to alcohol as a coping mechanism. I opened it up and started reading. With that bleak, dead fly as my witness, I read the book from cover to cover. What an adventure! As my eyes scanned the pages, I thought, "This is how I'm going to be okay." I was gloomy and sensitive, haunted by a nagging sense of loss I'd felt since the day I was born. Here was a girl who felt the same loneliness I did and for a few sparkly scenes found her fun in vodka-spiked watermelon. What was I waiting for? The answer to my pain was right here.

Of course, it was intended as a cautionary tale—a chaotic, problematic story, with an awful, tragic ending of a dead horse on a road. But I sidestepped the consequences and saw it as a how-to guide. I held the slim novel in my hands, knowing exactly what came next. As I slid the book back into its place on the shelf, I said,

"I'm gonna do this." I made a promise to myself: I would be the best alcoholic a girl could possibly be.

I stood up and went over to the game cabinet. Behind the green poker chips and the card-shuffling machine my dad would sometimes bring out for Saturday night card games stood the dusty bottles of party drinks. I reached for the tallest. It was a bottle of Amaretto. I screwed off the top and removed the wax paper stopper. In a sense, this was my last warning, but I didn't see it that way. I saw it as hope.

I took a swig. Not great, but not bad. It tasted like almonds, syrupy and sweet. I took a longer pull. "You're safe now, Baby Bear," I whispered aloud.

From that moment forward, Sarah T. became my inspiration, a mentor for how to crawl out of my timid body. Somehow, no one in my family took notice. I drank Beefeater gin. Miller Lite. Any bottle I could find. Just nips at first, then quick and burning sips whenever my anxiety would alight. Sunday mornings, I'd wake up early and take sips from the half-empty cocktails my parents left overnight in the sink. Every once in a while, I stole a bottle of Tanqueray and kept it hidden under my bed. I felt almost proud, as if I were grown up because I was doing this adult thing. I usually didn't get fall-down drunk; I barely even got tipsy. I just let myself have a little check-in, a tiny bit of warmth.

It wasn't until third grade that I got wasted again. My mother wasn't home. That night, after my sisters and I cleared the dishes, I crept back to the refrigerator. The light turned on, illuminating my face along with the jug of Gallo. I took just a little bit, a tiny sip, nothing to be alarmed over. But it kept calling to me. And as it did, I returned to the fridge for another swig, and another.

By the tenth trip, I was falling-down drunk. I staggered across the kitchen floor, past my dad on the couch bathed in the glow

of the nightly news, and finally into the powder room, where my stomach began to lurch. I vomited. (And vomited. And vomited. Sour splashes, evidence of my lack of impulse control.) My dad came in, held my hair away, and rubbed my back. Only then did he realize what had happened.

"Oh my God, Selma, you're drunk," he moaned, genuine concern playing across his face. "You can't drink this stuff; it's not for kids. It will make you really sick." He spoke in a soothing voice as he helped me clean up the sick. "I won't tell your mother about this," he said. I was grateful.

After that, I was on my own. I became an expert alcoholic, adept at hiding my secret from anyone and everyone. I was very careful. And no one was ever the wiser, at least until high school.

Some people say everything happens for a reason. I don't know if that's true, or just a line we repeat, over and over, to justify our bad choices. What I do know is that drinking happened to me. And once it did, it became my safety, a way of softening my jagged edges. As time went on, it happened with more and more frequency. It became the lede of my story. When I drank, I didn't know what drama I would find, but I knew it was drama that I would *feel*. I needed it. I looked forward to it. It was always my way out.

～

At Hillel, the families were very intact. Traditional. Parents knew what their kids were doing, and the kids seemed to have an instinct about what was healthy and what was not. I, on the other hand, had a different kind of family. Naturally, my parents wanted the best for me, and obviously that didn't include drinking. But there were four of us girls and I was the baby and both of my parents worked, so it was easy for things to go unnoticed. I was neglected, but not on purpose. Everyone did the best they could. No one hovered over me, and I was fast and secretive. I wanted to be older, to fast-forward to adulthood. I wanted to be my mother. So, I tried to follow adult social cues.

My school friends and I were in different places. I was reading *The Bell Jar* and trying to cultivate a profound, William Styron-esque depth. Meanwhile, they only cared about amazing bar and bat mitzvah parties and sweaters from The Limited. I didn't get a kick out of friendship bracelets and kid stuff. I was drawn to extreme situations, but my everyday life was very simple—wake up, take the bus, go to school, come home. I created my own drama.

My very best school friend was Marla. By fourth grade, we were inseparable, completely in love. We made each other barrettes braided with thin strands of ribbons, friendship safety pins with small glass beads, Keds painted with each other's names on the sides down in the basement.

One morning after a sleepover, Marla went home and my friend Ilysa and I walked over to play in the cool new park, past the field beyond my yard. We were the only ones there that morning, so I called my neighbor and kinda boyfriend, Danny, over to join us. I found a few half-empty forty-ounce bottles of Miller beer sitting on the platform that led to the slide. A nice drink before lunch. I wasn't worried about the alcohol, only the germs, but these bottles seemed clean enough. I figured the morning sun would have washed away any herpes germs.

I picked one up. It smelled warm and yeasty. I put the glass bottle to my lips and finished it, then burped so loudly that the two of them had no choice but to loosen up. But my peers were quiet. They took a purse-lipped sip when I handed it to them. We played a bit and the day petered out. I had no idea I'd shown my cards.

And then, in fifth grade, I got drunk in front of Marla. I misjudged. She was at my house on a Saturday night, and I drank a glass of wine after dinner. She didn't want any. Cool, I thought. I didn't think a thing. But that's when she disengaged. Before I knew it, she started siding with Ilysa instead of me. I felt ganged up on, confused as to what I'd done wrong. "Why do you hate me?" I asked her. That was my first fallout (due to alcohol). I felt hurt, rejected. It never occurred to me that she was distancing herself from me because of the drinking.

Her head was in *Ziggy* and *Garfield* posters and spending our allowance on bubble gum and greeting cards at the drugstore, not stealing alcohol and cigarettes. I would want my son to do the same. I wouldn't want my kid to hang out with me, either.

I don't think she ever told her parents.

After I lost Marla, the rest of my Hillel experience was hell. I sobbed every day, begging her to tell me why she turned against me. She never said. (In fact, I never knew until adulthood, when Marla visited L.A. and met up with me at the Chateau Marmont. She ordered a glass of wine as I sipped my coffee, then sober for years. "Was it my drinking?" I asked. "Yes, I think it was," she said. She shifted in her chair, still uncomfortable talking about it. "I also think it had something to do with the way you lived. You freaked me out. I'd never seen someone our age behave that way. And you were sick or lied about being sick. I don't even remember.") I'd lost my only best friend, whom I loved. I went through years of missing her, mourning what I'd lost, all the while being made fun of by her and the other girls. This should have made me reconsider my actions, but it didn't. It only made me keep them to myself.

Mimi and Katie weren't drinkers, but sometimes Lizzie would do it on the weekends, with friends. Once, when I was in fifth grade, we got our friend Emily so drunk that she poured a bottle of ink all over my mom's maple desk, which she'd had since childhood. We ran around, taking our clothes off, drunk and crying. We got away with that almost every weekend, Johnny Depp–ing our way around the basement. But that one weekend, Emily spiraled out of control. Ceiling tiles were popped out. Books were ripped, toys torn apart. My baby book—the only artifact I had that told me who I was—got destroyed. I hadn't anticipated this kind of fallout. When I drank, I never resorted to destruction. But what did we expect? You can't get a ten-year-old drunk and think it will go well. It was all my fault.

One Sunday when she was thirteen or fourteen, Lizzie came home hungover, a notch in her belt. "I was with Mia and Lisa," she told me—the cool kids—"and we got *so* drunk, and we went to the movies, and they said, 'Lizzie is glassy-eyed.'" Glassy-eyed! It seemed such an achievement of drama. That became my goal for the weekend. "Show me when I'm glassy-eyed," I said as we sat in the bathroom, drinking old bottles of Aperol and Grand Marnier. I would have a whole lifetime to explore that feeling. But I wanted to pack in as much drunk as I could.

Once Marla left me, I became best friends with Becky, the biggest outcast in our grade (who turned out to be an incredible friend). She was once a thumb-sucker and I had been way out of her league, but now blue-eyed Becky in her cool new Esprit clothes and newly ostracized Selma found each other. She had no judgment about any of the choices I made. I was feared, and alone, with her. That I made it through eight years of Hillel is thanks to three things: Becky, the long gulps of Tanqueray I snuck in most days before school, and Bradley Bluestone.

∾

Bradley Bluestone was the Brad Pitt of Hillel Day School. With goyish and boyish features: blue-green eyes, light brown feathered hair, thick eyebrows, and a button nose. To me, his face was delicate and handsome and perfect. He even had a lazy eye, like me. I wanted him on my arm and was determined to do whatever I could to make it happen. Every morning, when we said the prayer to Abraham, I took breaks to stare dreamily at Bradley.

Once, in sixth grade, Becky and I were talking by the swings at the park behind my house when she asked me, "Do you think you'll love Brad forever?"

"Yeah, I think I will, actually," I replied without hesitation. "Forever. He's the one I love."

"You can't be with him; he's a year older," she protested, as if it were impossible for him to "go" with me. But I wasn't having it.

"No, he's going to be my boyfriend. And I will love him forever."

And he was. By the next year, we were officially "going." From that point forward, I again firmly established myself as the most popular girl in school—besides Lizzie—the only one with a boyfriend who was older.

"You're so beautiful," he told me one summer afternoon, as we were lying in the sunlight, his face over mine as I lay back in the grass. "I can see every pore on your face." Mortified, I shut my eyes so he couldn't see me. He was the first boy to ever look at me up close, I guess. His observation shamed me. Bradley was my first kiss. His mouth tasted of sweet raspberries as we made out in front of my house next to the lilac bushes. It was June 24, the week after school let out. He drove over on his Aero moped—on a real highway! I was nervous and impressed. In my mind, he was all of it, like Jake in *Sixteen Candles.* His dad was a lawyer turned chiropractor! Doubly useful! He made my knees weak. It was young love, and it stayed for a while.

We'd split up and reconcile, as young love goes. I would call and

break up with him—or worse, have a friend call and break up with him on my behalf—just to try out dramatic adult behaviors I saw on TV. I was dead terrified of people so I pushed and bedeviled. "Stop bedeviling Bradley!" my mother would say.

Even later, as I was ending my time in high school at Cranbrook Kingswood, Brad and I confided in each other. We wrote love letters and talked late into the night, cramming as many song titles as possible into our congenial chats. His parents doted on him, though college had its share of emotional stress. He was still golden. He was still golden for me. BB + BB still made me smile when I opened his letters. Bradley Bluestone + Blair Beitner forever.

And then, on February 7, Becky called me. It was my senior year. I was sitting back in bed, taking my temperature while enjoying a Whitesnake song on MTV, watching the blur of motion and spotlights and Tawny Kitaen on a white piano, not a car, this time.

"Bradley is dead."

What? What?

"He died in his dorm room," Becky told me. "The funeral is tomorrow."

"What? How did he die?" I asked, my eyes filling with tears. "What happened?"

She said Anthony found him. His best friend since Hillel. She never knew what happened.

I couldn't speak. I wanted to drop the phone, to stop the words from coming out, to stop this from happening, from being true. But it had already happened. I held the phone with both hands and wept.

The next day, we went to the Ira Kaufman Chapel, where Bradley was interred.

As we shoveled dirt onto his expensive steel coffin, the shovel broke. There was a gasp. Sobs. His mother and I hugged. My heart broke for his parents. He was the love of their lives.

"To outlive your child is the worst grief," my mother said later that night as I sat on her bed crying.

"I can't stop thinking about him, rotting in the ground, all alone in there. Underneath. Mom!" I sobbed, too consumed with grief to care how I sounded. I tried not to think about the movie with the werewolves. I cried and cried. My mother said, "You will never really get over this." She was right. I never did. No one ever spoke of his cause of death; to this day it's still a mystery to me. It's almost as if his parents couldn't bear to put a label on what had happened to their son. They wanted to remember him as he was, unblemished. To me he will always be this golden boy who floated up to heaven like an angel.

I, Selma

THOUGH IT DIDN'T ALIGN with my mother's original ambitions for me, I found I loved to write. Every summer starting when I was six, the whole family would accompany Katie on her way to Camp Ramah, a Jewish sleepaway camp in Ontario, Canada. On our way, we'd make a pit stop in Toronto, where we stayed at the Four Seasons. One of the things I loved most about the Four Seasons was how the rooms had a pad of yellow paper and a pen next to the bed. I'm not joking when I say that before this I don't think I was exposed to a blank piece of paper of my own not meant for a school pad. A piece of paper where I could write something personal? Frivolous? This was a gift.

And so, I set about to write the story of my life.

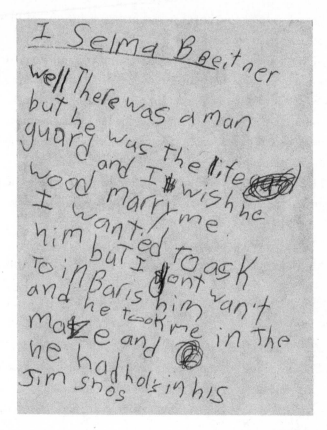

"I, Selma, am six years old, and I'm in love with a lifeguard. He has holes in his tennis shoes, and he took me through the maze. I thought he was sexy."

I shared it with my mother, who was so impressed. Praise did not come easily from her, and yet she loved my writing notes. It took only three sentences to win her over. If my mother approved, then I knew it was a worthy venture.

Back home in the basement, I began writing *I, Selma*. I wrote about how my sister Katie had smooth skin or some such irrelevant and clichéd finding. I wrote that I was scared to grow up, because I didn't know how I would make a living. (Valid.) I also wrote that I was fat. (I was not.)

While some of *I, Selma* was scrawled in childish print, some was done in cursive that was at once very pretty and very upright. (Now it slants every which way, like my mind, but at that time it was clear and straight.) It didn't take me long to see it was not a literary masterpiece, and so I gave up and eventually threw it away, embarrassed by my naivete.

Eight years later, I was in a bookstore with my mother when I noticed Tina Turner's new memoir displayed up front. It was called *I, Tina*.

"That's my title!" I said, pointing at the cover.

My mom laughed. "You gotta get up earlier than Tina Turner!"

⌒⌐

PopPop was a deeply literate thinker who also loved to write. He said he always hoped to publish a book one day about the pitfalls of conglomerating in the grocery store business. He even had a title for it: *Requiem*. But he never made much progress with it, as far as I know.

I like to think I inherited this yearning to write from him. From a young age, I privately wanted to be a writer, but I was too scared to say this ambition out loud. It felt at once lofty and also disappointing, since I thought it wasn't what my mother wanted, and my greatest wish was to please her. So instead, I wrote all the time in secret—stories and poems, random thoughts on scraps of paper. I poured my fears into my journals, along with details of every crush and rejection. Pretty heady and boring simultaneously.

When I was twelve, our teacher Ms. Nelson gave us a creative writing assignment in school, and I took the task to heart. Looking back, I wrote something incredibly trite but age appropriate, and I was thrilled when my poem won first place. (At a Hebrew day school not known for its writing, managing to open up in any way was worthy of praise.) I had never won a prize for anything academic since the "Pitzel Family" book I made in elementary school, and I couldn't wait to show it to my mother.

We were in the formal living room, the one lined with all the law books and the fly of yore, and I perched beside her on the cream velvet sofa. I wanted so to please her. To have her smile and say, "Wow. This is wonderful, kiddo." But apparently, her standards were higher than Ms. Nelson's.

"What is this?" She peered at the pages. I already suspected it wasn't her dish of tea—something she corrected me about all the time. ("Selma, it's not a cup of tea, it's a dish of tea." To this day, I still don't know which is right.) Still, this was worse than I'd predicted. When she was finished, she put it down and said, "Ugh, Selma. This is drivel. Sheer drivel. I can't believe they gave you something for *this*?" She thrust it back in my direction. "I don't want to see this shit again."

I looked down at my words. Now I could see there was something off about it. My mother was right. There must have been some mistake. I felt ashamed. I crumpled it up and threw it in the garbage.

I didn't view her as being hard on me; I trusted her word. Instead, I went in the other direction and stopped trusting others whenever they offered me praise. I internalized her words. It was the truth. (Later, when I was in high school, my mother actually told me I should write a book one day. "You write, I edit," she said.)

My older sister Mimi had the most beautiful friend, Gina Ferrari. My favorite. She was an artist, a painter, as well as loyal to my sister, a quality we all appreciated even then. When I was in fourth grade, she set me up at the table at her house with some of her watercolors and an iris in a vase. I painted what I saw. As it turned out, it was pretty damn good. It was chosen—again at Hillel—for another award. The painting was displayed at Sinai Hospital, of all places, and my mother was thrilled. (She loved the painting so much she kept it until the day she died.) If my mother praised something, then I knew it was worth pursuing.

⁓

I didn't share my writing again for a long time, but whenever I said something that my mom found to be exceptionally clever or nuanced or funny, she would sit up straighter, point her cigarette at me like Princess Anne, and order, "Put it in the box."

One time, my mother and I were in synagogue, and we were starving. I was in middle school. It was Yom Kippur, the Day of Atonement, and we were fasting, we were famished. Miserable. Bad breath all around. Even the handsome stained-glass wall of our Saarinen-designed Shaarey Zedek temple with its Chagall-esque vignettes of Old Testament scenes couldn't distract us. My attention rested on a woman in front of us, an old, old salon-coiffed lady focused on her prayer book, hunched, her clip-on earrings backward. I whispered to my mother, "Mom, look!" and pointed to the earlobes in front of us.

We were the only ones who could see the glimmer of two ersatz diamonds pointing in our direction, like headlights shining only on us. We found this totally hilarious. The backward clip-ons.

"Put it in the box," my mother whispered, laughing. "Put it in the box."

Then we went around critiquing all the other congregants' bad fashion choices. We were the mean girls of shul.

I was pleased. I didn't need a prize when I had my mother's approval. This became our refrain. Through college, through New York, through California, with every phone call. If I made my mother laugh, she pleaded to me between cackles. "Oh, Selma!" she'd cry, hands clapping. "Put it in the box."

∼

"Selma, you must write a book!" my mother would say.

"I have nothing to write about, Mom."

"Then write a song! Be a songwriter."

"But all the good melodies are taken!" I said.

"Put it in the box!" she roared.

∼

For a long time, I thought this box was purely symbolic, her way of acknowledging a funny story. But then, after years and years and countless demands to "put it in the box," I finally asked her, "What is this box? Is it a real thing?"

She told me PopPop had kept a box in his closet, and whenever he had an idea or a funny story for the book he hoped to write, he jotted it down and put it in his special box. I pictured a wooden bird box where all the winged thoughts were held, fluttering around like hummingbirds, until he was ready to write fully and set them free.

As the eldest, Mimi was the family authority on our grandfather. He named her his *ichiban,* a pet name, meaning "my first," that he borrowed from his travels in Japan. Not long ago, while talking to her about PopPop, I asked if she knew anything about a box where he collected his thoughts and musings.

There are people who live by words and those who lie by silence — both are shits — equally.

"I'm not even sure if there ever was a box," I said. "It's just, like, a metaphor. Something Mom said."

Mimi gasped and almost screamed into the phone, "No, I have the box! I have it!"

When he died, Mimi was given some of the contents of his apartment, including a box that fit this description. I couldn't believe it. She had the famous box.

Recently, Mimi sent me some of the contents. Much of it is random—newspaper clippings about his business, nonsensical quotes, restaurant receipts with a single indecipherable word scribbled on the back. But there are some jewels, little glimpses into his personality and biases.

A newspaper clipping, at the top of which he scrawled, "When the gov't becomes law-breaker—anarchy."

A handwritten note: "A woman should be charming."

And this: "Children make us young, but how can they keep us young when they make us so old?"

And this: "Requiem: In a family, some members often feel they 'own' you—but at the same time, do not feel the responsibility 'to' you."

Another: "Only a success wipes out the disgrace, etc.—but writing it out helps. Catharsis."

And my personal favorite: "There are people who live by words and there are people who live by silence. Both are shits equally."

Whenever I look at it, I feel a kinship with him, a string connecting us. A mystery closer to solving.

Written in a thick red script: "The value of life depends on dignity not success." I noticed the date. It was the last day before he retired.

❧

My mom didn't have a box, at least not in the literal sense. Instead, she had a cherrywood rolltop desk—separate from her makeup vanity, separate from her work desk—which we were *never* to look into on pain of death. The bottom drawer was very deep; from the outside, it looked like two drawers. Everything she liked of mine went in that bottom drawer. There were no photos of me. She kept all my stories, all my drawings, all my little pieces of paper. "Put it in the box." That is what she saved. I was the only child she did it for.

❧

The most important person I met at Hillel was probably Anne Frank. Her diary was the required reading in Ms. Nelson's fifth-grade class. I felt immediate respect. And kinship. Not since Sarah T. had I found a girl who spoke to me as intimately and urgently as Anne Frank did. For a child fifty years my predecessor, she still seemed alive and modern. I can see her face in black and white on the cover, her sweet, ever-familiar smile. Hair parted on the side. I carried that paperback with me everywhere, to keep her alive. My sister Katie once took my copy and hid it, as payback for when I hid her *Tiger Beat* magazine, and I ran through the house screaming, "Katie has hidden Anne Frank! Give her back! Give her back! Hasn't she been through enough already?"

Anne was my glorified shadow. Trapped. Intelligent. Optimistic. Unlike Anne, though, I did not believe people were mostly good at heart, and I didn't understand how she could maintain such faith in humanity. I couldn't wrap my head around what had befallen her. And yet I related to her as if she were a close classmate—romantic, passionate, and outspoken. She fought with her mother. She questioned her faith. She could be petulant and sullen. She had intense mood swings and periods of internal despair. She yearned for one true confidante to whom she could confess her deepest secrets, and the person she found was Kitty, the imaginary friend to whom she addressed most of her diary entries.

"Dearest Kitty," she wrote. "I am seething with rage, yet I can't show it . . . I'm stuck with the character I was born with, and yet I'm sure I'm not a bad person."

Relatable.

Of course, we are reading a diary of a lamb to the slaughter. What I really couldn't believe was that, as far as I could tell, Anne was going through this period of hiding from imminent death without losing sanity or self. I couldn't even manage a day of Hillel without a few sips of alcohol to calm my system, much less years of hiding in a secret annex, fearful each day would be my last. I compared my little life to hers and felt inner guilt and shame for all I had. For safety.

Anne was a different ideal from others I clung to. I loved her depth and that she was a secular Jew who wrestled with her belief in God, like me. I felt conflicted as to my own identity, so I truly, deeply identified with Anne Frank. It is the Selma and the Blair. Selma identifies as Anne Frank, while Blair is off trying to cultivate a Hitchcock blonde look, at least in photographs. Like the smile and the frown, they are equally a part of me.

Years later, in 2010, I was honored to be asked to read Random House's new audio edition of Anne Frank's diary. As we began in the studio, the script laid out on an easel, I was overcome. The first sentences I uttered were difficult; Anne's revered words, every one of which I'd read so many times, coming out of my mouth suddenly sounded so hollow. But once I gave in to the voice, I felt as though I had crossed over into something real.

When I first encountered Anne as a child, I didn't realize how much I would come to relate to her in truly unexpected ways—the experience of feeling trapped, of wanting to interpret her world and the world beyond but not being allowed to have a voice, of feeling as if you were no longer in control of your own destiny. Of wanting to find a way to cope. For Anne, it was through writing. For me, for a long time, it was through alcohol. It took me a long time to find another way. Unlike Anne, I would have the luxury of years to try to get it right.

Now I can say without hesitation that I am, and always will be, Jewish. In my everyday life, I am very Jew-ish: a secular Jew who is deeply spiritual, with a lot of faith and a big voice when it comes to remembrance. I don't belong to a temple. I still remember Passover, though I don't serve Manischewitz. (No fucking way!)

⌘

By the end of eighth grade, I came to resent Hillel. The religious curriculum was fine, but I struggled in math and began to clash with teachers who resisted my desire to change and grow up. I was too dramatic, too rebellious and restless. And Brad had gone on to high school, so I felt there was nothing left for me.

It was around this time that I developed constant throbbing headaches. Pain blossomed. My face ached. To soothe the pain, I began drinking more on weekends and feeling poorly as a result. I had little appetite, eating only breakfast and a small dinner when we all sat down as a family. I had even more trouble eating in front of others. It felt garish. Sexual. Provocative. Private. As winter came, I became thinner, my skin tinged with gray. I went repeatedly to the endodontist, believing the pain I suffered was caused by my teeth, and received several root canals, chasing what I now know was trigeminal neuralgia.

One November weekend, the seventh- and eighth-grade classes went away for a retreat called a Shabbaton, and everyone turned on me. My friends iced me out. I was friendless and depressed. When I came back home, I told my mother what a terrible time I'd had, and she suggested that I dye my hair. "You need a change," she said. "It will cheer you up." She called Cousin Helen, a distant relative just out of beauty school, for help.

It took hours, but I went from dark brunette to champagne blond. I looked like a movie star with a dash of Sylvia Plath. Still melancholy, but on the surface I was quite bright now. My face looked pinker. Sweeter. My eyes, framed by my dark, thick eyebrows, suddenly looked stunning. I was happy with my new hair. A lighter bang did mean a lighter face.

Especially as a bleach blonde, I found things at Hillel devolving. The final nail was hammered when my teacher, upon reading my class journal, kept me after the bell to discuss my work. She pursed her lips, holding her glasses in her wrinkled, thin, but manicured hands. Ms. Itzcovitz was always on top of things. She was sharp. Skeletal. Watching. But this time, she read it all wrong.

"Do you think it is peculiar that you go by two names? Selma and Blair equally? As if you are two people?" she asked.

I did not. But clearly she did.

"And now," she continued, pointing her eyeglasses in the direction of my newly dyed hair, "you have this situation."

I found this deeply ironic, because her own hair was dyed a brassy caramel color. I felt accused. Betrayed.

"I have two names," I patiently explained. "I prefer Blair. Some people prefer to call me Selma." It was simple. Sensible. True.

She nodded her head. As if she knew it all. Then she told me to think about it. Not for a journal prompt, but to *really* think about choosing one name only.

I have thought about it. I thought about my mother and the seldom referenced Roseanne. I thought about the two selves I was accused of having, Selma and Blair. About the smile and the frown. And this is where I've landed: There is no schism. My names are a wardrobe. Whatever I felt like wearing on that particular day. Over the years, I have grown into Selma. As I always knew I would. Or rather, as my mom did.

Ms. Itzcovitz was a fine teacher. But both Selma and Blair can now agree. Making me feel wrong was a rotten thing to do to a child.

Brigadoon

$\mathcal{F}$OR NINTH GRADE, my sisters Lizzie and Katie had gone from Hillel to the prominent prep school Cranbrook Kingswood, and I was finally following their lead. Cranbrook was pure enchantment. Reminiscent of *Dead Poets Society* or the dazzling world of F. Scott Fitzgerald. There were buildings by Frank Lloyd Wright hidden within the Saarinen-designed campus. Everywhere you walked, there was something to appreciate. High ceilings and wood paneling, grand foyers with polished brass, shiny malachite tiles. Wrought-iron windows specially made for the school. Every last detail had been chosen in the best taste and craftsmanship. Everything was exclusive, in a welcoming bent. It even *smelled* good, with fireplaces roaring on cold winter days. It still remains the most glorious set I've ever been on.

Classes were held in rooms that looked more like living rooms. Beautiful open spaces to wander, besting even the lobby of the Chateau Marmont, which has a similar lighting scheme. The environments were specifically designed to facilitate open conversation, stimulating questions, and discussions around big ideas.

As soon as I showed up, I saw there were so many people—a whole world, in fact—outside yeshiva. And they looked and dressed so much better. Coming from such an insular community, I was surprised to meet so many sunny blond athletic types who, despite their lack of being chosen ones, were doing just fine. When I was a student, Cranbrook was a haven of dazzling lacrosse players and VW Cabriolets. The students were, by and large, the products of generational wealth—the descendants of people who had important names. They came from beautiful homes in which they hosted parties like something out of a Jay McInerney novel, where the things that got broken were priceless and irreplaceable. I fell right in step anyhow, cultivating an aesthetic that was both dramatic and classically tailored, inspired in large part by my mom. One day I'd wear a full-on riding habit, the next a motorcycle jacket. I studied *The Official Preppy Handbook,* memorizing every word as if it were gospel. It was funny and kitsch, but really enjoyable. I had a new goal, and it was to master prepdom.

I also found that when it came to academics, I was utterly unprepared. At Hillel, I excelled in English and writing and social studies. But when it came time to keep up in math and science, I was in way over my head. I flat out failed, and my attitude was equally out of step.

It can take hitting a kind of bottom for a lazy person (and I counted myself as such) to find motivation. I found I had failed this gorgeous place, a truth far more disappointing than failing myself. For the first time, I saw that my choices affect my future. The positive side of my negative self is that I don't see what I have until it's gone. And then I do change.

I was expelled from Cranbrook, and I went to public school for a week. It did not go well. I didn't understand the hierarchy; I couldn't keep up in the large classes. I was lost. I was verbally bullied and physically pushed. Luckily, fate had other plans. During that first week as a student at Southfield-Lathrup High School, I

Box 801
Bloomfield Hills
Michigan 48013 USA
313 645-3000

Cranbrook
Educational
Community

CRANBROOK KINGSWOOD

Cranbrook Schools

September 11, 1987

Mr. and Mrs. Elliot Beitner
22445 Coventry Woods
Southfield, Michigan 48034

Dear Mr. and Mrs. Beitner,

I am very pleased to be able to write this letter to tell you that
Blair has been invited back to Cranbrook Kingswood School.

Blair has persuaded the faculty that she is serious about returning
to school. Her attitude has undergone a dramatic change. She has
shown she can be an outstanding citizen by her achievement this summer
at camp. Her willingness to see a counselor and to work with a tutor
in study skills demonstrates clearly to us all that she is actively
seeking to become a successful and self-confident student.

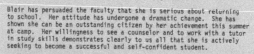 made a most wonderful presentation of Blair's petition to
return to school. His faith in Blair was the key element, I believe,
in the success of the petition. For a student to return to school in
this way is an exceptional occurrence. I cannot recall this happening
once during my last ten years as a teacher here. It is manifest to me
that the faculty have thought very carefully about Blair's situation,
believe she can be successful in the school, and will do everything it
can to support her and encourage her.

It was, in the end, Blair's own behavior that has persuaded us to readmit
her. I commend her, and I congratulate you.

Sincerely,

Dr. Jeffrey Welch
Academic Dean

JW:bjl

had an anaphylactic reaction to the long-term Bactrim I was prescribed for bladder infections. It grew so severe so quickly that
I couldn't breathe. My mom picked me up in the middle of the
day—I was never more grateful for an early dismissal—and I was
rushed to the emergency room. After that, I never returned.

By the time I was discharged from the hospital, I managed to
get invited back to Cranbrook. There was a meeting in Dean

Arlyce Seibert's office to discuss my future at the school. I fixed my eyes on Arlyce, on her welcoming posture, her gray blazer, the pale fabric of her pants. She told both my parents I would be readmitted, pending some academic and social conditions. My mom sat closer to me, her Burberry trench unfastened but still hanging on her slender frame. Once Arlyce finished speaking, my mom glared at her.

"You can just change the rules?" she said. "You're going to change the rules . . . for her?"

Despite her profession, my mother had a real distrust of authority, let alone one who altered the rules. (She might have said, "To know the rules is to break the rules," but her expectation was for everyone else to abide by them.) The magistrate in her could not let this positive moment pass without offering her two cents.

Elliot, his own Burberry draped across his lap, whispered, "Molly. Please?" He knew how much this school meant to me, that I couldn't manage without it. The grounds. The teachers. The students. The glimmers of hope. And just like that, I was given another chance.

To feel you have a second chance is one of life's greatest victories. I was grateful, humbled, not to mention relieved as all hell. This time, I promised, I would do better. I would never make the same mistakes again. I would remain present. I would try.

◦~◦

I felt I would not be long for this world if I remained alone, in the basement, without allies. I needed to get on someone's back, to have them navigate for me. I am a true case of someone who needs someone smarter, someone brighter, someone more together in my inner circle, to learn from. My mom often said about creative people, "He'll either be a great actor, or he'll wind up in jail!" You need the right crowd, she reminded me. To keep you in line.

Thank goodness for Sue. She was the only stranger who walked up to me at orientation day. Thank God she did. There I was, leaning against a wall, waiting in my thrift store clothes, at this very rich school, where no one wore such things. Royal blue Repetto ballet flats paired with black denim jeans and a royal blue letter jacket in the same shade as the shoes. It had "Dan Rose" stitched on the left breast. My hair was still blond with dark roots, grown out from the champagne blond bob that caused such a stir back at Hillel. I stood out, though I didn't intend to. I was nervous and curious. Self-conscious and intimidated. So I tried that mood on. I wore my mean baby face to keep people away till I could get sorted. But that didn't deter Sue.

I called her Suzy Sunshine. She was perpetually upbeat, my polar opposite, the best counterpart. Before Cranbrook, I had lived a small life. My entire existence took place between the orbit of Hillel and my home. Meanwhile, Sue was so blond, so Nordic, so never-met-a-Jewish-person-before. She was the light I gathered to.

From the first moment we met, Sue *saw* me. One of the first people who did. She saw me out of my fear. When she looked at me, she saw past the exterior, intuiting who I was at my core. After Sue came up to me, we never let go.

All I really wanted (other than to be tall and a model) was to be kind. I wanted someone to say, "You know Selma Blair Beitner? She is so sweet." I wanted to shake the ghost of the mean baby once and for all. But that's not what people did say about me. Instead, it was more like "Selma is crazy, you have to love her. Don't you love her?" or "That chick's on drugs," even though I wasn't. People either loved me or were repulsed by me. But they didn't see me.

Not for who I really was. Or wanted to be. I had no outline just for me.

Sue did. She understood that I was a likable, sweet girl who was also eccentric and tough. My mother scared people to earn their respect, and I learned that from her. Where there was fear, there was admiration. Where there was admiration, I could keep a distance.

"I feel so seen" is something people say now, often as a joke, but if you really dig down, it gets to the heart of what people want all their lives. I was surprised someone like Sue wanted to be good friends with me. Because she was so *good*. With a big strong family and healthy boundaries. She went to church and studied hard. She took me into her world, and mine became better under her care. I saw what it was like to be part of a loving family, the kind with spotless carpets and a chirping alarm system. Our home was tidy; we had a housekeeper. But it wasn't clean in that cared-for, shiny way. Whenever Sue would borrow something of mine, she

would say, "This smells like your house! It makes me so happy." Finally, one day I asked her what that meant, and she said, "Cigarette smoke."

Sue was *normal*. She was sunlight. My association with Sue kept me grounded. And in turn, I showed her another side, where things that are dark and broken aren't so scary, really.

Even though I was newly happy in my surroundings, I still suffered from depression and melancholy and mystery pains that settled in and went without warning. But I discovered I wasn't depressed when I was moving. For two weeks in March, I found an escape in Wilderness, a modified Outward Bound program and a Cranbrook rite of passage. We were given the opportunity to travel to the Smoky Mountains of Tennessee, to carry our food and shelter. It was extracurricular and very immersive. The teachers, who observed us all year, knew whom you were friends with and purposefully matched you with students not in your own social group.

I loved it. I did not excel in team sports. Though I was agile, I didn't have the stamina or the training for those kinds of endeavors. But realizing I could walk with a sixty-pound pack the same way the big hockey goalie could? That was something! Wilderness was its own team, in a way, where the point wasn't to score a goal. We slept under a tarp, nestling in to stay warm. Once, when it was 16 degrees, I had to put my frozen foot in Andrew Clausson's groin to warm it up. As the designated foot warmer-upper, he took each person's foot and nestled it in his ball area. I've never spoken to Andrew, I thought, and yet he is letting me warm my frozen feet in his sixteen-year-old crotch. What a mensch!

In nature, my depression melted away. Of course, on that trip, I also couldn't drink, which no doubt played a role. Without my usual escape hatch, I discovered camaraderie. Once I'd felt that love, with basic strangers, the sane part of me knew to seek it out again.

Outward Bound became my healthy distraction. Later in life, when I went through periods of depression, or MS flare-ups that I didn't yet recognize as such, I would sign up for Outward Bound. After a big project wrapped in Hollywood, I would take two weeks in the wilderness to restabilize. (Once I was already established as an actress, I registered as James Blair, hoping for anonymity. Which was short-lived because once we met at the airport before our treks someone would say, "You look like that actress." So it was back to Selma.)

It was just one of the many wonderful things to come from my experience at Cranbrook. It was like stumbling upon Brigadoon. Students were made to create art, to write, to think deeply and critically. What amazed me most of all was that everyone I met seemed to be genuinely interested in who I was and what I thought, even when I didn't feel I had much to share. We were valued. I've never encountered teachers like them again, even in college. It was a far cry from my dark house, where the grown-ups didn't seem to care for anything but work and cocktail hour. Here, we were treated as equals.

⌒⌣

"That's the guy," said my sister Lizzie's friend Anna, turning to the field hockey expanse by Kingswood Lake. It was just before the start of my freshman year, and we were at field hockey conditioning, running drills on a humid summer day. Anna was gorgeous and older and drove a Saab and wore Ombre Rose parfum, and like many girls at Cranbrook she had her hopes pinned on Chip. I looked up and there he was—long, lanky, slightly hunched, in

black sport shorts and a plaid shirt worn open over a T-shirt. Our eyes met. He gave me a shy smile. Fleeting, but genuine. And that was it. A match had been lit.

Even as a high school sophomore, Chip Fuller was a most gorgeous human. The high cheekbones, the straight white teeth. His face was framed by thick eyebrows that were slow to arch, like mine. His young, full veins showed visibly on his arms. He was a flesh-and-blood, real-life movie star boy. By the time we met, he was already well established as *the* guy at school. I didn't crush right off. But I was curious.

Our first kiss took place in my friend Cathy's den, her family's iconic art pieces as our witnesses. (I recall that a Rothko was present just outside.) One of us gurgled, an involuntary throat gurgle, prompting a smile. And then came a kiss. It was my first kiss since Brad, the summer before eighth grade. Chip smelled ever so faintly of salami, reassuring. I relaxed into it. And then I fell in love.

I arrived at high school inexperienced; I had only ever kissed one boy, nothing more. The truth is, I was so terrified of getting pregnant that I never had sex while I was in high school. Blow jobs, however, didn't scare me. If you couldn't get pregnant, it seemed okay. (Someone once wrote on a bathroom wall, "Lizzie and Blair Beitner give good head." I couldn't believe it. A good review!)

Nevertheless, Chip's mother was very worried we would soon have a sex life. One day, while meeting at Embers Deli to discuss their children, my mother put a proverbial bagel in her mouth by telling her it was a physical impossibility. "He's six four and she's five two! It's impossible!" And my mom truly believed it. I did not have sex with the love of my teenage life, and to this day Chip and I still laugh about it. (Although it was, in fact, physically possible. Sorry, Mom.)

Instead, he cheated on me with one of my friends. I went away to camp that summer after ninth grade, and he slept with her. (I honestly can't say I blame him. She was cool and worldly and sexy.) I didn't find out until the following winter, and it broke my heart. I forced him to call her right in front of me, as any young, insecure girl might do, and say, "I don't want to be friends anymore." They are still friends.

Later, that same friend gave me a beautiful book of photos, inscribed with the lyrics "When the mountains crumble to the sea, there will still be you and me," which I found ironic, because that was my song with Chip. But I loved her and kind of forgave her.

It was that time of life when many trespasses are made on our hearts. I forgive it all now. I did a lot of bad things myself—lied, apologized, begged for forgiveness. I once kissed the only boy that Sue liked, right in front of her. We had been drinking a bit. Thankfully, we're still okay. I've come to understand it's all part of the process of learning how to be human. And no repeats, please.

Even before I started at Cranbrook, I was acquainted with the Dean. Everyone at Cranbrook knew him. He had tutored my sister Lizzie in math before she enrolled and offered the same help to me in the summer before school began to catch me up to speed. (Coming from a parochial school, none of us Beitner girls were equipped for the academic rigor of Cranbrook, and we needed the extra preparation.)

The summer before ninth grade, I met with him in his office every afternoon after field hockey practice. It was warm and inviting, with wood paneling and built-in bookshelves. I can still picture the way the sunlight came through the wavy glass panes in his office, bathing the space in August light. If every corner of Cranbrook was like a big-budget set, the Dean's office was no exception. There wasn't a bad angle to be found.

For me, that office was a place of safety and comfort. He helped me understand polynomials and slopes and algebraic equations (barely—I'm still hopeless at math), and he helped me to be patient with my potential. He was kind and comfortable. He was funny. He was also handsome and deeply respected by the community. Everyone adored him. I was lucky to have this man in my corner.

He took me under his wing. He counseled me on everything— friendships, boyfriends, schoolwork. He began to treat me like his family. I thought he was the greatest man I had ever met. So thoughtful and well dressed. Handsome. Tall. So generous. I joked with him and sought him out and reveled in his attention. He was a kind and authoritative guiding force, the father figure I longed for but hadn't found in Elliot. All of my friends melted in the Dean's presence. Sue and I would say how much we hoped we'd find a man just like him when we grew up.

I'm sure you can see where this is all going. The pattern is so familiar, so obvious, it feels inevitable. But at that time, I couldn't have predicted it. I didn't know anything about consent. I trusted authority. I was just a teenager.

A few months into school, the Dean's embraces started to linger. He remarked I was pretty. Maybe inappropriate, but of course he was also married. To a woman I respected and found lovely. In fact, he and his wife once took me and my three best friends, Sue, Kelly, and Frances—we called ourselves the Fab Four—away for the weekend to their beach home in Tawas, Michigan. We all sang "Don't Leave Me This Way" together and threw spaghetti at the walls in the kitchen. I snapped pictures with my drugstore Kodak. I felt cherished by both the Dean and his wife, and I cherished them back, taking walks with them along the autumn paths.

I couldn't overlook how my interactions with him had started to seem romantic. But as best I could, I ignored the signs, as though my denial would somehow prevent them from getting too real. In my mind, we were more like peers. He cared about me and he helped me, and in my young point of view, that made us friends.

The problem was my grades were not up to par. I was failing. I was overwhelmed with math. I started to drink even more. I couldn't keep up with French. The only foreign language I'd learned at Hillel was Hebrew, and now I was far behind my classmates. I was so happy in my social life—I had a great circle of friends, I'd been a Homecoming Princess already as a freshman, I had Chip—but academically, I was lost, and as the weeks ticked on, I grew more and more anxious about my grades. More and more I turned to the Dean for help, and more and more he cast me in a romantic light.

One day right before winter break of my freshman year, December 1986, I was in his office. He locked the door. We exchanged gifts. He asked me what my scent was, an Hermès fragrance I'd

borrowed from my mom's friend Jane. I didn't know how to pronounce it at the time, and I told him it was "Hermies." I'm sure it
was too adult of a fragrance to enjoy in such a small room, a real
Saks Fifth Avenue scent. I felt ashamed.

I was already a little disarmed when he asked me to stand. We
embraced. It felt too long and too still and too quiet. I was a child.
I wasn't equipped for this. His hand went to the small of my back,
tracing the space just above my tailbone. His lips were on my
mouth. They were closed, but they were there.

I tried, everything I had, to put my faith in this. Please, I
thought. Please don't go under my pants, my dress-code-approved
Ralph Lauren khakis into which I'd carefully tucked a plaid shirt.
Please. You are a grown-up and I love you; please do not put your
hand inside my pants. But he did.

It was gentle. It was subtle. It wasn't far. But I was shaken. I froze.
My stomach clenched. In one moment, everything I had worked
for seemed in jeopardy. I didn't want to lose all the good I'd created at Cranbrook. But I knew I couldn't stay.

It was a simple thing. He didn't rape me. He didn't threaten me.
But he broke me. The Dean was my only touchstone there, and he
was no longer my friend. He had put me in a situation from which
I could not comfortably extricate myself. I wanted him to be the
man I met before I started at Cranbrook. The one who taught
me algebra. The man with the handsome jaw and eyes and a wife,
with such patience and affection and care, both for this school and
for me. Now the same man was making me unsafe. He was throwing me away. He was the Dean and he was respected. He was the
politician everyone loved. He knew I was fragile at this school and
was trying to regain my footing. Now I would have to play along
untruthfully.

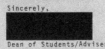

Box 801
Bloomfield Hills
Michigan 48013 USA
313 645 3000

CRANBROOK KINGSWOOD

Cranbrook
Educational
Community

Cranbrook Schools

December 7, 1987

Mr. and Mrs. Elliot Beitner
22445 Coventry Woods
Southfield, Michigan 48034

Dear Mr. and Mrs. Beitner:

I was extremely pleased with Blair's first quarter performance. She demonstrated that she was sincere about wanting to return to Cranbrook Kingswood. I did not doubt that she would have a good year, but it is now reassuring to know that is the case.

Blair is a very positive person in our school. She cares about her friends and our school. Her participantion in the sports program also speaks of her willingness to be part of the school in ways other than pure academics.

I hope the physical problems Blair has been facing will soon be resolved.

Please feel free to get in touch.

Sincerely,

Dean of Students/Adviser

█:js

I didn't know what to do, so I might have giggled when I ran out of the room, and promptly passed out in the vestibule right outside the Dean's office. Chip happened to be coming out from a class down the hall. He saw me and helped me up.

In the safety of Chip's car, I told him what happened. I wanted an ally. Chip believed me. He saw the Dean's favoritism and how it was possible. Chip became a good part of that story. He kept the peace; he was friendly to this man who was my mentor. But I knew he was always looking out for me. He didn't do much, but it was enough. He waited for me outside the Dean's door as often as he could after that.

I felt sad. I loved the Dean, but not as a lover. And he had dealt a huge blow. I had no designs on grown men. I needed the Dean for so much more than a sexual awakening. I needed him to help me learn to be in this world. I needed him to help me succeed academically, to thrive. I needed to do better in school so I could stay at Cranbrook. I felt shattered. I didn't understand anything. I was angry.

My grades continued to fall; I lost my way. I fell apart.

It was later that spring that I was told I would not be invited to return to Cranbrook for my sophomore year. I was devastated. It was the Dean who lobbied for me to be readmitted, and he prevailed; it was in part because of him that I was given a second chance. Despite his transgressions, he did fight for me. He was my ally. Except when he wasn't. That's why it hurt to discover the Dean was just a regular man. It was a sad awakening. Adults are just like you, but older.

For the rest of my time at Cranbrook, I did what I could to avoid being alone with the Dean. But in order to stay in my beloved school, I was under a contract to meet with him every day. I was in a bad spot. He kept trying to find me—taking me out of class, seeking me out. He was one of the most important men at the school, and I knew I could not refuse him outright. Sometimes when we were together, he tried to hold my hand or kiss me. Nothing ever happened again, but I still felt it could. I never felt safe. I was the mature one, the one to make sure we were never alone together for any extended period of time. I became cagey, laughing and deflecting and making jokes. Distracting. All the while I would pray, *Please just let me get through this year.* Still, I never told him to stop. Cranbrook had taught me so much, offered me a whole new vocabulary, and yet I didn't know how to say those two simple words. "Please. Stop."

Please. Stop. Are there two more important words in this world?

Please. Stop. Are there two words that are harder to say when you're a woman in a position like this?

Every time, I tried to get out of the room, I tried not to engage. But I never asked him to stop. I didn't want to consider what the consequences might be if I refused him. Saying no to him meant losing Cranbrook. And I didn't want to lose Cranbrook.

One night early in my senior year, my mother and I were lying in her bed. She was reading a Robertson Davies novel. I leaned into her shoulder. Apropos of nothing, she closed her book and said, "I think the Dean is in love with you." She paused. "Is he?"

I was overcome. I took a slow, deep breath, exhaled, and said, "I think he might be. He tried to kiss me."

My mother exhaled and said, "I knew it." She took a deep breath. "You must not tell anybody. He's beloved at that school. And you'll just be a troubled girl. Best to get through and get done." I knew she was right in saying this. I put my head on the pillow. I would evade. I would get out. I had done the right thing in confiding in her, and she would not embarrass me and make me react in any public way. My former ally was now an enemy of my ever-loyal mother.

"I'm sorry," she said, her focus far off.

My mother and I didn't speak of the Dean again. I did as she instructed and stayed quiet. But at the end of my senior year, on the night of my baccalaureate, he came over to speak to me. He congratulated me for winning a writing award and told me he was so proud of me. I was still holding the book I'd received in recognition, a hardcover collection of short stories engraved with the words "To Blair Beitner, the 1990 Strickland Writing Award, in Recognition of Her Passionate Commitment to, Joy in, and Success at Creative Writing." I clutched it over my chest. Armor. Then he turned to my mother and said, "And you must be so proud of Selma, too."

She stared at him but didn't say anything. She didn't even crack a smile. She just looked at him, stone-faced. Then: "I know what you did. Stay away from my daughter." He walked away. I graduated the next day.

❦

When I was a freshman at Kalamazoo College and felt worlds away from the Dean, a call came in from him out of the blue. I was in my dorm room. I don't remember how the conversation began; I had five roommates crowding near, waiting to go out together. But I do remember him telling me, "I need to apologize for what I did. I am so sorry, Selma."

I breezily said, "It's okay."

I hung up the phone. Then I went in the bathroom and threw up.

Two years later, a girl approached me on campus and asked, "What happened with the Dean? My mother is friends with his wife. She said she's furious with you. You ruined their marriage."

That broke my heart. I'd never have the chance to explain his transgression. There was no winning. I was the mean baby, the girl who had ruined this house. I was surprised that another adult—an adult I loved—thought I was culpable. I was surprised she couldn't see the truth: that the Dean had ruined me.

~

I still think about what happened. How handsome the Dean was, in his suede elbow-patched tweed coats over cashmere sweaters. How he was seen as so fair and great. How I chose him as my father figure because he allowed and encouraged me to. I think about how it all seemed on the up-and-up. He didn't rape me. He was too old-school, old guard and careful. What is so horrible to me, what hurt me then and now, what damages and hurts the scores of women who have been in similar situations, was that he extended the invitation to a vulnerable girl. That he dared to test out the waters, knowing full well I believed he was there for me, in my corner, as a trusted champion, friend, and mentor.

It took tremendous strength to see the situation for what it really was. To my fourteen-year-old brain, I was sensitive and lost and I wanted to trust someone. This man represented the sum total of what I thought I wanted someday. I wanted to grow up and find a man who was just like the Dean. To be a wife who was just like his wife. But his predation changed me. It was an insult to everything I learned to believe in.

I learned that this man, so beloved, was not—at least not entirely—who everyone believed him to be. I learned that when it came to marriage, I did not have much to look forward to. I learned that the people in charge do not always have your best interests at heart.

☙

Remarkably, my dealings with the Dean did not diminish my total awe and love for the rest of my Cranbrook experience. If anything, I built Cranbrook into a transcendent place. It was remarkable, and it was beautiful and otherworldly, but I made it into a full-blown fairy tale, maybe to compensate for how shattered I was by the actions of a grown man. But the institution of Cranbrook still saved me from my basement.

More than anything, Cranbrook is where I was exposed to great works of literature beyond the books I'd discovered on my mother's shelves. I loved books, just as my mother had always loved books, but Cranbrook gave me a vocabulary. Words, I discovered, are the salve for curiosity. Words are the connection linking me to everyone else, to all the people before and since. Words were a discovery, threads of humanity connecting us across time and place. Words were my saving grace.

The surroundings of Cranbrook made every book even more heartbreaking or winsome. The first book I studied in ninth grade was *The Catcher in the Rye,* taught by my young teacher who looked like a Salinger character himself in his L.L.Bean moccasins and wool socks. *The Scarlet Letter. The Odyssey. The Turn of the Screw. Invisible Man* and the works of C. S. Lewis and James Joyce. If my house were to catch fire, the two things I would save are my son and my first edition of *Till We Have Faces,* gifted by a dear friend.

I preferred the tragic tales then. *The Sorrows of Young Werther. The End of the Affair*—oh, that book broke my heart open! *The Wanderer,* by the doomed French novelist Alain-Fournier, in which the main character is ruined by his passion for an unattainable girl found in a fairy-tale estate in the woods. I fancied myself a chain-smoking writer, living in a garret and writing poems like Sylvia Plath and Ted Hughes.

We also read plays and short stories, by Henrik Ibsen and James Joyce. Shakespeare and Homer and Morrison. I learned that Raymond Carver said he didn't write long stories because he didn't have the endurance. Oh! I thought. You can use your laziness to your advantage. You can use your lack of focus and still create something beautiful.

At Hillel, we learned from the Torah. Our main Hebrew text was the Talmud. They were laws, and they were profound, but they weren't personal to me. At Cranbrook, the canon of literature they chose all felt so personal, an intimate conversation between writer and reader. It could be playful, easy, and sometimes confounding. To me, Cranbrook was a secret garden. Meeting so much literature in that setting, where everything felt so timeless, I found the thing that sang to me.

Books would save my life. I saw how they cracked me open in the best way. Pushed tears out or made me laugh with the fart that did fly in *The Canterbury Tales.* I learned how it feels when someone else's thoughts touch a part of you that you haven't felt before. Books are a great emotional lifesaver. A nightlight. A doormat.

Even if you're stuck in a hospital or in line at the DMV, it's all okay if you have a good book with you.

Books also taught me how to notice things, how a moment can be a whole story. I notice everything these days—the dust bunnies swirling into far corners, the long blades of grass living between the cracks in the sidewalk, the way my son flares his nostrils. These things, if you stop and take note, remind you that you're alive, make you feel that you still count. They silence all the worries for a moment.

By the time I was a young adult, I was just starting to arrive at that point where distance made one wiser. I wanted a permanent record. Something to prove I once existed. Something to hold on to. These books moved me; their words so beautiful that they became a part of me. I wanted to stay inside them forever.

But my hero was Joan Didion, whose work I devoured—*Slouching Towards Bethlehem, Play It as It Lays, The White Album.* I related to her aloofness, the refuge she sought in words. I read and reread her, dazzled by her brilliant mind and understated style. Her whole presentation thrilled me. I felt so pleased that, like her, I kept journals all my life. "Keepers of private notebooks are a different breed altogether, lonely and resistant rearrangers of things, anxious malcontents, children afflicted apparently at birth with some presentiment of loss." It was as if she were speaking straight to me.

If Didion was my idol, my English teacher James Toner was my first real-life mentor—the only person I'd ever met who had actually published stories in literary journals. I worshipped him. As a bonus, he didn't want anything from me other than for me to keep reading and writing.

I entered Mr. Toner's class as if I were walking into his church. For the first time, I was allowed to be seen as a person growing into a writer. It was a far cry from Hillel, where the girls were not even encouraged to study in the same way the boys were. Mr. Toner taught me that literature could be a salve. He nurtured my yearning to be a writer.

The very first short story I wrote was for Mr. Toner's class, and my mother served as my editor. "Selma," she said, her red pen slashing, "this is very rococo." But she had an eye for it. Ever the storyteller, she would find a good sentence and then build a simple narrative out of it. Somehow, without really adding a word of her own, she could turn a story into something great.

I am a procrastinator of writing essays. I saw this in school. They were too structured, too focused. You had to map it out, you had to outline, you had to be clear. Whenever I began to write, I thought, "Who the hell knows where it's going?" I wanted to force the words out. But in Mr. Toner's class, I discovered that writing could be so many things. I felt the power in the pages. He helped open up the possibilities. I wanted to be someone. I wanted to create something, too. In my dreams, I wanted James Toner to someday teach my words to other kids who felt shut down and needed a key out. I wanted to be seen. I wanted to run into the hills like white elephants and come out a writer. Instantly.

❧

We girls knew that my parents didn't have the sort of commitment to each other that would go the distance happily, and so I was not surprised when one day, I came home after visiting an Ohio college with Sue junior year and found my mother alone on the chaise in her sitting room, a cigarette in one hand and a book open on her lap.

"He's gone," she said, without a trace of emotion.

My father had moved out. My mother didn't make a big deal of it, and neither did I. Elliot had left and never lived on Coventry Woods Lane again. He rented apartments and furniture, as if the split were temporary. They finally divorced when I was twenty-three and never spoke to each other again. My relationship with Elliot was never going to build after the day he moved out. I chose a side, and I chose my mother.

∽

My literary ambitions took a major detour my senior year, when my first foray into acting was made. Ironically, the whole thing was James Toner's idea. I was struggling mightily with Shakespeare; I didn't care for verse and didn't find my way into his plays. This was, Toner thought, a deficiency in my education. He recommended I audition for the school play *As You Like It*. Perhaps onstage I would embrace Shakespeare's brilliance as a playwright. My audition went so badly I didn't even get a callback. I was dreadful! The text fell from my hands, I was unable to find my place.

I continued auditioning, at Mr. Toner's urging, and was rejected again. Finally, I tried one last time, for a student-directed production, and was cast as a lead in T. S. Eliot's *Murder in the Cathedral*. The play was not great in our hands: interminable and boring as hell. At intermission, much of the audience fled, including my mother (although she did comment that I looked gorgeous in my stage makeup and that I should keep it on indefinitely).

Looking down from the stage, I intuited we were losing our momentum and resorted to every trick I could think of to keep the fidgety audience engaged. I could have turned the performance into a burlesque show. The show must go on. It didn't matter what show.

By the end, there were only a few listless souls remaining in the auditorium. To my dread, James Toner was one of them. Mortifying! I wanted to melt into the stage. I couldn't believe he'd witnessed such a boring calamity. I felt certain I'd fallen several rungs in his esteem. After we took our bows, I sheepishly made my way over to him. "Blair!" he exclaimed. "You're an actress!" I was quiet. Crushed. I wanted him to see me as a writer. But he was unequivocal. His words played in my head. *You're an actress.* The power of a label yet again. At least I had more options now.

Later that night, I took a walk in the woods. Deep in the trees on Cranbrook's campus, there's a statue of Zeus's head, a kind of mantelpiece in a clearing, and if you stand on the right spot, tears fall from his eyes. I stood there alone, waiting for Zeus's tears. Mr. Toner's words replayed over and over in my mind. I wasn't a writer. I was an actress. I did not yet think that one could be both a writer *and* an actress, or that I had the power to set my own course. Not an overachiever. Or even much of an achiever. But I had been given another prophecy, and it was my destiny to fulfill it.

PART II

QUESTIONS

Kalamazoo

Because of my early academic struggles at Cranbrook, I didn't have a strong enough GPA or SAT score to get into the University of Michigan, where Katie and Mimi had gone, so I won a partial scholarship to study photography at Kalamazoo College, a small liberal arts school a few hours from home. I didn't think any school would ever compare with Cranbrook, so I never gave the lovely, ivy-covered Kalamazoo a chance.

From the day I arrived on campus, I was a recluse. I worked hard enough, spending hours every week in the photography lab or typing poems at my word processor. I didn't try to make friends. My suite mates were a decent group of misfits, but we never grew close. When I wasn't in class, I drank. But so did everyone.

I grew dangerously depressed and despairing. Away from the reign of my mother, so lonely, I felt lost and adrift. Grateful for the wine coolers, beer, and fancy Godiva liqueur I kept in my room.

My English professor Conrad Hilberry, an accomplished writer and a wonderful older man, became an appropriate mentor. He was elegant, with a wide grin and a big laugh and legs that kept crossing and uncrossing. He was also quite thin; if he turned sideways, his glasses appeared thicker than his torso!

His class gathered in an airy room, like my Cranbrook days. We sat around a table and read our work aloud. We talked about

Arthur Ashe, of whom we were all great fans and who was honored with the tennis courts in his name. He introduced me to the works of Charles Simic, Sharon Olds, John Donne, Joan Didion, Truman Capote. He was so pleased whenever the word would sing. When I was a freshman in college, he told me to keep writing. So, I wrote. Only poems, because I was still too unsure to put more words down on paper. Words that made sense anyway. Recently, I came across one.

Martini Olive

You started with the asking that summer.
Honey, will you hand me the lemon rinds?
My little hands willingly felt past
The warm milk and mushy avocados.

Peculiar how you were so happy in the day,
Buying limes, stirrers and olives
Orange pimiento caught inside that firm green flesh.

Strange to think I came out of you
Like the inside of an olive
As soft and as slippery.

But on the front porch,
Watching the mosquitos,
You never mentioned it.
Night would buzz down.
The glasses were still now,
But only that summer.
Later is a different day.

Before bed, your asking brought me running
Sliding on the pickled oak floor.

Summer, and you were afraid of dying in the tub,
Naked—undignified, you called it
And that made me cry.

Somehow, silently, my nose pressed against
Plaster, I waited for you outside our little bathroom
While you undid yourself and soaked.
I listened for the clink of glasses or
The smell of a martini that reminded me of
The geraniums we planted.

I imagined you floating down
Bloating with water like a martini olive
Sponging up the gin.

Conrad Hilberry died in 2017. I miss him. He sent word once
in a blue moon and continued to be a supportive presence in my
life, until I left for California. He encouraged me to dig deeper.
"Let yourself be provoked. Don't be afraid to get agitated," he said.
"What if I don't have anything to say?" I would ask him. "Just keep
searching," he'd respond. He always urged another story, a closer
look. I think he knew how much he meant to me. I hope he did.

When I was a freshman at Kalamazoo, I started dating Jason K., a
pretty boy who lived upstairs in the dorms. He was a catch, in that
college-boy way, easily cuter than anyone else there. One night,

we rode the bus into Kalamazoo for dinner and a movie, and he kissed me. For months I walked the stairwell to his small and cozy room, where I was greeted by the scent of his Calvin Klein Eternity cologne and the glow of the Christmas lights strung above his bed.

We tried, very sweetly, to make ours a love story. But we weren't cut from the same cloth. He didn't really fancy me deeply, a fact that became evident soon enough. He typed up a list of all the things he thought I needed to change about myself. How to Fix Blair.

I took up with another handsome fellow, Todd, a trainer at the barn where I rode for PE credit. We fell in love. One night, he told me he didn't love me anymore and that he wanted to break up. Devastated, I waited for him to fall asleep. Then I went into his closet, sat down on the brown marble shag carpeting, and decided my life was not worth living.

Tucked among his clothing, I took a full bottle of extra-strength Tylenol, which I got down with half a bottle of tequila. Then I closed my eyes and waited. I don't think I wanted to die in that moment. I just didn't want to be in pain anymore. Aka: alive. I believed I was unlovable. I wanted to go to sleep and maybe I could wake up as someone else. Someone right.

As I was about to pass out, I had regret. I woke up Todd and showed him what I had done. He found his mom upstairs and she called poison control. They drove me to the nearest hospital.

In the ER, they gave me a supersized charcoal slushie the consistency of blended Oreo cookies. I couldn't keep it down, retching violently, so the nurses pumped my stomach. The large tube they threaded through my nostrils broke my nose but sucked out most of the offending acetaminophen. I had diarrhea in the bedpan. By morning, I was released.

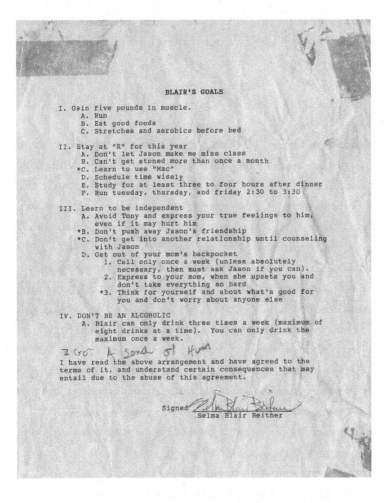

BLAIR'S GOALS

I. Gain five pounds in muscle.
   A. Run
   B. Eat good foods
   C. Stretches and aerobics before bed

II. Stay at "K" for this year
   A. Don't let Jason make me miss class
   B. Can't get stoned more than once a month
 *C. Learn to use "Mac"
   D. Schedule time wisely
   E. Study for at least three to four hours after dinner
   F. Run tuesday, thursday, and friday 2:30 to 3:30

III. Learn to be independent
   A. Avoid Tony and express your true feelings to him,
      even if it may hurt him
 *B. Don't push away Jason's friendship
 *C. Don't get into another relationship until counseling
     with Jason
   D. Get out of your mom's backpocket
     1. Call only once a week (unless absolutely
       necessary, then must ask Jason if you can).
     2. Express to your mom, when she upsets you and
       don't take everything so hard
    *3. Think for yourself and about what's good for
      you and don't worry about anyone else

IV. DON'T BE AN ALCOHOLIC
   A. Blair can only drink three times a week (maximum of
     eight drinks at a time). You can only drink the
     maximum once a week.

I got a sense of Hum

I have read the above arrangement and have agreed to the
terms of it, and understand certain consequences that may
entail due to the abuse of this agreement.

Signed _Selma Blair Beither_

I didn't say a word about it to anyone until months later, when I confessed to my father, who forced me to tell my mother before she saw it on the insurance bill. Over the phone, she calmly told me, "You are dead to me. How could you have done that to me?" I held the receiver to my ear and held back fat tears as my suite mates looked over. I thought she understood who I was. I thought she understood everything. So angry was she that we didn't speak much for two years. Todd, however, took me back, and we stayed together until I left for University of Michigan and then New York City.

～

Aside from Conrad Hilberry, the other bright spot of my time at Kalamazoo was that I finally had the space to pursue my childhood passion for riding horses. They offered riding for a gym credit, and I immediately enrolled. I was pleased to discover that somehow I was okay at it, a pretty enough rider. My body had learned more, I thought, and this time I was ready to ride.

That's how I met Todd. I noticed a trainer who was gorgeous in his riding outfit. He had a natural way with horses, and I wasn't surprised to learn he'd been riding since he could walk. He taught me how to jump. He taught me proper form. We spent frigid days watering horses and dropping hay bales in stables.

For two years, I kept riding and jumping. It was like a time-lapse sequence in a movie, where I worked at it daily, blundered and prevailed, and eventually I progressed into a decent rider. Practically, this meant that if I got on a good horse, I'd win a couple ribbons. If I got on a horse that wasn't so good, I'd fall. I didn't show a tremendous amount of promise, but I was obsessed.

My daydream was to be like Tatum O'Neal in *International Velvet*. I wanted to be a good rider. And like any actress, I also wanted to look the part. The style part I could manage. Ordering a hot dog and Diet Coke at a horse show, I looked like a serious contender. But when it came time to ride, it was anybody's guess. Where other girls would cry when they fell off, I would laugh it off, get back up, and finish the course. Everyone thought I had such a good attitude, but really I was just a mediocre rider who was pleased to get to ride instead of watching my sister.

My mom only opted to view one horse show. She was very disappointed in the dusty ring in Kalamazoo. "Where's my mint julep?" she asked. If my mom had to be somewhere she didn't want to be, there had better be a cocktail; otherwise she wasn't coming back. One and done. I'm sure she had a good book with her to get through.

Where riding brought me joy, it also caused pain. I broke bones, including my lower back. I crushed half my face in a bad fall. After college, when I left Michigan to pursue acting, I put it behind me. I left showing, I left the injuries, I left the dream of opening up a barn with Todd. But I never really left my love of riding. It would be waiting for me to return, someday, when I was ready.

I once stole a pair of jeans from the college laundry room. I didn't intend to; I was carrying my clothes back to my room when I saw a green pair of jeans crumpled in the pile. I didn't have a pair of green Guess jeans. They definitely weren't mine. But I made no attempt to return them.

Three years later, I rented a bright red summer-term house with a girl named Tammy. I wore those jeans all summer long, and it turned out they had been hers. By that point, I'd forgotten about it. She never said a word to me, but later she told a boyfriend that she knew I stole her jeans. Cringey.

Even though they were not particularly flattering, I remember feeling really solid in those jeans, because they felt like a hand-me-down from someone who wasn't my family. Meanwhile, the whole summer long, she thought she was living with a thief and said nothing to me. I wish she had told me! I would have said, "Oh my God! These are yours? Here, I'll give them back to you right now." And off they would go, returned safe and sound. I would have told her my side of the story and made it right. But she didn't have the same casual outlook on thievery that I had.

I'm still embarrassed about it. There is surely someone out there saying, "Selma Blair? From *Cruel Intentions*? She stole my jeans." I want you to know, Tammy, I've thought about you a lot. I was an ass, but only a one-time thief of jeans. I'm sorry.

Over the years, I've come to find that it means something big to have something of someone else's. Having another person's possessions feels a bit like love. A sharing. Maybe it started when I stole Marla's purple nail polish in fourth grade. Once I'd swiped it, I could never wear it, because then she'd know I had it. I just liked keeping it at home, because it belonged to Marla. A small way of keeping her close. I didn't tell her and felt guilty. I still do. For all the things I did wrong.

Of course, stealing things from people is in fact not an act of love. But I've discovered you can ask them. I stole a shirt from my high school boyfriend, Chip, well into our adult years. I went right into his closet and took it. I told him about it, after the fact. The next day. "It reminded me of you, and I wanted to have it." He was very unfazed by it, in a very cool way, and he said I could keep it. So, I'm still a bit of a thief, I guess. But now, at least, I go about it in a more kosher way. He told me to ask next time. Copy that.

❧

My junior year, I transferred to the University of Michigan. A chance for a fresh college start. Still, I didn't stop drinking. I couldn't. Alcohol was too much a part of me, a part of college life, a necessary emotional sustenance, as essential as air. I became anxious and scared if I didn't have a drink come evening. It was my regulator, a way to quiet myself quickly. I drank some before class. I drank after class. I drank all weekend long. I drank alone in my dorm room. I drank in the darkroom while developing photographs. I never drank water, only alcohol—wine or gin or whiskey or vodka. I fell down, I threw up, I stood up, I went to class.

My drinking grew worse when I befriended the hard-partying sorority girls of Kappa Alpha Theta, who invited me to join them on spring break. The whole group of us drove down to Key West, all the way from Michigan. My dad offered to get me a plane ticket, but I declined. I wanted to have a real college road-trip experience. As a solo drinker, I was curious to know what it felt like to be normal and sociable.

The day after we arrived at our rental, a few of us went deep-sea fishing. It was sunny, humid, and frankly kind of boring. There was a stocked cooler full of beer, and I made quick work of it. I was so bombed catching barracuda on that boat in the hot Florida sun that I began shamelessly flirting with the first mate. By the time we came ashore, I was dead drunk. Our group ended up at a fancy restaurant for dinner, where I retched in the bathroom nonstop. I could barely make it back to the table without vomiting more.

After I'd discharged a day's worth of sun poisoning and beer, I found the boy from the boat at the club. We went back to his little house, where his tiny bedroom smelled like fish, his work clothes piled in a corner. I knew nothing about him other than his first name, Tom. In a blackout, I started to have sex with him. Right away, he said, "We need a condom," and those words brought me back. What the fuck was I doing? "I have to go," I said. "I will call you a cab," he responded courteously.

But I needed air. I fled Tom's apartment and ran into the street, but I had no idea how to get back to our rental. I didn't know where I was. That I was miles away. This was before cell phones. I was alone.

I stumbled down the sidewalk, trying to find my way back to the house, or someone who could take me. The street was pitch black. I sat over by a cropping of trees. That's when two men found me. They held my hands down, kissed me, touched my breasts, laughed with each other. They were very aggressive; they didn't leave bruises, but they hurt me just the same. They flipped me over on my stomach. I don't know if both of them raped me. One of them definitely did. I made myself small and quiet and waited for it to be over.

I lied plenty when I was little, but I am not a liar now. I've never accused anyone of anything false, never spun a tale with details that aren't real. I wish I could say what happened to me that night was an anomaly, an isolated incident. But it wasn't. I didn't think of them as traumas. I have been raped, multiple times, because I was too drunk to say the words "Please. Stop." Only that one time was violent. They were total strangers. It was always awful, and it was always wrong, and I came out of each event quiet and ashamed.

Over the course of my youth, this type of thing happened more than I care to recall or admit. Crawling out of bars, waking up bloated and sick in hotel rooms. Not remembering how I got there. Not understanding what was taking place at the time. It is painful to write these truths even now. Looking back is the way to move forward. To meet it. There are many plot points I don't remember clearly, so many time frames upon frames lost. I numbed my body and left it an empty shell for the taking. I still don't know a lot of the details, and it's safe to say I never want to.

It started the very first time I got drunk at the Passover table and screamed and cried to my cousin Matthew, who was just a kid himself. Even then, when I drank too much, I would look to a male for comfort. In eighth grade, I hung out with a boy from the gas station, drinking and making out in a bathroom stall. As a teenager, I'd drink and wake up with a boy I didn't fancy on top of me. I was taken advantage of so many times. And then grown men—true strangers—overpowering, trespassing. I left my body and other people entered it. The real ways I was assaulted were not, and will never be, okay. Now I see how tragic and embarrassing this is. Reading it over on this one small page, all I can wonder is, how did this happen? How did I let this go on? Where was Blair?

I never said a word to the sorority girls I was with about the rape. That crowd wasn't as messy; I imagined they had better sense to never put themselves in such situations alone. So I didn't tell anyone, ever, until now.

These were the things I drank to forget. I didn't drink for attention; I drank to disappear. To find relief. I drank to numb the pain I was in. The mysterious aches and ever-present pains. And the more I drank, the more I drank out of the need to erase what I had done and who I was when drunk. It was a vicious cycle. But it was no matter. The desire to drink as much as I could, as often as I could, stayed with me and did not let go for more than twenty years.

New York

IN THE SUMMER OF 1993, I received a postcard in the mail at our home on Coventry Woods Lane. It said I could take summer classes at an acting school in New York City for college credit. My parents agreed to let me go, only because Katie was living in Manhattan and could keep an eye on me.

I lived on Twenty-Ninth and Second, in a grad student dorm that smelled of mildew and Clorox. The whole place was infested with tiny cockroaches. I had never seen a cockroach in person before, until one spun out of the toilet paper roll when I was ripping off a few squares. They hid everywhere—in the walls, under the bed, in the phone books. (I was forever scared to open the Yellow Pages, terrified a little roach might shimmy out and find its way inexplicably straight to my mouth.)

The acting school was through the Column Theater and Studio in Chelsea. All the students were around the same age as me. One pretty redhead named Dierdre had been in a Cherry 7UP commercial years before and I was in full admiration. She was the first person I'd ever known who carried around a water bottle. Odd but also sensible. She was ahead of the curve clearly, as well as the only one who'd signed with a real modeling agency, Wilhelmina. She had big, glossy white teeth and freckles, and was a full head taller than I.

One night after class we all went out drinking, and spied Matt Dillon across the bar. I'd been in love with him ever since he played Dallas in *The Outsiders,* and like my childhood poster come to life, there he was. Brooding, unattainable, absolutely gorgeous. Dierdre kept getting up from our table to walk past him, hoping he'd notice her. She was quite confident! But I knew I should stay put. I didn't stand up until I was ready to leave, and then I shuffled right past him, out of the bar, and back to my roachy apartment. Still, I couldn't sleep. Something about seeing Matt Dillon in person had flipped a switch in me. I had a goal: to be the one at the bar who captured others' attention.

After that summer, I returned to Ann Arbor for my senior year of college, but I was itching to get back to New York. I had to get closer to the energy I'd felt that summer. My aim now was clearer: I wanted to try to make it as an actor.

One week after graduation, I moved to New York City. My mom helped me pack my Hartmann suitcase, with "Blair" embossed in gold lettering on the side. She snuck in a pink-and-blue cotton quilt, so old and thin it was flat as a penny found pancaked on the tracks. (I have carried that blanket from house to house for more than twenty years.) I passed the long winter nights tucked under that blanket, rereading every story James Toner had assigned me and desperately wanting to be safe and successful and near my mother.

We wrote long letters to each other. She'd write that she missed me so much she'd go into my bedroom and put on my old clothes just to feel close to me. Sometimes we spoke on the black rotary phone, but only occasionally, because I had nothing glorious to report. I only wanted to share achievements that would make her proud. The struggle would not be of interest.

My sister Katie was just starting her career as a book publicist in New York, and we saw each other often, which helped our relationship. She showed me how to use the subway. She lived with a roommate in Murray Hill. For two nights I slept on her couch, but we quickly realized we were not meant to be roommates— ever. The plan was for me to secure my own room at the Parkside Evangeline, a women's residence subsidized by the Salvation Army, situated in the tony neighborhood of Gramercy Park. A prewar building with seventeen floors, the Parkside felt like a college dormitory, with its tiny rooms and simple built-in wooden furniture. My room had a desk with a lamp, a small twin bed, and a shared toilet, which smelled of age and Lysol. It was good. No kitchen, which was fine, since I didn't cook. It wasn't far from the Column, and I drank enough beer to keep my clothing snug.

The larger truth was, I couldn't afford food if I wanted to drink, and I wanted to drink more than I wanted to eat. So, I didn't eat. I was an evening regular at Pete's Tavern, the oldest standing bar in New York, right across from where I lived. Women got free chicken wings during happy hour, so I went there nearly every night for my small supper, where lots of men would buy me drinks. Not knowing what to order, I drank Bushmills, a drink Lizzie ordered. It took me that year to learn that amber alcohol was not for me, causing me to vomit and sway too quickly. I fell off barstools and stumbled back to my room, but the people at Pete's Tavern always took some care of me. I always made it back to my own bed at the all-women's residence. There were a lot of decent bartenders there, and someone usually walked me home.

⁓

My first week in the city, I found a palm reader on the street, next to a sign advertising her as both a psychic and a gypsy. She held my hands in hers, carefully studying the lines. I knew that whatever came next was utter BS. But a person holds a little power whenever you ask them to tell you what they see.

She considered my palms. "You will have a horrible disease and you will die a horrible death," she told me, before concluding with "Do not go overseas." Then she told me that if I gave her more money, she could lift the curse and reverse my bad fortune. I didn't go for it, but I told everyone I saw for the next week that I was going to die a horrible death. It wasn't even a good story, but I told it over and over, wearing my curse like a badge of honor.

⁓

I gave myself one year to find some traction. At night, in my small wooden bed, I prayed for a miracle. I asked for clarity about what to do with my life. If a job didn't materialize, I'd have to give up, go back to Michigan, and work at Dawn's Donuts, then marry rich. As if, in that fantasy, my mother would be pleased.

In the meantime, I took a job folding T-shirts at the Gap on Seventy-Fifth and Lex. I loved folding clothes on the folding board. I loved the Gap pens we won if we sold the most product that day. I loved the employee discount and the tap of the register keys as I printed out gift certificates and ran exchanges. In a way, working at the Gap was the perfect job for me, a place to channel my deep need for organization. To get there, I rode the subway more than fifty blocks uptown. It was worth it to emerge from underground and find myself on the Upper East Side. That location was regarded as the first class of the Manhattan Gaps, attracting only the finest shoppers. I sold Valentino a stack of white T-shirts, the perfect pocket tee. He couldn't get enough.

Then, after nearly ten months of the struggle, Jana Kogen found me. One night while I workshopped some scenes for this children's agent, a blue-eyed pixie watched me from the velvet row seat where she sat holding her clipboard. She looked amused as I performed a botched monologue from *Top Girls*. I was wearing lingerie and too much lipstick, clutching a cigarette and a highball, and speaking in a wonky southern accent. At least that's what I was going for. The agent said that perhaps my headshot should be updated. And that was all.

(I recently asked her if she remembered the monologue. Her eyes danced. "Terrible," she said with a laugh. "With a horrible southern accent!")

I was pathetic, but promising enough for her to see some potential in me, because she called me the next day at the Parkside. On my pager rather. I rang back. She was energetic and funny and encouraged me to keep going. Get some clothes. A new haircut maybe. She had no idea who I was, but we fell in love with each other. I needed a chance, and Jana is the one who gave it to me. She took me on, and we became a team.

Jana signed me, then sent me out on auditions. I dressed in my wardrobe of pocket tees and shorts from the Gap, purchased with my employee discount. After sixty auditions, I was offered my first movie role, Cousin Linda, in a film called *In & Out*. Three thousand dollars a week for the six-week shoot. I booked it.

It was a golden age for movies. I was on set with Joan Cusack!

Kevin Kline! Tom Selleck! And most exciting of all: Matt Dillon. The very one. The unbelievably model-gorgeous Shalom Harlow also made her debut as Matt Dillon's girlfriend. I remember watching her in the makeup chair, where she magically transformed from a pretty teenage girl with pubescent acne into a Hollywood beauty with clear skin and red lips.

In the end, my scenes were mostly cut, but I didn't care. I'd been "discovered." I had my first role and I was now a hugging acquaintance with Matt Dillon. I was on my way.

❧

A perk of living at the Parkside Evangeline was the free daily breakfast provided in the basement for residents. While I lived there, I became friendly with a woman from Scotland who also lived and worked at the Salvation Army. One morning over breakfast, she told me about a tea leaf and tarot reader she frequented. The woman charged $250 for a reading, which for me at that time was quite the hair ball to swallow. Still, I wasted no time seeking her out.

The reader was an old Turkish woman who looked, dressed, and acted like a vaudeville character of a fortune-teller. Every element of her home and wardrobe was straight out of central casting, right down to the Victorian furniture covered in plastic and the cat perched in the other room. Overall, the apartment was very nice, a spacious walk-up with wood floors and high ceilings.

She read my tea leaves. Gazing into the bottom of her little porcelain cup, she said that I had a boyfriend who recently died and that he was with me. Immediately, I thought of Brad. She said I would be in show business and that I wouldn't do that well, but I would stick with it. She said I would have a little dog that would help me. Then she said that someone with the initials M.W. would be a very important man in my life, that I would come across him later in life, and that he would help save me.

I looked for that M.W. everywhere. I always believed in it. The first job I got was on the series *Matt Waters*—I thought, there's the M.W.! Finally, a prediction that came true. To take it one step further, Matt Waters was played by Montel Williams, another M.W., who became my friend. It didn't dawn on me until recently, but Montel has MS and has been a huge help in my life. I could never have known, when I saw that tea leaf reader, the turns our lives would take. Montel became a hero of mine, and I don't hesitate to say this prophecy was fulfilled.

⁓

It was during this time in New York that I got my own place in Murray Hill and took up with a Cranbrook friend's redheaded stepbrother who I knew had a crush on me in high school. He was smart, complicated, and very fashionable. He took me to the Gramercy Tavern, Bice, Mezzaluna. He lavished me with gifts, buying me a new wardrobe at Calvin Klein, shoes at Prada, hats from Dolce & Gabbana. But the clothes did not change my essential character. Once we became a couple, a label he didn't seem to embrace, I drank even more, a cover for my insecurity.

On my twenty-second birthday, after a few too many dramatic arguments and hangovers, I admitted, "I think I need to stop drinking." I arrived at both the conclusion and the confession out of necessity. He rewarded my honesty by leaving the bar with another girl.

I was shook. Devastated. Crushed. In my acute panic, I rushed to self-destruction. I went back to my studio, where he often spent the night. I rummaged through his leather Dopp kit and took all the pills I could find. I didn't actually want to die. I just wanted the pain to end instantly. I wanted comfort and revenge. I hated myself.

I found my favorite Belinda Carlisle album and put on "Mad About You." In a world with Belinda, I didn't want to die. I called his sister and told her what I'd done. She said to call someone I trusted, someone nearby who could help me.

I had no friends in New York at the time, and I wasn't about to tell Katie. So I called a man whose business card I had—a photographer who'd recently taken nude photos of me for a project on alternative beauty. He came over right away, and the plan was to take me to Bellevue Hospital, which was right around the corner.

I was adamant about not using my insurance, because I didn't want my mother to find out and disown me the way she had when I was in college. But my concern was premature. Just as we reached the entrance to Bellevue, I fell and passed out. My face hit the pavement so hard that I broke a bone, the zygomatic arch, just beneath my eye. The photographer picked me up, and instead of taking me into the hospital, he carried me back to my apartment.

I don't remember, in my mental state, exactly what happened next. I don't know what was said, or not said. I don't know what I invited. I don't know what transpired. All I know is that I passed out, and when I opened my eyes, he was having sex with me. I came to just long enough to understand that he was on top of me, with Belinda still playing in the background. And then I passed out again.

The next day, Katie came over. We were supposed to have met earlier that morning for brunch, but I was so far gone I never heard her pounding on the door. She persuaded the super of my building to let her in. When she came inside, she found me sprawled on the floor, mumbling incoherently.

I was not well. After the drinks and the bottles of antidepressants, it was more than I could manage. Katie rushed me to the hospital, where they pumped my stomach again. The doctors told her I'd ingested a lethal amount. But I survived.

There was a lot of damage done. Physical and emotional. The hospital contacted my parents. We all agreed, out of necessity, that I would come back to Michigan and immediately enter an inpatient rehab facility in Pontiac.

Rehab is a tricky thing. It feels a little like going to camp or to boarding school; you're with a bunch of other people who are as messed up as you. This particular treatment center was more of a state lockup. There was no way out. At Fox Center, my roommate was a toothless meth addict from Las Vegas. My closest ally was a man by the name of Bob Evans (no relation to the sausage family), a wheelchair-bound diabetic with blue feet and a winning personality.

While I was in rehab, I fully owned that I was an alcoholic. It was absolutely clear to all of us. With the introduction of AA, I felt hope for the first time in my life. AA was a good tool at the time, though it became more difficult for me to maintain over the years once I became more recognizable, in part because I lost my anonymity. But back then, when I was unknown, the tools of AA forced rigorous honesty. On family visiting night, my mother pulled me into her lap, wailing, and cried, "My baby, my baby," over and over until the nurses told her that she couldn't have me sitting on her lap, because it was inappropriate. But she wouldn't listen. She held me in the way I'd always hoped she would, and we were being separated by the staff. She seemed relieved that I was an alcoholic. "It explains so much, so much," she said. It was a bigger comfort to her than thinking I was only depressed. Alcoholism, she thought, was something that could be fixed.

At Fox Center, we were kept inside, the doors locked. Smoking Newport after Newport in the kitchen lounge, I acclimated to various new prescription drugs, Antabuse and Trexan mostly, ostensibly to curb any wish to drink once I was released. One morning after a dose of Trexan, I felt especially agitated. Rageful, upset, frightened. I was having my first panic attack.

Earlier, my doctor, who was also a friend of my father's, had said I was welcome to read the Merck manual he kept in his office whenever I liked. This was a great comfort to me as a natural researcher and self-diagnostician. I was on my way to read about the side effects of Trexan when I encountered a nurse blocking my path to the doctor's office. Steadying my voice as best I could, I calmly explained to her that I felt out of control—triggered, trapped, distorted. "I've never felt this way before," I told her, adding that it must be because of one of the prescribed drugs in my system. She ignored me then ordered me to class. I repeated my story. I moved closer to the doctor's office door, but she pushed me away. That was it. I lost control. I punched her in the back with all my confusion and anger. She did her best to block my blows until three big security guards rushed over, restrained me, and carried me to a small room where I was given a sedative injection.

The doctors discontinued the Trexan. Poof, I was normal. My rage vanished. What I didn't know at the time was that my father had witnessed this entire episode. He had come to visit me and stood silently in the hallway watching the scene unfold. Later, he would use that episode against me.

∽

While home in Michigan, shortly before my release from rehab, my father checked me out for the day to take me to the eye doctor for a checkup. I'd been having trouble with my vision and was experiencing some unusual pain. I hadn't seen my childhood eye doctor, Leonard Lerner, in several years. But he was the same—thick mustache, kind face framed by round spectacles. I laughed, remembering how sweet he had been when I had to wear the eye patch as a girl. Now I was twenty-two, thin and pale and agitated from weeks of rehab and Antabuse and attempted starts on antidepressants.

In the dark room, staring into my dilated eyes, he asked, "How is your vision? Do you see all right?" I thought for a second before replying. "Um, I think so? Yes, I think so. I don't know."

The doctor looked again, sat back on his little stool, and said, "Well, the interesting thing is you have optical neuritis. An inflammation of the nerves in the eye." He turned on the light and said, "It's usually a symptom of MS. Multiple sclerosis." He looked at me, but I have to say it simply didn't register.

"I think it's all the medication I'm taking," I said. "I don't have MS," I told him.

I was eager to get back to Fox Center and cigarettes, so I imagine we made an appointment to return for a follow-up visit. During that time, the pain subsided or I figured it was my teeth. Or a side effect of the Antabuse, as my copy of the *PDR* informed me. Three weeks later, I was back in Dr. Lerner's chair. He examined both eyes, sat back, and confirmed, "I must have been wrong. The optical neuritis is gone."

On my release from Fox Center, I flew back to New York, newly sober, to pursue my acting career. I booked a real job, a movie with Adrian Grenier called *Arresting Gena,* where I was to play a struggling drug addict. The role was in my wheelhouse, and I was excited for it. Before I told anyone else the news, I called my father. I was proud to report the news after he had kindly covered my Parkside Evangeline bills. We spoke regularly in those days. He had a new girlfriend, a struggling TV anchor who was trying to break into show business, Katie told me. Elliot never mentioned her to me.

That's when the letters started coming. Twenty letters a day arrived via FedEx at the production office of *Arresting Gena,* all of them written by a mysterious sender. They contained bogus information about me and my "violence and addiction." They obliquely referenced my attack on the nurse at Fox Center. The letters mentioned heroin, which I'd never tried, and warned the director to fire me, claiming I was a liability. The return address was always from a place in Chicago called Faces and Places, a fake agency. I was fired before we even started shooting.

The letters continued for a year and a half, during which I was fired from every job I booked. I was quietly hysterical when, finally, I was contacted by a detective who was retained by the talent agency UTA. He said he had been hired to protect Drew Barrymore, the famous and adorable actress to whom I was supposedly writing death threats. After weeks spent trailing me, he realized I wasn't the perpetrator and got in touch to let me know.

He also had information. He said the letters were being mailed from my father's office building in Detroit. He gave me a description of the sender that just happened to match my father's girlfriend at the time, I found out.

The detective, Kevin, told me to lay a trap to find the culprit. I had secured a screen test at Universal for a movie called *Father's Day,* which seemed like as good a time as any to see if my father's girlfriend was the saboteur. At the detective's urging, I told three different stories to three different people: I told my ex-boyfriend that I had a screen test against Alyssa Milano. I told a friend I had a screen test against Alicia Silverstone. I told my father I had a screen test against Drew Barrymore.

Sadly, the name Drew Barrymore became involved in the story

again. The head of casting at Universal received no fewer than fifteen letters saying I was a violent and dangerous person who held a grudge against Drew Barrymore. The casting director showed me and my agent, Jana, the letters. Humiliated, I told my father he was now dead to me. I didn't speak to him for twelve years, and our relationship, already challenging, never fully recovered.

Years later, I begged my agent at UTA to get me an audition with Drew Barrymore for the new *Charlie's Angels*. Nancy Juvonen, Drew's production partner, queried, "Don't you know the history with Selma and Drew?" End of discussion. I was mortified. I had no idea the story had followed me for so long. I opened a bottle of white wine, drank it, and cried. I never tried to audition for Drew again.

When I finally met Drew in person at Tracey Ross, the L.A. clothing store on Sunset popular in the early aughts, much later, I discovered she'd never truly known the whole story, only that it was a father thing, a messed-up situation. I told her I was so, so sorry about the letters she'd received. She hugged me and said, "Don't worry. We all have wild family stuff," and her big embrace smoothed out some of those years-old anxieties. It's still a fright to me. The sabotage. The fear. But I count my lucky stars, the famous star is the dearest Drew. Who seems to have an unending source of compassion.

L.A.

AFTER AT LEAST sixty more auditions in New York, Jana told me it was time for Los Angeles. "You need to go west, young woman." It was pilot season. It was also time for a new era to begin.

I was happy to leave the roaches behind, along with the cold, numbing winters. And so, westward I went.

Jana set me up with two agents, Bonnie Liedtke and fresh-faced Julie Taylor. Perfectly suited, I was happy at the Oakwood corporate housing in Burbank, on Coyote Drive, which was close to the agencies and Warner Bros. I had a Murphy bed that came down from the wall and a cat named I Know, whom I adopted from a shelter back in New York. (The name came out of our first night together, when he cried and cried and I said, "I know, I know. You're hungry. You're sad. I know." It stuck.)

I was immediately taken with Los Angeles. The smell of jasmine at night. The vast highways. The lights. The novelty of eating a bagel while sitting under a palm tree. It was unbelievable to me. A vacation almost.

As part of my fresh start in L.A., I went really blond. Art Luna was *the* guy; he had a chic hair studio in West Hollywood. I saw Sherry, a blonde colorist to the stars. The first time there, Anjelica Huston was getting her hair done beside the wash sink where I sat. The movie *Prizzi's Honor* was a favorite of my mother's and mine, and now here she was, right in front of me. Anjelica complimented my straw wedge shoes. "I had a pair of those back in the day," she told me. Her presence was the perfect balance of commanding and fun. She asked where I got them, and I told her the truth—Steve Madden. The admission hurt. I wished I could say Cacharel, or anything, for that matter. But Steve Madden was within my budget, and Anjelica was kind. "How marvelous," she said, and told me she planned to get a pair of her own.

When it came to my career, Jana was my point person, along with Bonnie and Julie. All three of them were quick-witted and hilarious, pretty and stylish. (Bonnie is still a big deal in the film business; Julie went on to create SoulCycle and sell it.)

The very first job I booked there was a movie with Suzanne Somers and Chad Christ. As soon as I was cast, my brand-new sunny-blond hair was dyed dark brown. Suzanne was the blonde, of course, so I had to go dark. It was darker than I'd ever gone before, and that was how it remained. I already knew Chad from my time in New York, and I found him to be beautiful and cool. And Suzanne! I watched *Three's Company* when I was a kid ad nauseam, and I couldn't believe my great fortune to work with my favorite adult childhood sitcom star. She was glorious. Bubbling with excitement, a grand toothy smile, almost a caricature of herself, that's how strong her real presence is. I liked her immediately.

I remember the imprint of her long, tan toes in her rose-pink suede Bebe wedges. Alan, so in love, was ever by her side. One night, we went to dinner, and I can still picture her long fingers plucking a warm pita slice from the bread basket. "I love this bread," she trilled. "If a place has bad bread, forget it!" I was shocked that the food-combining master ate bread, and I told her so. "I love it. Of course you can. Just with the right things!" she replied.

I continued on audition after audition, learning lines in my green Levi's bought from an ex in New York. There were little sprinkles of fairy dust that kept me going. I got close on so many pilots. But I wasn't pretty enough, I wasn't shiny enough, I wasn't energetic enough. I wasn't "killing" them. I was too tough here.

Unable to afford the Oakwood any longer, I moved out and found a small apartment in a brick apartment building on Gretna Green in Brentwood, around the corner from where Nicole Brown was murdered in her front courtyard. I had a studio over the garage and dumpster. But I was hopeful. I was happy. I liked the warmth, the joggers, finding my way. I knew I was going to need big-time luck. But I also had these three women looking out for me: Jana. Julie. Bonnie. I had an inkling that somehow it would all work out.

My mother casually asked when I was going to come home. "Just come home, Blair. You can work at CVS." She acted as if my interest in acting were very foolish and impractical. She said she didn't understand the appeal at all. If I wasn't a success, why was it worth it? But I wasn't ready to give up and move home, as much as my mother wanted me back in Michigan.

Kevin Williamson wanted me to test for the role of Joey on *Dawson's Creek*. I auditioned and thought that I really nailed the part. I wore a beaded choker, my hair tucked back with a bobby pin, parted on the side. I tested against Katie Holmes. She was so tall, so pretty. She wore headphones and Birkenstocks. She kept to herself. Of course, I didn't get that part, and the rest is history, but I kept getting close.

Alec Baldwin saw a short film I was in at the Hamptons International Film Festival and wrote a little piece about me in a festival paper, calling my performance a display of "flat-out star power like a combination of Marlene Dietrich meets Debra Winger." He said the film "sagged slightly" whenever I was off screen. My mother was over the moon. "Movie stardom in abundance," Alec wrote. (Years later, I saw him in a bar at a restaurant in D.C. and thanked him for his words, which had given me hope. He smiled and said, "You're welcome! Well, I guess you owe your career to me!" I replied, "Don't celebrate quite yet." I haven't seen him since.)

I auditioned for a role in *Amazon High,* to play a cheerleader sent back to Amazonian times to teach women how to tame horses and rule the cannibals. It was a ridiculous premise but I wanted it. I went to the producer's offices at Universal and did the splits, then a cartwheel, then a flip, along with scripted cheers. My body could still do these things easily, without training, I was still a kid really. The next day, I got the part. I spent the next seven weeks in New Zealand for the shoot, most of which found me disoriented and melancholy, with all the time alone in a room while it rained outside during preproduction. I'd been sober since Fox Center, but I went to the land of the long white cloud and became out of sorts and homesick. I walked to the only liquor store I could find and bought the most expensive port I could afford. I gave myself a limit: only one tiny sip a day. I would drink like a normal person, I told myself. But then one night we all went out, and that one night was my undoing; I drank until I blacked out.

When I returned to Los Angeles, I was drinking again. I took on some bit roles here and there, but nothing was real. I was tired. I was always tired. I was in my mid-twenties and figured I would need to start fibbing about my age, telling directors I was eighteen or twenty. I felt ancient. Then I heard about a movie called *Cruel Inventions,* a contemporary riff on the French novel *Dangerous Liaisons* set in private-school New York. I was going to get the part, I decided. And if I didn't, I would consider giving up.

There's no other way to say this: the audition for the upcoming teen drama *Cruel Inventions* (the title was ultimately changed to *Cruel Intentions* in postproduction) was a Big Fucking Deal in Young Hollywood. Everyone was talking about it, buzzing about it, speculating about it. The established young stars Sarah Michelle Gellar and Ryan Phillippe had already been cast as the leads. Ryan's girlfriend, Reese Witherspoon, already a high-profile actress, was pending in the role of the ingenue. He would persuade her to take it.

The casting director, Mary Vernieu, had a small but busy office in Brentwood. I didn't actually yet believe I had any chance of getting the job, so when I went in to see Mary for the part of Cecile Caldwell, I was completely relaxed, not at all invested in the outcome. I had already been crushed losing the Joey Potter role on *Dawson's Creek,* so I chilled out. Like every young person in Hollywood, I wanted the role of Cecile. I had read the script, and while not *The Deer Hunter,* I found the whole thing compelling. At the same time, I felt somewhat drained by the constant rejection, maybe even ready to pack it in. I looked forward to getting back to photography or writing, or even a job in a shop.

When I strolled into the room, nonchalant, my hands in my pockets, the director, Roger Kumble, immediately asked, "So, how old are you?" I was done lying about my age. After fielding this question at so many auditions, I'd had it. I stiffened and spat back brattily, "How old are *you?*" At that, he sat up and listened.

I could see I'd piqued his interest. He was paying attention. I played it up. I told him I'd just gone across the border to Canada with some friends to buy alcohol, hoping he'd buy that I was under twenty-one without my actually lying. And then I did the audition using the same energy he brought out in me. I wasn't angry; I wasn't combative. I think I was just a little fed up that day. After doing seven auditions that week without being noticed, I felt I had nothing to lose. A little mean baby came out of me. But she saved the day, because she made him listen. I suppose Roger realized this was the saving grace for the character of Cecile. She didn't have to be the sad victim. His words: she could work humorously. She could be relentlessly irritating. There's a certain power in annoying the shit out of the people who are scheming to take you down. Clueless confidence saved her from a pathetic existence. In the end, it's often the confident people who are the most successful. And Cecile would be a great success.

A few days later, Roger and I met at a bar to talk about the part and how to get everyone on board. He talked to Ryan; he talked to Sarah. He really went to bat for me. The cast represented young Hollywood. I was so starstruck and happy I could plotz!

I was already acquainted with Sarah Michelle Gellar before we met in person, from a voice-over I'd done on *Scream 2*. Of course, I also knew her from her work. She was the epitome of a young TV star. She had been Kendall on *All My Children*! From day one, she was a friend to me, both in getting the part and in showing me the ropes. In a lot of ways, our real-life relationship mirrored our dynamic in the film, albeit without all the scheming. She is still one of my closest friends in the world. A mighty nurturer and talent is she.

At the table reads, when we first all got together to read the script, I sat next to Reese. She was the most delicate yellow flower. I was completely overwhelmed by the sight. She wore a pale blue cashmere hoodie, Essie Ballet Slippers on her nails, her blond hair thick and straight. She was lovely. It was clear to me she was going to be a superstar. Everything about her was impeccable and still is today: her nails, her cuticles. Her brain! She smelled freshly showered and kept her notebook tidy, her cashmere didn't pill, she never complained. Reese also had the prettiest feet. Even unpedicured, her feet are perfect. My mom loved Reese and her delicate ankles. "You look like you're a different species," she would say. "Don't you feel like a water buffalo when you stand next to her?" I did, actually. I always felt like the awkward outsider around Reese and Ryan. Ryan called her "doll" when we all went out to dinner, like Frank Sinatra and Ava Gardner. Just like Cecile herself, I was the goofy brown mushroom among the Upper East Side elite.

There was only one instance where I felt remotely cool. The cast had moved to New York for the shoot, and one night we all went out to the *Godzilla* premiere. It was a huge movie, and everyone who was anyone at that time was there. Prada lent me a dress, and the entire cast went together. I looked up to Reese and felt as if I couldn't let my guard down. I longed to impress her. At one point, Ryan came up and said, "We want to meet Puff Daddy. Do you know how we can meet him?" I saw an in. "Yes! I know him!" I didn't really, but we shared a manager. In dopey Cecile fashion, confidence in hand with cluelessness, I rushed up to Puff Daddy, Reese and Ryan in step behind me, and embraced him with a gigantic hug. The audacity! I didn't know you don't just walk up to the biggest star of the moment and introduce him to the stars of your own little movie.

The final image of Reese driving off in that 1956 Jaguar roadster while the notes of "Bitter Sweet Symphony" rise along with the camera is still one of the most iconic memories from that film, but I think the kiss between Kathryn and Cecile (me!) is a close second. That kiss! That wet kiss. (I'm reminded of it at almost every meeting with a group of younger people. As in, "Hey! You're that girl who kissed Sarah! Do you remember that?" Now perhaps they think I am so old I wouldn't remember . . .) I wasn't that nervous about kissing Sarah, but I was eager for the scene to be over and done with because we both knew it was going to be somewhat sensational and there was pressure on us to pull it off. We wanted to get it right, certainly.

I remember Sarah's lips were so soft. I wasn't attracted to girls, but I did enjoy the soft, whisker-free lips of SMG on mine. We kissed over and over. During one take, she pulled back and there was this long trail of spit between us. I thought, surely that won't be the one they use. Of course, the spit take won the day. It reminded me of the sexy scene of Marilyn Monroe's spit string in *Niagara*. When my mother saw the film, she was appalled that I was such a graphic, sloppy kisser. ("Honestly, Selma, did you have to use so much tongue? Your tongue, it's massive! Like a creature from *Star Wars* or something! When are you going to come home and get a real job?") Despite her feigned shock, I knew she must be relieved that I at least managed to get one real Hollywood job.

It felt grand. I hoped all movies would be this way, that everything in the world would feel like this. Magazines. Newspapers. My first *Tonight Show* appearance, wearing Dolce & Gabbana. I kept the name plate on my door. It was all easy and fun.

After *Cruel Intentions,* I was offered the role of Vivian Kensington in *Legally Blonde* because Chloë Sevigny, who had just struck big with the movie *Kids,* passed on it. At the time, I was the next logical choice, which made me feel that I was in very good company. I did have to audition for Robert Luketic. A few lines. It didn't seem there was a lot to the role. Fine by me. Reese. Yes, please. In the original script by Karen McCullah, Vivian ended up blond, bubbly, friendly, and best friends with Elle Woods. That part didn't play well, though. Elle was the true and only legal blonde. Vivian was to remain brunette and in the background.

To watch Reese command the room so aptly on *Legally Blonde* was clearly movie star magic. She had just given birth to her beautiful daughter, Ava. She was in excellent shape and worked so hard—always the first one there, always the last one to leave. As ever, she never complained. It made an impression. I learned.

When I was working on the movie, I told Amanda Brown (who wrote the original novel the screenplay was based on) how much I loved *The Wizard of Oz*. So as a gift, she gave me my very own pair of ruby slippers. That was the only time I've ever acted the part of a gleeful child. I jumped up and down, yelling, "I got the slippers! I got the slippers!" although nobody was at my house to witness this exuberant display. They were an exact replica, made especially for me, to my exact foot measurements. They even had the same felt glued to the soles, a sound deadener, which allowed Judy Garland to silently dance on a soundstage. (We use foam these days.) It was such a beautiful, thoughtful, personal gesture—the best gift I had ever received. It seemed to make up for any childhood neglect I ever felt I'd had regarding toys. The shoes live on my mantel, sparkling from the fireplace. More than any role I had, more than any movie, getting those slippers was the most thrilling discovery.

I enjoyed myself on that set; it was the first time I let my guard down in front of other people. Ever the goofy sidekick, I kept the crew and cast entertained while Reese did one great take after another in pink stilettos. One time while I was performing my own shtick outside as some of us stood around the craft services table, I started impersonating a *Billy Elliot* routine and got so amped up that I actually jumped up into the air. I don't know what happened, but my feet went out from under me. I couldn't locate them. Before I could make sense of it, I was parallel to the ground, then landed flat on my face. It was a colossal fall—even a Teamster ran over to make sure I was okay. Now I simply say "Billy Elliot"

to that crowd, and we all start laughing. When entertaining the troops, I go flat out.

The offers came in, some better than others. I was on a roll. I played the titular character in a TV show, Zoe Bean, of *Zoe, Duncan, Jack and Jane.* Zoe was the cute girl next door. It didn't take off. The label I'd been given was too embedded in who I was. I never figured out how to play the sweet, stable, capable, pretty person. I excelled at characters who might be called smug or ridiculous. Eccentric, weird prudes became my bread and butter. I never had an arsenal of gentle, weightless, girl-next-door glances. Always the mean baby, I played the girl who was misunderstood and set apart. Her default expression was a dry stare. A barb, her power. She is all the women in my life—my mother, my sisters—or a ridiculous child woman making her way. Or all these versions combined.

My career was on the rise, but I had a hunch I was not going to be a leading lady. I was a supporting player. That was who I knew how to be. It was also the easier label to give. Stars are few and not like me, I felt. If you take one message away from this book, let it be this: labels are sticky.

Still, I landed the cover of *Seventeen* magazine, a dream get for a young actress in those days. I felt so proud. It was June 1999. I showed up with my freshly cut bangs and was given a chartreuse shrug and a lime-green plaid maxi skirt. It's a casual shot: I'm seated, holding my knees, smiling. Beaming, really. But my eyes looked small.

I sent a copy to my mother in Michigan. She called me as soon as the package arrived. "Oh, Selma," she said. "You look so unimportant. When are you going to come home and get a real job?"

Hollywood

In many ways, my time in Hollywood felt to me like an extension of my Cranbrook days, in that I've taken a liking to almost everyone I've met. I was genuinely friendly and old enough to be damn grateful. As a supporting player, I didn't feel competitive. I've met everyone, it seems. I will have some story, some personal anecdote to share about them. While I like Six Degrees of Kevin Bacon, I'd bet if the game were changed to Two Degrees of Selma Blair, it would have even more wings. (By the way, Kyra Sedgwick and I get our hair done by the same colorist and talked just last week. See what I mean?)

I've met so many great people here among the shits. People I like to run into at the grocery store. The truth is, I don't know that

I would fit in elsewhere. It's much easier here, in this setting where people need a bit of a label to be understood. I don't know if they talk behind my back; I'm sure there are a few. But for the most part, I love the women in this town. I love them like my sisters. We talk, we text. We share stories and advice and support one another. I could rattle off big names. I won't. But I did spend a recent big holiday at Sharon Stone's house. Gorgeous place.

The first working actress friend I made was Amy Hargreaves. She was a commercial actress in New York while I lived there, and we moved out to L.A. at the same time. We were with the same agency, and we had been cast in the same first show, *Matt Waters,* back in New York. She was the star. Upon arrival in L.A., we went to a showcase and to dinner after at Jones on Formosa. It was dark inside, with red booths and poodle paintings over the tables. Decidedly Hollywood. Lo and behold, Matt Dillon strolled in. He saw us by the door, stopped by to say hi, and asked Amy if she was having any luck. Then he left. Amy moved back to New York and kept on as I did out West.

Early in my friendship with Reese, she invited me to a Billy Blanks workout class in Woodland Hills. I was so looking forward to spending time with her. Historically, I am never late. I thought I'd given myself enough time, but this was before GPS, I was coming from work at Warner Bros., and the drive took longer than expected. As it got closer to the start time, I began to panic. I saw a parking spot and decided to grab it. Little did I know that it was still two miles away. Wearing a full face of TV makeup, I walked and ran and sprinted. After around a mile and a half, all I could do was sprint. I am not a sprinter. This might very well be the only time I've sprinted a mile in my life. But I did it, fueled by the rage at my own incompetence.

I finally made it to the class, but I was late, sweaty, and wiped out. And now I had to slog my way through a Tae Bo class, a totally new concept. I was lost, totally inept. Halfway through, I thought I was going to die. Reese, on the other hand, sailed effortlessly through it. I had no doubt that if the roles were reversed and she'd somehow made the same idiot blunder I did, she could have run those miles and still made it on time, prepared for class.

After class we went out to dinner at Teru Sushi on Ventura and talked and laughed, Reese putting me at ease as she always does. Her world of work was so beyond my own, and I was fascinated. We chatted and caught up; she mentioned she had just worked on *Friends* or was about to and we both marveled at Jennifer Aniston's incredible physique.

I have a recurring nightmare that I'm meeting Reese again, but I parked too far away and only my legs can take me to her on time. I start running but my legs won't keep at it. So I allow myself too much room for error if I'm going to meet her for lunch. Invariably, I dawdle and fuck up. I always wind up late. And she always waits for me and greets me with a hug after texting back: "Just be safe."

In the early days of *Mad Men,* Bottega Veneta threw a party that January Jones and I both attended. I'd been feeling sick that day, slurring my words. I took a couple of shots and a nap, but I still felt off before the party. I figured it was because I hadn't eaten and the alcohol amplified everything. Now I see it was the MS. I was so out of it that I fell asleep mid-sentence during hair and makeup, and then threw up.

When I arrived at the party, I laid eyes on January, center stage, who looked stunning as ever. "January!" I called, making my way through the crowd. "You're Betty Draper!" I exclaimed, once I reached her. "Betty Draper! Betty Draper!" I kept repeating myself, aware of what was happening but powerless to stop it. January very calmly put her lovely hand on my shoulder, and said, "You do know I'm not Betty Draper."

It was one of those awkward social encounters, confirmation that I shouldn't have let myself out that day. "I should have more champagne!" I said, before backtracking. "Wait, no I shouldn't."

She gently took my hand and reassured me. "We should all, always, have more champagne," she said, smiling, before returning to the party. We were already good acquaintances, and it wasn't exactly as strange as it appeared. But I spent the night disoriented and sick and then resigned myself to more champagne. People noticed.

Another favorite, Amanda Anka, has a few stories like that about me too. One took place at the kickoff party for *The Sweetest Thing*. Amanda was a familiar face to me at a party, always amiable and inclusive, but I didn't know her well. "Have you seen Jason Bateman?" I asked her, gesturing across the room. "He is so hot. I love him. He's going to be my husband."

"That's so amazing!" Amanda said. "He's my fiancé." She was genuinely pleased and amused I made such a gaffe. That is an easygoing betrothed girl.

My closest friend is Claire Danes, whom I met at a Sunday night dinner party with my boyfriend, Jason Schwartzman. I remember thinking her skin was so clear. I watched her from across the table, her blond hair falling over her face as she leaned forward and pushed her hair behind her ears to listen to the conversation. I'd never seen her in person before, and I told her, on that first meeting, right as we were leaving, that I had bacne. And she, very nonjudgmentally, told me I should try Proactiv. No one was using it—no one had even heard of it—back then. She was totally unfazed *and* offered advice, so I thought, "Well, there's a practical friend." I decided never to let her go. She remains sacred to me.

In a crowded room, I also tend to keep an eye out for Kirsten Dunst, a longtime favorite actress as well. I have always been a bona fide fan. You see, I came to Hollywood late in the game. I'd already gone through college and spent a few years in New York, and by the time I arrived, I didn't feel like a young starlet. It felt strange that one minute I could've been in college in the Midwest, then suddenly find myself across from that actress from *Interview with the Vampire,* a movie that meant so much to me in my previous life. I always appreciated that.

In 2002, I saw Kirsten at a show for Jason's band Phantom Planet at the Standard in L.A. We arranged to meet for breakfast the next day. As we walked back to my house, I spotted a paparazzo with a long lens. "What do you do about those paparazzi?" I asked her, assuming such a major young star must have to confront them all the time. It had been a problem for me for years, though I was always photographed by default—by virtue of my neighborhood or the more famous people in the frame. Even so, it always left me feeling ambushed and worried.

"Oh, they never photograph me," she answered.

"What do you mean? There's one right there!" I pointed at the photographer crouching in the bushes. In that moment, I witnessed loss of innocence. She was genuinely surprised and befuddled, and in the ensuing years the paparazzi presence would only grow with the quick multiplication of invaders. I didn't realize how bad their monitoring of young female celebrities would become, nor what an issue it would pose for so many people.

Jake Gyllenhaal and I had become friends from *Highway,* a film we shot in Seattle, in which I'd played a hooker on the run, her only shoes a sparkly red pair, like Dorothy's. When he was shooting *Donnie Darko,* I stopped by his trailer to visit him. In recent days, he'd seen so many of his school friends having these big successes. "I wonder when it'll be my time," he said.

"It *is* your time," I said. History soon proved me right.

When all the pieces line up, Hollywood is captivating. I got to live through another golden age of Hollywood. I have been a witness to the new greats making their mark. Claire invited me to her Hollywood Walk of Fame induction years later, which I attended while my child napped at home.

                                             ✒

I have a manager. He was my publicist in those early days. We are a team now. Our first meeting was arranged by David Weber, who was my boyfriend (and lawyer) at the time. My first impression of Troy was that he was trim and handsome in a black shirt, black pants, and good shoes. The three of us sat in a big conference room overlooking Wilshire Boulevard, and at one point he leaned over to David and said something like "Just tell this one she's pretty." I was miffed. It felt condescending, dismissive. Invalidating of any talent or intelligence. I didn't say much.

"He was adorable, but I'm not sure he got me," I recapped with David at the elevator as we were leaving.

I may have misunderstood Troy's remark. In any event, I was wrong. He got me. Over the years, I'd had agents and managers I liked and admired. But I struggled to find a true focus or ambition. Troy saw me light up in the hands of a great artist. He knew this world, and he saw something in me. We've been inseparable ever since.

We are, in many ways, of brother and sister makeup. We play and annoy, we egg each other on. We call each other "monkey." We agree it reads a bit pathetic to have my main gay and cohort a commissioned employee. We are Elizabeth Taylor and Jason Winters, we joke, so fundamental to my life is he.

Troy is better than anyone at pushing what he believes in. For years, I thought he was the boss. For years, he thought I was. It was only this past year that we realized we are partners. (An epiphany that made us cry.) I have never had anyone stand by my side like this man.

Troy told me I was America's last great beauty, although he doesn't remember saying this (or I misunderstood the remark—again). He had me meet Krista Smith at *Vanity Fair,* another person with an incredible eye as well as a brain. The two became like parents to me, even if peers in age. Over the years, I appeared on the cover of *Vanity Fair* two times, for the Young Hollywood issue. For the first time, after a long day of *Zoe,* I flew to Miami for the cover shoot and got a horrible bloody nose on the plane. It wouldn't stop, so I called Troy for help. I was up all night, got my nose quickly cauterized, and showed up on set an hour later, still wiping blood from a spot under my chin, dazed by the greatness of Annie Leibovitz.

I was so looking forward to having my hair and makeup done for this shoot, to be made glamorous for *Vanity Fair.* I had studied the Hollywood covers and knew there was no skimp on gowns or glam. When I entered the room where Annie was setting up for the garden shot, she took one look at me and said, "Don't touch her." At the time, I was shocked. But now I see. She *saw* me. She saw me, exactly as I arrived, and thought I was the cool girl for that moment. "Don't do anything," she said. They wiped my face, added a dab of concealer, a swipe of mascara, and that was it.

It got better. "This is what you're wearing," she said, and handed me a polka-dot leather bikini, still on a hanger.

A voice trilled, excited, "Oh my gosh, you finally got someone to wear the bikini!"

Already feeling a little long in the tooth, there I was barefoot, in a leather bikini, void of major hair and makeup, and sitting next to my crush Wes Bentley and new friends Jordana Brewster and Paul Walker. When they turned the fan on, my self-consciousness blew away and I enjoyed the scene.

At one point, Annie was studying me, scrutinizing. She squinted. She whispered something to Sally Hershberger, who threw up her hands and comb. "What can I do if she has a bad haircut and a bald spot?" I think Sally dabbed a little eyeshadow in the widest spot of my part. Troy and I still laugh at this comment, a familiar one by now. From that point on, my bald spots became a short-lived obsession; for a while after that I carried around a Bobbi Brown eye shadow to touch up my scalp before auditions.

The second time, Annie shot me again, this time for the Young Women in Hollywood issue. Older and wiser, I came armed with a haircut by Chris McMillan. I thought for sure I would be put in a gown, lengthened and made stunning.

I waltzed on set in a black turtleneck and a pair of jeans, lean and fresh-faced. Annie glanced up, hugged me briefly, and called out, "Oh, Selma. Perfect! Nobody touch her." That was my blessing and my curse.

With some photographers, they saw me, and there was an instant connection. Tired, dark circles, jeans, whatever. That's Selma; she is who she is. My look didn't translate into the greatness I needed for Hollywood. It didn't align with what it takes to be a leading woman. But it still led me to this incredible life.

Troy stayed away on those days. To let me be. To honor the reputation of these masters. And when he popped in, freshly buzzed hair, new Prada pants, we always laughed. And made others laugh, too. (Possibly at us.) But we all had an all right time.

My greediest, happiest moments were spent in front of a camera. The glory of my life was that I became the first actress ever to grace the cover of Italian *Vogue*. In those days, Italian *Vogue* was everything in fashion. When I got the cover, that was my Oscar. I was Edie Sedgwick in Warhol's house. Steven Meisel waited with his huge brown eyes, long eyelashes, the bandanna over his head, and in those days a cigarette. He processed the pictures in a little tent I couldn't see, and then he emerged to show me. "There. That is the lighting test." He laid them out, right there, in a spread. I looked like the cover.

If only I could have Steven Meisel's eye and light frame me forever. That superseded everything. I didn't celebrate this moment. I couldn't fully contemplate it. I was so grateful for it I didn't know how to put it into words. That was my glory. My dream alongside my mother's.

Looking down the lens at Michael Thompson or Peter Lindbergh or Steven or Annie and having them see me and approve, that's the stuff. Lindbergh and I sent postcards after he shot me— just once, for the Pirelli Calendar, on the Sony lot. He was charmingly old-fashioned and old-school in the way he created a whole environment, with the cold and the fog. Because I am not tall, I am often given underwear to wear, since it does not require alterations. On this Pirelli shoot, I was in underwear and heels, and I was chilly in the manufactured rain and fog, so wardrobe gave me a tuxedo jacket to wear, and I walked toward Peter. "I love this energy," he called. That became the shot. The makeup artist Gucci Westman gave me a red lip, which I loved. She was the first to pull that off on me. I couldn't wait for my mother to approve. I was finally playing the part she wanted me to. I'm not sure she ever even saw it.

My mother always wanted a full report. "What were the compliments, Selma?" Like when Michael Thompson confided to Joe Zee that I moved better than most models, up there with Kate Moss. I didn't allow the sublime glee I felt to get out. Not to anyone, not even to Troy. I was afraid. Afraid I would attract attention. Afraid Elliot would somehow ruin it, or me. So I became private about my successes.

And then there were the duds. As soon as a photographer says, "Relax," I know it's all over. All he sees is a short Jewish girl from the Midwest whom he needs to make into a star. "Relax" makes me feel inadequate and stiff. I never knew how to behave in those moments when I knew someone couldn't see me. Inwardly, I would disappear.

These days, I see myself everywhere, quite literally. As I write this, I am surrounded by large, framed portraits of yours truly that hang all over my home, relics of these indelible gifts. I'm a *Saturday Night Live* sketch of a Hollywood actress. A house wearing its owner on its sleeve.

⁓

Then there were the powerful, magnificent cheerleaders, the prophets of some great promise I am still waiting to fulfill. The writer, editor, and cultural figure Ingrid Sischy was that person for me. From our first meeting, at a *Vanity Fair* dinner, she saw a glimmer of something in me. She saw me, in all my awkwardness, and believed in me fully.

Ingrid was born in South Africa and became a fixture in the

New York media scene as the editor in chief of *Artforum* and later *Interview*. She invested in it all—art, celebrity culture, music, and fashion, especially. With her big warm questions and welcoming face, she was a tastemaker who set people in motion. She was so encouraging of others. Of people with talent. Miraculously, she became my mentor.

She would tell me about the people I should know—really know. Miuccia Prada and Karl Lagerfeld. And I would tell her whom she should: Amy Adams and Kate Bosworth and Scarlett Johansson. One day long before Kanye West was famous, Ingrid and I were sitting in an upstairs Japanese restaurant sharing one of our first lunches. "Kanye. You gotta know him," she said. "He has an album coming out soon and he's brilliant! Brilliant!" She connected me to everyone and everything that was fabulous, and she did it single-handedly, because her influence was that big. She created this energy around artists and interactions, and for some reason she really saw me as a star, or a fellow changemaker.

Soon after we met, I became guest West Coast editor of *Interview*. Because Ingrid's two closest friends in fashion were Karl and Miuccia, she made sure I was part of something. A muse. I was doing campaigns for Prada and Miu Miu and Chanel. Ingrid did know I was prone to severe depression, and she gave me places to go, things to do. She gave me work and assignments and a direction. She kept me afloat.

I lived a dream in the fashion world largely thanks to Ingrid, under Troy's approval. She was an incredible woman to have in your corner. When she died of cancer on July 24, 2015, at the age of sixty-three, the media world was shaken. I was shocked.

From Graydon Carter's obituary: "Ingrid was a great friend and therefore she had a lot of friends. And they will be utterly bereft for the next little while, so be kind to them. They will be the ones wandering the streets, or just staring off into the middle distances, lost in the knowledge that a beloved original in an age of generics has gone somewhere else and left them behind."

Now I really see how much she did for me, and I wish I'd known how to run with it then. But I was quiet. God, how I wish Ingrid were here. I would do anything now—anything she asked, without hesitation. For so much time, I was breathless with appreciation, and I didn't even know how to address it. *One day,* I thought, *I'll be able to tell her.* I figured that eventually she would teach me enough so I could finally find the right actions to say thank you, to make her proud to have found me and believed in me.

❧

It was through Ingrid that I found my way to Karl. He actually came to my house on Cynthia Street to shoot me for *Interview* magazine. Ingrid came in from New York, as well as L'Wren Scott, who was the stylist that day. Before Karl arrived, L'Wren and I decided it would be fun to dress me up as him. This was right when he'd lost the weight and was in the sexy libertine, rocker chic look, with the cravat and the tight jeans. His were so tight, so pegged, with the balls to the right. I made a comment about the crotch area. Again, the audacity of me!

When he saw me dressed as Karl, he gave a smile. We embraced. I wanted to do more. More theatrics! More drama! But instead, he had me take it all off, keeping only my own tank top on. Just a touch of mascara and gel in my spiky hair.

It was swelteringly hot that day. I spent most of it trying to look serene in the skylight of my very small house. Karl looked around, aiming for the best light. He pointed to the skylight and asked if I would get up there, go right up to the light. I climbed on the shoulders of his muscular companion, a gorgeous young man, naturally. I balanced there, like a young girl playing chicken fight in a pool, looking down at Karl. "Good. Good. This is you," he said. And we were done.

On our lunch break, Karl's only request was a Diet Coke. I didn't have a Diet Coke in the house, and that was his only request. Forevermore, I keep a Diet Coke on hand, in honor of him. (For years afterward, Ingrid raved about the lunch I provided that day. Which was and still is hilarious to me, because I'm pretty sure she provided it. I am many things, but I am no hostess.)

From that very first meeting, I loved Karl and felt at home with him. Karl and I became friends, actually. He was obviously the most brilliant man I have ever met. He was spotless. He even smelled clean. His hands were like a mechanic's—handsome worker hands. Not rough, just big and capable. He was incredible. He was the revered one. Everything about him was otherworldly—his shape, his presence, his style. I don't think there will ever be another figure in fashion so suited for greatness.

Karl always sent pink peonies when we shot together, a sumptuous bounty of pale full blooms. Heavenly. I remember opening the door to my hotel room in Paris and discovering the entire space was infused with the scent of these arrangements. Oh, to have a small, perfect room on the Left Bank, filled with peonies sent by Karl. I mourned having to leave them so soon, still fresh. I hope someone at the Hotel Montalembert saved them after I'd gone. Sometimes I look back and I still don't know how I got there. I don't know how Karl shot me, and loved me, and put me up in a hotel filled with such glorious petals that my hair and clothes still held the scent even after I got home.

Throughout my years of being a still life, I have only one regret. I wish I had picked up my own camera more often. I regret not having stood on the other side of the lens. I was exposed to so many phenomenal artists, but I never shot them. I worried I'd be seen as an intruder. An outsider.

At the *Vanity Fair* shoot in Miami, I had gathered that Penélope Cruz brought a camera everywhere she went. She'd just bring the camera to her beautiful face and—click—took photos of everyone else. She had such a lovely European way about her, it never looked invasive. I felt like a clunky American girl, so I rarely brought my own lens. Now I wish I had. Regrets, I have a few!

On Cynthia Street, Karl posed with me before leaving. It was the one time I dared to pick up my little vintage ecru camera. "Let's have a shot!" I ventured. He accepted. "Yes! Here is good?" he asked. We stood on the edge of a fountain, the sunlight slicing our heads. The snap is framed on my desk, unflattering to both of us in the harsh glare. But the only shot I have.

I lived well in those years. Paris and shows, diamonds and gowns with provenance. Dresses from the archives. In the moments when I dared to consider it, it felt wonderful. I've had an enchanted life. I still consider myself one of the luckiest girls in Hollywood.

The Man and the Muse

During a lighting setup on *Cruel Intentions,* I went searching for Reese. I found her next to Ryan, talking to a handsome man I didn't know. He had height and bore a resemblance to JFK Jr. He looked good, and I'd learn he looked even better on paper.

Roger, the director, brought me over and said, "This is Ryan's lawyer, David Weber. He'll probably try to sign you—don't do it." I shook his hand and said it was nice to meet him. He looked bored. *Well, then,* I thought, *I'll be off!* I left him with the two cherubs and went on to craft services.

I was surprised when after our meet-cute, which was not very cute, he asked me out. After running into each other at a function where he gave me a wave hello—barely an acknowledgment—he called and asked if I would like to go to Roger's birthday dinner with him.

"I will come get you," he said. And I said, "Sure."

He picked me up in his long silver Volvo station wagon, which felt very lawyerly. I was still living at my first apartment then and felt intimidated by his professional air. Over the course of the next few weeks, David came to really like me, and I came to like him, too.

⁓

David was solid, adult, steady. And gorgeous. We fell in love. The adults in my life celebrated our relationship. I felt, based on some vague societal standard, that I was supposed to be moving forward, toward something, in a direction. I was an adult and adults were meant to find a person to commit to. David represented exactly what I thought that was.

Our relationship progressed, and he bought us a Spanish 1920s house. It was idyllic, right down to our neighbors, Reese and Ryan, who lived in a charming bungalow up the street. Across the street from them was Winona's house, with big, incredible yellow trumpet flowering trees that smelled heavenly, like jasmine, but are in fact very toxic. Crazy-making if brewed or eaten.

David planned to propose to me, one ill-fated weekend at a Cranbrook Kingswood reunion in 2000. I was afraid he was going to ask. When we arrived in Michigan, I became very ill with a fever and headache. He had told my mom his plan, and had even bought the ring, but once he saw how sick I was, he put a pin in it.

He did eventually ask me, the morning after a *CosmoGirl* photo shoot. He presented me with an elegant, emerald cut diamond. Bravo, David Weber. It was so flawlessly beautiful that I tried to hide it when out, worried what people would think of someone so young and inexperienced with such a perfect ring.

So, I was engaged. But it was not so simple.

David was my ideal. But I was about to meet my muse.

❧

The first time I saw Jason Schwartzman on-screen in Wes Anderson's charming *Rushmore,* David in the theater seat beside me, he took my breath away. I'd never seen anyone like him—not Dustin Hoffman, not Tom Cruise. He was charming and captivating and pure. The prep school where *Rushmore* took place reminded me so much of Cranbrook, and Jason's character's love for his school reminded me of my own commitment to my school. He had such charisma. I was enamored. When the movie was over, I turned to David and said, "Wow, he was great." And he said, "You know, that's Talia Shire's son."

I kept returning to Jason in my thoughts. When *Cruel Intentions* premiered, I went on *Total Request Live* on MTV, where I was asked, "Do you have a celebrity crush?" And I answered, "Jason Schwartzman, from *Rushmore*." As if I could will him to me. I had no bones about making my infatuation with him public, because in no universe did I ever imagine that we would wind up together.

Months later, at a photo shoot, I learned that the photographer shooting me knew Jason. I persuaded Jazzy to get Jason to come to the shoot as a special request. "I'll stay longer if you can get him to come," I begged. Then, there he was.

His eyes were unreal in person, the color of a passionate storm sky. I was smitten. I was in a black tuxedo and skirt. He handed me a daisy he'd picked from the grass and gently kissed me on the lips. The moment was captured in a tiny contact sheet frame that I still have on my shelf. He was a boy, only nineteen. I was twenty-five or so. I thought of him as a child, and myself as a much older woman.

I was madly in love from the moment I met him. It felt like a homecoming of spirit, as if I'd known him forever. Destined. A simultaneous heartbreak and joy.

Much later, he came to my house—the home I shared with David, who was at his office in Beverly Hills. Jason looked around, taking in all the trappings of adulthood. "You really are a grown-up," he said. When we got to the part where I showed him the view and the balcony, he sat on the edge of the tub, looked around, and said, "Wow. This is a lot."

We already knew we loved each other. I looked at him, knowing full well that we would have some future together. "If we fall in love, this will end badly," I whispered. I was immediately angry at myself. It sounded just like something my mother would say. Sabotaging it before anything had even taken hold. Jason looked at me and rested his chin in the heel of my hand. And that was that.

In many ways, a relationship with Jason felt like an impossibility. I was living with another man. I loved David very much, but I felt too big a pull toward Jason. I was immediately in love with him in that emotional, overpowering teenage way. I knew it wasn't possible to move forward with both of them. My heart chose Jason.

My breakup with David was murky and sad. I remember listening to *Play,* the Moby album, on repeat as I packed up the home we'd shared. Sadly, I gave back the perfect ring when I called off the engagement. Though we never did tie the knot, I remained married to David, in a way, for decades, because he continued to be my lawyer.

A few months later, Jason and I became a couple.

Once, after he bought a new Prius, Jason drove us all the way up to Yosemite to visit my mom, who was visiting her cousin Stella and her husband and son at their home there. Jason played guitar, made us laugh, talked about spirits and horse ghosts rumored to roam the property. My mom got a little bit tipsy and ordered us to take off our shoes. We studied our feet. He had Fred Flintstone feet, he joked—big, thick, comical, and adorable. I loved them. Stella said they were a sign of a passionate character.

We stayed together, off and on, for several years. His mother called me beloved. But I never publicly embraced the relationship as much as I wanted to, because I was ashamed. Not of Jason or my feelings for him, but because I thought I should be getting married, and I didn't want to drag Jason toward that. I didn't necessarily *want* to get married. I calibrated my expectations based on what I read in magazines, or other people's experiences, or the pervasive cultural attitude about what someone my age should be doing. I couldn't fully own how I felt about him, worrying that our eight-year age difference must be inappropriate, that my mother wouldn't approve of this match, snatching such a young boy. I imagined I was way more grown up than I was. But I believed, at the time, that I was already too old for such things like infatuation.

I loved the abandon and purity of youth that he represented. But I didn't know how to let myself be a young girl in love. Instead, I kept him somewhat hidden. Afraid he would be ruined by Elliot.

He was young. But we both were. We got jealous. Things happened. I flirted, as was my habit; he made out with supermodels. Hearts were broken, repaired, broken again. I was hurt by his actions, though they were more age appropriate than the relationship we were destroying. By the time we were finally "ready" to be a real couple, we had broken each other apart.

⁓

We went to see an astrologist. Jason's mother, Talia, was very into astrology, to the point where she consulted the stars as a road map to her life. She conferred with the cosmos before making plans. If one of us was going out of town, she would look to the stars to see if it was a good time.

She sent the two of us to a highly gifted and reputable adviser, who printed out a whole series of charts. As he explained their meanings, I circled the things I found exciting. At the time, all I wanted to know was if Jason and I would weather our age difference and be together forever. The astrologer considered this from every angle. The stars all agreed we would end up heartbroken.

⁓

Time away working on a film allowed me to focus, offering a respite from the cycle of self-flagellation, doubt, loneliness, and neuralgia. But when I was in Prague filming *Hellboy,* I floundered in my solitude. On my weeks off in the Czech Republic, I resembled a pinball careening from wall to floor to wall to hallway and finally gripping pillars holding arches carved out of stone. From catacombs to car to bar to bed to bathroom, crying to myself out loud on the floor. Sometimes I lost myself in the comfort of memories of my time with Jason. We had a rocky farewell. After time apart, I knew we were done, but I couldn't let him go.

Late one night, as I sat in my trailer smoking countless cigarettes and grieving my loss while playing "Under Pressure" by Queen and David Bowie, I called Jason for what must have been the fortieth time that week. It always went to voice mail, the dreaded click-to-beep. But that night, he picked up. His voice. Both my heart and my gut froze.

"Finally," I whispered, my spirit on the precipice. I knew there was a vastness before us but I did not see the turning away to come. He was clear and resolute; love and heartbreak had grown him up. And then the little black phone in my hand, the only channel to him for months ahead, was of no use.

I had never felt more sure my whole future would be a loss now.

Heartsick, I flooded myself with champagne and vodka, fresh mojitos in dark bars in the old part of town. I drank, surrounded by girls made up like prostitutes. Pale, skinny. Tacky, glamorous. Faded already and not even twenty. Men in square-toed loafers stepped on my feet, sliding past. These were the bars I left every night, out onto the Charles Bridge as the beggars cried on their knees, shrouded in black robes, silent and bowed.

In the morning, I'd report to set and perform in a big movie. I was crushed. Silenced. I didn't see the miracle that was my life. I didn't see the wins, the fabulous directors, the famous friends. I saw only heartbreak. I didn't believe I would recover.

July 29 - 30 2:15 A.M.
Wrap later today.
This journey is almost
over. A memory.

The pain and Growing I
have gone through in Prague
as immense.

Love

Shooting *Hellboy II,* several years later and still grieving, I called him one more time. That's when I accepted it was over for good. We spoke. He told me he was in a great relationship, with the woman who would later become his wife, Brady. He was happy. He was so clear in his devotion to her that my heart found grace and was healed. I loved him enough, I realized, that I actually felt relief. He forgave me and wished me well, he said. Then we said goodbye.

Not too long ago, my son, Arthur, and I ran into Jason at the drugstore. He was carrying a big box of diapers. Arthur asked, "What's that?" To which Jason replied, "Pillows! I come here to get my pillows!" My son laughed. And I thought, *Wow. This did not end badly after all. This ended perfectly.* Finally.

❦

Even as my acting career continued, as lovers came and went, as friendships deepened or trickled off and time marched on, I would return to drinking. To be clear, I did not drink on set. When I worked, I was totally sober. Those were sacred moments, where I was given a job and I did it. But left to my own devices, I let sleep, sadness, and drink take over. I'd go for periods when I didn't drink at all or didn't drink as much, and then I'd go all in again, crippled with pain and fatigue, bingeing until I passed out, welcoming oblivion.

Before shooting *Storytelling* in New York, I wound up going back to rehab for a second time. I wanted to go, it was my idea— I didn't feel safe with myself. I was worried about my overall health. I entered the Sierra Tucson center for treatment of my alcohol addiction and depression. The intake nurse reviewed my form and assigned me to the eating disorder unit. I told them I didn't have an actual eating disorder, which I thought true. While I knew I wasn't one to nourish myself adequately, I did not feel I had an eating disorder. Though I did mind my weight, I didn't count calories, I didn't starve myself (my middle school years were another story), I didn't follow any of the patterns that accompany disordered eating. But I doth protest too much.

Ironically, the experience gave me a full-blown eating disorder for a long time. I substituted an eating disorder for drinking. The people I met there taught me how. Everyone sat around obsessing about calories, competitive with weighing and measuring and packets of artificial sweeteners. I became embarrassed to gain weight there, and I was given less to eat than I normally would have, because they didn't want to trigger me. I see now that it was always in me. Latent, waiting. I just needed someone to prompt me to be better at it. To compete.

Once I left the program, regulating my own starvation became a bigger theme in my life. I read the book *Stick Figure,* not as a cautionary tale about the danger of eating disorders, but as a how-to guide. It was like encountering Sarah T. all over again, trading out shots of vodka for withholding food.

On the other hand, I did stay sober for a while. But it would not be for good.

Alcohol had been the salve, the relief, the warmth. I thought I found a way to stay on this planet with my wine. But the electric anxiety and loneliness found a friend to creep around with in the dark halls. Alone in my bedroom, I was like Alice, sampling what the order "drink me" could bring. Nothing good.

Wink

THERE ARE DAPPLES of light in my story, all along the way. Wink was one of them.

When I was still with Jason, I suffered a bout of despair and chronic trigeminal neuralgia that had me searching for a distraction. So I took a volunteer job walking dogs at a local animal shelter, the Lange Foundation. There was this mutt, a forgotten one-eyed corgi mix named Wink. She could not stop jumping whenever I walked past. She reminded me of a Hanna-Barbera cartoon doggy on a pogo stick. At night, alone in my house, I couldn't stop thinking about her delightful, boundless joy; she bounced around in my head, even in my dreams.

One bright morning over buckwheat pancakes at Quality, I asked Jason what he thought about taking Wink home for a night. "And then I'll write a glowing personal report to pin on her crate at the shelter, to help charm a potential forever-home adopter," I said. When we went to collect her for the overnight evaluation, I had little intention of keeping her. I'd never taken care of a dog on my own before, and besides, I didn't want the added responsibility as I tried to build a career and stay awake, really.

On our way home in his Prius, with Wink snuggled happily next to me in the front seat, we stopped by Jason's mother's house. Talia wanted to meet her and Wink replied in kind. "This is a great dog!" Talia shouted as her three pugs and Wink chased one another around the lawn. "You have to keep this dog, Selma," she insisted, before she adjourned inside to read more Pirandello, still grieving her beloved late husband, Jack.

I took Wink home that night and with me she stayed. It was a miracle to have found her. She was my Steinbeck companion. My *Travels with Wink.* Everybody loved Wink. Wink, who once ate an entire pumpkin pancake from my plate at La Conversation with such swiftness I never even saw her do it. She sat contentedly on my lap through so many meals, eyeing my steak frites, ever hopeful. She sat quietly in my lap, still while makeup artists readied me for camera, away on location. She accompanied me on every trip and to every movie set, for every sleep and every waking.

When I was overwhelmed by melancholy and wiped out for weeks, she brought me mice and rats and even a possum. Loyal little dog was she, staying tucked beside me when I retreated to my bed, or howled in pain, whether from a broken heart or the pain in my face, or from missing my mother. She was a dear witness to all of it, the happiest dog I've ever known, fearful only in thunderstorms. One spring night in Budapest while I was filming *Hellboy II,* the sky cracked with lightning and driving rain. As Wink trembled in my arms, I hummed deeply into her heart, the vibration soothing her to sleep. Guillermo del Toro honored her in the film by naming a character after her. I cared for her as tenderly as I would a human child, cherished her above all else, every night and every morning gently kissing her and thanking my angels for her company. I could not imagine a life without her.

Carrie

MEETING CARRIE FISHER was another bright spot. As soon as she found me, life grew softer. My world felt kinder and more exciting with her in it.

Now, I should preface this by saying: I was not a Princess Leia fangirl. I'd seen *Star Wars* in the theater, when it was first released—Lizzie, Katie, Mom, Dad, and me. I enjoyed it. The famous font scrolling by, accompanied by the dramatic, sweeping building orchestra. C-3PO lost in the blurry haze of the desert. Katie liked C-3PO best; he was skinny like her. Lizzie was Chewbacca, cute and strong. I was relegated to being R2-D2 because we were both the smallest. I was not amused by this. My parents bought me a shirt with an R2-D2 decal on it, and I was so upset that I screamed and screamed until my mother locked me in my room. That was the only time I can recall her doing that, although Katie would trap me often.

But the Force! I missed the whole point. "May the Force be with you" became my rosary, my mantra, my wish. In my young eyes, Darth was the real star. The cape, the breathing, the mask. A presence. Dramatic. Frightening. Imperious. Who wanted to be R2-D2 when you could be Darth? That, to me, was the true meaning of the Force. He reminded me of my mother.

⁓

Fast-forward to 2001, at a Women in Hollywood luncheon. *Cruel Intentions* and *Legally Blonde* had put me on the map. I was dating Jason Schwartzman, deeply in love. I was riding high and thin from late 1990s fame, thinking the world would only keep getting better. I was wearing a gray Jane Mayle dress that Jason had purchased for me on the advice of his cousin Sofia Coppola, Gucci boots, a vintage Hermès Kelly bag on my arm.

The parking lot of the Beverly Hills Four Seasons swarmed with gorgeous, important women. One of them came running up to me from across the way. I didn't recognize her at first. She was middle-aged, attractive. Her long scarf trailed behind her, where it latched onto the back of her shoe like toilet paper. She was comical—dropping things, carrying on, adorable. As she got closer, I realized the woman was Carrie Fisher. She looked right into my eyes, grabbed my arm, and said, "It's my birthday, please come to my party!" Bruce Wagner, her tall, handsome sidekick, wearing a boilersuit, took my number for her and promised to call me with her address. The citizens of Los Angeles can be flaky, so I was pleased when he actually did.

Jason was a huge *Star Wars* aficionado, so we went. We drove out to her home, a sprawling estate off Coldwater Canyon. It had once been owned by Bette Davis, followed by the Academy Award–winning costume designer Edith Head. Carrie had it redone in a colorful, kitschy way, filling every inch with London flea market finds and folk art. As we drove up the driveway, signs pleaded, "Please Do Not Enter." They looked as if they were written by charming trolls. A chandelier glimmered from a tree, and tiny bulbs twinkled in all the lace-boughed branches. There was a swimming pool with an old-fashioned slide way up on the hill. The whole place was whimsical, marvelous. Every corner of the house told a story of her life.

Jason and I walked into the party arm in arm. Carrie greeted us, so genuine and friendly. "Don't stand too close to each other; you'll look like garden gnomes," she quipped, in a good-natured joke about our short stature. She reminded me she was once married to Paul Simon and together they reminded her of salt and pepper shakers.

The people whose work I admired on-screen were suddenly mingling about. George Lucas waited in line for the bathroom. Michael Keaton at the bar. Robert Downey Jr. on the bar, but not drinking any longer. Meg Ryan, looking like Meg Ryan, dressed in her combat boots and tights. Tracey Ullman and Téa Leoni and David Duchovny. It was like the Mad Hatter's tea party come to life. A who's who of the old guard.

After that party, Carrie was in my life as though she'd been there all along. We'd smoke cigarettes in her bed and watch Turner Classic Movies as she wrote on her yellow pad. She always kept one by her side, as my mother used to do. (Now I do, too.) Carrie was very skilled at her trade; she knew she had to fucking write, so she sat on her bed and she wrote. Every now and then she'd look up and go on these riffs. I'd roar! She was so enthusiastic. Sometimes she'd get dark in her writing. She'd read a passage aloud and I'd suggest edits. "You're right, you have to leave room for laughter," she'd say, nodding, trying to build up my confidence. Sometimes, like with my mother, she'd admire one of my quips. Always, she wanted to help me, knowing I was not yet ready in life.

We'd have long dinners, her stained-glass light boxes of saints glowing behind us. She knew a little about every subject under the sun. The most brilliant wit. One night, while talking about the filmmaker Buñuel, she stopped mid-sentence and said, "Let's go down to Mom's house and scare her!" Her mother, Debbie Reynolds, lived on the property.

Once Carrie got an idea in her head, she ran with it, full steam. We'd slink around and play ding-dong ditch and dress up in her Leia costume, drinking Diet Coke. One of the best parts of Carrie's world was that you didn't have to be polite. You could just be you. Messy and raw. I felt compelled to fill the silence. But Carrie justified everything. She would wave her hands and say, "Who cares?"

At Carrie's house, you could wander around. You could say what popped up. You could go deep, talk about something for twenty minutes, have a Diet Coke and maybe a cigarette outside, while she dropped glitter on my head, and then leave. Or you could stay forever. She didn't have expectations. Carrie took the responsibility off things. She knew how to make people comfortable. She was the kind of friend I could handle.

Plus, she sent a good email. No one sends a good email anymore. She signed them all to me "Leia."

We would talk about being misunderstood. "I know," she'd say. "It's all a misunderstanding. And all of it is true."

After attending a couple of Carrie's gatherings, I noticed that she often made her way to bed even before the party was over. She really did try to live each day, but she struggled. Sometimes she'd disappear into the bathroom and come back talking gibberish. I never asked a question, never brought up the pills. I respected her too much, and I didn't feel it was my place.

We never once drank together. We never once took a pill together. Only once ever did Carrie see me drunk. It happened to be the last real time I saw her.

Arthur was a toddler. I'd checked us into Shutters on the Beach in Santa Monica for a night of relaxation. The front desk sent up a bottle of champagne. I wasn't drinking much then, but that day I was sobbing uncontrollably about some child-proofing issue I was nervous about. I would fall into spasms of sobs unprovoked, and it could all be too much. I couldn't stop crying, so I poured a glass. I decided, why not? (This was the first of only two times in my life when I drank in front of my son.) At one point, I stumbled down the hall, already exhausted again, a champagne flute in one hand, Arthur balanced on my hip, and there was Carrie, walking with Bruce Wagner. We screamed and squealed and hugged. She was such a hugger. Unlike my mother, she loved human touch. We couldn't believe it! We couldn't believe it. We hugged again and again. I didn't want to let her go.

She invited me to come up to her room. "Bring Arthur!" she said. But all I wanted to do was hide in my room and cry and drink. So we hugged once more, swaying back and forth in each other's arms, and that was it. We walked away, promising I would make it to her room. I did not.

⁕

A couple weeks before she died, I was at Barnes & Noble in L.A. with Arthur, my beau, Ron, and his daughter, Chloe, when I noticed all the characters from *Star Wars* wandering around the store. I went up to a guy dressed as Boba Fett and asked him, "What is this? What's going on?" In a voice muffled by his armor, he said, "It's for Carrie Fisher's book party." I squealed. "Carrie's book party!"

It was a huge crowd. There were so many costumes. So many Carrie Fisher admirers. I gave Boba Fett's female companion a message. "If you get a chance to meet Carrie, please tell her I was here, but I have to get my son home."

Later that night, Boba Fett's friend found me on social media and sent me a note. "I gave Carrie your message and she said, 'Goddammit where is that bitch?' And then she called out looking for you. 'Bitch! Bitch!!! Where are you?'" I laughed and wrote back, "I hope you told her this bitch had already gone." I pictured her standing on a chair, searching the rows and rows of books, trying to find me in the crowd, just as she had years before.

I was home alone when I found out she'd gone into cardiac arrest on a plane and was in a coma. It was Christmastime, and I'd just put up our tree. I sat next to it and sobbed. She died four days later, on December 27, 2016. When I heard the news, I couldn't breathe.

Someone once told me that grief is love you can no longer express, and that's certainly how I feel about the loss of Carrie. I loved her. I did take Carrie for granted. I thought she would always be there. She was larger than my life. I didn't think she would ever go—I didn't think.

I really, really miss her. We were true loners, Carrie and I. Real recluses. But because of her, I learned how to listen. Because of her, I learned that it's good to idolize the people who are here now, the ones who really mean something. Because of her, I try to always say "I love you" to those I take for granted. Because of her I keep a tree lit and decorated with ornaments all year round, as she did. Her Leia figure hidden in the plastic branches.

~

I didn't go to her funeral. The only person who would have invited me to it was Carrie herself, and she was dead. We'd never worked together. I wasn't on anyone's list. I was only on Carrie's list. They'd put her ashes in a Prozac bottle, a kitschy object from an old pharma display. She would've laughed.

The loss was so huge. When there was an auction of some of her things, I bought her dollhouse, her trinkets, the molded modern furniture, her light-up Saint Francis, her hanging Lucite chair. I couldn't bear the thought of her things going to anyone else. I wanted to hold on to her. I spent too much money on it all, just as she did. "It's expensive being Carrie Fisher," she lamented once.

I did talk to Carrie on the night before her funeral. I told her I wanted to leave a rock on her grave site. (We both had Jewish fathers, and that's what Jews do.) "I have to bring a rock," I said out loud. "I need a heart-shaped crystal." And I swear I heard her voice reply, "Please don't leave a heart-shaped crystal! Just write something, you lazy asshole!"

"I don't own any yellow legal pads," I said to her. "And I don't have anything to say."

Missing her voice, I started to reread her memoir *Shockaholic*, but it was too fucking painful. I put the book down, thinking I'd get to it later. I placed it on the far side of the room, right next to a lamp she'd given me. And then I forgot about it.

A few days later, I went back over to the book. Right on top of it, there was a big, amorphous crystal. It was a smoky quartz, and if you look at it just so, you can see it's in the shape of a jagged heart. As soon as I saw it, I started shaking. A feeling of warmth washed over me. I felt her presence.

I screamed, "Oh my God! Carrie Fisher! You're real!"

A voice back: "Fuck you, I'm real."

"This is so special," I responded. "I'll never tell anyone about this."

(I have told anyone who will listen.)

❦

After Carrie died, I met with the clairvoyant medium Tyler Henry. I felt unmoored after losing her, and I wanted to talk to her. I needed a bedtime story. I was so intent on meeting him that at one point I actually called E!, the network that airs his show, *Hollywood Medium,* and said, "I'm going to go on the show, if that's the only way to get a reading." And that is exactly what happened.

I do believe that some people can see spirits, the same way I can see lint on other people's jackets that they don't seem to notice. Personally, I've never seen a spirit. And aside from the day I found Carrie's rock, I've never *felt* a spirit. But I am open to it.

The reading took place in my home. I brought Tyler three objects connected to loved ones: Bradley Bluestone's photo, the crystal Carrie left me, and a picture of Wink. I set them down in front of him, with the photos turned over so he could see only the backs.

The first thing we discussed was my career. "I'm ready to get back," I told him. I'd been feeling stalled, sick, weak for years, and I needed good news.

"I don't really see you acting," he said. "You're going to be more of an advocate." This was not what I wanted to hear.

"Oh, fuck no." I laughed. "I'm not a giver like that. I am a privileged, miserable white woman who struggles with depression, so I can't even offer a self-help spin. Advocate for what?" This was before my MS diagnosis, and I could never have predicted what was coming. (He was right, of course, just as he was with Alan Thicke's impending heart attack.)

We started with the objects. Tyler picked up on everything from Brad. He felt Wink come through loud and clear. "Wink!" he said, without any prompting. He said he'd never had such a big energy between dog and person. He told me Wink was so glad I made a memorial for her, and I began to cry.

I thought, out of everything, Carrie's rock would explode, but Tyler held it, and nothing happened. He shook his head. "I don't see anything. I'm not getting anything from it at all."

To this day, I have no accounting for that crystal and its appearance. It is the only instance in my life, aside from making a baby, that was my one real account of magic. When I saw it, I picked it up and felt such warmth in my chest. It was so tangible. The rock is still here, but it doesn't have the magic anymore. Almost like an expired birthday wish. I let time dissipate my belief it was really from her.

"You know," Tyler said, putting the rock back down, "this reminds me of the time Beverly D'Angelo wanted to talk to Carrie Fisher. She wouldn't come through. She just didn't want to be public anymore." Oh, Carrie. I apologize.

The Julies

WHEN I LOOK BACK through my childhood diaries, it's mostly about boys. Boy after boy after boy. And misery. And body pains. *What did I do wrong? How can I get him to like me? What could I do to keep him?* And *My face burns. I can't take this pain.* I had it all backward. I was looking for help, love. I wasn't even looking for attention or approval. I was looking for a Julie—a soul mate, a confidante. Someone who sees me for who I am and loves me in spite of it all.

I collect Julies. Everyone needs a Julie, but preferably a handful.

A Julie is one of those stable, well-adjusted, loving, and utterly grounded women who comes into your life and makes it better in every way. I owe the major steps of my life to the Julies of the world. As much as is humanly possible, I surround myself with their love.

I met my first Julie on the first day of Cranbrook Kingswood. (This Julie was actually Sue.) She was everything I wasn't—blond, tall, good to the bone, properly ambitious in life. After high school, my friends Kelly and Fran and Chip and I revered her so much that whenever we found a good person, we'd call her a Sue. When I moved to Los Angeles, I met another Sue, but her name was Lisa. And she stayed by my side, sharing my adventures over a glass of wine. Then I met Julie when I moved to my first house. Now, whenever I meet a good person, I call her a Julie.

The house on Cynthia Street was a charming little bungalow, once a pied-à-terre for Groucho Marx's mistress. The day I moved, in the summer of 2001, a little girl, a precious sprite with long brown hair named Anna, came over to say hello. She bounded up the driveway, trailed by her mother, to give me a welcome hug. The affection from that girl has never wavered, but the greatest gift was the woman standing behind her, her mother, Julie De Santo, whose three other kids and husband, Elio, were waiting at home, next door.

Julie brought out home-cooked Italian meals, welcomed me into her family, became my confidante and my cheerleader. She and Elio owned a restaurant in L.A. for years, and she was a devoted mother who ran what was basically a day care out of her house so she could be with her four children. After her kids were grown, she followed her calling to become a trauma therapist. I watched in awe as she transformed her family, and her life, through her understanding of how trauma and pain are held in the body and how we can recover from them.

In December 2015, I met another Julie. I had just started working on a film called *Mothers and Daughters,* and my life was in a desperate place. I had been experiencing aggravated, unidentified MS symptoms for years, and I was really in bad shape. I probably weighed eighty-five pounds, if that, and was in constant pain, with tight, burning, inflamed skin. My financial situation wasn't much better. I hadn't worked since 2013, when I was fired from *Anger Management* after I called Charlie Sheen a "menace to work with"—at least that's what I read. I was broke—my funds had dwindled so much, I shouldn't even have splurged on going out to dinner. This job offered me three paid weeks in L.A.

On the first day of work, the car showed up with a young, pretty woman at the wheel, ready to transport me. She wore a big parka and sensible running shoes. Her name was Bonny. During the next few weeks, she cheerfully and skillfully managed my life on that shoot, taking everything in stride. She made sure a constant supply of nourishing snacks was eaten by me. She was extremely capable and grounded; in other words, she was a Julie. I learned she'd been a Montessori teacher for five years but had burned out and, like me, she was looking for a change. In the car home one evening, we discussed life plans. She came on as my assistant and stayed by my side through it all. She was and is a beautiful and reliable woman. It was as if she'd been sent to me by some benevolent force in the universe. I don't know what I would have done without her at this time.

So now everyone who knows me calls the good people in their lives a Julie. Another piece of advice: Find yourself a Julie—those guardian angels who walk among us. And then hold on to her.

⁓

I first saw the ethereal brand of Julie known as Jaime King on a magazine cover in 1996 with a story by Jennifer Egan titled "James Is a Girl." I fell in love. I'm a sucker for beauty, and she has one of those faces that made me grateful and envious. Grateful that such a face exists, anxious it wasn't mine.

Later, in California, Jaime and I auditioned for the same role in the movie *Slackers*—Angela, the pretty girl—and she got the part. Jason Schwartzman was also cast, and suddenly, instead of admiration, I felt jealousy. Not only did I think Jaime was heartbreakingly gorgeous, but certainly my boyfriend would, too.

I'll never forget the name Angela, because Jason had to shave an *A* into his chest hair as part of the movie. Now I saw the *A* in the shower and when we were intimate. A constant reminder of this girl who was now playing the girl who steals my love's heart.

I drove to Riverside to visit him on set, but I accidentally passed the exit, driving hours out of my way. By the time I arrived, I was hungry and dehydrated. When I saw Jaime in person, I couldn't believe there was a creature so beautiful. She was Grace Kelly, a young Brooke Shields, perfection magnified. It was otherworldly. She wore Birkenstocks, and all I could think was, "Of course they look good on her." When I wore mine, I looked very Seattle coffee bean, or as my mother said, like a potato picker, but they looked stylish on her. *Alors.* When I saw how perfectly she presented even in a Birkenstock, I excused myself from set.

If ever she and Jason had dinner in his room together, I became paranoid. "Don't trust her," I told him. "Don't be alone with her." I'd never seen her act inappropriately toward him, but she was friendly, flirty. "What's her deal?" I grilled him. "Why does she want to be alone with you?" Whenever I went to set, I grew silent and judgmental. Eventually, I saw she'd done nothing. I'd been making her into something she wasn't.

A couple months later, I called her from the bathtub, where I went to think. "You know, I'm really jealous of you," I admitted. I apologized for being cold and distrustful. And Jaime was true. "Thank you so much," she said, with so much grace. She offered me a lot of grace. From there, we fell in love, as young close friends do.

I had a dream the world was ending. Gravity had disappeared and everyone was slipping into space. In this dreamworld, as I tried to hang on, I noticed that I was holding Jaime's hand. In the morning, Jaime called me. "I had a dream about you," she said. "I dreamed that I was holding your hand." Ever since, it's been understood that we are sisters of a sort.

I love her. She pulls through for everything. She's generous beyond. She's a real seeker of things. She's a long hugger—maybe a little too long. Julie always said everyone should hug for nine seconds to really feel it, but nine seconds is a long time. Still, as with most things, Jaime easily gets away with it. Minutes. Hours. Years. Holding on to me, please.

Ahmet

I DID GET MARRIED ONCE. It happened, in part, because of a horoscope.

I was thirty-two at the time, a rag doll, way too depressed and exhausted, still living in the aftermath of my ruined relationship with Jason Schwartzman, the love of my young life.

One day, my friend Amanda Anka asked me, "Who are you dating?"

I was very much not dating anyone.

"I think I have your husband," she said.

"Really? Who?" I asked.

"Ahmet Zappa." She waited for my reaction.

"The bald guy who was on MTV?" Not the reaction she was hoping for.

"He has a crush on you!" she said. "He just asked me, 'When are you going to introduce me to my wife?'"

So, I met Ahmet for breakfast at Hugo's in West Hollywood. His first impression of me was that I looked like, as he put it, "a brown clown." Like my mother before me, I am heavy-handed with a blush brush, which I believe is the sign of either an insane woman or a great artist. I was trying to look sun kissed, but instead I showed up caked in bronzer.

"Hello, brown clown!" he said when I sat down.

We got engaged eight days later.

Ahmet was sweet. He had a kind face and big, warm eyes with lashes like a Snuffleupagus. When he blinked, I felt like Beyoncé, with my very own wind machine. He was tall and cuddly, inappropriate with a remark, and fun. With his friends, we made up stories that we told in silly accents. I played a woman named Donatella who made hoopskirts for ponies. "Dis hoopskirt is the height of fashion for the pony who wants more girth!" Ahmet laughed and laughed.

The week after we met, I took him to my Julie's house. She approved and we all cozied up in her daughters' room as the girls got ready for bed, laughing together, which made me happy. Deeply entrenched in that new-couple glow, we picked up a book—a zodiac book on astrological love matches. It was one of those tomes you find for $1.99 on the bargain shelf at Barnes & Noble. The book told us that Taurus and Cancer were the ideal match. He was a Taurus. I was a Cancer. Clearly, I was someone who had trouble straying from a forecast. Whatever the prophecy was, I felt I had an obligation to fulfill it.

When we got in the car, Ahmet asked, "Will you marry me?"

I laughed and said, "What?" A moment passed. I could see he was serious, so I giggled again and said, "Well, where's the offering?" He fumbled in the glove box, found a yellow highlighter pen, and repeated, "Will you marry me?"

It was so Zappa. Very impulsive. I thought, *This is what I need. Someone spontaneous. Someone who is going to jump off the edge for me, because I'm pretty far down.*

I was happy that it was written in the stars. With Ahmet, I could wipe off my brown clown and be myself. So, I accepted the highlighter. And just like that, we were engaged.

After I said yes, Ahmet remembered how his father, Frank, had proposed to his mother, Gail, with a ballpoint pen. It was another sign: this match was meant to be. Why I thought either of these stories was romantic, instead of hasty and impulsive, I do not know. We were two loving people who hadn't yet found their person. We walked in blindfolded but holding hands.

When I called my mother to tell her the "big" news, she sighed loudly. "Oh, Selma." Then she asked, "Who are his people?"

"He's a Zappa," I said. Still, she was indignant. "Well, I'm not going to throw you a wedding when you're only going to get divorced. You're like me; you're not meant to be married." Ever the rebel, I did it anyway. Though her words haunted me.

The whole wedding was somewhat wonderfully ridiculous, as many of these things are. I was shooting a John Waters movie with Tracey Ullman at the time, and when I announced to her that we were engaged, she immediately called Carrie Fisher, with whom she was close. On speakerphone, she screamed, "Carrie! Carrie! Carrie, are you there? I have Selma here! Don't you want her to get married at your house?" And that's exactly what happened. Carrie Fisher generously offered to host my wedding at her home—when she was strong-armed into it by a trio of celebrants.

Karl offered to make my wedding gown, which *Vogue,* under Anna Wintour, covered in a piece by Plum Sykes. I went to his studio in Paris for the fitting. He drew a simple column in a very pale pink, with rhinestones on the satin ribbons wrapping around my neck and down my back. At first, I protested. "No, no! This is my wedding! I want a big giant fairy princess ball gown!" But Karl said, without skipping a beat, "Darling, the ball gown will be for your next wedding." He made an identical dress in black, for the party, so I could drink red wine without concern.

Our rehearsal dinner was held at the Chateau Marmont. Everyone in attendance had a copy of Carrie Fisher's latest book, *The Best Awful,* which had just come out. It was dusk, and we were about to play drag queen bingo, with prizes donated by Carrie, from her eclectic personal collection. My mother appeared at the door of the bungalow, backlit by the evening sun. She looked very, very shaken. "Helmut Newton just dropped dead," my mother announced. "Here. Right in front of me." Soon after, the food arrived, and the meat in the burgers was still frozen because the kitchen had gone into a tailspin after Newton's heart attack. He was a resident, and they were horrified. (And boom. This is the part where the fortune-tellers weigh in, and the signs are clear. The universe was telling me to run.)

Nothing felt right. I felt sick. I wanted to go home, back to Michigan, with my mother and Sue, Kelly, and Frances, my Fab Four group from high school. Instead, I picked up a glass. I found someone's abandoned red wine and drank what was left. I sorted my fishtail linen skirt, which I'd bought in Milan with Lizzie and her husband while on a break from shooting *Hellboy* in Prague, and tightened my ponytail. Well, I thought. At least my mother will go home having witnessed something memorable: Helmut Newton's death.

The wedding itself was small, around forty guests. I didn't invite many people, because I don't think I actually believed I was getting married. The entire guest list was made up of my closest friends from Cranbrook, my sisters, Reese, Troy, Julie, Jaime. My heart wasn't in any of it. (Apparently, neither was Carrie's; she forgot all about the wedding time and showed up at her own home after the ceremony was over, after having a fresh salon cut.)

Our engagement might have been written in the stars, but believe you me, a year into that marriage I went to see another intuitive. But in the end, I couldn't really get answers. How was I supposed to know if I should get out of the marriage when I barely understood how I'd gotten into it?

After the wedding, Ahmet and I traveled around Europe and Japan for the *Hellboy* press tour. In the Frankfurt airport, Ahmet bought me a brown stuffed rabbit he named Snoobles. We got along well on that trip, relishing the company and the music and the food, the smell of chocolate in Zurich, the clean air. We were young and hopeful, and we really did love each other. But there was no deep sexual attraction between us. It wasn't totally foolish, but it wasn't built for the long term. We should have been goofy friends who saw each other for dinner every two years, joking about what a fun couple we'd make, then going on our merry way.

We might have done that if we were not so impulsive, so wanting, so wounded.

Our relationship did not provide the comfort I needed. Once I married Ahmet, the emptiness came back. I lost hope and drive. I didn't know what I wanted to do, how I could secure another good job on-screen. I felt sad and terrified. Claustrophobic. I had trouble sleeping. I would sob and laugh at the same time, or wake myself in paroxysms of grief. It felt as if I were falling apart. It felt like a slow treading of water, of things falling away. I couldn't keep up mentally or physically. I didn't recognize myself. I was in bed. Under cover. Literally and figuratively. Swollen, wet with constant tears.

I started drinking, and I wanted to drink alone. I didn't recognize how fragile I'd become. Or that it would ever change. My spirit couldn't get comfortable in my shell-shocked, love-torn, glass-near-empty mindset. And I couldn't wake up. By the end of the marriage, I was drinking at lunch, drunk by dinner.

I wanted a divorce, I told him seriously. We had just come home from Julie's grad school graduation and reception. She was going to be a trauma specialist. It was evident she was living the life she wanted. And it made me realize, in stark relief, that I *wasn't* living the life I wanted. I still didn't know what the fuck I wanted. All I knew was that I wanted to be drunk and be done with this marriage.

Ahmet and I did try. Together, we went to therapy. Eventually, he gave in to my request for a divorce. In the end, we had an important, short relationship that wasn't meant to be.

When I called my mother to tell her that Ahmet and I were divorcing, I made sure to lead with the part where she was correct. "You were right, Mom," I said. "I shouldn't have gotten married. I'm not capable of so much compromise."

"That's okay," she said. "At least I didn't pay for that wedding. And my *God,* your hair was *awful.* Good thing you didn't invite anybody. Now that's over. Like Karl said, 'The next one!' Maybe you will fix your hair next time. Do you have to pay him alimony? I hope you had a prenup. Silly. Just silly. I still love you."

After we split, I decided that was it. My mother was right. I wasn't meant to be married. I would *never* make that mistake again.

I hadn't changed my name to Zappa, so I didn't need to give it back. The responsibility of being a Zappa, with my personality, hit too close. I did get stationery with my married name, though—*Selma James Blair Zappa.* Sometimes I still use it. Every now and then, I'll write to someone giving them that unexpected gift of history.

Bite Me

 $W_{ITH\ THE\ EXCEPTION}$ of high school or spring break, where everyone does stupid things, I hardly ever drank around other people. I was not a social drinker. "How much did you drink?" a friend would ask. "Nothing," I would shrug. I didn't get publicly sloppy from booze very often. I didn't want to make mistakes. I already felt bizarre and uncomfortable, and I didn't need alcohol to exacerbate those qualities for all to worry or judge. For me, the act of drinking was only ever a last resort (more like a common resort), a way to pass out and go into the void.

One night after my divorce, I was at the Chateau Marmont, drink in hand, and lo and behold, there was Sienna Miller. Everyone had told me how much I would love Sienna, and she didn't disappoint. She had such a great smile, with a dimple and white teeth. I couldn't begrudge her for any part she was winning over me.

So, I grabbed her arm and bit it, playfully, as if it were an apple.

Even as I held her forearm in my mouth I was aghast at myself. I thought, *What have I gotten myself into? Or her? This is horrible behavior.* Followed closely by, *Please, Selma. Please don't leave the house again.* I have very sharp canines. But Sienna couldn't have been more charming. She kind of screamed, "Opa!" as I do whenever someone breaks a plate. "You bit me, didn't you? You really did!" she said, in her charming accent. She didn't shame me. For this, in my book, she will forever be the belle of the ball.

There was another such incident that did not go as well. The thought of it still makes me redden. Scarlett Johansson and I had met while working on the movie *In Good Company* and were on our way to becoming friends. When she invited me on a trip to Las Vegas with a group of her friends, I didn't hesitate to accept.

It started out well enough. We got to fly on a private plane. I liked her friends. The room was great.

On our first night there, we all went downstairs for great sushi. Because I wasn't good at social drinking, I did not realize how drunk one can get while seated at a table, eating. (In fact, it's quite possible the last time I'd done it was that Passover seder all those years ago.) One minute, I was sitting there feeling fine, the next, I stood up and I was right back at Pete's Tavern. I was the kind of drunk where you're crawling off the stool and the room is spinning and finding your way to the bathroom feels like circumnavigating the globe.

After dinner, we needed to make an appearance at some very loud club. I did my best to work it out, dancing halfheartedly, Paris Hilton–style. I was wearing a dress and cape by The Row, and I remember reminding myself how Ashley Olsen would advise I go to bed. This didn't have to be.

My friend the actor Seth Green was at the club that night, and he came up to me and said, "I want you to meet my friend." He proceeded to introduce me to Seth MacFarlane. I love Seth Mac-Farlane! I was starstruck. What do I do in public situations where I admire someone, but feel as if I don't bring anything to the party? I bit him on the hand.

"Whoa!" he yelled. "That really hurt." It wasn't a disaster; I didn't break skin. But I soon hated myself.

The following week, there was a story in the *Enquirer* about how I met Seth McFarlane and how shocked he was when I bit him. The story did not die there. Seth was the voice of Johann in *Hellboy II,* and he told Guillermo del Toro the same story. ("Did you really bite him, monkey brain?" Guillermo later asked me. Monkey brain was a nickname he gave me because my eyes cross when sleepy.) By the time of this telling, I had been sober for a while. But the story lived on. Anytime I met anyone connected with Seth, which is not a small number of people, I would ask, "Do you know I bit him?" And invariably, they would say, "Yeah."

Scarlett has never invited me anywhere since.

The truth is, I am a person who is meant to stay home and read books, maybe have a nice dinner, and then put myself to bed. That is the life I'm built for. It's all about the setting. When I'm out in public, it's as if my system gets overwhelmed and instantaneously short-circuits. I turned the phoenix into ashes, by accident, in small ways, all the time.

In my life, social interactions have been cumbersome. I worried about my mental state for a long time, because I didn't yet understand that the MS symptoms accruing over the years were something real. I just thought, *My God, I'm a fucking mess!* Falling and dramatic, affable or ridiculous in public.

To my family, I'm brooding and quiet. To the world, I'm like Phyllis Diller in drag—attention seeking and big. I'm a loner, but when I talk to people, I overcompensate and try to give them their money's worth (even if no one asked and no one paid). But it doesn't always have the intended effect. I get overstimulated, unreadable.

Thank goodness there are the Sienna Millers of the world. Those who are willing to play. Those who are willing to see. Once a person has patience for me, I calm down. But first I throw everything at the wall trying to see what sticks, trying to connect. I'm a slow burn. Someone has to really like me in order to be with me. It's just one of the reasons I love the friends I have so much—the ones who understood me and loved me just the same.

❧

The first and only person to bite me back was Kate Moss.

Kate and I were friends of a sort, through Robert Rich. In the heyday of Marc Jacobs, he was the PR director and celebrity liaison for the brand, and he held court from his basement office on Mercer Street. Some of my best days were spent in that basement, taking Polaroids, drinking rosé out of a can. An inner circle.

"You're Kate Moss," I said, when I first met her. But my intimidation melted quickly, because she was so fucking funny and cool. For a stretch of time, whenever she came to New York, or whenever I went to London, we would hang out.

After a Marc Jacobs show, a bunch of us were lounging around in a big suite at Claridge's London. I had just started taking Adderall again, which I was prescribed for depression. It worked, in a way, because it got me out of bed. It also made me able to drink more. That night, and well into the morning, Kate and I were having a great time, taking Polaroids with Robert. And then I bit her finger. She laughed. And because she laughed, I did it again.

The second time, she did not laugh. With annoyance, she took her other hand, the one I hadn't bitten, and punched me on my back.

"That really fucking hurt!" she said.

Then she bit me back. She grabbed my thumb and crunched right into it. This was the first time I had any inkling of how much I might hurt people when I bit them. Immediately, I transformed into a shamed nursery school kid.

"Oh my gosh," I whispered, "I am so sorry."

I looked down at the little bit of blood on my thumb, and thought, "Oh my God. This could scar." (No. It couldn't.) I felt so happy. I hoped it would. I'd have a scar forever—a scar that came from Kate Moss. (Sadly, it didn't leave a mark.) I loved how she bit me back, 'cause that put an end to that.

Personality-wise, Kate and I exist on very different planes. One night, we were standing on a balcony at the Chateau, when she said, "I want to stay up tonight! Give me a number."

"Eight?" I guessed. I had no idea where she was going with this game. She looked at me, expecting me to continue.

"Four?" I supplied. This went on for longer than it should have.

Of course, she wanted a phone number for a person. A low-key, high-end connection. Weed, or whatever. I was just a run-of-the-mill drunk. I had no such number. Robert and I still crack up about that. Every time I see him, that's the joke. "Give me a number!"

⌒⌐

The idea of someone asking me for a number is particularly funny if you consider the fact that I had never done cocaine and didn't enjoy pot. The one time I tried snorting, it was nothing short of a disaster. It was the night before the Met Gala in 2009, and I was staying at the Carlyle. In the room above mine, there was a gathering. A spring breeze floated through the open balcony doors. At one point, I went in the bathroom, where someone had laid out a single line of white powder. I'd never tried cocaine, or any recreational drugs for that matter, for the simple reason that if I acted as weirdly as I did when I drank, best to abstain from hard-core drugs. But it was a small, wealthy group of icons, and it wasn't a huge amount. So I figured this was the time to do it.

It tasted horrible—unspeakably awful. It was so bad that I had to remove myself from all festivities for the rest of the evening. *How do people do this?* I wondered. It was easily the worst thing, other than a Tic Tac in my youth, I put in my nose. It cut a burning trail of bitterness all the way down my throat. My sinuses were on fire.

As I made my way back to my hotel room, I didn't feel any type of stoned. Not a lift, not a buzz, nothing at all. I went into my bathroom and opened a tiny bottle of champagne. I drank it, then inexplicably passed out on my bathroom floor.

The next thing I knew, I woke up hungover. But this wasn't a typical hangover. It was the lowest I've ever felt in my life. I'm talking teeth-chattering, body-shaking illness coupled with over-whelming nausea. It turns out that what I'd taken probably wasn't cocaine at all. It was probably crystal meth. But by this point, it was far too late to do anything about it.

Chris McMillan came to nurse me to health but I was sicker than I'd ever been. I spent the day vomiting, wondering how I would possibly make it through. My face was puffy from throw-ing up all day. To make matters worse, I had lost most of my hair due to an autoimmune issue, but thankfully the hair genius Teddy Charles put a long fall, like my mother would have worn, on me to disguise it.

I pieced myself together enough to make it to the gala, where I gave Anna Wintour a hug in the receiving line. (You do *not* give Anna Wintour a hug.) I might even have kissed her on the cheek. It was a serious gaffe. I knew better. But I loved her with deep admiration. I'm expressive. Maybe it's because I was so out of it, or maybe because Ingrid and Karl liked me, I had a momentary lapse in judgment, where I thought I could get away with such behavior. But I am fully aware this is not how it's done with Anna Wintour. (Thank you, Anna, for being so gracious.)

I wore a black Marc Jacobs minidress with Louboutin Kate sti-letto heels that had me in pain. No one took my picture at the event. I was confused. Later, I realized that no one recognized me with fake hair and a swollen face, or maybe illness rendered me invisible.

Luckily, I kept it together. No drunk shenanigans, no further embarrassments. In fact, nothing horrible happened to me that night, except that the only man who spoke to me was Donald Trump.

While everyone dispersed to their various cool spots, I was standing, floating where I had sat, lingering at the end. I was next to Carine Roitfeld, and she said, "Don't worry, I'll take you home." Just then, Donald Trump sidled up to us.

The first thing he said to me was, "Wow. Amazing hair." I could tell it was *genuine.* "That hair. You have beautiful hair. Really. That is sensational hair. Don't you think so, Melania?" Melania was back three paces. She took a step forward, holding her expensive clutch, and politely agreed.

Carine was talking again about rides home, and Donald said, "You need a ride? I'll take you!" But I turned him down. I preferred to go with Carine, of course, because she was the coolest.

My brief conversation with Donald Trump is funny to me now, for a couple reasons. The first is that it was a very positive exchange. He really liked my hair! The second is that I was wearing fake hair that night. Of course I didn't tell him.

⁓

A bad thing happened. I took up with a new guy, hereafter known as the Monster, who turned out to be toxic in every sense of the word. (I actually met him at the Chateau the same night I bit Sienna Miller.) From the moment he pushed into my scene, everything fell apart.

The Monster barged in when I was particularly vulnerable. I was making a real effort to go out and make friends again, but unfortunately that often went hand in hand with drinking. The MS hit me really hard at this point, but I didn't yet understand what it was. I let go of my nutrition, too shut down to digest; I was smoking, I was drinking, and all of it was affecting my looks. My personal life was disintegrating.

Emotionally, I was in the perfect position to fall for a toxic person, a fact he instantly got. I wasn't even into him, but he was persistent. Quite possibly the most persistent suitor I've ever encountered.

People warned me about this guy. My dear Quinn, a newly made close friend, warned me he was a con man, not to be trusted. He was just after the spotlight, he only wanted his picture taken. But he wormed his way into my life. He was, quite literally, all about appearances. He hung around the Chateau, leaving a trail of heavy cologne in his wake. He wore colored contact lenses but denied it. His self-tanner left brown spots on the white bathroom walls. As soon as we started seeing each other, paparazzi appeared in places they had never been. They kept turning up—at the dog park, not on Robertson Boulevard, where it's expected. It became apparent afterward that he was the one calling them.

When I went away to work, he set up camp at my house unin-vited. He looked through my journals, read my private thoughts. When he found something, some fact that he could use to his advantage, he stayed silent. He never divulged that he knew. He uncovered every weakness, cataloging them for later use, to bribe and extort me. As if that weren't bad enough, he remained in my home, living there while I was gone. I was on the other side of the world, and I couldn't get him out.

He became vicious. If we disagreed, he would turn on a dime. He spouted nonsensical things, telling stories that never happened and saying things that weren't true about people I happened to know. At first, I thought he was gaslighting me, but it seemed as though he truly believed them himself. I didn't know how much a person could scare me until I met him. When it became clearer, I tried to extricate myself.

This was that time—that Juicy Couture track suit moment—when the internet exploded. Gossip websites like Perez Hilton and PopSugar were hugely popular, and they began posting awful things about me, prompted by his insider machinations. One site, the Evil Beet, was the worst of all. I was late to the internet gossip thing, but while I was shooting *Hellboy II,* I became acquainted with a computer and discovered that you could search for your own name and a slew of information would pop up. That was the first time I ever googled myself, and it just about undid me. I was already not in a great place, and that put me firmly over the edge.

Back in L.A., the Monster posted lies all over the internet—that I was crazy, that I did drugs. He changed my Wikipedia page to include his vicious untruths. I tried to defend myself, taking it upon myself to call these bloggers and explain the situation. But there was only so much I could do. It's not that I was some highly credible character; there were already stories out there about me biting people.

It continued this way for a year. Eventually, investigators I hired went to his home and told him how the evidence was traced to his router in L.A., as well as to his parents' home in the Midwest. I had already blocked him. But so much damage had been done.

The first few years I spent regaining my balance after the divorce were an awful, awful time, a fun-house mirror of bad experiences. I felt totally lost. I would stay in my house, trying to will myself not to drink. My life was messy, ugly, unfocused. I was lonely, I was puffy and hot, and I was tired. Always, always tired. I couldn't keep it together. In my attempts to self-medicate, my drinking grew heavier as my mind grew less and less focused.

After another bad binge, Troy contacted a rehab specialist who got me into Promises in Malibu. I didn't trust that I could get better being alone in my home. Though my insurance would have covered it, I paid for it in cash, too afraid someone might find out. As with all my stints in rehab, I tried as best as I could to keep it to myself. I didn't want to be labeled, as either an addict or a depressive, because I worried the stigma could impact my ability to get work. It was all a humiliating weakness. I didn't tell anyone—only Troy and a couple close friends.

I was in a state of constant terror.

As it turned out, the biggest star in the universe, Britney Spears, was also recuperating there. I loved her right away, recognizing she was incredibly dear.

At the time, she had a shaved head and wore a cheap platinum bob wig. After we became friends, I suggested she ditch it. I took her wig and told her that she couldn't wear it anymore. It was associated with the "crazy" label, this tumultuous time in her life, and she was ready for the next chapter, I thought. And told her. May the record stand, I did not steal it—though I did ask her for it, and she gave it to me. I held on to Britney's wig because I wanted to protect her. I told her she was beautiful, and she really, really was. She was so gamine and young, but in a horrible situation.

She also wore wedged flip-flops; you could hear her coming

and going from rooms away. Since she asked me what I bought, what I wore, how I knew what to do, I felt she wanted advice. So I secretly dropped the worn sandals in the trash, hoping it might inspire her to get some real shoes. Instead, she found them in the garbage minutes later and was hurt. "Who threw away my flip-flops?" she cried. I never told her it was me. I thought I was being helpful. I've since come to feel terrible about this. Here was the biggest pop star in the world, in the middle of managing her own public and personal crisis, which her family trapped her in, and I'm throwing away her flip-flops. I meant well. I was just being a girl (not yet a woman).

(Britney, I want you to know I'm sorry I threw your flip-flops in the trash.)

She was an angel, with wisdom and sweetness in equal measure.

I had no real idea of the extent of her suffering. I still have her blond wig. It lives in my closet, in its own little time capsule. A relic of a bygone era. I truly love that girl.

We didn't keep in touch; her number changed a week after she left.

Family

AFTER MY TRIP TO HELL with the Monster, I resigned myself to being alone. I was working long hours on the set of *Kath & Kim,* weary and bloated from eating Doritos and Cinnabon rolls on film as my lazy, snack-driven character. I was juggling both a TV show and press for *Hellboy II,* which made it easier to distract myself with work and promotion. We traveled through Mexico with Guillermo and the main cast for a pampered while. My makeup artist, Rachel Goodwin, and I sampled mezcal worm tacos at the Four Seasons in Mexico City with Guillermo explaining how he dreamed about these tacos, soft white worms delicately seasoned. I couldn't swallow the bite, my American brain stubborn as ever. There were long, jubilant nights at candlelit tables in Berlin and Madrid, laughter and stories from our cherished director himself, well-deserved hangovers along with somber and reverential visits to the Holocaust and Anne Frank museums. My best friend at the time, my dear Quinn, traveled with us and delighted in it as much as I did, even finishing a shallow dish of soup with a baby bird presented in the center. At the chicest, gastronomically superior, six-table restaurant in the Spanish city. When pressed, Quinn appreciatively told the table that the bird was soft. The beak and bones only slightly crunchy. I closed my eyes and had a sip of cold water. And we smiled as we strolled the streets after-ward, all spiffy and high-heeled was I.

When the festivities ended, I headed back to L.A. Months passed. In short order, a girlfriend set me up on a date with Jason Bleick, the designer of a clothing brand I admired called Ever. I had a sweatshirt, the logo of a leaf on the right arm. Jason was quiet and reserved, muscular and gentle, with piercing eyes that were impossibly clear and blue, like a Siberian husky's. I thought he was handsome and sexy, but we didn't connect instantly.

He lived in a giant teepee in Topanga, where we had our first date. When I arrived at his little compound, he had candles lit. They twinkled in the tiny tiled bathroom in his studio there, and a beautiful hinoki-scented one danced in its flame atop a large stack of Rizzoli art books. The effect was lovely. The smell of a familiar fig candle Victoria Beckham had been burning on a few visits to her stunning house was gently wafting among his sketch pads and leather samples. I also noticed he was nervous. I actually tried to cancel the date because I'd crushed my left hand earlier that day from a forceful horse kick while out galloping in the hills of Sun-land with another friend. But instead, Jason sent a car for me. I was charmed by his thoughtfulness. We walked to dinner at the Inn of the Seventh Ray. And as we ate in relative quiet outdoors that evening, with twinkle lights all around, he cut my food because I couldn't use my knife. I noticed he was strong, with good taste, a good eye. A special kind of man. But he was reserved. Also intrigu-ing. I couldn't get a real read on him.

After dinner, we went back to the teepee with its wood-burning stove in the center. We casually lay down on the bed, each staring up, nestled among the fur blankets. It wasn't romantic as much as it was . . . just being present. At one point, a spider quickly spun down from a beam of the teepee, heading for my face! I rolled over, pressing into his side. It was just a reaction. But he rolled away. I was sensitive and it hurt my feelings.

"Well," I said, "I guess it's time to go."

The car arrived. We said goodbye. We shared an awkward hug. The whole interaction felt platonic, confusing. I left, bemused and fine. I didn't expect to hear from him again.

A week later, he sent a text: "When can I see you again?"

It was funny to me. And now I was curious. Why would he want to spend more time in my company? I didn't know him, how reserved he was in new situations especially, though I would come to understand he is a man of few words.

He arranged to pick me up to go to an art gallery. M+S was the name of it. A small, cool space with an exhibit by a great artist who does pool photos. And oceans. Not Slim. Someone else. But someone great. He was visibly nervous; he didn't speak much in the car. His speech seemed kinda clipped. Quiet. So I talked a lot. As I do. "I like this song. [It was Jay-Z and Alicia Keys. "Empire State of Mind."] You know, I stopped listening to anything. But I like that you do. Listen. To music." Silence. He smiled and got us to the space. I was amused. I didn't know what to make of it. When we pulled up to the gallery, it was closed. He had the date wrong. He was stricken, mortified. Stunned. I laughed and said, "Don't worry! Let's get a coffee." Coffee turned into dinner at Pace in Laurel Canyon. We sat in a cozy booth in the farthest corner. At some point, he took my hand and held it. I held his hand back. When he dropped me off at home, I went inside and cried. I felt inexplicably forlorn. And I kept thinking of his hand holding mine at the table. I knew. I just knew we were connected until the end. And I felt hard times in it.

On our first day date, he took me paddleboarding at Topanga Beach. He drove us to the Malibu Country Mart on a rich-looking customized black BMW bike. We wound around the late after-noon canyon sun to get there, both wearing Ever leather jackets. We held hands, already in love. For the first time in my adult life, I felt I had a man on my arm who was suitable for me. I smiled and leaned in as the ever-present paparazzi snapped a few pho-tos as we strolled. Earlier, I took a picture of him unstrapping the boards from the top of his Mercedes G wagon. I sent it to Troy, who approved. And so, we were a couple.

My heart grew full and in love. I found him fascinating and specific. Passionate about Dan Eldon and his family, about fonts and branding. His hands were handsome and strong with long nail beds, which my mother and I always favored. We were mad about each other. He thoughtfully customized my riding helmets, mak-ing leather bands to go around the sun-soaked velvet, complete with my initials embossed by him. Loving gestures . . . to say the least. I gave him my soft cotton hankie to use for his allergies when we drove up to ride my horse, Dark. I loved the way he slowly walked with a coffee in his hand. Pleased to be doing just that. He liked real cinnamon sticks in his coffee. (He once told me that was all he needed from me—cinnamon sticks in his coffee. It turns out that wasn't true. Or maybe it was, and I was the one who was after something more.) I still have jars of cinnamon sticks, waiting to be plunked in his dark brew.

Soon after, he left to go on a trek with his best friend, Scooter, visiting ancient monasteries in Tibet, while I flew to New York to shoot another movie, *Dark Horse,* with Todd Solondz. The film was a major win for me, an honor. Todd being my favorite director to work with, and knowing my mother would be pleased.

"*Happiness* is pitch-perfect," my mother would announce. "PERFECT!" We were in wholehearted agreement that Todd Solondz was our personal story hero. Mom couldn't make it in the winter to visit, but Jason came to visit me twice. Todd liked him. He was likable, a good man.

Like a hopeful teenage girl, I scrawled Jason's name all over my notebooks. I wrote his name over and over on the soles of my Converse, along with the word "ever." I was smitten.

On October 13, 2010, he flew from Nepal to New York to be with me. It was the first time we'd been together in several months. I was staying at the Standard Hotel in the Meatpacking District, my friend André's hotel, and ran downstairs to greet him. We had the most healing and enduring hug that I've ever had in my life. I was so overwhelmed with gratitude and love I could barely catch my breath. In love. In hope. Miraculous. A fellow guest at the hotel, laying eyes on the two of us, reunited, and in the elevator, going back up to our room, said, "You're both so beautiful. Look at that happiness." It was truth.

That night, our son Arthur came into existence. It was a perfect night. I wasn't impulsive or lost. I was there, fully present. Everything about that moment was very loving. We were safe and didn't have any idea a baby was in the cards. When I found out I was pregnant, six weeks later, all I could think was how desperately I wanted this baby to be safe. I wanted him with all my heart. Whatever that meant.

The tide of my life was turning toward a new north star. Every decision I made, every stumble and success, brought me to this moment. Arthur was growing inside me. A miracle, a reason. Oceans upon oceans upon oceans of love swelled inside me even before I saw his face.

PART III

ANSWERS

Motherhood

THROUGH ALL THE MESSAGES and predictions I'd heard in my life, from all the mystics and healers and energy workers, there was always a common refrain. They all noted I had a darkness around me.

Early in my pregnancy, I drove to Woodland Hills to see a man named Kit. He had more of a pedigree than I was used to; apparently, he read for presidents. I hoped this time might be different.

"You'll have a hard time with the baby's father," he told me. "You won't stay together." I didn't have any intention of being a single mother. But I also think Jason and I knew that it probably wouldn't last. "You and your son will be inseparable until he's three, at which point he'll be closer to his dad also." He paused before continuing. "You will go through a very hard time. You've gone through a hard time already, and you will be tested for the next ten years."

He called it all.

Another seer, Bobby, said, "This kid's going to take everything from you. You will live in that moment between the lightning and the thunderstorm. And in the end you will not be afraid." He told me I needed to keep the circulation going in the spot where my brain stem meets my neck. As it turns out, that is my problem area—the place where I have the most damage.

Right before Arthur was born, I went to see Kit again. He told me that in Arthur's last life, he was an Irish fisherman with an anchor tattoo. Maybe it's pure coincidence, but now Arthur's biggest passions in life are deep-sea fishing and swearing like a sailor.

～

The truth is, I was scared to death to have a child. I knew I had love to give. But otherwise I felt ill-equipped.

I was afraid of how much help would cost.

I was afraid of how I'd adjust, because I'm such a loner.

Other pregnant people would touch their bellies and smile, proclaiming, "I don't care if it's a boy or a girl, I just hope it's healthy!"

My version of that was, "I don't care if it's a boy or a girl, just let it be a puppy!" Until I got pregnant, I was never someone who dreamed of having a child, so I thought maybe, just maybe, the doctor would pronounce it a puppy. My only dependent up to that point had been Wink, my precious rescue dog.

Even my mother was skeptical of this unexpected turn in my life story. "This is awful, Selma," she moaned when I told her the news over the phone. "How will you work?" She was afraid for my career. I'm sure it also brought up memories of the hardships she had experienced during her own single motherhood and how strong she had to be, going to law school in the midst of it.

My pregnancy was bookended by destabilizing pain and bladder and kidney infections. But the rest of it was magical. The truth was, I'd never felt better. What I know now is that pregnancy can put MS into remission. It was amazing. I had energy, clarity, hope. I ate well. I didn't touch alcohol. It was, for many reasons, the happiest time I'd ever experienced up to that point.

All my life I'd always felt most comfortable dressed in black—

it was my wardrobe staple—but now I was so blissed out that I started wearing pastels. (In multiple magazine interviews about my pregnancy, I'm quoted as saying, "I am just too happy to wear black!") I was photographed looking healthy in white sundresses and wedge heels.

Jason and I went down to Mexico for a babymoon. It was such a joy to be sober, back in the water, and to feel safe, bobbing up and down like a seal, feeling the large waves lift me up and down. I was photographed in a tiny bikini, my belly a watermelon, my entire face a smile.

I loved my obstetrician, but I'd watched Ricki Lake's documentary *The Business of Being Born* and felt inspired to have a home birth with a midwife and a doula. I wanted my son to work his way here. I wanted him to come in comfortable, prepared. More than anything, I didn't want to repeat my mother's scheduled C-sections, her rigid birth schedule. For me, childbirth would not be a chore. I wanted this baby with every ounce of myself.

When I was in the second trimester of my pregnancy, at what was otherwise one of the healthiest and happiest times of my life, Wink suddenly fell ill. She lay on the floor at the foot of the bed all morning and didn't move, her spirit subdued. "This is the end," I said to Jason. He said she would be okay, try not to worry. But I was worried. That afternoon I took her to the vet, and they decided to keep her for observation.

A few days later, the vet called to say she'd blown a clot. They were keeping her alive so I could come and say goodbye. "You need to come now," they said. When they gave her the shot to end her suffering, I held her against my pregnant belly and willed her back to me. I prayed harder than I ever had. But she was gone. A wall of pain surrounded me as they wrapped her up so I could take her home. Other than Bradley, losing Wink was my biggest loss up to that point. I could barely breathe. They'd even died on the same day: February 7. I still feel a bone-deep pang on that date every year, my body remembering.

Jason dug a hole in our backyard. I wrapped her in my forest-green monogrammed towel, a graduation gift from Cranbrook. I set her little head against the embroidered letters of my name and gently placed her in the ground, cursing and blessing God for taking her from me now when I still needed her.

⚬

A month past my due date, Arthur showed no signs of budging. The midwife had no choice but to let me go. When I went for that last scan, my obstetrician said I'd gone too long and needed to be induced right away. It was evening by that point, and I hadn't slept in days.

The Pitocin took a terrible toll on me, but still I refused a cesarean, or even an epidural. Thirty-seven hours of labor later, Julie rushed home early from a vacation to sit with me. She rubbed my head and encouraged me to get an epidural.

"I'm scared. I don't know how to be a good mother," I said.

"It doesn't matter if you don't know how to be a good mother," she told me, over and over. "You just have to want to be good enough."

Finally, she persuaded me to get the epidural, which only worked on half my body. I'd never felt such asymmetrical pain. Another epidural followed. I wasn't dilating enough. The baby was in distress.

And then I pushed. His head came out. My body finally realized he was ready and let him go. I reached down and pulled him from me and placed him on my pelvis.

When Jason first caught sight of him, he yelled, "Wow! He looks exactly like you! This is crazy!"

I placed my handsome baby on my stomach because I wanted him to find his own way to me. Everyone in the hospital room watched as he slowly started his army crawl to my right breast. I'd heard of this phenomenon, but I couldn't believe it until I saw it happen with my own eyes. I couldn't believe my damaged body, my enemy for so much of my life, had done this one good, heroic thing. I still can't believe it. Giving birth to a baby even in the best of circumstances is nothing short of miraculous.

He latched onto my breast, where he drew out the colostrum and fell asleep. Even Julie, who'd given birth four times by then, had never witnessed a baby do this. From his first moments on earth, we were all very impressed with Arthur Saint Bleick. As I held him to me, I thought of Wink and thanked her over and over again. Thank you for getting me to this place, sweet girl. I wouldn't be here without you.

❧

That first night in the hospital, Arthur slept. "What an easy baby!" I thought. Once again, he had other plans.

Arthur was anything but an easy baby, and I was not at ease. I was stiff and weak. Everyone assured me this was normal, it was my body normalizing, this was all normal normal normal. But I felt as if something were terribly wrong.

From the first instant I saw him, I loved Arthur more than I could ever dream of loving anyone. But when I got home from the hospital, everything hit me at once. I was not well, and I would not be well for many years to come. I was broken.

I was exhausted to the point where I couldn't see straight. I'd gone through periods like this before, but now I had a child to care for, and it just felt completely overwhelming. I'd never planned on having a baby of my own, and now, at home with this tiny creature, the buyer's remorse was brutal. I was woefully unequipped.

Early on, I called a cranial-sacral postpartum specialist. I explained through sobs that my pain was too "impractical." Tears led to further exhaustion and dehydration, but I was too deep in it to care. I couldn't stop crying. "I don't like any of it," I said. "Eating my encapsulated freeze-dried placenta hasn't helped for shit." She worked on me; she was patient. She listened. She advised healthy fats and restorative rest.

Before I had a baby, I had been able to check out whenever my body betrayed me or made things hard. Back then, I had solitude. I had Tanqueray. I knew how to numb the pain and disappear out of myself. Suddenly I was hit with a terrible realization: now that I was a mother, I would never be able to check out again.

⁓

The nanny I hired for Arthur had worked for me for only two weeks when I decided I had to let her go. I needed a live-in. She didn't want to be a live-in.

I paid her severance. We agreed to part ways amicably. Or so I thought.

A few days later, *Star* magazine called Troy to say that a former nanny was calling to sell a story about me. Of course I knew who it was. I paid five thousand dollars to quash the story. A year later, when she had a child of her own, she sent me an email saying her boyfriend at the time persuaded her to do it as revenge for firing her. She said she was so sorry. "We figured you were rich. I am so, so sorry." I wrote back, "I understand."

～

From the moment I gave birth, pain blossomed throughout my body in ways that were both familiar and entirely new to me. Every joint, every muscle grew stiff and brittle. My neck and shoulders spasmed. I couldn't walk to the bathroom; I couldn't get out of bed. The doctor explained how every woman who gives birth feels this. The ligaments just needed time to adjust, I was told. I believed this, I accepted it.

My eyes were red and irritated. My skin broke out. My mind broke down. It was hellish and it felt as if there were no way out. All I could feel was exhaustion. Arthur cried and cried and cried. No matter what we did, he cried. Unless he got exactly what he wanted, he cried. I was flailing and felt like a failure.

I wanted to die, but I couldn't die, because I didn't want to leave Arthur motherless. I went into survival mode. I had room in my life for only one other person and that was Arthur. I didn't have room for Jason. I lacked life force, so I prioritized, I thought.

My sense of smell was still so extreme, I couldn't stand myself if left unshowered for a day. Needless to say, Jason took the brunt of this because I couldn't take his smell either. Which is undetectable to other noses. Jason drifted, and I did, too. Our love vanished, replaced with a new feeling that was just as overwhelming. I wished a city bus would run him over. He felt the same way about me. So afraid were we both we would lose precious time with baby.

Jason had his house. It didn't make sense for both of us to go unrested, I said.

He started sleeping at his house more and came every morning before work to have coffee and son time.

We said goodbye, both of us knowing that though we would no longer be together, we would both raise Arthur. Somehow.

When Arthur was born, I prayed he'd latch on to nurse right away, and a big part of my job would be done. I'd be a mother. To this I warn: be careful what you wish for. From the moment Arthur arrived, he only wanted to nurse. He was relentless. He nursed as he slept. He wanted everything, sucking the marrow from my bones. He once nursed for twelve hours straight on a flight to Venice. I was drowning. When I nursed, I never felt the oxytocin sense of calm that some women experience. I could never sleep, knowing he was going to wake up and need me.

When Arthur was a toddler, I hired a woman to help me be a better parent. She asked him what his favorite food was, and he said, "Boob soup."

The woman turned to me and said, "You've got a great kid. He's cool. He'll be fine."

Then she taught me about boundaries.

✿

I told him, "I don't want you to have a girlfriend while you still recall nursing!"

Without missing a beat, he replied, "Why you always gotta be so stressy?"

He no longer latches on. He's ten, though.

✿

Once, in an effort to establish said boundaries, I went into the bathroom to change.

"Mama, what are you doing?" Arthur said.

"I just need some privacy, Arthur. Sometimes I need time to myself."

He replied, without missing a beat: "Mama, don't be embarrassed of your itty-witty boobies. I think they're cute."

❧

My son looked like an angel. But his lion child tendencies were strong. His roar was not characteristic of our family laugh. It was, and still is, deafening, demanding.

Once, I told him he would have to wait. His heel indented in the stairway wall. A kick of rage because he was not immediately placated. Waiting for him to calm down, I scrambled him eggs. He smiled and placed the buttery cooked yolks in my morning coffee, with a shit-eating grin. "In Mama's coffee?" he asked. Sweetly. Curiously. I roared and kissed him. My very own to love. My little "Saint."

❧

I decided I needed to break some of my bad habits in order to give Arthur a shot at a happy, normal life. First and foremost, I wanted him to have a healthy relationship with food. It's taken me until writing this book to realize how malnourished I've always been. I don't have a goal weight, I don't get on the scale, I don't limit myself, I don't have an active eating disorder. But clinically, I have anorexia. Because for years and years I didn't eat.

My mother was the same way. For her, thin was the only way. On a weekend, if we were home, she would say, "Cut yourself an apple and a piece of cheese." And that was enough. Even though it was never enough.

When I was younger, I didn't eat, because I had a nervous stomach, or I wanted to disappear or stave off puberty. Now I don't eat because my MS makes it both too hard to cut things and too easy to choke on them after I do. In some ways, learning to feed myself has been my greatest teacher, because I needed to see that the way to get the most out of life, out of this body I've been given, is through real nourishment. I never had the patience to make something for myself. On some level I believed I was not worth the effort. Plus, every time I turned on the oven, I thought of Sylvia Plath. I have lived a whole lifetime not feeding myself properly. There's no secret here. I write it because I need to admit it to myself.

I wanted Arthur to have the opposite experience. I wanted him to associate his mother with nourishment. Shortly after I bought our house in Studio City, I planted rows and rows of leafy greens. They grew wild and spicy in the sun-soaked garden. When Arthur was just a year old and exploring the backyard, I would wander to the greens—romaine, chard, butter, and arugula—and snap off what the earth had made. Exhausted from nursing through the night, I would whimper as I brought a jagged piece of arugula to my mouth. With bees hovering by the flowers, I stood hunched and ate. Slowly chewing until I had no choice but to swallow. When I brought Arthur over to try some, he screwed up his face and announced, "Too spicy." I thought so, too. Hot and peppery. I shoved leaf after leaf into my mouth. It was all I could eat that first year. I was like that character from *Into the Woods*. Greens, greens, nothing but greens. Bitter greens, mustardy and hot.

At the table, when I set down Arthur's much preferred butter lettuce with olive oil and lemon juice drizzled throughout, I gently told him it was okay to eat with his little hands. I didn't mind. "Eat, eat!" I said. I only wanted him to eat some food. Natural, wholesome food. I pureed yams and peas, butternut squash and strawberries mixed with sour cream and honey. Macerated into a delicious kind of sweet stew. Meatballs made from bison in a marinara sauce his godmother Julie always made. Eggs in butter, warm croissants from the local bakery owned by two Russian women. He shook his head and walked to me, his toddler arms out like Frankenstein's monster: "Nurse." That is all he wanted.

He wanted every vitamin and mineral from my own bones, and I gave it to him, the only thing my body did well all on its own. His needy body groped until it settled into the soft flesh of my full breasts. The plates full of tiny portions, cut up for a tiny mouth, sat in the sink while we nursed upstairs, tears falling from my swollen eyes.

One weekend his dad took him for visitation. Seeing Arthur go always left me empty and in terror. I nagged his father about a toy knife or a screwdriver I saw in my son's grip in a photo text he sent. Nervous, I asked him to be careful. He was too young to hold such a weapon. He was too young to sleep away from his mother, I thought but could not say. I could only pick apart safety hazards.

One Sunday, his father reported how Arthur ate his salad with his fingers.

"I think he got that from you," he said. I could see he was embarrassed. He was right. I eat salad with my hands, dipping each piece into just the right amount of olive oil.

At least he eats, I wanted to say. But I bit my tongue.

❧

Back at home, I watched as Arthur picked up each damp green leaf of lettuce from the garden and dipped it into the small bowl of Wish-Bone Italian dressing he favors, which I had carefully placed next to him. He took a whole folded leaf and stuffed it into his perfect little mouth. Some oil smeared on his chin. He went in for another, his bitten nails just skimming the flavored oil when he dipped. He was eating. He was happy. This small boy was so different from the fearful, sensitive girl I was, trying to impress my family, trying to understand the rules, hiding under the bed in shame. He was the complete opposite of me, in fact. Arthur didn't care. He made his own rules. He doesn't fit under any of the beds in this house. And he would never try to. Unless to scare you. Naturally.

When Arthur was six months old, I knew I needed to bring in an income, so I "landed" a job. But he had no intention of giving up nursing. One night during a terrible thunderstorm, I tried to make him wait, and he started what I thought was breath holding. After a few moments, he turned the color of the kitchen counter when the lights were off: rigid and unresponsive and gray.

I ran to the door, Arthur cradled in my arms, not knowing what to do. The phones were down from the lightning. I couldn't call anyone. I couldn't reach out for help. The thought that kept repeating in my mind was, what will I tell his father?

I put him down on the ground, his body so gray on the glossy white floor, and started CPR as I'd learned in infant CPR class. *Thirty pushes, two breaths, thirty pushes, two breaths.* His body was as stiff and rubbery as the dummy I'd learned on. It wasn't working. He wasn't coming back.

I held him with my right hand, trying to keep his head down so his brain wouldn't lose what oxygen was there. I swung open the bedroom door and raced outside. I ripped his clothes off, hoping the cold would shock him. Nothing. I placed him carefully on the ground and started CPR again. I screamed to God, so loud that there wasn't even any sound. *Please save him.*

The rain landed on his eyes. He didn't flinch. I started CPR again, and this time he brought his eyes back to me and smiled. I brought him to my breast, and he latched and nursed. He drank almost as if he were unconscious. Back inside, I held him all night long, praying he would be okay.

In the morning, the sun came out. I called Jason and told him what had happened. As I said the words, it felt almost as if it hadn't been real.

Six months later, it happened again. This time, Jason witnessed it. Anytime I tried to make him wait to nurse, or to pry something out of his little baby hands, he would hold his breath and turn gray and collapse. I would do CPR, and he'd come back.

With each month that he got older, it happened again and again.

I devoted all my time to trying to heal him. By the time he was three and a half, his pediatrician was out of possible answers. No one could find what was wrong.

Finally, a diagnosis: reflex asystolic syncope, a nervous system issue.

When the human body goes into fight or flight, it releases adrenaline. The nervous system is what regulates that adrenaline. But Arthur's nervous system didn't regulate; instead, it shut down all the adrenaline, which in turn shut down his heart. His heart actually stopped beating. He really took playing possum too far.

When he was little and had these episodes, I nursed him. Even after he stopped breast-feeding, I needed to feel his body close to mine. It was the thing that seemed to regulate him the most. The attacks continued until he was six.

It happened at a mall in Topanga, with dozens of terrified parents looking on. It happened when Arthur was doing ninja moves in the living room, while I sat near him making stencils. That time, his whole body sucked in like a paper bag. He looked so different. It was the most violent episode he'd ever had. In between doing CPR, I called Jason and said, "Get over here. I don't think Arthur's going to live." I called 911. By the time they arrived, I had gotten him breathing again. I threw the stencils away.

I recently started taking him on roller-coaster rides so if it happened then, with me, I could help him. I'm terrified it will happen when he's alone, or with a friend who can't help him. I've done everything I can to expose him to adrenaline, like immersion therapy.

Once, I showed him a snake on Animal Planet. I was curious if it would trigger him when the snake bit a man on-screen. "Do we need to turn it off?" I asked. We were lying down. "No." He continued watching this grisly scene, while I kept watch over him, studying him. He looked weird. He went gray. I got him down off the bed and did CPR until he came to. We've never watched Animal Planet again.

⁓

Anyone who cares for Arthur now knows that he needs to keep his head down. The doctor said he'll grow out of it. He should be able to recover on his own. The last time it happened, my assistant, Bonny, was in the kitchen and Arthur was going to the door to wave goodbye. He must have hit his hip. There was no blood. He came up to me, pale and clammy, and reached for my hand. As he held it, he said, "Mom, it's happening." It was the first time he'd ever identified it himself.

I had a fire going. I laid him down by the warm flames. I started CPR. The area around his mouth was already tinged with dark blue. I heard a gurgling, but I also felt how hot he was. I screamed for Bonny to help me. She stayed calm because she's a pro in all situations. "Keep his head down, grab his feet." I did CPR again, and he came to.

I once read about a girl who had this condition who died at age fifteen. She was hit in the head with a softball, but she didn't die of the injury; she died from the seizure that followed. I think of her all the time.

Split/Screen

WHEN I LOOK BACK on Arthur's early years, I see the images play out on a split screen. On the one side there's me with my gorgeous, sparkly-eyed, adventurous, and curious boy, exploring the bright world together in an Instagram filter of pure joy. And that is all true. We had many, many happy times. Every day with him has a bit of magic to it. He's such a vibrant kid. Being with him requires me to be so present I almost can't focus on my own body.

But on the other side there's me in a filter of gray. I am stumbling. Throughout Arthur's early childhood, I was off more often than I was on. I now know these were MS flares. I'd fall down our carpeted stairs. My legs would give way for no reason. I felt confused much of the time. Exhausted. I would make a pot of coffee, and instead of pouring it into a mug, I'd pour it down the drain. My face grew puffy; I had boils. I'd wake up on weekends with a new cut on my back not remembering how I'd gotten it. I had to pee constantly. I thought I was stressed, battle scarred. I thought I'd brought this on myself.

Jason thought I was drinking again. I promised him I wasn't. I swore I wasn't. I was sober then, mostly. Occasionally, when Arthur was with Jason, I'd allow myself an airplane-sized bottle of tequila, dipping my toe back into the pleasures of disappearing for only a little while, of erasing the pain and numbing the discombobulation. But I wasn't drinking the way I had when I was younger. I was trying so very hard to be a good mother. Something else was going on inside me. I could feel it growing and spreading, but I had no idea what it was.

Elliot Again

WHEN ARTHUR was a year and a half, I decided I needed to make amends with my father and introduce him to my son. It felt wrong to me that he'd never met his grandfather; I hoped seeing my beautiful son would help us start anew. Elliot had been trying to reconcile; he had sent me some money, for which I was grateful. He was trying. I wanted to reciprocate. He was in his early eighties by then, and in poor health, with a failing heart. I made plans to visit him in Michigan for Thanksgiving.

A few days before my trip, Katie called to tell me Elliot had died. When she told me the news, I felt so sad. I felt sad for the relationship we never had, and more than anything for the pain I knew Katie was in; she was Elliot's favorite, and her grief was profound. He'd called Katie from a hotel suite to tell her he wasn't feeling well, and that he was scared, and by the time she arrived to try to bring him to the hospital, he was gone. She lay next to him, wiped his brow, dressed him one last time.

Arthur and I flew to Michigan for the funeral, using the tickets I'd bought weeks earlier in hopes of a reconciliation, never guessing I'd be going to bury him instead. I wanted to see him one last time, so when Arthur and I arrived at the funeral home, I went straight to the room where Elliot lay in his coffin. He looked the same. Young for his age, full head of thick black hair. He was still with that awful woman. He still played tennis. He had never met my son. I touched his cold forehead and whispered a prayer of mourning. And then I took Arthur outside to the car. He was restless and fidgeting and wanting to nurse.

Rock Bottom

IN JUNE 2016, Jason, Arthur, and I traveled to Cancún as a family. We stayed in the Presidential Suite at the Hard Rock Cafe, as part of a Father's Day promotion.

Here is what Arthur, who was almost five at the time, remembers:

He remembers seeing me eat toast with butter and a piece of fish.

He remembers seeing an iguana.

That's all he remembers. For this I am eternally grateful.

Here is what I remember:

I was falling apart. The exhaustion and anxiety were destroying me. I couldn't hold it together even for Arthur. I lost control and spent every stolen minute I could alone in our hotel room, drinking. The last night of our trip, I fell over the sink and vomited three times, then lifted my head and searched for my eyes. My eyes, my eyes, my eyes. They were floating around the mirror, detached from my face.

"Why do you hate me so much?" I said to my own reflection. "You're fucking up, Blair. You're fucking up, you fuckup, you fuckup, you stupid fucking fuckup." And then I fell into the closet and reached for the bottle of tequila—the big gallon bottle I'd brought in from the huge bar in the living room—that I'd hidden in my room. I unscrewed the metal cap and spilled the tequila on my face and down my throat. Then I collapsed on the bed and cried myself somewhere into oblivion.

I don't remember much else from that week, except constant vomiting, running into walls, and bruising myself from going to get more alcohol from the other room. It was a place I had never before been in my life. Thus far. With responsibilities. A child! The pain I felt in Mexico—I could've been dead, and I wouldn't have known the difference. It was four days. It was the longest, most destructive binge I'd ever had.

❧

When we got to the airport to fly home, I was exhausted, dehydrated, hungover. I thought, if I can just get some rest, I'll be able to function as a mother again. I figured I would get some sleep en route, wake up alive again, and everything would be okay. Ish.

We boarded the plane, took our seats in first class. Jason, holding Arthur, was seated one row ahead of me. The man next to me ordered me a glass of wine. When it arrived, I drank it very fast, eager to get on with it, back to feeling livable. Then he asked me if I needed to sleep. I said I did. He offered me an Ambien, which I don't normally take, but I thought, "Oh, what's the difference?" So, I took it.

I remember feeling agitated, kicking the seat in front of me, trying to irritate Jason.

The next thing I remember is waking up in a hospital, with an IV in my arm.

Later, I found out there were nurses tending to me for the entire flight.

Later, I found out I nearly died from dehydration and elevated blood pressure.

Now I know I had MS symptoms that I was trying to self-medicate with booze, but at the time I thought I was losing my mind.

As all this was unfolding, Jason, petrified, continued holding Arthur, who miraculously was asleep with headphones on. (He has never slept on a plane, before or since.) Jason didn't move, didn't react to the commotion, so as not to wake our sleeping child. Arthur slept through the entire flight. I will forever be grateful.

The story was all over the news. CNN, the *Daily Mail, People, TMZ,* Refinery29. A blurry photo of me, taken by another passenger, appeared in all the papers. Quotes from a witness popped up overnight. When I got out of the hospital, the paparazzi were all over the house, wildcats bored and hungry to humiliate.

There is something unexpectedly freeing about public humiliation of this magnitude. It can't get any worse until it gets worse. It wasn't until Cancún that I saw how I had zero concept of how to take care of myself. Now I understood. I needed to make a change. (With all things, we see, this must come from within.)

I had never fully saturated myself in personal responsibility, but now I had Arthur. I had gotten drunk—beyond all control—in front of my son. The worst feeling of all was that he had witnessed it. I felt, for a mother, that was a lockup offense. My mother had taught me as much. Throughout my life, she remained a fearsome, strong figure, with full conviction that a child needed to have a sense of fear and boundaries in order to feel safe.

Now I was putting fear in my son, but it was the opposite fear—the worry that I wouldn't be able to care for myself. Even as a drunk who had done dangerous things to my own self, I would never put my son in danger. Knowing that my son, the person I created, that I am now responsible for, was present at a time when I lost all sense of myself—the clarity of that shook me to my core.

Nothing truly tragic happened on that trip. It could have. And that was enough. That was the wake-up call. It knocked me out of Selma. It knocked me out of my own discomfort long enough to say, I won't do this anymore.

I am so sorry to everyone I disturbed on that plane. Even if one of the passengers was cruel and recorded it, or exploited it, I was the one in the wrong. It was reckless. It was sad. I was the one who put myself in that position, and I saw it for just how pitiful it was.

After the flight, a doctor was tending to me in the hospital, and I asked, "Can I get up and go home?" This doctor, this woman, could not have been clearer. She shook her head, looked me in the eyes, and said, "Girl. If this ever happens again, you will be dead. So, if you make the choice to walk out of here, please know that."

It was a mental switch. I finally got it.

Get out of your own way.

You have to treat yourself as you would want your mother to treat you.

You have to treat yourself the way you would treat your son.

You've got a kid.

This isn't just about you anymore.

You cannot let this get you down so hard you won't recover.

You will not kill yourself over this.

You will not kill yourself.
You must break the shame.

I saw, suddenly, in a new light. I understood that I needed to love this person, this human being whose body I was in, broken as it was. Otherwise, it would be a total waste.

I stood up. And that changed me forever.

⁓

The episode needed an explanation. Troy offered to send out a press release on my behalf, but I told him not to. I wanted to write something myself, in my own words. I apologized in a statement to *Vanity Fair:*

> I made a big mistake yesterday. After a lovely trip with my son and his dad, I mixed alcohol with medication. That caused me to black out. It caused me to say and do things that I deeply regret . . . I take this very seriously and I apologize to all of the passengers and crew that I disturbed and am thankful to all of the people who helped me in the aftermath. I am a flawed human being who makes mistakes and am filled with shame over this incident. I am truly very sorry.

I saw that not only could I not do this to myself anymore, but I also couldn't do this to the people I loved.

My friends were incredible. Troy and Bonny were so supportive. Reese wrote to me immediately: "You're going to be OK, kid." She said the best course of action was to be honest and move on.

When Carrie found out what happened, she called me. I told

her how ashamed I was to nearly die on a plane. She said, "You're not doing that! You can't die on a plane. You know if anyone dies on a plane, it's going to be me." She was joking, trying to make light of it by saying she'd do it better. Her words haunt me every single day.

CRUS

A note from Bonny after Cancún:

> The jig is up. You need
>   1. Detox.
>   2. Treatment.
>   3. Therapist.
>   4. Daily Schedule.
>   5. Accountability.
>   6. No more bullshit.

The hangover lasted two weeks.

I returned home. I wept and wept. The sadness poured out of me. I realized I had something that was even more out of control than my addiction. I needed to fix my emotions.

I vowed I was going to break this cycle. But how was I going to go about changing everything I'd built my whole life? How was I going to rewrite an existence that relied on alcohol as the only fire door when my body needed soothing?

I immediately set to work. I started with food. For the first time in my life, I was really nourishing myself. Detoxing. Replacing alcohol with what my body needed: meat, strawberries, gluten-free muffins, tempeh, squash, all sorts of greens.

Within two days, I started to feel like a grown-up. I felt as though I were taking responsibility. There was a shift in my brain. It was my first real step in saying, "I will do whatever I must to learn to be a healthy person."

From there, my entire relationship with alcohol truly changed. I had hit my rock bottom and I fully surrendered. Years of AA only amplified my gratitude, humility, and commitment to sobriety. I abandoned all old patterns and ways of thinking. I opened myself up, and it was transformational.

Throughout the process, I told myself: *Go basic. Your brain is like an analytical maze from childhood. So, let's start from the beginning.* I looked into my genetics, which proved insightful. I discovered I had the *MTHFR* mutation, as well as the *CBS* mutation, which was causing my body to produce too much sulfur and ammonia—real, measurable toxicities that were activated and severe.

I needed to move more. I thought back on my experiences with Outward Bound and how those wilderness trips had helped me through rough times. When I was in motion, the depression lifted, was replaced with a task.

When I look back on my recovery process, I recognize that one of the main pieces was Jason. Before the Mexico trip, our relationship had been plagued by a contentious custody battle and an air of sadness and mistrust. After that trip, we dropped it, but now we were standing together, on the same page, trying to solve it.

When we got home, Jason returned my son to me, under the condition that he would help ensure that it was safe. We had a long discussion about what we could do, how we could work together, to make things all right with my drinking. As part of this, he gave me examples of behaviors that concerned him—emotional outbursts and events where he thought I was drunk. I'd trip and fall and I didn't know how to explain it. I told him, truthfully, that I hadn't been drinking on any of those occasions. The Mexico trip notwithstanding, I never, ever drank around Arthur. I was just being who I was at that time; we didn't yet know that MS was stalking me.

Still, I couldn't believe Jason could trust in me after such an extreme, public breakdown. For Jason to continue to have faith in my ability to be a good mother, even after seeing the very worst I could pull out of a hat, was an enormous act of generosity on his part. I'll always love him for that. Always. Jason stood by me and helped me get better, and my family gave me the will to never drink again.

I believe that once you've become an addict, of any sort, to anything, it changes you. I think it changes your brain, your personality, your drive. I think it changes your character, and as such will always need to be maintained. I know firsthand: It's a relief you will chase forever. That first feeling of warmth. That first moment of comfort.

But seeking that comfort in the old ways is not a possibility for me. It really hit home this time. Before, I would leave myself a bread crumb, a way to get back to myself. Now I saw that I needed to start over.

I stayed sober. I have had vices. But I haven't had a drink since that day.

Every day, there are prayers. There is work. There is acknowledgment. If I ever have a drink again, I will have the accountability. (Though I plan on never doing that.)

The truth was, this epic humiliation was the wake-up call I'd been waiting for. I imploded publicly, in the ugliest way possible, but miraculously I didn't hurt anyone. Throughout my years of searching, that's all I ever prayed for. I was lost and I wanted hope, and that was such a clear, final warning. I will forever say, "Thank you. Thank you for allowing me to hit that bottom without really harming somebody."

❧

My mother's mind was already slipping when the *Daily Mail* called her for a quote. "Selma was my last daughter and she's really quite difficult! She gets me upset when these things happen." (Let's be honest: my mother herself was probably a bit pickled when she gave this sneak-attack interview.) "She took an Ativan and had a glass of wine and went crazy! She's a lovely girl! She's never had any problems with airplanes or flying before!"

❧

I wish I could see what I would have been like without alcohol. I would truly love to know.

My mom was a big drinker, but she wasn't a drunk. Molly was functioning. Molly was responsible. She was always—always—on top of it, just as she was on top of everything. She never fell apart the way I did. She kept her shit together.

But is it any wonder? All my life, I saw a stunning, capable woman who was able to smoke and drink. I idolized her, in all ways. Of course, I was going to copy that.

I watch Arthur like a hawk now. I don't even want him to try it. I don't want to project my thought patterns, my own experiences, onto him. I don't want him to relate to the side of me that's not as capable as I want to be.

His memory of my drinking years is minimal at best. He

remembers once getting in a fight with me in Mexico, one of the two times I drank in front of him, over the game Chutes and Ladders. (A sloppy moment. Did I throw a Chutes and Ladders piece at my kid? Was I that pathetic?) Thankfully, he doesn't even recall a drink in my hand. He doesn't question it. He doesn't know me as a drinker. It's not something his mom does.

I hope some good has come of my failing. I hope that I've broken the cycle.

Ducky Manor

I WANTED TO CREATE a safe space for Arthur. In 2012, I bought an old Cape Cod–style house built in 1950, a hodgepodge of small rooms. I loved that it was cozy and dark, with windows that were bright but dirty, more Cambridge than Studio City. I gave it a tailored ambience—walls painted in shades of hunter green and "Polo blue" and lined with bookshelves. It's intentionally reminiscent of a prep school. I wanted it to feel like Cranbrook, the place that changed me. I filled it with things from people I've loved, reminders of the places I've been. My home tells the story of my life.

There are lemon and lime trees in the backyard, and a swimming pool built into the slant of the Laurel Canyon hill. I planted jasmine on our terrace, and every April it blooms wild, its fragrance synonymous with springtime.

Our home has been our cocoon. Arthur feels safe in this house. I feel safe in this house. It has held us through the nights. In the time that we've lived here, our home has seen so much. It has seen death and loss. But oh, my Lord, it has also seen resilience.

Arthur and I named the house Ducky Manor after our first dog together. Ducky was a rescue we brought home on a hot, sunny late summer evening. I was trying to fill the hole left by Wink, who had been my soul mate before Arthur was born. I still missed her terribly.

Arthur and I had stopped at every adoption stall, but no luck. No little dogs captured our attention. As we resigned ourselves to leaving empty-handed, I spotted a small white dog whose eyes were so big I later joked that I could only see Maggie Smith in her expression. "What about her?" I asked the woman from the rescue. She gently coaxed the dog out of her cage. Arthur looked at me pleadingly. I told him to sit down crisscross applesauce, and she walked right into Arthur's lap. She settled there, already home. She was perfect. We named her Ducky.

One evening when Arthur was four, I let Ducky out to pee in the backyard, and a moment later she was gone. It happened so fast, in an instant. I barely had a chance to make sense of what had happened. One moment, Arthur was playing in his tree house, and the next he was screaming and crying for help. "Ducky!" he yelled as he climbed down the ladder, his little boy voice ringing out in the evening air. "Ducky!"

I ran up the rocks by the pool to help her. I thought perhaps she had fallen, broken a leg. But then I saw her, lying on a rock in the blue-and-white sweater she always wore. There were puncture wounds in her abdomen, as if she'd been attacked by something. An owl maybe, or a coyote. I had no clue what had happened, only that I'd failed to protect her. Ducky was shaken. I did my best to stay calm, but I could tell her breathing was shallow. We rushed her to the animal hospital, where the vets tried everything to save her, but her injuries were too severe. Sweet Ducky died in my arms.

I was immediately overcome with that same familiar feeling. I'd let us all down. I had tried to create a place for Arthur and me, a safe life anchored around this home. And yet I let something horrible happen to our family.

And then I had to tell my son that Ducky was gone.

&

For years animals have appeared in my home as warnings, signs, gifts. The possum Wink brought me during a years-long depression. A gift just as vulnerable as I was. The owl who perched in the backyard in the early years of Arthur's life, standing guard. The scorpions, exotic and dangerous, raising their white bodies in the brush on our hill. I keep a clean house, but the animals don't care. Nature finds a way.

Once, there was a drowning deer in our black-bottom pool. She had fallen in and couldn't find her way out. She thrashed, bleeding, on the edge, my own heart caught in her twig legs. She was more frightened of me than I was of her, so I corralled her to the shallow end. She looked at me for four long seconds, before regaining her senses. Like thunder, she flew up the hill. Like the dreams I had that have come to seem like premonitions, I remember her.

Sometimes the warnings are gentle, and sometimes they are not.

The day Ducky died, when I saw her sprawled on that rock like a dead rabbit, my first thought was that a great horned owl got her. But the vet said no, a bird wouldn't lift a dog with a sweater on. They were certain, very certain, it was a coyote.

Looking back, that violence should have been a sign of some of the losses ahead. How fragile and vulnerable we are. The way life can change instantaneously. As with most great losses, it was also a reminder of how life does go on.

⌒⌒

After some time, we adopted our dog, Pippa. Before she came home, I did everything one could possibly do in order to coyote-proof the yard. Still, out of an abundance of caution, we never leave her alone.

The other day, I was sitting under an umbrella in our bricked backyard when I heard a crash. My adrenaline picked up, and I raced into the grass to discover a red-tailed hawk swooping down at 120 miles an hour near the rock at the top of the hill. I immediately covered Pip, thinking, *I will die before I let another bad thing happen to my son.*

"This is what happened to Ducky," my boyfriend said. In an instant I realized he was right. A hawk tried to pick her up, then left her on that rock. For years, I'd been on high alert, looking for this coyote. But it wasn't a coyote at all.

That's life. It'll blindside you, that thing you didn't know about. Especially when it's been there all along.

Diagnosis

THAT THING you didn't know about. It had been there all along.

The pieces started falling into place.

I'd suffered from symptoms that would come and go ever since childhood. Fevers, urinary tract infections, nerve pain and numbness, depression. Symptoms I tried to dull with alcohol, but the effect was temporary. Symptoms that only grew stronger over time.

Right around the time I met Jason Bleick, I began to lose feeling in my legs in a way I never had before. They started to give up, inexplicably. I'd been riding again, which I loved. One day, I was walking down a hill with my horse, when out of nowhere I fell. The ground just slipped out from under me.

I wasn't binge drinking then. In fact, I felt I was in a good place: Jason and I were happy, I was active, I had work. I decided, since I wasn't drinking, it must be diet related. I hired a chef to make macrobiotic, mostly vegetarian meals, inspired by Alicia Silverstone's *Kind Life*. I ate tempura and fish in special sauces, made pots of green soups. I went to chiropractors, energy workers, every kind of healer. (What's ironic to me now is that I spent so much of my life consulting experts, looking for signs, when all along there were signs right in front of me.)

Then I got shingles. Intense nerve pain, unlike anything I'd ever experienced, shot up and down my leg, up into my hips. The shingles cleared up thanks to antivirals and rest, but I still felt unwell. My leg still gave out. Doctors told me it was postherpetic neuralgia—the body's memory of the shingles virus.

This continued, off and on, for several years. Some episodes were petrifying. When Arthur was about three and a half, we took a trip to Palm Springs for the weekend. In the car, my legs began shaking uncontrollably. There was nothing I could do to stop it. I was scared to drive, so I pulled over and told Arthur I was okay, I just needed a minute. I got back on the highway and drove for five miles before having to get off again. It took us hours to go just a few miles. Arriving at our hotel felt like summiting Mount Everest. When we finally pulled in, I practically fell out of the car. I told the concierge, "You have to help me. Something is seriously wrong."

In all my medical journal snooping, as I dug into depressive symptoms and alcoholism, searching for a link, I never once looked up movement disorders. It was unthinkable.

Over the next three years, there were more and more episodes like that one. It would come and go. The symptoms grew worse. I saw every doctor under the sun. They blamed hormones, depression, anxiety, exhaustion, malnutrition, my "neurasthenic" nature. One doctor went so far as to tell me I might feel better if I had a boyfriend. Through all the symptoms, all the visits, I never once had an MRI. The only doctor who had ever mentioned MS as a possibility was my eye doctor who saw me for eye pain when I was twenty-two. I see now that most of those doctors, well intentioned as they were, truly believed this was mostly in my head.

In early August 2018, I went to Miami alone to visit friends. I was shooting a movie in Atlanta and dragging from fatigue. I hoped the Florida sun and warm ocean water would invigorate me. It was a trip made for Instagram. I bought a tiny Eres bikini and Hermès shoes. Our friend wanted to enjoy the ocean on his new yacht. When we were out on the water, no land in sight, I walked to the edge of the boat and leaped high in the air. As soon as I hit the water, I knew something was terribly wrong. I couldn't swim. The act of jumping had taken everything I had out of me.

I knew then that the body I lived in had dramatically changed. I found my legs and with all my might kicked my way to the surface. Unsure of what to do, I floated on my back. For a long time, I stared up at the clouds, keeping what had just happened to myself. I didn't want to alert anyone. I turned it into a meditative moment. When I finally floated back to the boat, my friend Amy had to help me back onto the stern. I felt cradled by love and concern. She showed me the photo she had taken of my final leap into the air. I'm flying and it is glorious. My hands are outstretched ballerina-style, my

legs are tucked under, my toes pointed. My mother would be so proud of my perfect form, thin in my bikini, tanned with blond highlights. I looked great.

If you didn't know, you wouldn't know. But I knew. That's when I really, truly knew.

It was right after this trip that I finally got the diagnosis. It happened so randomly that it's a miracle it happened at all. I had posted on Instagram:

> Monday. So, I am in pretty intense pain. Whiplash a few times on my horse and sitting on planes . . . and now I am in a real musculoskeletal bind. Hanging in though. Hoping I can rehab it and get back to riding and writing again soon. #chronicpain is a real challenge. Love to all of us.

My friend the actress Elizabeth Berkley, whom I actually knew from Cranbrook, saw it and sent me a message. "Are you ok?" she asked. I told her all my symptoms; I would tell anyone who would listen at that point. "You need to see my brother right away," she told me. "He's a spinal neurologist. Maybe he can help. I'll call him now. Stand by."

That's how I came to Jason Berkley's office in Beverly Hills. Social media can be noxious, but it can also be miraculous. On that day, it saved me.

He performed the Romberg's test, a simple examination where you put your feet together and close your eyes. My legs gave out beneath me. I fell backward, dropping like a plank onto the exam room floor. He ordered an MRI on the spot.

With my eyes shut, I had no sense of where I was, but gravity did. And then, finally, answers.

The scan was my new fortune-teller. The only one I needed. It revealed a number of midsized MS-related lesions on my brain, six of which were problematic because they were active. Little fires burning from canyon to canyon on the synapses. The connection between my brain and my body demyelinated. It all made so much sense now. Dr. Berkley saw it first, then referred me to an MS specialist, Dr. Silver, who confirmed what Dr. Berkley suspected. He gave the news to Dr. Berkley, who then called me.

When Dr. Berkley said the words "You have MS," I felt an adrenaline rush of emotion. It felt like giving birth. The release of it. The catharsis of it. But more than anything, I was overwhelmed by a sense of relief, like the way you feel when an ocean wave breaks right at the shore before taking you under. For years, my symptoms were dismissed as "anxiety" and "emotional." It was all in my head, perhaps. It's psychosomatic, they suggested. For years I'd known they were wrong (and right—it was in my head, only not in the way they thought). And now I had a map to follow. I had information. A label. This time, one that fit.

There are words that explain what is wrong with me.
It's not my fault. At least . . . I hope it's not my fault.
I can work with this.
I can learn how to cope with this.
It can't get any worse than this. Or it can.
I will teach myself how to be okay.

I thought back to the time when my mother cried with relief upon learning I was an alcoholic and suddenly understood why she felt comforted. There is great power in words. In an answer. In a diagnosis. To make sense of a plot you could hardly keep up with any longer.

⁂

In the moments after I received the diagnosis, and in the days that followed, I stayed surprisingly composed. I was so tired. I was too tired to be sad, I think. Too tired to be angry at all the time I'd lost. When Dr. Berkley first gave me the news, I did cry. Loud, choking sobs poured out of me for exactly two minutes. And then I was done. I was supposed to return to Atlanta to finish filming *After* the next day; the film was my first foray back to work after a long hiatus. I didn't want to let the director down.

"I'm getting on that plane. The show must go on," I said dramatically.

"You can't go to Atlanta," Dr. Berkley warned. "You're in an MS flare. You cannot get on a plane. You have to cancel your trip."

I didn't understand. "This disease is incurable, right?"

He didn't understand either. "You must cancel it."

"But it's chronic, right? It will still be there, will still be incurable, when I finish. It will always be there."

"Yes. Always."

"Okay, then. So it's possible for me to work."

"It's possible," he finally admitted. "But you have to understand, it will be hard."

(Truer words have never been spoken.)

I didn't cancel my trip. The show did go on. But right before I saw Dr. Berkley, I'd made the mistake of getting a steroid injection in my neck to stop the spasms, not knowing at the time that I had MS and that the shot would exacerbate my symptoms. My body raged. I was in a bigger flare than normal, and at the same time I was trying to resurrect my career. On the plane to Atlanta, shuddering in pain, I googled my disease for the first time and was shocked to find Joan Didion had MS. My idol. I couldn't believe it! Joan Didion! If Joan had it, then I must be in really good company. There was a certain dignity about it.

I learned that Joan was diagnosed in 1968 after suffering from periods of intermittent blindness and extreme vertigo. When I got back from Atlanta, I pulled her essay collection down from my shelf and reread "The White Album," in which she describes receiving the news in a doctor's office in Beverly Hills, perhaps not far from where I had received my own diagnosis, and the way hearing this news slammed her face right into her own mortality. It was a jarring experience for her. As she wrote, "I had, at this time, a sharp apprehension not of what it was like to be old but of what it was like to open the door to the stranger and find that the stranger did indeed have the knife . . . I could be struck by lightning, could dare to eat a peach and be poisoned by the cyanide in the stone."

I felt so grateful to Joan for giving us this essay. She gave coherence to what I felt. It was the realization of possible limitations, grief, and fear. She so elegantly offered me a reference point. I no longer felt alone.

In many ways, I related to her initial reaction. It's life changing to be given a diagnosis of MS, or any other chronic disease. Even if you've lived with the symptoms for years, the story now has a name. It has a label. There is language for your experience. The future you imagined for yourself begins to morph before your very eyes. Your plans, even the ones you didn't realize you had, start to look radically different. In a moment, your life divides itself into the before and the after. You realize this body you've inhabited for so many years—this bizarre collection of cells—has turned against you. It's more than a betrayal. You feel trapped, a hostage inside your own skin. You are a stranger to you.

It was a long time coming. My whole life I felt lost and wanted an answer. I'd looked for truth anywhere I might find it. I'd asked sages, healers, the universe. Now, finally, here it was.

My diagnosis was the validation I'd been searching for—that I was human, and that it was okay.

I am so grateful that I was sober at that point in my life. When I progressed into a time lapse of MS, I did not go the way that Selma would've gone. The biggest realization is that I wasn't a victim. I was done with self-sabotage. Now it was time to use every resource I knew.

I saw with overwhelming clarity how every stage of my life has offered me incredible lessons. I had been given blessing upon blessing. My whole life I couldn't get my shit together. But now, from this new vantage point, I saw how there is a natural order, if only you slow down and listen. It's ugly and it's messy, until it's not anymore. This is how we progress.

⁓

I announced my MS diagnosis on Instagram on October 20, 2018. I was working on a new show for Netflix and wanted to thank my wardrobe designers, who had accommodated my symptoms and helped dress me with loving patience and care. The producers told me, "Everyone has something," as they held me through my tears. The entire Netflix team was so supportive.

My doctors urged me not to go public. They said people wouldn't understand my diagnosis. They worried I wouldn't get work. They said the disease might not progress beyond what I'd already experienced, so why share it? "You're an actress; your body, your voice, it's all you have."

But they were wrong; it wasn't.

I agreed to an interview and photo shoot with *Vanity Fair,* and when the magazine invited me to its annual Oscar party in April, I knew I wanted to be there. I wanted to wear high heels, but because my gait had grown increasingly unsteady, I'd need my cane. My stylist found the most gorgeous Ralph & Russo dress. It had a cape and a choker around the neck, which I appreciated because at the time I was having a lot of trouble with my voice. I felt cocooned in this dress. Protected. I wore my hair gelled up and back—no side part anymore. I've never felt more beautiful.

When I stepped out on the red carpet, with my beautiful dress and my cape and my bejeweled cane, and saw the cameras waiting for me, I broke down sobbing. Troy came over and helped me collect myself. I was just so astounded by it all. This act—this very public act—of being open about who I am overwhelmed me. There was no turning back.

To my utter amazement, when the photographers noticed I was crying, they put their cameras down and stopped shooting. They waited, quietly, as I dried my face and found my balance. "You look great, Selma!" a paparazzo shouted. "We love you!" I'd never seen anything like it. I smiled and readied myself to pose. And then they started up again.

The next morning, the headlines talked about how brave I was. They called me a warrior. In that moment I didn't feel like a warrior, or any kind of hero. But I did feel a new sense of peace and purpose. I felt, for maybe the first time in my life, fully and completely myself. I was doing what I'd done for much of my adult life—just trying to get through it all as best as I could.

Didion again: "There's a point where you go with what you've got. Or you don't go."

I made a decision. I would get up and go.

Years ago, when I was in high school, I saw a girl walking beside her mother at Sue's country club back home. She was young, maybe eight or nine, and her body lurched uncontrollably when she walked. It was a wonder; it was a terror; it was a shame. I'd never seen anyone like her.

Later, I described her to my mother. "What was wrong with that little girl?" I asked. I replayed the girl stepping jerkily over the concrete squares near our lounge chairs. Fragile, pathetic, awkward. My mom explained it was some kind of dyskinesia. "That poor girl," my mother said. "And her poor, poor mother."

When I play the scene now, I can still picture fat drops of pool water on the girl's thighs catching the sunlight on her skin like an ill-fitting sequin dress. She was indomitable. I see now how beautiful she was in that innocent determination. And then I realize something: My mom was wrong. So wrong. I wish I could go back and tell her how wrong she was. This girl was not to be pitied. She did not want our pity. Pitiable and determined are simply not companions.

> I wonder how many people I've looked
> at all my life and never seen.
>
> —JOHN STEINBECK,
> *THE WINTER OF OUR DISCONTENT*

Living

WHEN I WAS DIAGNOSED with MS, my life finally did markedly change. I became a kind of face for the disease. Just as Tyler Henry predicted, I am an advocate for something that matters to me. Though it's a role I never thought I would play, it has become who I am.

The community of people I've found, and who have found me, have comforted me. They see the real me and accept me as I am—weak, raw, humbled, dependent, free, honest, sensitive, scared, hopeful. The mean baby is still there, but her edges are softer, wiser, kinder.

I don't talk about MS as much as I craved someone talking about

MS when I was first diagnosed. Now I realize that the simple truth is I can't be a spokesperson for someone else when every person's experience is so unique. Joan Didion's MS is not my MS. As anyone who's had MS for long enough would tell me, "It'll be different for you." Our experience is ours alone, and I'll never know the extent of someone else's.

At the same time, I think it's important to talk about it. When it comes to chronic illnesses, there's a lot of shame in disclosing one's experiences. People judge. People dispute your symptoms. People say things can't be proven. Let me assure you, this stuff is real.

Living with MS is not as bad as I thought it would be. It's also way worse. My particular experience with this disease is that it has affected every inch of my body, from scalp to marrow.

If I stand up too quickly, I fall.

If I'm triggered by anything where I don't know the outcome, I can't speak.

I sweat through my clothes, but I'm freezing.

If I don't take my meds, I cannot feel my body. I don't know if I'm sopping wet or getting frostbite. Without my meds, I also lose the ability to speak.

When I'm in a flare, I sound like a tantrum-throwing toddler, distraught and gasping for breath. I sometimes choke when I eat. I am sometimes incontinent. Like. Enough!

The West Coast sun is impossible. The light is impossible. The weather is impossible. I no longer see all the way to the horizon.

There is no hanging out with my son and following the trajectory of our conversation. I will always be more disorganized and emotional than I want to be.

My gait will always be affected. I pay my toll in fatigue.

There is more—there's a lot more—that feels too complicated to share. In some ways, I'm doing amazingly well. I could dance for an hour if I wanted to! But the next day, I need a cane to get around. It's also hard to quantify, because it is ever-shifting. The shape of my experience changes from day to day, and conversation to conversation. It occupies a vast terrain between good and bad.

I don't have a lot of energy, and there are weeks when I sleep most of the day. That's a very common part of MS. But then I think, some people don't have the luxury of sleeping, and they have to get up and take their meds and go to their jobs and fight the fatigue.

Then there are times when the dog pees in the house, because I myself am busy trying to pee, but it takes too long for me to get there, and I wet my pants. I am one of the lucky ones. I will always have another pair of pants. I know this. I'm grateful for this.

I understand why people with MS spend a lot of time in their homes. Self-preservation. These small things add up. In my bedroom, on the floor that I'm used to, I can dance. But if I step off a curb wrong, I'm liable to injure myself.

When I announced my diagnosis, to the outside world it seemed as if "it hit so hard so fast." But they didn't see the constant fatigue or the years of inflammation or the signs that presented themselves all along. I'd gone through a lifetime of knowing. The only thing that changed was that I was given a name for it. I lived with so much self-hatred for so long. But now that I know what I've been living with—as best as we can determine, for at least twenty years—I can be gentler with myself. There is no "Why me?" anymore. There is just me.

This is part of my healing. I go easier. I try to be the best person I can be. I figure out small solutions to get by. I find moments of grace and I hold on to them.

On some level, MS is an adventure. It wasn't the one I wanted, but it was already there. So, I do my best to embrace it. Ironically,

I'm more comfortable in my skin now than I've ever been, even if my actual skin is uncomfortable. I love using my prop of a cane. I love my service dog. If I'm going to fall down, I want to look good while I'm doing it. I'm going to lean in. I'm going to embrace every perk I can, and I'm going to flaunt it.

In the end, I realize I'm just one of more than two million people on this earth who have MS. But I hope that because of my platform, I can do for others what Joan Didion did for me. I hope I can help erase the stigma attached to MS, bring increased awareness to those living with disabilities, and help people who are coping with chronic illnesses—or even just the painful experience of being human—to realize they are not alone.

Here's another realization I've come to as I write this book, now, at the age of forty-eight: every person on this earth needs just one person who sees them and roots for them. Deeply, truly. One person. It's what we all need to get through. The more the merrier, but let's start with one. Because of my illness, there are so many people I see now. And there are so many people who see me. But it wasn't always this way.

For years, I had a recurring nightmare that I was trapped in a burning house and couldn't get out. I'd wake up drenched in sweat, panicked and frightened. What I realize now is that the nightmare has become my reality: I'm trapped in a body that is often in rebellion against me. But I'm very much awake. I'm very present.

As Didion wrote, I've met the stranger with the knife. I've faced him head-on, but I still have the strength to push him aside and see all the good that exists behind him. I still have a chance to set my record straight.

I've always been a researcher, since I was a little girl. After I received my MS diagnosis, I had the chance to put that inclination to use. More than anything, getting the diagnosis was a wake-up call. *How can I continue to live?* It gave me a new outlook. Each time a challenge appeared, I would rise to meet it, instead of crawling under the bed. My diagnosis gave me a point of reference. It gave me tools.

Because I was diagnosed during a severe flare, I was able to begin a series of treatments to halt the progression of the disease. The onset of my worst symptoms was dramatic, so it made sense to me that the treatment needed to be similarly dramatic.

My sister Katie was the first one to mention HSCT—hematopoietic stem cell transplantation—as a possible therapy to slow the progression of my disease. I wasn't sure: the procedure was new and risky, and the idea of being immunosuppressed for several months while trying to raise a little boy struck me as foolhardy. But then, a few weeks later, again through the power of Instagram, the actress Jennifer Grey helped get this baby out of a corner. She messaged me about a friend whose own brother had undergone successful stem cell treatment at Northwestern and urged me to consider it.

Slowly, I warmed to the idea. The procedure appealed to me on two levels. Practically, it would use cells from my own blood, so I wouldn't need to match with a donor. And spiritually, it felt like the chance to reboot my whole system—to rid myself of all the darkness I carried in my genes and bring in more light. To be reborn.

In the spring of 2019, with my symptoms growing more severe and unmanageable by the day, I found out that I qualified for the program and that my insurance would cover the cost. I opted to move forward with it. I knew it was extreme, a Hail Mary pass. I knew there was a chance I wouldn't survive it. I knew it wasn't a cure. But if this treatment could improve my quality of life, and allow me to be here longer, for Arthur, then I decided it was worth it.

The treatment would quite literally suck the life out of me. Old cells purged. New cells from my own body pumped in.

I would spend two months in Chicago, followed by three weeks in isolation. I would need chemotherapy beforehand. It came with significant, terrifying risks, but on the other side was hope. I made a vow to focus on the hope.

In the days leading up to the procedure, I felt as if I were watching my funeral. All my Julies came out to Chicago to see me. My three sisters with their families. Jason. Troy. My lawyer, David Lyon. Bonny.

Arthur stayed by my side constantly, rolling around the city with me until I had to go into isolation. I was happy just to look at him. When he left for Los Angeles on July 9, I felt a sense of peace knowing that if something happened to me, he would be surrounded by so much love from all the people who had shown up for us. I knew that he would be safe.

I chose to do stem cell because I believed it would help me. It made sense to me at this point. It was the only treatment that offered rebirth. It was a sprint. My container was full. I had to take out the garbage, or the flies would still be there. I saw that I was where I was, my disease is progressing, and I'm not willing to go without a fight. If I fail, if I don't get to the end of the end, well, I tried. I wasn't scared. I was hopeful.

As plans were falling into place, I made another decision for which I'll be eternally grateful. One day, as Troy sat with me, I told him, "We need to shoot this. For Arthur. Plus, there are people like me who want to know about this." Cass Bird, who shot for *Vanity Fair*, introduced us to an extraordinary documentary filmmaker named Rachel Fleit, with whom I felt an immediate affinity, not least because one of her first films was a documentary short called *Gefilte*, about a Detroit family coming together to eat gefilte fish during Passover. It was *bashert*! I'd never pursued a starring role in anything, ever. A supporting role was my comfort zone. Playing the sidekick was who I was. But now I felt a calling. I wanted to do this for myself. I wanted to do this for Arthur. I wanted to do it for Troy, who stood by me through it all and always said I should have a one-woman show. I wanted to do this for everyone who suffers from physical pain, whether they know the label for it or not. I wanted to show the reality of life with chronic illness. I wanted to allow myself to be truly vulnerable.

When I was undergoing the process in my room, the film crew wasn't allowed inside, so I had to use my phone to capture footage. I was alone, with my blood whirring through the machines, receiving these gifts in the quiet wing of the hospital. It was during this time that I really looked at the unfinished puzzles in my life through new eyes. I thought of every snapshot I was ever shown. Riffled through every photo album in my mind. The rape in Florida that I never told anyone about. The Dean's hand tracing the small of my back while I froze, unable to run. All the wasted hours I spent looking into the bottom of a glass.

And then I brought in the happy images. I was determined to balance out the pain with joy. Heartbreak and beauty both. I summoned the sun-dappled beaches in Puerto Rico with my family where we could have ice cream from a cart. How my mom packed Christmas presents one year—an entire suitcase filled with gifts. All the charming people I had shared something with during my Hollywood life. All my friends. Bonny, who always made sure I got home. Arthur. Arthur telling people he loves boob soup. Arthur at the playground, running toward me. Bathing him in Julie's kitchen sink. Sometimes, she would take over with her strong, loving hands while I stood next to her and learned how to be a mother.

I promised myself that even lighting a candle would be appreciated after stem cell.

To have been so lucky.

Stem cell—and the diagnosis in general—were an extreme kind of TED talk (for me) on growing up. And growing older. In real time I felt and saw the generations I held in this body. I closed my eyes and willed myself to let go of everything I held inside. To let go of pain. To embrace a totally new life.

Bonny was at my side for the last couple of weeks and brought me back to L.A. When we arrived at my house, I kissed Pippa, I cried over my desk because I was still tired, and I knew a marathon recovery awaited me. I was alone in the house with leaves filling the pool. And then Arthur was there, Jason standing behind him. I

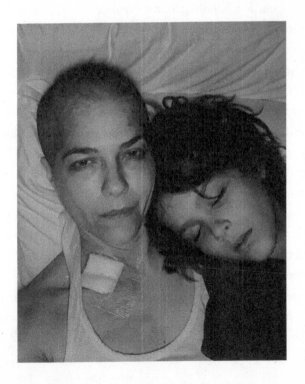

bent down to hug him, and I wrapped him in my arms and smelled him, and I was so grateful for that moment that I felt I could die happy.

Once I returned from Chicago, I felt worn down, weak, and vulnerable as my system worked to rebuild itself. Steroids coursed through my blood. My life became much smaller—occasional trips to the farmers market, visits from friends. It meant a lot of time at home, resting and healing, which my inner loner did not mind.

People called to see if they could stop by. They asked what they could bring for me, their offerings so L.A. I had to laugh. Celery juice? Acai bowls? Marijuana? "No, no, no," I answered, giggling. "Just bring logs." I'm sure they would've preferred celery juice. But it's logs I needed. Kindling for my fireplace.

I made a fire every day, no matter the weather. I tended it well. I curled up in front of it and watched the flames.

When you're quarantined, it feels as though there is nothing but time. Long, slow stretches of it. Time to confront the things you've been avoiding. Your consumerism. Your regrets. Your mistakes, dreams, desires. Everything gets clearer as the outside slips away. It's like being trapped at a casino in Las Vegas. Day? Night? Doesn't matter. The hours, days, weeks, bleed together.

I no longer felt tied to the mystery of death. We're all going to die. Not as a way to drama, but as a part of life. Before I accepted this fact as truth, I always felt either inspired or paralyzed. But now I feel as if I've exhausted it all. I want to be here now.

How can I continue to live?

I used to pray to the world, or to God or spirit or life force, whatever it is, that I would die knowing joy. Now I also wanted to live knowing joy.

This was going to be tough. But I was committed to trying.

By October 2019, my immune system was strong enough for me to get on a plane, so I went back to Cranbrook for homecoming weekend. In the weeks before that trip, I'd started feeling better. My new cells were agreeing with me. I could feel my body rebuilding itself, however shakily. But I was still struggling mightily with balance, my gait jerky and uneasy. As soon as I arrived on that campus, I was held in memories so strong it was as if I were turning my mind and body back in time. There was land, wide-open sky, no paparazzi. (The photographers do trip me up in Los Angeles. It's brutal when you are working through a challenge and you have cameras pointed in your face, recording your every slip and fall.)

It's the strangest thing. With MS, if I have new experiences, my body freezes. Each new eye line can cause a glitch in my brain. Demyelination of nerve fibers. I can't find the ground. I can't speak easily. I crave familiar terrain. Routine. But as I walked around that exquisite campus, I felt the support and freedom of my time at Cranbrook rushing back to me, lifting me up. I could transport myself. My body believed it was young again, without missing myelin sheaths.

I feel about Cranbrook the way a sports lover probably feels about a favorite team. Devoted, even when it fails me. Inspired, even when it disappoints me. I went walking into the same woods I'd journeyed through years before, with Chip. Once again, I went searching for the head of Zeus. As I made my way, I noticed I was really ambling along quite comfortably. For the first time in months, I hardly needed my cane.

That was when I knew, with total certainty, that the stem cell treatment was working. Later, my doctors would confirm that I was in remission.

After Cranbrook, I stopped in Plymouth to visit my mother, who had aged significantly since I'd last seen her. The cancer that she didn't know she had was taking a toll, and her mind was going. She didn't smoke anymore, but she still punctuated her sentences like Princess Anne with a cigarette, only now with a vape pen. Her nails were perfectly painted thanks to my sister Mimi, who took her for weekly manicures. She still had the same hacking cough she'd had since she was forty. She was in a wheelchair, tiny and frail. Perfectly dressed in Chanel ballet flats. Refined as always. This pleased me. I couldn't admit to anyone what was happening, but we all knew she was dying. But she didn't know. She wouldn't understand. As I was learning to understand my brain anew, she was losing hers.

She didn't recognize me at first. Maybe not at all. I was bald from the chemo, my face puffy from steroids. I used a cane. But

she didn't seem startled by my appearance or even my gait. Her wig was lopsided; mine was totally off. Nevertheless, she was in charge, regal. "Mom, it's me," I said. "It's Selma." I set my cane down and knelt beside her and took her hand. She said, "Selma, I saw the magazine," referring to the cover story about my MS journey in *People*. She looked around in her lap for the magazine, which was lying open on the table. (I do this, too. I'm always rummaging around for things that aren't there. Small things.) "It was good. It was good." She paused. And then I asked her for a kiss, and she gave it to me.

જ

I set other goals for myself after stem cell. To swim again. To break into a run again. To ride a horse again. My wonderful horse trainer, Kelly, is one of the biggest doctors I have right now. Four years ago, I confided in her that my dream was to become a successful amateur owner/rider. "I want to ride, I want to show, I want to be the best," I told her. At that point, I was pretty well established as an out-of-work actress, and by most measures buying a horse was not a good move. But I told myself, when I get down, I'm not going to drink; I'm going to go riding. This would help keep me together. This was an investment in myself.

The barn is out in Calabasas, in the Santa Monica Mountains, and whenever I go there, it brings back the feelings I had when I first came to California. I'm bowled over by the scenery, by the mountains and the air and the sky. I get caught up in the thrill of being in such a beautiful place, doing something I never thought I could.

There was a time when I felt as if I owed my life to horses. It was during that high point that I started to notice how broken my body was. I was doing something I loved, that brought me so much joy. Normally I could push through the fatigue, but I was passing out after every ride. When we went over fences and my horse took it a little long, the jarring action of his athleticism only amplified my deteriorating state. My neck would pinch. "Get into your hips," Kelly would say. And I'd say, "Where are my hips?" I truly didn't know. Once upon a time I was able to do a perfect backflip without a second thought. Now I couldn't get into my own hips. I blamed myself. Getting old is hard, I thought. You get older, and suddenly you can't feel your left leg.

I'm back in the saddle and that's a start. I don't have a lot of endurance to ride, but there is still nowhere else I'd rather be. Even though I'm not shiny, even though the fences I jump are more of a tiny crossrail.

I will ride in a show again; I'm not giving up on that dream. One day, I will wear a shadbelly coat, and I will win at least one class at the Thermal equestrian show. If I can manage to "relax" in my own way, if I can learn how to just feel him, the horse knows what to do. He'll take care of the going.

Memory

I HAVE SHORT-TERM memory loss. It's unclear whether it's caused by the MS itself or if it's a side effect from stem cell. I suspect a combination of the two. In practice, it means I can't always remember what I said ten minutes ago or what I ate for breakfast. But I have intricate, precise, and revealing thoughts.

My long-term memories are vivid, a high-def screen that plays inside my head. I sift through the images, as if searching for prisms of light. Pathways of glimmering, flickering candles guide my way as I work through my past.

I have no ability to organize. I can only choose one memory at a time, turning it over and over in my mind, like a stick of Juicy Fruit. I work on it until the flavor is gone. It never lasts as long as I hope. I do this over and over again, memory after memory, refreshing the old and dulling the new.

Focus is now my main problem. My brain is fatigued from the simple tasks I ask my body to perform: Getting out of bed. Making coffee. Brushing my teeth. Even just walking to my closet.

I stare at the rows of Chanel heels, the Isabel Marant sandals that are too complicated to fasten. Every movement I make now requires herculean effort. It takes so much out of me that my mouth is left unable to form words. Only grunts emerge. Twisted and spastic, I smile big to convey that I am okay. I smile so much these days.

❧

On good days, I have a deal with my new brain. "Okay," I tell my brain. "Since you now seem intent on dissolving all my recent memories into particles of dust, how about this? I will give you a few irritating older ones to throw in the pyre." And so, we agree, my addled brain and me. We shake on it. I start tossing out unpleasant, needless memories like yellowed bills from 2001. The Winnie-the-Pooh cake topper goes into the fire, the colors melting into swirls of orange and red like an abstract painting.

For a while it works this way. I am fascinated! I summon a time I felt hurt or sad or betrayed, take a mental picture of it, and away it goes. I get cocky and toss in a random doozy of a memory. I can't even decide if it's gloomy or not. And poof! Fizzle fizzle, it's gone.

And then, suddenly, an image floats up, unbidden: Arthur as a toddler appears in the frame. He's at the beach in Santa Monica, waddling in and out of the waves, bending down to splash the water. He's at the playground, running up to me, play slapping me before he falls into my arms and collapses into me. Wait a minute, I say. Now wait just a minute. Arthur is not part of this game. This is a mistake. A terrible trade. Please, please give me back this one. I don't want to spare a single memory of my time with my son. I scream this in my head, as if I were yelling to an imaginary friend. But I can't control it. In my mind the image of a fire appears even though I try to resist it. I watch, helpless, as this photo gets tossed into the flames. I jump in to try to save it, but I'm too late, it's already gone.

I must be careful. Very careful. No more trades. Pain and joy together.

❧

One night, I am alone in my house. I'm sitting near the fire, and it's heating my right side, my good side. I have a yellow legal pad next to me, and a black ballpoint pen. I have become my mother, always a yellow legal pad by her side. I am channeling Carrie, who wrote in bed. My head aches. I can't think. Black hole. Black sky. Maybe if I stay here, the fire warming my cheeks and my limbs, I won't start the chain reaction of pain. Maybe I can just *be* for a while. Curled into a woman ball, I wait for it to get dark. The flames make loud, satisfying pops and the wind chime sways and sings. I imagine my dog, Pippa, is already waiting for me under the covers in the spot on my bed where I usually sleep. I know I won't move for hours.

I think of my mother again. Every day, I think of her. I imagine her, at that same moment, across the country on a chair in her parlor in Plymouth, Michigan, an aide sitting nearby and with my oldest sister, Mimi, as her caretaker and only regular visitor. My mother. Her mind is going; she's sick. I picture her crying because she can't get home. "I missed the bus again," she moans to someone she can't see. She says this frequently. There is no bus. She is already home. She's not going anywhere. She almost never leaves the house anymore. Neither of us does.

I am so sorry I can't help you, Mom. I say this out loud into the dark. The sun is setting here in Los Angeles with its orange good night. I could go out now into the gloaming, with the sun beginning to sink into the earth. This is my golden hour. It's the daytime that is treacherous for me. The glare of the California sun is decimating to me and my condition. Another way to describe this feeling of disorientation: it's the physical equivalent of a tongue twister. Sally sells seashells by the seashore. That's the sensation. I try to breathe. The wind chimes are saying something.

I have to pee. I really, really have to pee. I'm not ready to get up yet, to shoulder the pain in my neck, the pain in my legs, my feet. I can't seem to care that I will wet the floor where I dropped myself when my son left. I am safe because he won't see this. I let it come, like a puppy marking her turf. I'll clean it up before he returns in the morning. I've given up on dignity. The only dignity I have left is to be kind. Kind to myself. Kind to others. The puddle sits on the floor. Another secret my house will keep. Well, until now.

∼

My mother always said, "When in doubt, get in the water." When I'm not sitting by the fire or watching Arthur swim in the pool, I'm in the bath. There are days when I'll bathe five times. It's the only place where my muscles don't spasm. It's the only place where I can lower my head, relax my breath, and hold time without interruption. I submerge myself and feel cool and young, permanent and formless.

My mother took a bath every day. Strangely, she liked to see proof that her tub was cleaned every week, so she always asked the housekeeper to leave a trail of Ajax at the bottom. I wondered if she bathed in the Ajax or simply liked the smell? Or did she just like to watch it run through the drain? I'll never know.

She once told me she was afraid of dying in the bath. This was particularly true during thunderstorms. Her tub was situated in a small bathroom near a window, framed by the lower boughs of elm trees. In her mind, the location practically invited a lightning strike. Sometimes she had me wait outside the room for her, my ear pressed to the door. I go back to this again and again. What a big job I had. If the water stopped swishing and I called to her and there was no answer, I would need to break down the door, get her dressed, put on her makeup, take off her turban, and fix her hair. All the things she never let me witness her do, but that I knew how to do all the same. I'd studied and prepared, whether she knew it or not.

I don't know who was waiting to save the other.

Later, when she was in a wheelchair with her hairdo on sideways, she would talk about her father, wailing and crying about how much she needed him. By this point I no longer knew if she took baths. Did an aide, or perhaps a nurse, give her one? She would have hated that. I wonder if she ever called out for me, the interloper, the last child she didn't want but learned to love. I was always waiting outside the bathroom door. That is my life: anticipating the lightning.

After losing my hair to chemo, my new mane grows in thick and gray, like a salt-and-pepper schnauzer. For a while, I shaved it, but now I think it's going to seriously protect my head. From me.

One day, I find myself reaching under the railing on the stairs to retrieve Pippa's damn pink-and-yellow fetch-until-you-trim-your-claws-to-nubs ball. Easy. But then I forget where I am and jolt to stand up. Impatient, quick, putting all my strength into a thrust up. Cracking into the oak rail. Fuck-shit-fuck-shit. I must be missing my spatial awareness more than I gathered.

I hold my head together as if it might split open. The pain causes drool to fall from my mouth, down onto the plaid runner. I am cracked open like a Babe Ruth fielder. Sparks. Wailing. Laughing. Fire behind my eyes. I don't feel the blood on my good right hand as I cradle my skull, which I had imagined as lambskin, like a football.

Wow. Turns out, I am actually okay. Not concussed, no stitches needed. I am whacked but I am fine. The lump on my head is five inches long and feels tender for days.

Still, I don't learn. I do this same thing all the time, sometimes six times a day. Like a Bugs Bunny cartoon on repeat. Major short-term memory loss causes bumps and bruises. I can see why people with MS are tempted to stay in bed, indefinitely.

Me? I won't, of course. I need to keep going. It's rooted in who I am.

Selma means battlefield.

Blair means Helmet of God.

I've been geared for battle my whole life. But I make a note to look into buying a helmet.

One day, I kept hearing parts of a concerto, the swell of violins and a piano. It was really lovely, but I couldn't tell where it was coming from. I searched everywhere. I kept checking my phone, but it was off. I got in my car and there it was again. I put the radio on and turned the dial up to high, until it drowned out the sound of the violins.

When I stopped the car, there it was again. That's when I realized the music was playing inside my ear. As it turns out, I have symphonic tinnitus, which is like a mellifluous version of ringing in the ears. Practically, this means that sometimes music plays inside my head.

Historically, I'm not a musical person, so this was exciting! How mind-blowing that at age forty-eight I finally had a musical ear.

When I got home, I listened to my ears for an hour. I tried to record it, because I wanted to remember. *Am I becoming Mozart?* I wondered. But the melody was pretty simple. I am an amateur musician at best.

I wrote a text to one of my best friends that said, "I can hear music! In my ear! It's really pleasant! I'm not worried."

"That sounds incredible!" she replied.

I wanted to tell my mom. I wanted to call her and say, "I have a song in my head, and I think I wrote it!" I'm finally composing the songs she told me to write in childhood. But I can't tell her.

I wish what I heard instead was her voice as she opened the basement door and called, "Selma! Dinner!"

Every night, when I say, "Arthur! Dinner!" I think of her.

The Moth

Mother's day, May 2020.

All day, I thought, *I need to call my mother.* But I never did.

We were well into COVID by then, accustomed to isolation. It had been two months of this. Days bled into days. I was in bed that week and felt nervous that if I called, she wouldn't know who I was. My sisters and I had been texting continuously about our mother's rapidly declining health. She was suffering and afraid; her mind was foggier than mine. It was as if our bodies were mirrors of each other. I didn't want to face what was happening to her.

For most of my adult life, I called her once a week. Even when I was younger, when her mind was all there, she would say, "Selma, you're boring me," and hang up. She had no tolerance for a shaggy-dog tale. You had to make her laugh and get out.

These days, she would trail off. She would go on tangents, talking about the baby in the next room, even though she knew I was no longer a baby. I was embarrassed on her behalf. I couldn't bear to witness her no longer being feared. And so I stayed away.

Arthur decided to go for a swim at sunset. I sat on a child's chaise near the deep end, holding Carrie's rock. Again, I thought, *It's Mother's Day. I should call my mother,* when, suddenly, a moth alighted on the stone in my hand. I have a mortal fear of moths. It was huge—bigger than a sparrow—with swirls of gray and brown and fuchsia covering its pretty wings. It looked almost like a Proenza Schouler print, or a blazer from the late 1970s. Two velvety black patches colored either side of its body, like a suede vest. It was both beautiful and terrifying, breathtaking and strange. I felt a moment of knowing, as though I had seen it in a dream.

Immediately, I thought of my closest dead loved one, Carrie. In my fortune-teller mind, where all the dots always connect to make up a story, I *knew* this moth was Carrie. It must be a sign. Perhaps she was trying to send me a message.

"Who are you?" I said to the moth. "And how lovely of you to come here so impeccably dressed!"

Later that night, I googled moths and discovered that this particular species, the sphinx moth, lives for only about a month or so. They're rarely found in Los Angeles and eat grape leaves. Ah, but of course. This moth was here to feast on the vines I'd planted and then die. Why else would it grace me with its presence? I invite death and loss like a magnet.

Maybe, I thought, my mind drifting again to Carrie, *this is my chance to say goodbye.*

The next day, I went out to the pool to discover that, improbably, the moth was still there. Still perched on Carrie's rock. I was so fascinated to see that it hung around that I went right up and touched it.

(My mother hated moths. They attacked our Burberry jackets and our Talbots blazers, ate our designer rugs. Like so many things handed down from her, I inherited this grudge.)

The moth kept me company, sleeping beside me all day. As I wrote on my legal pad, the moth tried to fly, but it was so weak it could only flutter its wings without ever leaving its perch. Its wingspan was huge—a flow of energy radiating from its epicenter. It took my breath away.

Day after day, the moth remained. It stayed with me, near me, sometimes even fluttering inside at night. We went for a swim together, the moth perched on my wrist. It fluttered up onto my shirt. Arthur and Bonny kept watch over it. "Wow," Bonny said. "It's been a week." The moth stayed, but as the days went by, I

couldn't help but notice it was getting smaller. I worried it was withering and would soon disappear.

A week later, on Memorial Day, my boyfriend came to my house. We sat outside, the moth still on its rock beside me. "That's crazy! How is that the same moth?" He put his hand out and the moth went to it, landing nimbly on his finger. It was fat with life. And then the moth flapped its wings and began to fly. It flew into the woods and was gone with such energy it left me speechless. And that's when I realized: It wasn't dying. It had only just been born.

The intensity of my error shocked me.

I clapped my hands with delight, like my mother whenever she thought I looked beautiful. "Brava, brava, brava!" Off it flew, into the woods, so high and so fast, off to greet its life.

After we bade the moth farewell, I went inside for my morning meditation, a COVID-inspired ritual. I had just settled in and closed my eyes when the phone rang. I glanced over and saw my sister Mimi's name, but I didn't answer.

When I was done, I listened to her message. Her voice sounded tight, as if she'd been crying. I replayed her message again. And again. And again. Until, at last, I understood.

My mother was gone.

When I was little and realized my mom would one day be dead, I cried into my worn pillowcase. I held the weight of it so tightly that I didn't sleep for weeks. I carried it with me, the truth of it too heavy to bear but too prescient to put down.

My whole life, I had been braced for it. And now it had happened.

My mother died.

My mother is gone.

We knew it was coming. And yet. And yet. When her firstborn, Mimi, called me, I knew. Her voice was composed as she said the words. She'd been my mother's only visitor during the pandemic. We shared group texts and FaceTimes. The last time we talked, Arthur had danced around adorably, alight with mischief. We all laughed, including my mom. I knew the next call would likely be the one to say she was dying. I didn't know it would be to say she was already gone.

I sobbed into the phone. Mimi asked if I needed to be alone. "Yes," I said. "Yes, thank you."

I wrote my mom a letter, the words flowing from pain. I begged her to come back and take care of me. I got out her crochet sweater and wrapped it around me. I closed my eyes and pictured her wearing it, back when I was a little girl. She looked like some kind of enchantress.

My sister Katie sent a picture of her. She doesn't have a stitch of makeup on. Her hairline is dotted with fine, silver strands. She looks both young and ancient. Pure. Her hands are elegant and thin. I put the picture away and wrap myself up in her warmth.

My mom's feet were beautiful to the end. Very bony, long, and pretty. She always took good care of them and they never aged. When she died, her toenails were painted red. This gives me some small amount of comfort.

We can't have a funeral or even a memorial service for now because of the virus. But my mom is not buried in the dirt, suffocating and cold. She is in a sprinkling vase on top of her hutch, waiting for us, her four girls, to reunite after the pandemic so we can put her back in the earth. (My mother would *hate* this urn. Black with gladiolus—she never had gladiolus.)

In the meantime, Mimi sends me things of hers, boxes and boxes of my mother's belongings. Unboxing Mom, I call it. Mimi is so sentimental that, left to her own devices, she wouldn't get rid of a single thing. So, I let her pay to ship it all to California, where I can be the one who decides what to send off to Goodwill.

I sit with my mother's possessions, unsure. What do I do with her dolls? Do I bury Skinny and Checkers? As soon as I see them, run my fingers across their filmy rag doll faces, I know that I can't.

For months, I comb through piles of my mother's precious shit. All of it is old. All of it smells like cigarettes and mothballs and a hint of Opium. Some boxes are a thrill, like the one with the turban from her second wedding. Others are just horrific.

This is our inheritance.

The truth is, I never dreamed of an Oscar. I've never given the pretend speech to the mirror, never even imagined it. That wasn't my thing. The lock of my mom's hair from her childhood—too precious for me to even open the envelope—that is what I treasure.

☙

I talk to my mother. Casually, as if she will answer me.

"Will you give it a rest, Selma?" I hear her say. Or, "How did you learn to be so funny, Selma?"

I miss her. I call her every day. Her answering machine is still set up, and I leave her messages.

A phrase I once read plays on a loop: grief is love you can no longer express.

I light cigarette after cigarette, hoping they will lead me to her.

Sometimes, I put on all her things so she can find me easily.

I love the way I sound like her sometimes. When I really cackle, I can hear her.

"Good night, Mom," I whisper every night. May all our dreams come true. Even the ones we haven't dreamed yet.

Arthur

I'M TRYING TO BREAK the cycle, but I'm facing a challenge. Arthur can be a mean baby!

It's true!

As an infant and later as a toddler, Arthur was not one to dole out a smile.

When he was about two, we went to a birthday party thrown by Rachel Zoe for her older son, who is Arthur's age. At one point, Jason Bateman came up to us with a big grin on his face and said, "Hey! Arthur!" Oh, the look Arthur gave him. As Jason so succinctly put it, "It just went dark." His words so perfectly encapsulated what I hadn't been able to describe. Then it hit me: what I observe in my son every day is exactly what people must have thought about me.

❧

At home, Arthur chases me around the house, attacking me with his Nerf gun until I spasm out. His constant assault of foam weaponry leaves me contorted and moaning, my posture rigid as I melt into the white wood floor.

My child sees me flopping around like a dying fish and keeps shooting, laughing. I grunt. Try to yell at him. But it's horrific. I get more rigid and weak. I drop. The demon child keeps pelting me. It stings now. My brain clutches. I'm furious.

And then I laugh. I laugh and howl and let go of the rage. I crawl to him and we laugh and smush and kiss. My body relaxes. He hugs and clings and punches gently, all over my body.

Eventually, I learn to set boundaries. The rule is, when I say, "Arthur, stop," he has to stop. Immediately. He understands that I am his playmate, but I am still, and most important, his mother. I may be fragile, but I am still in charge. Even if circumstances provide detours along the way.

Recently, for the first time in his life, I showed him one of my movies. On-screen, my character was smoking and drinking, looking weird and young and beautiful, and all he wanted to know was, "Is that *real* alcohol?"

"What do you think?" I asked him. "Do I look the same?"

"Yeah, on opposite day!" he yelled, pointing at the screen. "Because that girl is pretty, and you look nothing like her!" He roared with laughter. Before I had a chance to respond, he was already out of the room, grabbing his Nerf gun to shoot me with.

Jason tells me he did these things with his mom, whom he loves to no end. Luckily, Jason and I now have the best co-parenting relationship. It took a while to figure out—in the early days, letting my baby go for visitation was crippling to me—but now we are a proper family. For many reasons, I am glad that Jason is my father's son. Since both Jason and Arthur are babies, both wonderful boys that their mothers love, they're going to need each other. Honestly, I don't know who the hell is ever going to love them the way we do.

My favorite time is when Arthur is sleeping, and I can listen to him breathing. When he's asleep, I can pretend he's nice to me all the time. I spoon him. Sometimes he lets me; sometimes he pushes me away. But he has told me he loves me more than anything in the world, and that's going to have to do.

After all, mean babies like us have to stick together.

I am well aware that I am creating a horrible husband. I have made the person that I hope to never marry. For starters, I love carrying my son.

When Arthur was a toddler, he would yell, "I can't walk!"

"You *can* walk," I would say. "But if you want me to carry you, I will." And he would reply that yes, he wanted me to carry him.

"Mom! I want you to carry me to the bathroom!" he yells from his room. Because he is nine, many would argue that he is far too old to be carried. But I still carry him to the bathroom at night, practically dropping him along the way. But it benefits us both.

I find the only time I can walk, and walk well, without huge focus is when I'm holding Arthur. I have bad proprioception, from frontal cortex damage due to MS. But carrying my son always helps me to know where my body is in space. As soon as I drop him, I'm lost, which is both confounding and pretty tragic, because he's nine, and I'm forty-eight, and it's time to move on.

"God help me, un-koala yourself," I'll say, though I don't fully mean it.

I remember my own mom carrying me once in my whole life. It was such an anomaly that I wrote a poem about it. "Wow, my mom is strong enough to lift me," I thought. I truly had no idea. I knew she had other strengths, the kind involving high heels and going to work, but this one left me amazed.

Jason's mother, on the other hand, carried him all the time. This is how "horrible husbands" are made. Jason's mom is an angel woman (as I am now, ha), but in my book she was also a husband ruiner, and I once called to tell her so!

A bit of background: Arthur was a baby, and Jason and I were mid-breakup. We were walking together with the stroller, arguing about something that shouldn't have been such a huge deal, but custody and fear and fatigue and anxiety threw up their signs, and

I grabbed the stroller away from him and screamed, striking out at him, screeching in alarm and fear and stress that he didn't know anything.

I wasn't trying to hurt him, really. I was scared witless. It was the kind of episode where, if my friend recounted the story to me, I would have said, "It sounds like you had a bad day. Why don't you guys go take a breath, take some time apart." Instead, Jason called the police.

Holy shit, I thought, *I am dealing with a crazy person.*

"I've just been attacked," he said into the phone.

Meanwhile, I'm saying over and over again, "I didn't attack you, I didn't attack you, I didn't attack you."

In the end, he didn't file a complaint, because I was the mother of his child and because he wasn't at all hurt. But the whole ordeal served to cement that we were better off apart.

Later that day, I called his mother. I stood in my backyard, in tears, and said, "This is your fault. You raised your son to get everything he ever wanted. He's done this sort of thing to you for a million years, but I can't do the same to him, because you enabled this man-child!" That's how I felt. She was sad this was happening. I was on the brink of real self-harm, terrified Arthur would be taken from me.

I have since forgiven her (and she me—she is the sweetest person and the most loving, doting grandmother in the world), because I realize how hard it is to be the mom of a boy. I realize how hard it is to be a mother, in general.

I know that one day I might get a phone call similar to the one I gave Jason's mother. I won't be surprised. I am a husband ruiner, guilty as charged. But in my defense, Arthur does know how to cook. He does understand that women need naps. And I hear that outside the house he's very empathetic and wonderful. And Jason likes me well enough now. Besides the husband ruiner bit. And it's not even true anymore. Time heals.

Portland

AFTER I GOT SOBER, I went to Portland.

A group of us drove up to visit a psychic. A caravan of seekers, all in search of answers. We were nervous, anticipating. We acted as if it were a big deal. The psychic was pretty wardrobed up, but in practice she turned out to be terrible. Of all the working intuitives I've met in my time, she was the quickest to grab a buck, the quickest to say I was full of doom. I still took the bait for a while, gave her a couple phone calls on the credit card, because she picked up on my sadness. My vulnerability was palpable. You don't realize how much you're in it until you're not. Until you decide to change the story yourself.

❧

When you're a seeker, what you're really looking for is someone who speaks your language. You never give up hope of finding true connection. It's a little like hunting for a Birkin bag at an estate sale. There's always that glimmer of possibility. In a world full of fakes, maybe you'll find a *real* person who can give you the answer you've been after. Maybe you'll hear something that finally resonates. Maybe you'll stumble across the truth.

Here is what I've learned: you can make anything real.

I used to go looking for answers. I used to crave a warning, a map, a how-to manual, the secret code to hold myself together. I sought protection, largely from myself. I wanted permission to allow someone else to love me.

But this is new territory. In a way, MS has cured me. I've gotten enough advice from doctors to last me a lifetime. If a crystal ball fell in my lap, I would still gaze into it. I would listen to what it had to say. But now I take everything people tell me with a grain of salt. I no longer feel as if there were anyone who knows more than I do.

(I can be my own fortune-teller. Ready? I'm going to be the world's oldest supermodel.)

The truth is, I'm due for a visit to a psychic. But if I saw one today, what would I want to hear? I don't have the same fears I once did. I don't seek the same answers.

I want someone to tell me that my son is going to have a happy life. That I'm going to be okay. That I won't be a burden. That I'll see my loved ones again. I don't know that anyone else can tell me that. Or any of us.

~

Every night before bed, I get on my knees and pray. "What can I do," I ask, "for me, for my son, for other people?" (I've gotten a little lofty as I've gotten older.) Then I wait, listening for the answer.

The older I get, the more I see how interconnected things are. I think there must be something larger at play, that we exist to fulfill some teaching or some destiny. Otherwise, I can't explain the inexplicable love you feel for some people, or our inherent need for connection. It makes it better to think there are signs along the way. It feels more powerful if a message comes through. If something brings you comfort, I say, all the better for it.

There were times when I had to believe in fairy dust. Sometimes, I still do. I want to believe in magic, because I want to maintain there's more to it than *we're born, then we love, then we die.* But I also believe we make our fate. We can get in line and create a stronger story for ourselves. We can write it however we want. That is the wonderful, realistic part of magic.

I can't profess to understand the mysteries of the universe. All I know is that I desperately love a story. We all have one; I carry mine inside me. You carry yours inside you. I can hear mine now, in my own voice. Strong and clear. All it took was to stop listening to the stories everyone else told about me. I hope this helps you, too.

Dear Arthur

THIS BOOK IS DEDICATED to you and to my mother. But really, it's for you. Everything I do, even waking up, is all for you. I have loved it all—in its glorious, horrible, life-adjusting chiropractic-nightmare type of way.

You have heard all of this before, I know. But bear with me for just a little longer.

I am telling the old stories because I am learning a new way of living while we spend our time together on earth. I am undoing certain patterns of behavior. I am changing what I can.

Right now, I save the light I have to laugh with you. To feel the whole day and night with you. I will be with you as long as you need or want me to.

The other day, I watched you do a full flip in the pool, and I widened my bleak eyes in shock. *When did you get so brave?* I wanted to ask. The transformation was imperceptible. I missed the shift, and then you went and did it even as I was starting to say, "Hey, that might not be safe!"

You did it. And you survived it.

You you you. I have oceans of love for you, my baby boy. My eyes don't just light up when you walk into the room; they pool up when you leave that room in tatters. My God! You have a way of making it all seem wrecked in the most gorgeous way I could ever imagine. And you always help me tidy.

Always help to tidy up the messes, okay? We all make them. It's okay. Just clean up when you can. We have to help each other.

I hope you'll experience real joy. That you'll choose kindness over any alternative. That you'll surround yourself with people who see you for who you are. That you won't feel trapped, as I did. That you'll see people who might otherwise be invisible to the world. People who are broken, lonely, or sick. People who need someone to root for them.

Thank you for being someone who sees me.

I also want you to know that my disease is not a tragedy. Please don't forget this. For as long as I am here, I promise to live in a way that is an example for you and for myself. Because this is it. The only life we get. Let's make the most of it.

As for me, I will continue to be me for as long as that's possible. I will continue to love a good gown, or a suit, from Christian Siriano or Chanel. I will put in my mother's emerald earrings and show up. I will smile, but with my mouth closed. (My teeth, I feel, tell a story I am done telling. So I keep them hidden. I will explain this to you.)

I will always be happiest by a fire.

I will remember those I've loved and lost. Bradley, Chip, Jason, Jason, Jason. Ahmet. Ingrid. I will remember Carrie. I will yearn for my mother.

I will tend my wounds.

You are asleep in your room now. Happy, safe. I tucked you in. I watched you fall asleep. I laid out your school clothes and turned off the light.

Anchored,
Mother

Acknowledgments

I would very much like to acknowledge and thank my mother for allowing me to write anything about her. That's a lie. She's dead. But she was the first one to tell me I should write a book. I was seven. So I hope she understands how self-centered one's own stories can be. We could be a bit hard on each other. I'm sorry and miss having her here on earth so much it makes my teeth hurt. And, Wink, the three of us will meet again in the next imaginings. I like to picture our small pack walking together, contentedly in the shade, Wink chasing ducks along the shore.

To Elliot Sir, Daddy Sir! Thank you for some big-ticket school years. I wish you hadn't traded me in for lies. I wish it hadn't hurt us both so much. I hate hurt. Thank you for being the one to carry me on the escalator. I was really scared.

To my sisters, Mimi, Katie, and Lizzie. Thank you for supporting me in everything I do. KK, yes. *You* have been the most encouraging of my writing a book. Noted. With love. Rooting around in your room growing up, reading the candy section in *All in the Family* books, planning our trip to Sydney Bogg—with a whole dollar each!—or trading rainbow Spencers Gifts clear stickers on a short winter day, while Mom told you to "turn down the Victrola," are some of my most comforting memories. Now we are both published authors in the same book! Arthur and I love you very much.

Mimi, the best big sister with the shimmery pink lipstick I couldn't wait to apply every Saturday night between *Dance Fever* and *The Love Boat*. You are always so much fun and your summer visits with Jim meant the world to us and your care of Mom did, too.

Lizzie, my person. I know how you hate these group texts, so please just know I love you and can't wait for us to cuddle and play like puppies again soon.

Aunt Sally, for the love and attention and stories. Strangest thing to have become my mother but still have Little Blair with me now. Thanks for giving me acknowledgment all these years. Oceans. Arthur James Rubiner, you are wicked with a line. Beloved by all of us, even Molly. How she appreciated your Selma for turning her out so chicly, when her shithead husband left her and Mimi in Detroit. I love you, Uncle Jimmy, and all the cousins, Joey, Meg, Julia, and Matthew.

Jason Bleick. I love you. I love Arthur more. I know you feel the same.

Troy Nankin. We have been through almost all of it in our adult lives together. I can't wait to share the rest of it with you. What you did with *Introducing, Selma Blair* was the greatest gift. I thank you. I also thank you for rarely mentioning my neck and the pull of gravity in menopause. It's brutal for a team who admires the great beauty makers. You know where to find them, so we still have a few golden years left. I will always keep your mother's pendant of you with me. You are my partner and my family here, and I love you forever. Even when pulling over to rest and complain on the never-ending drive from Mary Vernieu's office. And thank you for the girls you love. For example:

Krista Smith, the most brilliant and solid woman in any room. Thank you for being my Dear Margot, my confidante and mentor, actually. Troy and I affectionately and solemnly recognize you as Mother. We defer. You have literally and metaphorically driven us to home and safety. A couple years out of college and new in town, meeting with you for that Vanities piece was potentially terrifying. I wore a Loro Piana black cashmere coat while you had on Chanel heels I admired. We sat in the burgundy-and-gold glow of the Four Seasons and became forever friends. Do not ever die. Or before me at least. Thanks.

Parker Posey! My word! You are as divine as everyone hopes. The support and love and friendship you have given me in this often brutal but incredible life is a major highlight. You are an amazing icon and I loved all our times together. I still have the journal where I glued a cutting of you from a *Fashion* magazine next to a list of seventy-nine auditions I had gone on with only two small jobs to show for them. I was a hostess with blisters on my feet, a student, and a salesgirl at the Gap, living in the Salvation Army when I discovered you on-screen. You take my breath away, and sentimental me can't believe legendary you is on my side on this earth. I am forever on yours and am hoping for a big-time *Columbo*-style show together in any event.

Mary-Louise Parker who over the years has been the incredible same-same sister I have looked to for light when the roads turned and grew over. Thank you for being the first to read this book and giving me your brilliant insight. Dazzling you.

Nothing would have kept *Mean Baby* moving without the love, support, encouragement, patience, and unbelievable care of my angel, Brettne Bloom. Nobody else could have accepted late-night text notes of lyrics to "November Rain" when I was crushed by remembering young love lost. Thank you for seeing silver linings in the hundreds of scraps of my heart. Some indecipherable, some just *chazerai,* and some simple truths I would not have found without your enduring belief in the value of our stories. I know how lucky I am to be embraced by the women of The Book Group. Julie Barer, your support and presence have been invaluable. Thank you for being another Julie in my life.

My editor, Jenny Jackson. You are a godsend and I am so proud to be with you and Knopf on this first leg of my journey, on this second act of my life. A dream come true. Thank you. Stories ahead! God willing. I can't wait to find them and write them under your eye. Since the day I warbled out "Big Spender" in Sonny's office, I was so grateful to have found my home with you. I'm also grateful to the entire team at Knopf for giving this mean baby a place on the shelf, most especially: the late, great Sonny Mehta. Reagan Arthur, Paul Bogaards, Jess Purcell, Sara Eagle, Maris Dyer, Nicole Pedersen, Anna Knighton, Janet Hansen, Erinn Hartman, I'm so grateful to all of you.

Caroline Cala Donofrio, your hours of attention and work on this book are so deeply appreciated. Your knowing and soul, I appreciate even more. Thank you for everything.

Hylda Queally. The strength and serenity of spirit you have given me by the power of your presence in my life has me thanking my lucky stars. I welcome this era of our days and hold it highest. Thank you, your Grace.

Kevin Huvane. From dinners with Ruthie and Weber twenty years ago, to graciously paying our bill when Ahmet and I took a stroll to dinner sans wallets, you covered it! To embracing me now as warmly as always. I kiss the ring with wholehearted thanks and love.

Berni Barta, Andrea Weintraub, Donovan Tatum, and my team

at CAA. I am honored to be on this leg of the journey with you all. Thank you so much.

Megan Moss Pachon. The perennially fresh-faced, wholesome beauty I first worked with almost twenty years ago is also the most capable, clear, protective, wise, efficient, incredible, and irreplaceable ally and publicist. Thank you for always being here and there. And Sloane Kessler who is remarkable and beloved. Thank you for making sure every *i* is dotted—metaphorically.

Elena Hansen. I thank whatever algorithm has put you in our lives. I would like to be like you when I grow up. You are great. Thank you. And Swim Social.

Bonny Burke, whom I believe angels sent to that funny set for me on a rainy winter morning. Oh, and you stayed and moved to L.A. to take care of us to help love me—and I fell in love with wonderful you. I am forever your family too and am convinced your path will be glorious. Karma owes you only the best. Now come back!! As if, rockstar.

Julie De Santo. How could I know you would become the foundation of my life? How could I know you merely thought Karl Lagerfeld looked familiar when you popped over with the girls as he stood before you? How could I know your love and faith would heal me? Please keep me forever. I couldn't love you more. And to you, Anna, Elena, Daniel, and Luca. Thank You. Understatement.

Ben Gaynor. Thank you for picking up the duties of the best older brother to King Arthur and for being my Boy Friday. If that can be a thing. You are a top mensch and I am so grateful for you.

Our entire documentary family: Mickey Liddell, Pete Shilaimon, and Troy again. Rachel Fleit, I hope this is just our first bird. Bird by bird. Cass Bird! Oh my! The miracle of Cass Bird joining up these birds. I love you both forever. And there are birds galore for us. See you tomorrow, Fleit, alopecia kisses and oceans of love.

Shane Sigler, Sloane Klevin, and Raphaelle Thibaut, who made the most extraordinary and heartbreaking soundtrack to my life. Igal Svet, for making sure everyone heard it.

Billie Lourd, we all loved your mom, and she loved you with all of her. Big love.

Sarah Michelle Gellar, you have been taking care of me since the day we met, feeding me from the get-go and showing me the ropes. I'm so happy the only real on-screen kiss of my career was with you, the great SMG! And to think Cecile and Kathryn have stood the test of time. I love who you are and how you live this life on-screen; your family is cherished over here and you are the gold standard of friends and stars.

Reese Witherspoon, the only person my beloved yet critical mother could find no flaw with. Your love of reading and even passing along favorite books to me since the early days was a wonderful thing. I am so in awe of what you have built from the true spirit of you. The most incredible woman. The world knows it, and I feel very cool loving your gorgeous brilliance in real life, too.

Clairus Danes, my truest and closest friend from this recluse existence. A little Blairus goes a long way. I think you do understand how much I cherish you. There is no better conversationalist and witness to go through this life with. Oceans of Love. Send a video right now.

Michelle Pfeiffer, I love you so much. For returning my texts and calls, for giving me the greatest encouragement to simply smell the scent of light and hope and to string a few words together and for you to pronounce them good. You are the brightest star in my orbit, and I'm floored by your grace. Thank you. And thank you, David E. Kelley, for giving me a great job once. Appreciated. The whole family.

Rajiv Joseph, Rebecca Taichman, Brad Fleischer, the horrible perfect greatness that is our *Gruesome Playground Injuries.*

Guillermo del Toro, the most astounding director and amazing friend, whose mere journals outrun everyone else in the race. My lord! You are an amazement and I am honored. Also, I do not have Liz's necklace. I wish I did. Some shit must have swiped it. But not this mean baby.

Todd Solondz who made my mother's favorite films. And mine. Thank you for the honor. The night is still young, buddy.

Roger Kumble, *mein Direktor.* We are a team somehow. What's next? Major love.

Ingrid Sischy. The way you lifted me up, put me to work at *Interview,* put me on the masthead, introduced me to Karl and Miuccia and Donatella. You gave me a table at Pastis. You gave me every single thing I would need to fly. And I got sick. I couldn't keep up with how wonderful the view was. But I have the images in my mind. Nothing will be lost on me now that I'm waking up, dear Ingrid. I wish you were here. Every day really. You were the most important woman I ever admired and loved. And to think you loved me unconditionally. You were truly the greatest witness of our time. Please come see me sometime. I'll set the table by the fire. You were exquisite, Ingrid Sischy. I see your kindness even more now. Just what I need.

Anna Wintour for making my first Chanel moment in Paris so perfect. André Leon Talley, how I have loved sitting on your lap, whether in custom Chanel or color blocks of Isaac Mizrahi. William Norwich, for documenting the date night at the Met Ball, when my plane had to be caught so soon into the night. *Quel dommage*. It was a resplendent evening and your words the tiara on top.

Applause for Karl Lagerfeld. You were sublime. I cannot believe what a puppy of a child I could be with you. I loved you so and will until I die. Wrap me in Chanel.

Steven Meisel, you are the answer, really, to every dark day. I wish to find myself in front of your lens again, Pat McGrath painting a perfect lip.

Inez and Vinoodh for seeing me. Laughing with me, being amazing people.

Joe Zee and Michael Thompson for the most striking and gorgeous *W* cover.

Peggy Sirota for the image on the cover of this book and for our day of shooting. It was one of the best days I can recall, along with meeting Chris McMillan at the end of it.

Christian Siriano, I love you. I never felt sexier than when next to you in a bathroom selfie in Toronto to celebrate your book launch. Thank you for inviting me to sit at your table.

Jaime King, every song I think of you, every prayer starts with you. How we found each other in this huge world will always be a sacred gift I love forever. My beautiful blond sister.

Jana Kogen Breitbarth for finding me and loving me. Bonnie Liedtke, Julie Taylor, and Andrea Pett-Joseph for taking me on.

Dr. Burt. You saved my system. Thank you.

Thank you, John Danhakl.

Jennifer Grey, there isn't enough love.

Matthew Perry, for looking the part of Cary Grant the night we met, and for being my real true friend ever since. Thank you for getting me home safely as you recovered yourself.

Jamie Lynn Sigler, the total knockout. Thank you for being an example and my beautiful friend.

Christina Applegate, one of my messy sisters and (looks like) forever friend. *Gah,* I'm probably on my way over to get in bed actually. Nah, too tired, love you. Night.

Ann Eagleton and Winch and Pretzel and Jim, I don't think I could have made it without you coming here to Cali every summer for our walks in the sand. You will always be in our memories and now my favorite texting mom.

JLCurtis, your hand could not have come sooner.

Azura Skye, you know you are my favorite and your talent is so ethereal and stunning and raw and dignified. As are you. God I love you. And thank you for being at every stage of my life here.

Jason Schwartzman, you are beloved.

Gia and Jacquie, as are you.

Ron and Chloe Carlson. This deeply loved family who manages to all cater to . . . Prince Arthini! I love you, Ron, and my red-headed stepchild.

The Strickers. Boundless love and thanks, you held me at my worst. You hold us still. We can't wait for our next trip with you.

Kelly Jennings and HRH Nibbles. You both know how I feel, but it doesn't cover it.

Britney, you did it. So much love to you, the Queen, the Lion. How does a girl get in touch with Britney Spears?! Xo, Saintly.

To David Weber, the tall and handsome man I loved dearly.

Bill Nighy, my most elegant friend, I hope we dance one day very soon. Thank you for your beacons of hope through the years, love and oceans.

The Cranbrook Kingswood mix tape of everything I love. For the Fab Four, Fran, Sue, and Kelly. And Chip, Chris Keogh, Art Tavee.

Todd "Meathead" Kessler, you will always amaze me with your writing. Your mind. I am so proud of you. Love, Archie.

Art and Caroline, my personal photographers, please carry on. With massive love.

James Toner, where are you?

Christine Goodale. Thank you for changing my life. In the best way. Photography saved me. You seeing me saved me. I loved your art rooms. And you.

Gina Ferrari. "Watercolored Iris" is due for an update. My idol as a wee Blair, I love you still.

Skunks. From *Rushmore* to now . . . I feel we've been through it all together. Thank you. I love you and cannot wait for the best in your life.

Quinn Olmsted Spilsbury. You saved me from the possum, from the Monster, from the bitch monster, and another monster. You are forever my Pugsley and I your Wednesday. Those early years of Arthur, we saved each other until you found your love, your own family. And a beautiful family you have. Always and always BFF, Squish.

Lori Petty. I mean, I can't sometimes. And I know you always know what I mean. Thank you for having me in your movie. And meeting my first children, Chloe and Jennifer. It's been a whole thing, and I hope to find you again, my friend.

Ellen Pompeo, from our NYC days to now, you have always been top shelf.

Constance Zimmer, I am overjoyed to be your friend, thank you.

Karen "Spring Break" McCullah, the biggest jolt of sunshine.

Janey Lopaty. I love Janey From Juicy. I love Janey.

Amanda Anka, and Tanda . . . all blessings already are . . . but you make them bigger.

Sharon Stone, your brain, your being, your strength . . . thank you for being there when I most need it. Coming over to float and hang, I'll tell you in person.

Thaiba, my yellow heart, thank you.

Hoora Smart and Julia Chastain, my beautiful girls of Instagram, I love you.

Courtney Ferguson. Rest in Peace, angel girl.

Jim LeBrecht. I love our friendship so much. My admiration is boundless.

Andraéa LaVant. Formidable and stunning and patient with me. I will never greet your service dog in the same manner. Now that I have my own, I do not know how you did not drive over my feet in frustration. More to come! Love you.

Keah Brown. To see you smiling across the room was the best surprise on a fall night in the Hamptons, you anchored me and I love you. Thank you for your talent and friendship.

To the disability community. I'm humbled and honored to be one part of a representation. I am an ally. Thank you.